Grantmakers for Effective Organizations Endorses *Foundations and Evaluation*

Grantmakers for Effective Organizations (GEO) supports effective evaluation practices in foundations, as described in this edited collection. GEO is a community of grant-makers dedicated to building strong and effective organizations. GEO's mission is to maximize philanthropy's impact by advancing the effectiveness of grantmakers and their grantees. Through research, conferences, its Web site, publications, and other activities, GEO highlights knowledge and practices in the field that advance the organizational effectiveness movement.

More information on GEO and a host of resources and links for funders are available on our Web site: www.geofunders.org

FOUNDATIONS
AND EVALUATION

FOUNDATIONS AND EVALUATION

Contexts and Practices for Effective Philanthropy

Edited by
Marc T. Braverman
Norman A. Constantine
Jana Kay Slater

Foreword by
Richard T. Schlosberg III

Past President and CEO, The David and Lucile Packard Foundation

JOSSEY-BASS
A Wiley Imprint
www.josseybass.com

Published by Jossey-Bass
A Wiley Imprint
989 Market Street, San Francisco, CA 94103-1741   www.josseybass.com

Jossey-Bass books and products are available through most bookstores. To contact Jossey-Bass directly,
call our Customer Care Department within the U.S. at 800-956-7739, outside the U.S. at 317-572-3993,
or fax 317-572-4002.

Jossey-Bass also publishes its books in a variety of electronic formats. Some content that appears in print
may not be available in electronic books.

Readers should be aware that Internet Web sites listed in this work may have changed or disappeared
between when this work was written and when it is read.

Credits are on page 315.

Library of Congress Cataloging-in-Publication Data
Foundations and evaluation : contexts and practices for effective
philanthropy / edited by Marc T. Braverman, Norman A. Constantine, Jana Kay
Slater ; foreword by Richard T. Schlosberg III.—1st ed.
     p.   cm.
  Includes bibliographical references and index.
  ISBN 0-7879-7077-8 (alk. paper)
  1. Endowments—Evaluation. 2. Charitable uses, trusts, and foundations—
Evaluation. 3. Evaluation research (Social action programs) I. Braverman,
Marc T. II. Constantine, Norman, date. III. Slater, Jana Kay.
  HV16.F68 2004
  361.7'632'0684—dc22   2004014546

Printed in the United States of America
FIRST EDITION
HB Printing 10 9 8 7 6 5 4 3 2 1

CONTENTS

PRESIDENTIAL PERSPECTIVES

PART ONE: UNDERSTANDING FOUNDATIONS AS A CONTEXT FOR EVALUATION

PART TWO: BUILDING CAPACITY FOR EVALUATION PRACTICE

TABLES, FIGURES, AND EXHIBITS

Tables

Figures

Exhibits

FOREWORD

The David and Lucile Packard Foundation's interest in evaluation is grounded in one of our core values: a commitment to effectiveness. David Packard and the Hewlett-Packard Company pioneered "management by objectives" and implemented Continuous Quality Improvement. These policies and practices have been fundamental to HP's operations and have contributed to the company's success. With this heritage, our trustees and staff have committed to identifying strategic opportunities and to evaluating the effectiveness of our major lines of work. Our founders' vision continues to guide our work to this day.

As we develop and refine evaluation processes at the Packard Foundation, we keep in mind our role as stewards. It is our responsibility to ensure that the resources entrusted to us by our founders are used effectively. We are committed to reporting evaluation findings to our board and to informing our grantees and the public of our progress. Simultaneously, we see evaluation as a powerful tool to advance learning within the foundation and with our partners to help improve our long-term program strategies.

Evaluation serves many purposes in foundations. As my colleagues and fellow foundation executives point out in the following pages, using data from evaluation is important in informing board members, grant seekers, and foundation program staff to advance strategic directions and learning. Overarching evaluation frameworks enable us to gauge progress within and across our organizations' activities and to make improvements.

Clarifying early on the primary purpose for undertaking any evaluation of our work has been one of the most important factors for increasing evaluation use and effectiveness. In planning evaluations, we seek to identify why we are doing an evaluation, who the main audience for the evaluation is, and how the information gathered from the evaluation will be used. Continually asking and answering these questions has helped us select and carry out better evaluations. In addition, we see the value of employing different evaluation tools, based on the unique characteristics of a program and approach.

Although establishing clear guidance for when and how to use evaluation is fundamental to its effectiveness, important questions remain. Foundations often work in areas that are constantly evolving; social and environmental problems are complex and rarely static. Efforts to demonstrate impact require a diversity of approaches and a long-term view. Questions of attribution and causality are sometimes difficult—even impossible—to answer. And in some cases, the financial cost of conducting sophisticated evaluations is prohibitive. Although we recognize the contributions of evaluations designed according to the medical model (we have funded them on occasion), we also see the value of "theory of change" approaches to evaluation that specify the logic of a program and that measure key steps during the life of a program. Identifying evaluation approaches that advance learning and that remain feasible continue to pose challenges to us and to the field.

It is an exciting time in the field of philanthropy. The focus on evaluation and foundation effectiveness continues to guide many of our discussions. The merger of Grantmakers for Effective Organizations and the Grantmakers Evaluation Network highlights the importance of evaluation in organizational effectiveness. Foundation and nonprofit evaluation issues continue to be prominently featured at the American Evaluation Association and at foundation industry meetings. We anticipate more activity and energy in these arenas and look forward to lively and productive exchanges.

We are pleased to have funded *Foundations and Evaluation: Contexts and Practices for Effective Philanthropy*. The idea for this project began at the foundation in 2001, and a partnership was formed with the Public Health Institute (PHI) and the University of California, Davis, to bring it to reality. We are particularly pleased that our partners at PHI and UC Davis have brought leadership to this work; their efforts and vision are reflected in these pages. We are also grateful to the distinguished evaluators who have contributed their best and most current thinking and to those colleagues deeply steeped in the world of philanthropy who have shared their insights on this topic.

This book highlights some of the important issues that surround the use of evaluation within foundations and demonstrates how diverse viewpoints and varied opinions lead to more productive evaluation methods. It will certainly help us continue the discussion of how best to evaluate our work and will be critical in helping foundation boards, staff, grantees, and evaluation professionals improve their vision, understanding, and practice. I hope that you will join me in considering these perspectives and in applying the best ideas to help better achieve the important missions we all pursue.

June 2004   Richard T. Schlosberg III
                                                              Past President and CEO
                                                              The David and Lucile Packard Foundation

PREFACE

This book is the product of a grant by The David and Lucile Packard Foundation to the Public Health Institute (PHI) and the University of California, Davis. Under this grant, we were able to bring together a notable group of experts from the fields of evaluation and philanthropy to discuss and strategize how evaluation could be better employed to serve philanthropy's needs. The participants included foundation executives and staff, evaluators, university scholars, and consultants. All had extensive experience with foundations or evaluation practice, or with both, through a variety of venues: working in foundations, working with foundations as external contractors, and studying and writing about foundations and evaluation.

Our workgroup met initially for three days in May 2002 at the Packard Foundation headquarters in Los Altos, California. At that meeting, we discussed how evaluation could be used to better support and enhance foundations in their roles as reflective, learning organizations. The group decided on a series of papers that would analyze the variety of issues involved, and members took on writing assignments. These papers make up the contents of this book. Not all workgroup members authored manuscripts, but all participated actively and creatively in the formative discussions. In addition to the chapter authors, the workgroup included the following individuals: Paul Brest (The William and Flora Hewlett Foundation), Michael Cortés (University of San Francisco), Ernest House (University of Colorado), Barbara Kibbe (The David and Lucile Packard Foundation, currently with

The Skoll Foundation), Judith Kroll (Council on Foundations), Carol Larson (The David and Lucile Packard Foundation), Kent McGuire (Manpower Demonstration Research Corporation, currently with Temple University), and Carolina Reyes (The California Endowment, currently with Cedars-Sinai Medical Center). In addition, some colleagues were brought into the group as authors shortly after the meeting. The workgroup members met again in November 2002 in Washington, D.C., to continue our conversations and consider plans for disseminating the papers. Finally, we asked three current foundation presidents—Hodding Carter, Michael Howe, and Risa Lavizzo-Mourey—to provide short essays setting out their perspectives on evaluation and how it serves the ongoing work of their foundations.

As part of the chapter development process, each draft (other than the presidents' essays) was sent to several peer reviewers, who were invited to provide feedback, based on their familiarity with the topics being discussed. They provided detailed comments and suggestions. Roughly half of the reviews were made by members of the workgroup (some on more than one manuscript) and half by scholars and experts who were external to the project. The internal workgroup reviewers were Lester Baxter, William Beery, Deborah Bonnet, Wendy Constantine, Rodney Hopson, Ernest House, Judith Kroll, Victor Kuo, Laura Leviton, Melvin Mark, Michael Patton, and Edward Pauly. The external reviewers were Martha Campbell, Maria Casey, Rebecca Cornejo, David Ferrero, John Grove, Michael Hendricks, Mark Lipsey, Lisa Korwin, Garth Neuffer, Linda Neuhauser, Susan Obarski, Sara Peterson, Dana Phillips, Emil Posavac, Tracey Rutnik, and Susan Wisely. We are grateful to all these colleagues, who generously offered the benefits of their time and expertise. The review process was collegial and constructive, and we trust that all of the papers are stronger as a result.

We also thank Johanna Vondeling and Allison Brunner, the editors with whom we worked at Jossey-Bass. They provided guidance, patience, and advice and were particularly sensitive to the highly collaborative processes on which this book was built. We extend our appreciation to the two anonymous reviewers recruited by Jossey-Bass at a later phase in the process, who provided feedback about the book as a whole. They offered many insights, and we are grateful for their input.

All of our workgroup members contributed to the project in innumerable ways, but as project conveners and then as editors of this volume, we were especially fortunate to have the counsel of an internal advisory group consisting of Ross Conner, Judith Kroll, Laura Leviton, and Edward Pauly. This group provided essential guidance at several critical junctures for the project.

We wish to extend our deepest gratitude to our project funders at The David and Lucile Packard Foundation. Victor Kuo, our program officer, has been a tremendous source of guidance, support, and encouragement, in addition to being a tireless and valued team member. Carol Larson, president and CEO of the

Packard Foundation, has provided wisdom and vision for how the efforts of philanthropy can continually be made more effective and valuable. And we offer our deep thanks to Gary Henry, who was the director of Evaluation and Learning Services at Packard when our project was funded and was instrumental in helping the project get off the ground.

We also thank Michael P. Smith at UC Davis and Donna Sofaer at PHI for numerous helpful and practical conversations along the way.

Working as a team in leading the grant project and editing this volume, we shared equally in the numerous tasks associated with the endeavor. The alphabetical ordering of editors is reflective of our shared workload.

Finally, on a personal note, we thank our daughters, Blair Braverman and Mara Constantine, whose adolescent wit and energy helped keep us buoyed throughout the course of this project.

June 2004

Marc T. Braverman
Davis, California

Norman A. Constantine
Lafayette, California

Jana Kay Slater
Davis, California

THE EDITORS

Marc T. Braverman is a Cooperative Extension youth development specialist in the Department of Human and Community Development at the University of California, Davis. His specializations include program evaluation design and adolescent health promotion, and his applied research involves University of California programs across the state. Braverman was the founding director (1994 to 1998) of the 4-H Center for Youth Development at UC Davis. He has consulted with the California Department of Health Services, the federal Centers for Disease Control and Prevention, the American Cancer Society, and numerous local organizations. In 1998–99, he was a visiting researcher at the National Institute for Public Health in Oslo, Norway, where he worked on adolescent health promotion studies and projects.

Braverman has been the editor or coeditor of two volumes in Jossey-Bass's *New Directions for Evaluation* series: *Evaluating Health Promotion Programs* (1989) and *Advances in Survey Research* (1996). He teaches graduate courses at UC Davis in applied research, program evaluation methods, and adolescent health behaviors. Prior to his appointment at UC Davis, he was an evaluation specialist at the Northwest Regional Educational Laboratory in Portland, Oregon. He received his M.S. and Ph.D. degrees in educational psychology from the University of Wisconsin–Madison.

Norman A. Constantine is senior scientist and program director of the Center for Research on Adolescent Health and Development at the Public Health Institute and lecturer in epidemiology at the UC Berkeley School of Public Health. He has many years of experience conducting research and evaluation studies in adolescent health, parent education, and infant development. His current interests include policy use and misuse of research evidence, and the heuristics employed by evaluation consumers to appraise conclusions about program effectiveness. He recently helped develop and enact the *California Comprehensive Sexual Health and HIV/AIDS Prevention Education Act;* the evidence-based advocacy campaign he led in this regard received the Public Relations Society of America's Compass Award. Constantine has taught graduate courses in evaluation, statistics, and measurement, and currently teaches a seminar on public health interventions. He is senior methodologist with the UC Berkeley Center for Community Wellness and its statewide evaluation of the California First 5 Commission's *Kit for New Parents,* and previously served as director of the California Interagency Data Collaboration, codirector of the California Healthy Kids Survey, founding director of WestEd's Assessment Services Program, and analysis director for Stanford University's national randomized trial of the Infant Health and Development Program. Constantine received his Ph.D. in educational psychology from the University of Oregon in 1984.

Jana Kay Slater is senior research scientist at the Center for Research on Adolescent Health and Development at PHI. She has over twenty years' experience evaluating health education and prevention programs for low-income and high-risk populations. Her current interest is working with grantees as an "evaluation coach," converting grantee anxiety and discomfort about evaluation into support of the process and building local skills for collecting and using evaluative information for program improvement. From 1987 to 1998, Slater was a research and evaluation consultant at the California Department of Education. Prior to that, she was an evaluation specialist at the Northwest Regional Educational Laboratory. The American Evaluation Association (AEA) awarded Slater the Marcia Guttentag Fellowship Award (1982) and the Robert Ingle Service Award (1997). She has served in multiple leadership roles for AEA, including as a member of its board of directors. Slater has taught graduate courses in applied research methods at the University of California, Davis, and at California State University, Sacramento. She was coeditor of *Advances in Survey Research* (1996), a volume in the Jossey-Bass *New Directions for Evaluation* series. Slater received her Ph.D. in applied experimental psychology from Southern Illinois University.

THE CONTRIBUTORS

John Bare is director of program development and evaluation at The John S. and James L. Knight Foundation in Miami. He directs research, planning, and evaluation efforts for the foundation's journalism program, its venture fund, and its community-based grantmaking. Having joined the foundation in August 1997 as its first director of evaluation, Bare helped integrate evaluation into the foundation's mission. He created a system to track quality-of-life indicators in Knight's twenty-six communities of interest and helped the foundation develop ways to manage risk across its grant investments. A former media research consultant, Bare holds a Ph.D. in mass communication research from the School of Journalism and Mass Communication at the University of North Carolina at Chapel Hill. In his research on journalists' attitudes toward the communities they cover, Bare developed a way to measure public journalism as a belief system. Prior to joining Knight Foundation, Bare worked as a writer and researcher for the Education Statistics Services Institute of the American Institutes for Research in Washington, D.C., and a columnist for the (North Carolina-based) *Chapel Hill Herald-Sun*.

Marian E. Bass joined the staff of The Robert Wood Johnson Foundation in January 1998, following an eighteen-month consultancy with the foundation. During that time, she helped to establish the Grant Results Reporting Unit, which she now co-manages. From 1990 to 1996, she was with The Rockefeller Foundation, where she led the Central Evaluation Unit from 1992 to 1996. Her prior positions have been with the New Jersey Department of Human Services (where she headed the Office of Evaluation, Planning and Analysis), The Pew Charitable Trusts, the Hospital of the University of Pennsylvania, and the Pennsylvania Department of Public Welfare. Bass's past board service includes work on the executive committee of the Grantmakers Evaluation Network; Isles, Inc., of Trenton; the Princeton Education Foundation; and the People's Emergency Shelter of Philadelphia. She received a master's degree in city and regional planning from the University of Pennsylvania and completed her undergraduate education at Brandeis University.

Lester W. Baxter, chief evaluation officer at The Pew Charitable Trusts, develops and oversees the implementation of evaluation policies for one of the country's largest public charities. In this capacity, Baxter advises the Trusts' board, executive management, and program staff on the design and performance of program strategies and on research and policy issues affecting the charity's work. He has developed evaluations of the Trusts' programs in campaign conduct, campaign finance reform, climate change, public health, wilderness protection, and youth voting, among others, and is the coauthor of *Returning Results: Planning and Evaluation at The Pew Charitable Trusts.* Before joining the Trusts in 1997, he held positions at Oak Ridge National Laboratory, the California Energy Commission, the University of Pennsylvania, and the East-West Center in Hawaii. Baxter is the author or coauthor of more than seventy professional publications on topics in public policy or philanthropy. He holds a B.A. in anthropology from Northwestern University, an M.A. in anthropology from the University of Hawaii, and an M.A. in demography and Ph.D. in public and urban policy from the University of Pennsylvania.

William L. Beery assumed his position as Group Health Community Foundation vice president in 1997 and has responsibility for the foundation's program, evaluation, and grantmaking division. He also directs education and prevention programs at The Hope Heart Institute. Beery holds the rank of professor (affiliate) in the University of Washington's School of Public Health and Community Medicine. He has had previous appointments at Duke University Medical Center and the University of North Carolina's School of Public Health. His evaluation and research interests have focused on community-based health promotion and prevention programs for low-income and high-risk populations. Prior to his move to Seattle, Beery directed health promotion and disease prevention demonstration, evaluation, and research programs at UNC's Cecil G. Sheps Center for Health Services Research. He also served as director of a community health education program at Duke and a community action organization in Virginia. Beery served as a Peace Corps volunteer in Senegal, West Africa, and later was the health program director for the Peace Corps in Malaysia and Thailand.

William E. Bickel is professor of administrative policy studies in the School of Education and a senior scientist at the Learning Research and Development Center, University of Pittsburgh. His research interests include evaluation methodology and research on evaluation utilization in various organizational and policy contexts, as well as educational reform policy and implementation studies. His evaluation work is focused on investigating how evaluation in educational systems and related organizational and policy settings can contribute to improved practice. This question is addressed, in part, by conducting evaluation studies for policy- and decision makers in a variety of reform and community settings. Recent work has emphasized investigations of the role that evaluation plays in private foundations in the United States. Bickel currently directs an evaluation partnership with the Heinz Endowments for their regional educational initiatives focused on "performance-oriented," school-based reform, preservice education policy and practice, and technology dissemination in urban systems. He is past director of an institutional evaluation partnership between the University of Pittsburgh and the Lilly Endowment (1990–1997). In the past several years, Bickel has been a consultant to a number of foundations, including The Robert Wood Johnson Foundation, The W. K. Kellogg Foundation, The Pew Charitable Trusts, and The Wallace Foundation, on matters concerning the effective use of evaluation-related processes to support organizational learning. Audiences for Bickel's work include educational practitioners and policymakers, organizational leaders in philanthropy, and the evaluation community.

Deborah G. Bonnet became vice president for evaluation at The Lumina Foundation for Education in 2001. In addition to designing and managing evaluations of the foundation's grants and research work, she is responsible for evaluation of the foundation as an enterprise. Since entering the field in 1974, Bonnet has conducted more than one hundred evaluation studies in a variety of fields, including education, health, human services, community development, leadership, and the arts. Before joining The Lumina Foundation, she headed the Indianapolis-based virtual firm DBonnet Associates, specializing in evaluation services for private foundations and nonprofit organizations. Bonnet has served on the board of the American Evaluation Association (AEA) and on the advisory board of Jossey-Bass's *New Directions for Evaluation* quarterly journal. She has authored several articles on evaluation for trade publications, including the *American Journal of Evaluation, Educational Leadership: Journal of the Association for Supervision and Curriculum Development,* and the *Journal of Research and Development in Education,* as well as a chapter in *Applied Strategies for Curriculum Evaluation*. She has been a frequent speaker at AEA meetings. Bonnet holds a master's degree in business administration from Indiana University, a master's degree in industrial engineering and operations research from Virginia Tech, and a bachelor's degree in psychology, also from Virginia Tech.

Hodding Carter III joined The John S. and James L. Knight Foundation as president and CEO in February 1998. He held the Knight chair in journalism at the University of Maryland College of Journalism from 1995 until 1997. Carter began his newspaper career in 1959 at the family-owned *Delta Democrat-Times* in Greenville, Mississippi. He served as a Washington-based opinion columnist for the *Wall Street Journal* for ten years and was a syndicated columnist with United Media/NEA in the early 1990s. He is author of *The Reagan Years* (Braziller, 1988) and *The South Strikes Back* (Doubleday, 1959). Carter has also served as host, anchor, panelist, correspondent, and reporter for a variety of public affairs television shows on PBS, ABC, CBS, the BBC, and CNN, including *Frontline* and *This Week with David Brinkley*. He was president and later chairman of MainStreet, a TV production company that specializes in public affairs television (1985 to 1998). He won the Society of Professional Journalists' national award for editorial writing in 1961, four national Emmy Awards, and the Edward R. Murrow Award. Carter worked on two successful presidential campaigns—Lyndon Johnson's in 1964 and Jimmy Carter's in 1976. He served in the Carter administration as spokesman for the U.S. Department of State and as assistant secretary of state for public affairs. Carter holds a bachelor's degree from Princeton University (1957) and was Nieman Fellow at Harvard University (1965–66).

Ross F. Conner is associate professor of social ecology and director of the Center for Community Health Research at the University of California, Irvine. Conner received his Ph.D. and M.A. degrees in social psychology and evaluation from Northwestern University and his B.A. in psychology from The Johns Hopkins University. His research focuses on the evaluation of community health promotion and disease prevention programs. His newest project is a multiyear collaborative effort involving the university and three community-based groups that is focused on innovative, culturally based cancer-control programs in the Chinese and Korean communities (funders were The Robert Wood Johnson Foundation, California Endowment, and The Irvine Health Foundation). He is collaborating with colleagues on an HIV-prevention program for Latino men (funders were the State of California, Office of AIDS and Universitywide AIDS Taskforce). Conner is the author-editor or coauthor-coeditor of nine books and numerous papers. He is a past president of the American Evaluation Association (1989) and continues to serve on special AEA committees. He has assisted a number of foundations in their evaluation work, including the Rockefeller, Kellogg, James Irvine, Paso del Norte Health, St. Luke's, and Levi Strauss foundations. He co-teaches (with foundation colleagues) an Evaluators' Institute class, "Evaluation for Foundation Program Officers." Much of his work involves multicultural populations, an interest that began when he served in the Peace Corps in Tunisia.

Wendy L. Constantine is an independent evaluation consultant with a focus on programs promoting child and family well-being. She currently serves as study director for the three-year, statewide evaluation of the First 5 California Commission's *Kit for New Parents*, based at the U.C. Berkeley Center for Community Wellness. Her thirty-year professional career has spanned the disciplines of program evaluation and survey research, resulting in practice-based expertise in employing both quantitative and qualitative methods. Areas of investigation have included parent education, infant development, family conflict resolution, and leadership training. Her methodological specializations include study design, questionnaire development, multisite data collection, and project management, with particular emphasis on longitudinal research. She has previously served as project officer for the State of California Judicial Council's research grant program in family law, field operations director for Stanford University's national randomized evaluation of the Infant Health and Development Program, field operations manager for the Survey Research Center at the University of Illinois at Chicago, and survey director for the National Survey of Youth at the National Opinion Research Center (NORC). She has a B.A. in sociology from Lake Forest College in Lake Forest, Illinois.

E. Jane Davidson is associate director of the Evaluation Center at Western Michigan University (WMU) and director of WMU's new interdisciplinary Ph.D. in evaluation, which spans the colleges of Arts and Sciences, Education, Engineering and Applied Sciences, and Health and Human Services. Davidson's current research in evaluation centers on developing and translating evaluation logic and methodology into user-friendly "nuts and bolts" tools and methods for practical application in real-world settings. She is author of the forthcoming book *The Multipurpose Evaluation Guidebook: The Nuts and Bolts of Putting Together a Solid Evaluation* (Sage) and creator of *Organizational IQ Test*, a tool for assessing an organization's learning capacity. Davidson has worked for several years in both internal and external consulting and training roles in government, nonprofit, and business organizations and is director of New Zealand-based Davidson Consulting Ltd. Her primary content specialization areas are in personnel evaluation and performance management, organizational learning, and the evaluation of organizational change. Davidson holds undergraduate degrees in chemistry and psychology, a master's in industrial and organizational psychology, and a Ph.D. in organizational behavior, with substantial emphasis on evaluation.

Jennifer C. Greene is a specialist in educational and social program evaluation at the University of Illinois, Urbana-Champaign. She received her Ph.D. in educational psychology from Stanford University in 1976. With academic appointments at the University of Rhode Island, Cornell University, and, currently, the University of Illinois, Urbana-Champaign, she has concentrated her scholarship on making evaluation useful and socially responsible, in terms of both theory and practice. Greene's work has emphasized the development of alternative approaches to evaluation and applied research, notably qualitative, democratic, and mixed-method approaches. Her work has also emphasized the sociopolitical role and value commitments of evaluation, within an argument that evaluation can best serve democratic and public interests. Greene's evaluation practice has spanned a diverse array of educational and social programs, including federal remedial and compensatory education, public policy and natural resource leadership development, youth development, high school science reform, arts education, and intergenerational storytelling. Greene has held leadership positions in the American Educational Research Association and the American Evaluation Association, and she recently completed two terms as coeditor-in-chief of *New Directions for Evaluation* (Jossey-Bass).

Peter Dobkin Hall is Hauser lecturer on nonprofit organizations at the John F. Kennedy School of Government (KSG) at Harvard University. Hall is a graduate of Reed College and SUNY-Stony Brook. His publications include *The Organization of American Culture, 1700–1900: Private Institutions, Elites, and the Origins of American Nationality* (New York University Press, 1982); *Inventing the Nonprofit Sector: Essays on Philanthropy, Voluntarism, and Nonprofit Organizations* (The Johns Hopkins University Press, 1992); and *Lives in Trust: The Fortunes of Dynastic Families in Late Twentieth Century America* (Westview Press, 1992). He coedited *Sacred Companies: Organizational Aspects of Religion and Religious Aspects of Organizations* (Oxford University Press, 1998) and the chapter on nonprofits for the forthcoming *Millennial Edition of Historical Statistics of the United States* (Cambridge University Press). Before his appointment at KSG, Hall served as director of Yale's Program on Nonprofit Organizations and held teaching appointments in Yale's Department of History, School of Management, Divinity School, and Ethics, Politics, and Economics Program. Hall's current research interests include the development of the modern welfare state and social welfare policy, the role of educational institutions in creating leadership and civic engagement, and the emergence of transnational institutions, communities, and identities.

Rodney K. Hopson is associate professor in the School of Education, Department of Foundations and Leadership, and faculty member in the Center for Interpretive and Qualitative Research (CIQR) at Duquesne University. His recent manuscripts related to evaluation extend the ways in which the larger field, profession, and major professional organizations come to terms with research on, issues about, and interests that impact people (and scholars) of color and traditionally underserved communities. Hopson's work emphasizes the need for evaluators to have a new set of skills, frameworks, and ethical considerations around culture, diversity, and social justice in evaluation. Other manuscripts in drug research and educational reform emphasize his use of qualitative and ethnographic evaluation techniques to contribute to understanding the social context of HIV/AIDS in inner cities and the notion of educational resilience in challenging schooling environments in southwestern Pennsylvania. Hopson serves on several evaluation-related editorial advisory boards and was awarded the Marcia Guttentag Award in 2000 from the American Evaluation Association. He received his Ph.D. in educational evaluation from the Curry School of Education, University of Virginia.

Michael M. Howe is president of The East Bay Community Foundation in Oakland, California. The foundation connects donors in Alameda and Contra Costa counties to community needs and opportunities, using community knowledge and leadership. Howe works with various programs and organizations that improve people's lives and contribute to the strength of communities. He was one of the cofounders of the Foundation Consortium and a board member of the National Funding Collaborative for Violence Prevention, the John Gardner Center at Stanford University, the Coalition of Community Foundations for Youth, Buck Institute for Education, and the Volunteerism Project; he is a founding board member of the Oakland Child Health and Safety Initiative, as well as the East Bay Public Corridor Safety Partnership. Howe came to the foundation from The Marin Community Foundation, where, from 1986 to 1993, he helped create and develop The Marin Community Foundation as its senior planning and evaluation officer. Over the years, he has supported the creation and expansion of community foundations across the nation. Between 1968 and 1980, Howe served as professor of sociology and founding dean of the College of Professional Studies at the University of San Francisco.

James R. Knickman is vice president for research and evaluation at The Robert Wood Johnson Foundation. He is responsible for external evaluations of national initiatives supported by the foundation and is a leader in shaping foundation-funded research initiatives. Prior to joining the foundation in 1992, Knickman was on the faculty at New York University, where he directed the Health Research Program and conducted research on a range of issues related to health-care delivery. He serves as vice chair of the board of directors for the Robert Wood Johnson University Hospital and is a member of the board of directors of the Academy for Health Services and Health Policy Research. He received a Ph.D. in public policy analysis from the University of Pennsylvania and a B.A. from Fordham University.

Mark R. Kramer is managing director of the Foundation Strategy Group and co-founder, with Michael E. Porter, of the Center for Effective Philanthropy. Kramer has over twenty years' experience in the foundation world as a trustee of three family foundations, a cofounder and former chair of the Jewish Funders Network—a national organization of seven hundred foundations—and a writer and researcher in the field. He is coauthor of the *Harvard Business Review* article titled "Philanthropy's New Agenda: Creating Value" (November/December, 1999); he is a regular columnist for *The Chronicle of Philanthropy* and a contributor to *American Benefactor Magazine* and *Foundation News & Commentary.* For the past twelve years, he has been president of Kramer Capital Management, Inc., a venture capital investment and consulting firm. Kramer holds a B.A. from Brandeis University, an M.B.A. from The Wharton School, and a J.D. from the University of Pennsylvania Law School.

Victor Kuo is a research associate in the Evaluation and Learning Services Department at The David and Lucile Packard Foundation in Los Altos, California. Prior to joining the Packard Foundation in early 2002, he had served in the evaluation office of another large, California-based foundation since 1999. In 2003, he was elected to cochair the Nonprofit and Foundation Topical Interest Group of the American Evaluation Association. Kuo has participated in evaluations of California state and federal class-size-reduction programs and has conducted research on education policy formation of state school finance programs and comprehensive school reform efforts. He is from Anaheim, California, where he taught high school biology and life science for English language learners. He completed his doctorate in educational administration and policy analysis and a master's degree in sociology from Stanford University, as well as a master's degree in science education from Columbia University and a bachelor's degree in biology from Pomona College.

Risa Lavizzo-Mourey became The Robert Wood Johnson Foundation president and CEO in January 2003. She joined the foundation in 2001 as senior vice president. Prior to joining the foundation, Lavizzo-Mourey served in a variety of roles while at the University of Pennsylvania, including director of the Institute on Aging and Sylvan Eisman Professor of Medicine and Health Care Systems. She also served in the U.S. Department of Health and Human Services as deputy administrator of the Agency for Health Care Policy and Research (now known as the Agency for Health Care Research and Quality). Lavizzo-Mourey served as a consultant to the White House on issues of health policy and on the President's Advisory Commission on Consumer Protection and Quality in the Health Care Industry. She recently completed service on the Institute of Medicine (IOM) Committee that produced *Unequal Treatment: Confronting Racial and Ethnic Disparities in Healthcare.*

A former RWJ Clinical Scholar, Lavizzo-Mourey earned an M.D. degree at Harvard Medical School, followed by an M.B.A. at the Wharton School of the University of Pennsylvania.

Laura C. Leviton is a senior program officer of The Robert Wood Johnson Foundation, overseeing evaluations for initiatives ranging from fellowships and scholarships to health-care quality. Before joining the foundation, she was a professor of public health at the University of Alabama at Birmingham (UAB) and, before that, was on the faculty of the University of Pittsburgh School of Public Health. Leviton was president of the American Evaluation Association in the year 2000, coauthored *Foundations of Program Evaluation* (Sage, 1995), and serves on several editorial boards for evaluation journals. She received the 1993 award from the American Psychological Association for Distinguished Contributions to Psychology in the Public Interest for her work in HIV prevention and health promotion at the workplace. She served on an Institute of Medicine committee to evaluate preparedness for terrorist attacks and was a member of the CDC's national advisory committee on HIV and STD prevention. She received her Ph.D. from the University of Kansas in social psychology and postdoctoral training in evaluation research at Northwestern University.

Melvin M. Mark is professor of psychology at Pennsylvania State University, where he is an award-winning teacher. He is currently editor of the *American Journal of Evaluation,* a journal of the American Evaluation Association. Mark received his Ph.D. in social psychology from Northwestern University. His interests include the theory, methodology, practice, and profession of program and policy evaluation. His writings address issues such as the role of stakeholders in evaluation, systematic values inquiry, mixed methods, and quasi-experimental design. He has been involved in evaluations in a number of areas, including prevention programs for at-risk youth, federal personnel policies, technology assistance programs for small manufacturers, and higher education. He has written over eighty articles and chapters. His latest book (with Gary Henry and George Julnes) is *Evaluation: An Integrated Framework for Understanding, Guiding, and Improving Policies and Programs* (Jossey-Bass, 2000), and he is coeditor (with Ian Shaw and Jennifer Greene) of a forthcoming book titled *Handbook of Evaluation* (Sage). Previous books include *Evaluation Studies Review Annual,* Vol. 3 (Sage, 1978), *Social Science and Social Policy* (Sage, 1985), *Multiple Methods in Program Evaluation* (Jossey-Bass, 1987), and *Realist Evaluation: An Emerging Theory in Support of Practice* (Jossey-Bass, 1998).

Marli S. Melton was vice president of programs at The Community Foundation for Monterey County from 1987 until 2003. Serving as associate director from 1991 to 2001, Melton saw the foundation grow from $6 million to $70 million in assets.

Melton started the foundation's evaluation program, served as lead staff for the installation of comprehensive integrated data management systems, and oversaw donor adviser services, special programs, and annual grants of about $5 million in arts, education, health, environment, and community and social services. As vice president, she supervised three responsive grant cycles per year, in addition to Neighborhood Grants (an ongoing bilingual initiative with a leadership development component), Management Assistance and Organizational Development, and an initiative for Education and Employment Development for Teens in East Salinas. Melton has taught nonprofit management, grant writing, economics, social sciences, and mathematics at the university and college levels. Born and raised in Seattle, Washington, she has a B.A. in economics, with an emphasis in interdisciplinary social thought and institutions from Stanford University and an M.A. in economics from Yale University. Currently the director of development at Chartwell School, Melton is assisting with the development of a new campus at the former Fort Ord, emphasizing healthy, sustainable design to improve outcomes for children with language disabilities.

Ricardo A. Millett is president of the Woods Fund of Chicago, a Chicago-based philanthropy that focuses on reducing poverty, eliminating barriers to equal opportunity, and increasing access to civic life for disadvantaged people and communities. Before joining The Woods Fund, Millet was at The W. K. Kellogg Foundation in Battle Creek, Michigan, where he served as director of evaluation. He has a Ph.D. in social policy planning and research from the Heller School at Brandeis University. He also has an M.S.W. in social policy and an undergraduate degree in economics, both from Brandeis. Millett shares The Woods Fund's commitment to helping people who have been historically excluded from the democratic process and to equality and social justice. Since leaving the university, Millett has devoted himself to increasing opportunities for the disfranchised and helping society understand how to hear and expand minority participation.

Patricia Patrizi, founder of Patrizi Associates, works with a broad range of nonprofits and philanthropies in the areas of evaluation and organizational learning. She is currently the editor and principal investigator for a series of studies titled *Practice Matters: The Improving Philanthropy Project*, which are aimed at examining and improving the practices and strategies of foundations. This work is funded by The Robert Wood Johnson, Ewing Marion Kauffman, John S. and James L. Knight, and David and Lucile Packard Foundations. She is also chair of The Evaluation Roundtable, a group of evaluation and program executives at the nation's largest foundations, dedicated to improving evaluation practices across philanthropy. Other recent work includes (1) design of systems of evaluation, accountability, and organizational learning for The W. K. Kellogg Foundation, The Rockefeller Foundation, The Edna McConnell Clark Foundation, and The William Penn Foundation; (2) evaluations of *Join Together*, a national substance abuse prevention and treatment resource, and *CADCA: Community Anti-Drug Coalitions of America*, both funded by The Robert Wood Johnson Foundation, and (3) a study of foundation practices in evaluation and organizational learning for The W. K. Kellogg Foundation. Previously, she served as director of evaluation at The Pew Charitable Trusts for eight years. At Pew, she was responsible for the design and oversight of over 150 evaluations in the fields of health and human services, education, the environment, religion, culture, and public policy. Patrizi holds degrees from Bryn Mawr College and the University of Pennsylvania.

Michael Quinn Patton is an independent organizational development and program evaluation consultant. He is former president of the American Evaluation Association and author of *Utilization-Focused Evaluation* (3rd ed., Sage, 1997), *Qualitative Research and Evaluation Methods* (3rd ed., Sage, 2002), and *Grand Canyon Celebration: A Father-Son Journey of Discovery* (Prometheus, 1999), which was a finalist for Minnesota Book of the Year in 1999 (creative nonfiction category). Patton is recipient of both the Myrdal Award for "Outstanding Contributions to the Use and Practice of Evaluation" from the Evaluation Research Society and the Lazarsfeld Award for "Lifelong Contributions to Evaluation Theory" from AEA. He serves on the graduate faculty of Union Institute and University, a nontraditional, interdisciplinary, nonresidential, individually designed doctoral program. He spent eighteen years on the faculty of the University of Minnesota (1973 to 1991), including five years as director of the Minnesota Center for Social Research. He received the university's Morse-Amoco Award for outstanding teaching. He helped design and train participants in the Leadership Labs on Outcomes in Minnesota, which has worked with over six hundred nonprofit, government, and philanthropic executives on leadership for results.

Edward Pauly, The Wallace Foundation's director of evaluation, leads the foundation's efforts to gain practical knowledge from the fund's initiatives. The Wallace Foundation's evaluations seek to provide powerful findings that are widely used by leading organizations and policymakers. Pauly has developed major evaluation projects for the funds on education, youth development, adult literacy, and public participation in the arts and culture. Previously, he was the first coordinator of education research for the Manpower Demonstration Research Corporation. His books include *The Classroom Crucible: What Really Works, What Doesn't and Why* (Basic Books, 1991), *Homegrown Lessons: Innovative Programs Linking School and Work* (Jossey-Bass, 1995), and, with Judith M. Gueron, *From Welfare to Work* (Russell Sage Foundation, 1991). Pauly received his Ph.D. in political science from Yale University.

Debra J. Rog is a senior research associate with the Vanderbilt University's Institute for Public Policy Studies and directs the Washington office of the Center for Mental Health Policy. Rog received her Ph.D. in social psychology from Vanderbilt University, a master's in social psychology from Kent State University, and her bachelor's degree from American International College. She has over twenty years' experience in program evaluation and applied research and has directed numerous evaluations and research projects for both philanthropic and government sponsors. Rog has to her credit numerous publications on evaluation methodology, housing, homelessness, poverty, mental health, and program and policy development and is coeditor of the *Applied Social Research Methods Series* (Sage) and the *Handbook of Applied Social Research Methods* (Sage, 2004). She has served on the board of directors of the American Evaluation Association, and is a member of the American Psychological Association, the American Psychological Society, and the American Public Health Association. She has been recognized for her evaluation work by the National Institute of Mental Health, AEA, the Eastern Evaluation Research Society, and the Knowledge Utilization Society.

Michael Scriven holds degrees in mathematics and in the philosophy of mathematical logic at the University of Melbourne, as well as a doctorate in philosophy at Oxford. He has held full-time appointments in the United States, Australia, and New Zealand, in departments of mathematics, philosophy, psychology, the history and philosophy of science, and education, including twelve years at the University of California, Berkeley, and at the Center for Advanced Study in the Behavioral Sciences (Palo Alto) and as a Whitehead Fellow at Harvard University. Brief or honorary appointments include those at the Center for Advanced Study in Theoretical Psychology (University of Alberta), the Educational Testing Service (Princeton), the Center for the Study of Democratic Institutions (Santa Barbara), the Academy of Social Sciences in Australia, and the National Science Foundation. His 330 publications are mainly in the fields of his appointments and in the areas of critical thinking, technology studies, computer studies, psychiatry, and evaluation. He has been on the editorial boards of forty-three journals in these ten fields and edited *Evaluation News* and *University MicroNews*. He is a past president of the American Educational Research Association and of the American Evaluation Association; he is currently professor of evaluation at Auckland University and of psychology at Claremont Graduate University.

INTRODUCTION: PUTTING EVALUATION TO WORK FOR FOUNDATIONS

Jana Kay Slater, Norman A. Constantine, and Marc T. Braverman

The modern grantmaking philanthropic foundation is largely an American creation. Launched in the early years of the twentieth century, the first foundations were based on endowments from private citizens who had enjoyed spectacular successes in the business world. Their reasons for donating money through a formal grantmaking mechanism were diverse. Many donors were motivated by a sense of social responsibility and the sincere desire to do good in the world. Others sought tax advantage so that much of their money could remain under the control of themselves, their families, and their business partners instead of going to the government. For others, the motivation might have been vanity: they were attracted by the notion of a powerful, admired organization bearing their name and doing good deeds after they were gone from the world. And, of course, for some donors these various motivations were probably operating simultaneously, making this new option for structuring their wealth irresistibly appealing.

Whatever the mix of reasons that spurred this early growth, the concept took off, expanded, and differentiated. There is no question that over the past hundred years, American society has been changed in innumerable ways, large and small, through the contributions of philanthropic foundations (see, for example, Nielsen,

We thank Laura Leviton for her valuable input on the content of the discussion. The three authors contributed equally to the development of this chapter.

1972, 1996). Increasingly, their work is having an impact in other parts of the world as well.

Many variations to traditional single-donor private foundations have arisen over the years. *Community foundations* are publicly supported institutions with multiple funding sources that serve the interests of a specified geographic region. *Corporate foundations* are established by private corporations as philanthropic grantmaking institutions and generally focus on issues related to the company's products, geographic locations, or employees. *Health conversion foundations* are established from the proceeds of the conversion to for-profit status of health maintenance organizations and nonprofit hospitals.

The past generation has been the period of most rapid growth for foundations, both in numbers and assets. According to the Foundation Center (2003), in 2001 there were 61,810 grantmaking foundations in the United States, which together controlled an estimated $477 billion in assets and gave out approximately $30.5 billion in grants.

The amounts of money distributed by philanthropic foundations each year are not large compared to outlays for social programs by the government sector, or even compared to the total of individual giving in the United States. It has recently been estimated that 88 percent of contributions to nonprofit organizations come from individuals, through both direct gifts and bequests (Dowie, 2001). Yet it is clear that the resources distributed by foundations are both significant and impressive.

Foundations as Social Engines

Early and traditional views of philanthropy centered on charitable giving, aimed at providing direct assistance to the needy members of society (Bremner, 1994). But many foundations have a very different view of their own mission and purposes. They are dedicated to changing society in ways that their donors, trustees, and staff believe will provide important and lasting benefits to individuals and communities. This is certainly an ambitious ideal, and, indeed, some of foundations' greatest successes have resulted from the pursuit of sweeping visions of society, science, human health, and the environment.

Observers have noted that foundations are particularly well suited to serve as engines of social change. One reason, of course, is the financial and intellectual resources that they can bring to bear on finding resolutions to pressing social issues. Beyond this, however, is the unusual position of foundations among other institutions in society. They do not have the constraints that are characteristic of either the public or private sectors. For example, government agencies are accountable to the electorate, and their fortunes and activities are closely linked to changes in political administrations. Most government agencies must operate with high degrees of transparency and must be prepared to deal with criticisms and demands from taxpayers, legislators, and assorted watchdogs. Corporations are accountable to their stockholders to produce strong financial performance, and both corporations and privately owned companies are subject to the competitive pressures of the marketplace.

Universities, like foundations, are characterized by an atmosphere of intellectual freedom and exploration of new avenues of knowledge. However, universities have a complex set of ongoing responsibilities beyond their research functions, do not have the ability to apply the intense institutional focus to specific areas of investigation that is found in foundations, and are accountable to multiple external audiences (with some variation, depending on whether they are public or private).

In contrast, foundations have their own funds, and no mandate to be financially profitable. They are not formally accountable to any bodies except their own trustees. The major constraint on their operation is that they must pay out each year an amount equal to 5 percent of their previous year's asset base, in order to maintain their favorable tax status. Therefore, within the boundaries established by their charters, they are freer than virtually any other type of institution to pursue objectives in accordance with the interests, inclinations, creativity, and expertise of their trustees, administrators, and staff. Certainly, this is a propitious basis from which to pursue bold societal visions, long-term timeframes, and a search for new knowledge.

How well have foundations taken advantage of their unique opportunity? The work and accomplishments of individual foundations run the gamut along the dimensions of innovation and effectiveness. Many foundations have had little effect, whereas others have achieved moderate accomplishments, and a few have had extraordinary impact, as becomes particularly clear when viewed over the course of years or decades (Nielsen, 1996). Modes of practice have been permanently changed; intellectual directions in the sciences and the arts have been nurtured and flourished; universities, research centers, and other institutions have been strengthened or built from the ground up.

Furthermore, the impact of foundations will probably grow larger, based on projections of the growth of foundation assets over the next several decades. Because of the remarkable growth of the economy in the 1980s and 1990s (and despite the economic contraction that has occurred over the past few years), a tremendous amount of wealth has been created and will be transferred across generations. If applicable laws governing estate taxes and foundation operations do not appreciably change, a substantial proportion of that wealth will almost certainly flow into foundations. Dowie (2001) cites estimates that place the amount conservatively at several trillion dollars. With that escalation in resources, the role and potential of philanthropic foundations will be even greater than they are now.

Potential Contributions of Evaluation

Given foundations' ambitious goals of promoting social change and the importance of their activities, many questions can naturally arise. Examples may include:

- How do foundations learn from their experiences and those of the programs they fund?
- How do they determine their organizational priorities?
- How do they know what they have accomplished or assess their degree of success?
- What do they know about the effectiveness of their grantees and the factors underlying grantee outcomes?
- How can like-minded funders share knowledge to advance a field?

The need to address these and many other questions is where evaluation enters the picture, and this invokes the purpose of this book. In light of the goals that foundations set for themselves and the amount of resources they commit in pursuit of these goals, it seems that evaluation would be naturally embraced as a significant and central practice of philanthropy. Evaluation, after all, is a broad class of activities geared to understanding the operations and outcomes of programs and policies. It is surprising, therefore, that foundations' use of evaluation has been relatively modest (Wisely, 2002). Nevertheless, the field of philanthropy has reached a crossroads, where many voices are calling for a greater effort to understand what, why, and how much its activities accomplish.

Attention to the practice of evaluation is increasing in the foundation world—how it is done, where it can be used, what it can accomplish, what it costs, how it varies, and why it is needed. Many of the larger foundations, as well as regional grantmaker associations, take evaluation very seriously. Evaluation is discussed at grantmakers' conferences, and a number of insightful analyses have been issued. Within philanthropy, the literature on evaluation and its relationship to effective organizational practice has been growing, primarily in the form of limited-distribution reports but spurred in recent years by the wide accessibility afforded by the Internet. A recent example is *Practice Matters: The Improving Philanthropy Project*—a series of papers on organizational effectiveness that has been funded by five major foundations and is published on-line by the Foundation Center (2004).

Yet evaluation is still at the cutting edge of most foundation activity and has not been incorporated in a productive way into the mainstream of foundation operations. Certainly, most foundations do not systematically or rigorously make use of evaluation. In practice, due to the lack of evaluative information connected to their grantmaking, many foundations, especially midsize and smaller ones, would have difficulty in objectively reporting what the impacts of their grants have been, why particular patterns of results were obtained, and what has generally been learned from their grants that can influence the course of future practice.

For its part, the practice of evaluation has evolved dramatically over the past decades. The field has progressed from a reliance on a small number of generally favored models and approaches to a continually enlarging domain of perspectives, drawn from a variety of other disciplines. Today, the creative and methodologically skilled evaluator is able to select from a broad constellation of tools and methods. As a result, one of the major problems confronting evaluation users, which is considerably more complicated than it might appear at first glance, is how to match the needs of the program situation with the most appropriate methods of evaluation inquiry.

Similarly, in the development of evaluation as a profession characterized by service to a growing variety of clients, it became evident that the group of people identifying themselves as evaluators was diversifying. Increasingly, these individuals displayed substantial differences in the viewpoints, skills, emphases, and methodological preferences that they brought to their professional practice. Recognizing this diversification, the American Evaluation Association (AEA) initiated the development of a set of guidelines for the practice of evaluation (Shadish, Newman, Scheirer, and Wye, 1995). The resulting statement, Guiding Principles for Evaluators (see Exhibit I.1 for a summary), was endorsed by the association's membership in 1994. The complete statement of guiding principles appears on the AEA Web site, as well as in each issue of the association's flagship journal, *The American Journal of Evaluation*. As evaluation grows in the nonprofit sector, these principles provide a basis from which clients can determine what they may expect from their evaluation collaborations and contracts.

This book is intended to promote effective evaluation practices within the philanthropic community and to help foundations work toward their ambitious goals of changing society in beneficial ways. Evaluation is a complex field of endeavor, infused not only with concerns about knowledge generation but also with a necessary focus on politics, economics, pragmatism, and the everyday details of making programs work. The discipline itself is already represented by an extensive literature, but what the authors in this book seek to do is to explore evaluation with

EXHIBIT I.1. THE AMERICAN EVALUATION ASSOCIATION'S GUIDING PRINCIPLES FOR EVALUATORS.

The American Evaluation Association (AEA), the professional association for evaluators in the United States, strives to ensure ethical work in the evaluation of programs, products, personnel, and policy. To guide the work of professionals in everyday practice and to inform evaluation clients and the general public of expectations for ethical behavior, the Association developed Guiding Principles, which establish criteria related to:

A. *Systematic Inquiry:* Evaluators conduct systematic, data-based inquiries about whatever is being evaluated.
B. *Competence:* Evaluators provide competent performance to stakeholders.
C. *Integrity/Honesty:* Evaluators ensure the honesty and integrity of the entire evaluation process.
D. *Respect for People:* Evaluators respect the security, dignity, and self-worth of the respondents, program participants, clients, and other stakeholders with whom they interact.
E. *Responsibilities for General and Public Welfare:* Evaluators articulate and take into account the diversity of interests and values that may be related to the general and public welfare.

Note: The complete Guiding Principles are available on the Web site of the American Evaluation Association, www.eval.org.

Source: Used by permission of the American Evaluation Association.

specific regard to the world of foundations and their distinct characteristics, needs, operating modes, and partners. On this topic, there is still little published literature, but there is a great deal of material for analysis and discussion.

Audiences for the Book

We have two primary audiences in mind. First, we hope to reach foundation officers and other personnel who commission, plan, and use evaluations to answer questions such as those we have posed. Second, we wish to reach evaluators who work directly with foundations or with nonprofits on foundation-funded projects. Together, these audiences can have a powerful impact on improving the effectiveness of philanthropic efforts by putting evaluation to work for foundations.

Organization of the Book

We open with perspectives from three foundation presidents; each presents his or her foundation's vision for evaluation. Hodding Carter III, president and CEO of The John S. and James L. Knight Foundation, discusses evaluation in relation to foundations' obligations to understand their own philanthropic aims, planning processes, and impacts on society. Michael M. Howe, president of The East Bay Community Foundation, describes how evaluation is incorporated into his foundation's processes of organizational learning. Finally, Risa Lavizzo-Mourey, president and CEO of The Robert Wood Johnson Foundation, describes how evaluation plays a pivotal role in RWJF's program development and funding processes. Although evaluation use is far from ubiquitous among philanthropic foundations, these and other foundations have developed positive visions to guide their development and use of evaluation in support of effective grantmaking.

The remainder of the book is organized into two major sections. Part One, titled *Understanding Foundations as a Context for Evaluation,* contains readings that analyze foundations' unique organizational attributes and the background perspectives that help one understand the application of evaluation to what foundations do. Part Two, titled *Building Capacity for Evaluation Practice,* describes factors that can increase the capabilities of both foundation personnel and evaluators to plan, conduct, and disseminate useful evaluations in support of effective foundation practice.

Chapter One, by Laura C. Leviton and Marian E. Bass, includes illustrations and vignettes about implementing and using foundation-sponsored evaluation, based on their own experiences and those of colleagues. The vignettes provide engaging illustrations of what happens to evaluation practice when important *internal factors* (foundation size, culture, and the organizational location of responsibility for evaluation) and *external factors* (foundations' power in society, their vulnerability to criticism, and grantee perceptions of the evaluation process) are (or are not) taken into account. Leviton and Bass use these points to discuss the potential role of evaluation and the contributions it can make.

In Chapter Two, Peter Dobkin Hall examines the historical development of foundation perspectives regarding the use of evaluation. As he describes, the 1970s were a formative period in which a number of influential foundation voices laid down strongly expressed support for evaluation as an enterprise that foundations should use to learn more about the value and effects of their activities. The ensuing developments in more recent years have not unfolded according to the script one might have envisioned from these early calls. Hall describes how foundations' use of evaluation has been problematic in a number of respects.

The practice of evaluation itself also broadened in that period of time. Yet the interest in evaluation within the nonprofit and philanthropic communities has grown steadily. He explores the interplay of these phenomena and analyzes how changing views and perspectives have brought us to the present point.

Mark R. Kramer and William E. Bickel explore, in Chapter Three, why current foundation-sponsored evaluation does not generally produce greater benefits for foundations in the areas of organizational learning and the sharing of knowledge. The reasons, they propose, lie in a number of systemic and cultural barriers. On the foundation side, these barriers include insufficient attention to foundation performance, implicit acceptance of professional autonomy for managers and program officers, and the time pressures of the grant cycle. On the evaluation side, the barriers include the difficulties of determining the qualifications of evaluators, the political pressures on evaluators, and evaluators' tendency to focus on individual grantee projects rather than overall foundation strategies or organizational development. Despite these challenges, Kramer and Bickel provide several current illustrations of exemplary foundation practice and suggest several strategies for positive change, beginning with a call for strong leadership and management on the part of foundations.

Relationships between foundations and their grantees can be affected by evaluation plans and requirements. In Chapter Four, Michael Quinn Patton, John Bare, and Deborah G. Bonnet review several types of foundation-grantee relationships, as well as ways that these relationships can be strained at various points in the grantmaking process, including the special tensions related to evaluation. The authors argue that clear and ongoing communication can alleviate some but not all of these strains. The process of risk analysis is then presented as a promising strategy for enhancing communication and otherwise alleviating stress.

In Chapter Five, Jennifer C. Greene, Ricardo A. Millett, and Rodney K. Hopson focus on an educative vision of evaluation; they extend this to a democratizing vision that can directly confront the evaluation challenges of privilege, power, and authority via meaningful participation, voice, and engagement of program beneficiaries and their communities. They make a case for the importance of foundations in realizing this vision of evaluation and provide key principles and strategies for conducting educative and democratizing evaluations of foundation programs.

Laura C. Leviton and William E. Bickel, in Chapter Six, present seven types of foundation cycles that collectively determine the fundamental work routine of foundations. Foundations' evaluation activities, argue the authors, must be integrated into these fundamental routines if those activities are to prove useful. The cycles relate to the course of a funded grant project, the life cycles of programs, the annual payout requirement (that is, the program decision-making cycle), business cycles affecting the foundation's endowment, the life cycles of nonprofit organizations, board voting schedules, and the waxing and waning of areas of institutional emphasis. What are the attendant challenges of these complicated patterns for individuals concerned with evaluation efforts? The individuals must recognize the cycles, the concomitant points in time when the organization is most in need of evaluative information, and the questions that most need addressing at each of these points.

Resources are usually more limited than one would like, even in foundations, and evaluation can be expensive. In Chapter Seven, Melvin M. Mark and William L. Beery address the issue of how allocation decisions regarding evaluation resources can be made. Two major questions must be tackled every time an evaluation planning decision is at hand. First, *what* should be evaluated? This might include the individual grant, a group of grants with similar activities, a group of grants with similar purpose (though different activities), a foundation's strategic initiative, or some other option. Second, *at what level of intensity* should this evaluation be conducted? The intensity dimension has implications for the standard of rigor to be applied, the degree of oversight that the evaluation will require, and the choice of an internal versus third-party evaluator. Mark and Beery describe the criteria to use in resolving these planning decisions, and they illustrate their points with a recent example from the Packard Foundation.

Foundations are complex organizations, and evaluation is a flexible endeavor that can take many forms and answer many questions. Ross F. Conner, Victor Kuo, Marli S. Melton, and Ricardo A. Millett have worked for and in foundations of various sizes, small to large. In Chapter Eight, they share their perspectives on four important foundation factors that influence evaluation planning, implementation, and use. First, what is the effect of resource level on evaluation activities? Second, how do factors within the foundation context influence decisions about the focus of evaluation efforts? Third, is the foundation's organizational climate supportive of evaluation for accountability purposes and improvement learning? Finally, how are evaluation activities influenced by the diversity of stakeholders and the questions they would like addressed? When these factors are acknowledged and their influences are used productively, evaluation is more likely to be embraced and to be useful to the foundation's operations.

In Chapter Nine, Patricia Patrizi and Edward Pauly take a strong position on the importance of adopting a field-based approach to evaluation. To increase effectiveness and accountability, philanthropy is urged to open up its planning and decision-making processes to new sources of information and perspectives. Evaluation will become more relevant and useful if foundation and field leaders work together to define the goals of evaluation and specify its questions. Field-based evaluation and field-generated questions would address issues of deeper significance and, in turn, enhance philanthropic effectiveness. The authors attribute foundations' disappointment with evaluation to the habit of conducting narrowly defined studies that have not taken into account the larger field context. If evaluation is to contribute to social betterment, it must look at two larger questions: (1) What would enable the whole field to be more effective in meeting society's needs? and (2) What does the field need to know to be truly effective?

The majority of foundations in this country are small, with few or no regular staff and little if any experience in using evaluation. Yet these foundations can benefit from using systematically collected data to answer questions about the programs they fund. Chapter Ten addresses this audience of small foundations. Marli S. Melton, Jana Kay Slater, and Wendy L. Constantine discuss low-cost approaches to evaluation. This chapter is most relevant for foundations in the initial stages of incorporating evaluation into their ongoing activities. The chapter begins with evaluative approaches for internally reviewing a foundation's grantmaking practices. Next, methods are suggested for introducing evaluation to grantees, including logic modeling. Finally, evaluative methods for making site visits are suggested. Throughout the chapter, examples of reporting forms are provided to illustrate their potential in building evaluative practices into grantmaking, at both the foundation and grantee levels.

With increasing frequency, foundations are funding complex community initiatives that can involve multiple delivery sites and, in some cases, cooperative grantmaking across foundations. These initiatives are multifaceted phenomena that pose sizable challenges for description, coordination, and measurement. In Chapter Eleven, Debra J. Rog and James R. Knickman discuss the difficulties inherent in conducting outcome evaluations of such initiatives. For example, the initiatives usually require long timeframes of several years or more to become well established and ready for evaluation; they also evolve over time, and local project sites develop unique features, based on the unique characteristics of their communities. Yet the investment in such projects can be considerable, and evaluation is often deemed an essential component. Rog and Knickman therefore offer several suggestions for evaluation efforts, based on the need for strategic evaluative thinking.

Questions about program effectiveness are central to much of evaluation practice and potential use by foundations, yet rarely does evaluation provide simple and conclusive answers to questions about the effects of funded programs. In Chapter Twelve, Norman A. Constantine and Marc T. Braverman discuss important issues in appraising evidence on program effectiveness. The main goals of this chapter are to motivate and support more critical appraisal and better use of effectiveness evidence among evaluators and evaluation consumers. Common sources of ambiguity and misinterpretation are discussed, with strategies for recognizing and dealing with these challenges. Examples from several influential evaluations are used to illustrate these points.

Chapter Thirteen is written directly to foundation-funded grantees. E. Jane Davidson, Michael M. Howe, and Michael Scriven explain how grantees can build evaluation and evaluative thinking into their projects in ways that benefit their own organizations. Examples and suggestions are provided on using evaluation to develop more compelling proposals, increase the chance of project success, inspire and focus project staff, provide a means of demonstrating the value of an organization's activities to its supporters and critics, and contribute to our understanding of what works in achieving social betterment. This chapter is oriented toward building on a grantee's existing strengths, minimizing evaluation anxiety, and expanding payoffs to grantees.

Finally, in Chapter Fourteen, Lester W. Baxter and Marc T. Braverman discuss the communication of evaluation results. They propose that one of the reasons for the limited use of evaluation findings is the lack of attention paid to the communication process and the needs of specific audiences. They present an analysis of potential evaluation audiences, including those that are internal to the foundation (trustees, managers, program officers, and in-house evaluators) and those external to it (grantees, government, other foundations, the public, and media). The authors also present a range of communication modes and discuss the use of these modes with the various types of audiences. They emphasize that communication decisions must be made strategically to optimize the value of the information for the people who will be using it.

The Need to Demonstrate Evaluation's Value

Two central themes that can be discerned through all the chapters in this volume are (1) the challenges for evaluators in accommodating the ways that foundations are structured, and (2) the benefits evaluation can provide to foundations, given their unique organizational characteristics. Foundations deal in information. Through the reports they commission, the scholarship they promote, and the work they support, information is one of their primary stocks in trade. One might wonder, then, at the factors that make the practice of evaluation such a difficult challenge in the foundation world. Why, after all, wouldn't foundations eagerly seek the information that evaluation promises to provide—information about their own plans, activities, operations, partners, and achievements?

One answer, of course, is that along with the potential benefits there are significant costs to the use of evaluation. The information produced must be seen as worth these costs, which include the diversion of financial resources, the need to ask difficult and sometimes painful questions, the tensions inherent in organizational change, and the attempt to impose transparency and rigor on decision processes that might otherwise be comfortably arbitrary or political. As we have noted, foundations, for the most part, are not required to conduct evaluations. Other institutions in society, by contrast, are subject to pressures from multiple internal and external stakeholders, who demand the forms of examination that are inherent in evaluation. More than any other type of organization, foundations are free to conduct evaluation and to demand it as an activity by their grantees *only* if they see the value in it—or, to state it more simply, only if they want to.

Therefore, as foundations operate today, if evaluation is to become a vital and indispensable component of how they function, it will need to be because of the inherent value that evaluation provides. Unless foundations' operating environments change (and that is certainly possible), their adoption of evaluation will not be compelled by outside requirements or pressures from external audience demands. This unique characteristic of the foundation world demands both imagination and pragmatism on the part of evaluators who work in the nonprofit sector. In that sense, philanthropic foundations represent one of the most challenging of all laboratories for the discipline of evaluation to demonstrate its value.

References

Bremner, R. H. (1994). *Giving: Charity and philanthropy in history.* New Brunswick, NJ: Transaction Publishers.

Dowie, M. (2001). *American foundations: An investigative history.* Cambridge, MA: The MIT Press.

Foundation Center. (2003). *Foundation Yearbook: Facts and figures on private and community foundations.* New York: Foundation Center.

Foundation Center. (2004). *Practice Matters: The Improving Philanthropy Project.* Available on-line at http://fdncenter.org/for_grantmakers/practice_matters. Accessed January 22, 2004.

Nielsen, W. A. (1972). *The big foundations: A Twentieth Century Fund study.* New York: Columbia University Press.

Nielsen, W. A. (1996). *Inside American philanthropy: The dramas of donorship.* Norman, OK: University of Oklahoma Press.

Shadish, W. R., Newman, D. L., Scheirer, M. A., & Wye, C. (Eds.). (1995). *Guiding principles for evaluators.* New Directions for Program Evaluation, no. 66. San Francisco: Jossey-Bass.

Wisely, D. S. (2002). Parting thoughts on foundation evaluation. *American Journal of Evaluation, 23*(2), 159–164.

PERSPECTIVE

Hodding Carter III

President and CEO, The John S. and James L. Knight Foundation

E valuation requires a baseline, a commonly recognized starting point. Herewith is a handful of observations to establish my own baseline of preconceptions and prejudices about evaluation, if only to provide some perspective on the comments that follow.

Newspaper folk, in whose number I was counted until my mid-forties, learned a basic lesson about "truth" very early in their careers. Not all readers who regularly demanded that we print "the truth" actually meant what they said. What many if not most of our critics wanted to see reflected in our newspapers' pages was *their* truth.

That understanding has been of considerable solace over my five-plus years as a somewhat bemused instant foundation executive. In this world, also, it turns out that not everyone who participates in the elaborate minuet that defines relations between foundation funders and nonprofit grantees actually wants rigorous evaluation of what we fund, how we fund it, and what it produces. Unsurprisingly, often the first instinct on both sides is to seek confirmation that good intentions given life by philanthropic dollars have created tangible, lasting results.

It also turns out that the men and women who work in this field have skins almost as thin as journalists'—which is to say very thin indeed. It is more than a little strange, but something that experience convinces me is an absolute fact, that those who are professionally involved in pointing out the flaws in other people's efforts and society's workings have remarkably little tolerance for criticism of their own. When faced with probing questions, our gut reaction is hostile and defensive. We'd rather pick at the nits than deal with the fundamental differences. This admission comes from someone who in his previous life wrote about 6,500 editorials—more than a few acerbic about the failings of others—and was everlastingly unable to handle negative comments with maturity or grace.

I also worked in the U.S. Department of State for a few years and encountered (and sometimes shared) another mind-set not unfamiliar to the nonprofit and foundation worlds. Many of the foreign service officers and high-ranking political appointees responsible for the foreign policy of the United States were certain that their work was of such complexity that no outside auditor could possibly judge it with adequate sophistication. Suspicious of the motives of those in the Congress or media who demanded cause-and-effect accountability, wary of the potential for serious harm that interim judgments about long-term policies could cause, and ever mindful that some of the demands for instant assessments came from partisan politicians more interested in embarrassing the administration or a foreign government than in correcting course, they believed passionately in working behind closed doors. "We work best without being constantly second-guessed," went the refrain. Only history can judge us fairly, and then only when all the facts are in.

To put it another way, we are all human—prickly about our work and touchy about outside criticism. That translates into a high hurdle for the introduction of systematic evaluation into any undertaking, not least philanthropy. It does not help that some of evaluation's apostles make ridiculous claims for its scientific accuracy that are unsupported by the record or common sense. It is positively harmful that others tout it as a way to punish failure rather than point the way toward success.

And yet, grudgingly but with growing momentum, the movement to bring informed judgment to bear on the grand work with which we in the independent sector are engaged gathers force. Well it should. What we attempt to do matters too much to too many people to be carried forth under the banner, "What we don't know won't hurt us."

Most grants are not sought or disbursed casually, after all. Many are the end product of elaborate bureaucratic procedures that consume reams of paper and countless staff hours. Petitioners and givers initiate, respond, negotiate, elaborate, and activate, accompanied by mutual pledges of commitment and performance. Funders require bona fides, work plans, and regular reports after they fork over the cash or to keep it coming. Grantees promise results that will justify the grantors' investment and advance the meaningful work in which they are engaged. In all this, it is well understood that everyone is living up to their fiduciary, as well as programmatic, obligations.

But even when there is consensus that evaluation is a good thing, there is the untidy problem that although *evaluation* is easily definable as a word, it is anything but commonly understood as a process. And, as you will note in some of the chapters that follow, even when the process is understood, there are deep divisions of opinion about how the results should be used.

Finally, the more deeply ingrained the problem that is being addressed—the more bound up it is with the muck and mire of life as it is lived by those who are not society's winners—the harder and also the more necessary the evaluation task. It is because Knight Foundation has, over the past decade, moved increasingly toward trying to deal with such problems and the social change necessary to address them that we now place so much emphasis on evaluation as an indispensable tool going in and coming out of our grants. This is a new thing for us, when measured against our fifty-four-year history. It is a new thing for me, when measured against my somewhat longer life experience, and thus I make no claim to profound insights. That is for the experts represented elsewhere in this volume.

But for us at the Knight Foundation, after years of serious internal study and discussion, the debate is over. We have decided we owe it to everyone—from the Knight brothers, whose bequests launched us out of relative obscurity, to our grantee partners, to the larger society whose tax laws make private philanthropy possible—to gauge as accurately as possible the effects of what we do and the lessons that can be drawn from those efforts.

This is not to say that all grants require elaborate evaluation. In a number of grant categories dear to many who give and many who receive, evaluation is relatively simple. A performing arts center is proposed. Foundation K gives money toward its construction. The project is completed according to the architectural plans on the agreed-upon site. At a gala event complete with glitter and glamour, the doors are flung open. Verdict: success; money well spent.

Yet even in such straight-line projects, life is not actually that simple. Why was the new center proposed? To be an adornment? To stimulate local performing arts organizations to higher levels of achievement and financial stability? Or both? How is its debt going to be serviced? Can local organizations actually carry that load? Will taxpayers be hit with a bill they did not expect? Or will the new structure have to be filled with touring Gong Shows or their equivalent to draw more paying customers? What then of the community's artistic growth? What then is the evaluation verdict? What are the lessons learned?

If the tough questions were not asked before the project began, before baselines were established and statements of defined outcomes negotiated, there is no way to offer an informed assessment. Time will tell, but it will be telling about a constantly moving target, as the arts center's managers adapt their mission statement to changing circumstances. And the next time, in another community, when a similar opportunity presents itself, Foundation K will again be able to offer money if it wishes, but will be unable to offer informed advice about what works and doesn't work beyond how to build a civic monument that may or may not be able to justify its existence.

Now move to grantmaking whose objective is to benefit, activate, or empower people whose needs are as immense as the nation's record of failure in meeting them. Here the need for honest evaluation is matched by the difficulty in producing it. The Knight Foundation allocates a majority of its annual outlays to highly focused programs chosen by community advisory committees, in close cooperation with Knight liaisons and content specialists, in each of our twenty-six communities. Early childhood and primary and secondary education are favored targets. So are neighborhood and economic development aimed at distressed neighborhoods. Goals have been established and measurable outcomes established. The foundation has committed resources for a minimum of between three and five years for each community objective. Community work plans are living documents rather than inflexible master plans. Knight is committed to remaining involved with its partners throughout the process, measuring, offering feedback, and evaluating as we go.

At the end, we hope we will have succeeded in each and every undertaking. We know that we won't. Risk capital is what we claim to be offering, and in the world of venture capitalism, far more ventures fall on their face than make a profit. But as with venture capitalists, we want to learn from our failures and be relatively ruthless about applying the lessons learned. In the real world of public money, indeed in the more limited world of charitable dollars, our funds are very small indeed. They should not be thrown around like so many snowflakes in July. It's not okay to be ignorant, even if it is not possible to know everything.

That said, only ideologues or idiots can claim that evaluation in the arena of social change can possibly offer absolute clarity. We are not dealing with laboratory guinea pigs or mathematical formulations of elegant precision. Our communities are not hermetically sealed, uncontaminated by unanticipated variables. We are dealing with—we are ourselves—mortal humans attempting to overcome implacably difficult circumstances around which swirl a universe of contingency.

To repeat, the Knight Foundation's communities' plans of action are carefully contrived to include starting point, baselines, mutually agreed-upon objectives, systematic review, and final conclusions. But having a built-in process and having built-in certitude about what you will be able to prove are not the same thing. Our dollars are limited, even within the context of our tightly circumscribed community objectives. Those objectives are heavily dependent on a wide array of other forces and circumstances over which neither we nor our nonprofit partners have much, if any, control. The national economy may wallow; so may the local economy. Changes in local government may produce changes in emphasis or cooperation. The flight from the center city may be too advanced to reverse; a continuing flood of immigration may swamp the school in which an imaginative youth development initiative is located. A charismatic principal may suddenly quit or be transferred.

It is also quite possible that, careful as the preliminary analysis may be, as thoroughly vetted as the plan of action may be, the partner organization will not measure up to the task for any one of a wide variety of reasons. In such cases, "failure" will be as easy to assess as "success" was in the case of building a performing arts center—as easy and as meaningless. The fact that a program failed in such circumstances may well say absolutely nothing of value about the central idea.

All of this must be noted, admitted, and absorbed in ongoing evaluation work. We cannot anticipate everything in our planning process; pretense of such infallibility is long buried, I trust, with the Soviet Union's five-year plans. But the certainty of imprecision makes the case for evaluation properly understood all the more compelling.

What we can try to extract is every bit of evidence available from the data. What we don't know about how and why things work, or don't work, is the enemy. Whatever we can learn about why things work or don't work is an asset. It is feckless to worry about not knowing everything; the best is, in such cases, always the enemy of the good.

Yet even when we think we have learned everything we can from our evaluation process, it will rarely be enough to justify hard-and-fast conclusions about what works and doesn't work in each and every similar circumstance. There are no final solutions in the world of social change. For those of us who believe that evaluation is an invaluable, integral component of foundation work, humility must be the byword. Failed certainties in social science litter the landscape like so many elephant bones bleaching in the African sun. Honest hard scientists never claim final answers; good social scientists shouldn't either.

And that is my final point. The context for evaluation is no less meaningful than what evaluation can help us learn. The context is this: we set clearly defined objectives, such as preparing children to learn. Programs are the methods we adopt to achieve those objectives, but they are not the objectives and should be judged against them. A common tendency, whether in government, the private sector, or the independent sector, is to confuse one with the other. To take the political example, the tendency is to wrap the flag around failed policies and equate honest evaluation with an unpatriotic attack on national values. What honest evaluation does is to peel off the flag and let us see the difference between the ideal and the real. It is therefore the ally, rather than the enemy, of the ideal.

I began with some musings about what I think I learned about human nature from my previous vocational lives and how it relates to evaluation in my present one. Let me conclude in the same way. Investing in a particular program as though it were the be-all and end-all is well-nigh irresistible to its creators and just about guarantees losing sight of the purported goal. Having worked for two presidents, however peripherally in each case, proved that to me for all time.

Evaluation—thorough, clearly understood in its intentions, and restrained in its conclusions—helps us maintain intellectual honesty. If fundamental social change is an objective, learning must accompany doing, hand-in-hand. There are no easy answers in this field, but ignorance is a sure prescription for failure.

PERSPECTIVE

Michael M. Howe

President, The East Bay Community Foundation

Although evaluation has long been referred to by philanthropy as an essential part of our organizational fabric, in practice only recently has it been used in the ways it was originally intended. Many foundations have required evaluations of some (usually those with larger grants) or all of their grantees. Unfortunately, in most cases the evaluation results have not been used by foundations as planning and assessment tools for their own work, let alone as a guide for new or ongoing grantmaking. With the development of internal evaluations of foundations, grantee evaluations are becoming more important, not only as reports on the effectiveness of grantmaking but as an assessment of the efficacy of the foundation's work.

The East Bay Community Foundation in Oakland, California, is striving to become more proactive in our philanthropic work. For the past ten years, staff and trustees have built a base of information, reports, and data associated with the work we have done in the East Bay. We have one of the most diverse populations in the country, with representative communities from virtually every racial, cultural, and language group. We have rural, urban, and suburban areas with every socioeconomic group one could imagine, from the wealthiest to the poorest communities in California. With a geographic area larger than some states and with a population base of approximately 2.4 million people, it is important that the foundation provide clear and concise information about the nature and effect of our work.

At The East Bay Community Foundation, we believe that evaluating our work, as well as the work of those whom we fund, is one of the most important elements of what we do. Why is this? First, as a community foundation we rely on donors investing in the foundation and, through us, in the community. Today's donors are not simply interested in our good work or the good work of those organizations that are supported through foundation grants. Today's donors want to understand the strategies that we, as well as the organizations we fund, use to change the conditions that continually cause problems within our communities. They also want to see evidence that these investments are achieving the proposed outcomes in these communities.

When we think of donors, we most often think of individuals, families, or corporations. However, the public sector is our most prolific donor. In the 1990s, the foundation was asked by the city of Oakland to assist with the administration and evaluation of the Kids First grant program. In 1996, this program was put on the ballot by youth and approved by voters to allocate 2.5 percent of Oakland's general funds to support programs for Oakland youth. Once it was passed, the city had a difficult time with the administration and management of the Kids First program. Hardly anyone was happy with the process the city used to distribute the funds, and there was virtually no feedback as to the effectiveness of the funded programs. As a result, the city asked the foundation to assist them in re-designing the administration and evaluation of Kids First. After a thorough assessment of the program, the foundation agreed to take on the program administration and evaluation temporarily, with the understanding that once the systems to accomplish these functions were in place and operating successfully, Kids First would be returned to the city.

Over a period of four years, the foundation restructured the administration of the program to better reflect the goals outlined in the legislation and instituted an evaluation system that provided feedback to the grantees for program effectiveness, to the city for evaluation and re-funding purposes, and to the community to report on outcomes and impact. After four years, Kids First has been transferred back to the city of Oakland, with a completely reorganized administrative structure and an evaluation system that the city uses for planning and allocation purposes, that grantees extol, and that the community understands.

In taking on Kids First, the foundation believed that the investment of our staff time and expertise was a wise venture, given the fact that many of the programs funded by the city were also funded by our foundation and others. The result was that once the first evaluation was published, it was used by both public and private funders in making funding decisions. In subsequent years, the evaluation reports have been used by Oakland funders to leverage their resources through collaborative funding. In addition, grantees serving the same clientele are now collaborating across disciplines, using the foundation's broadly based evaluation system. Without that system, the city would not be able to bear witness to the effectiveness of the funded programs, the funded programs would not be working together, and funders would be funding programs in isolation from one another.

These days, applicants to the foundation for funds are much more likely to want to discuss evidence that the foundation uses to make our grantmaking decisions. Without data that are clear and representative of the programs in which we choose to invest, we find ourselves discussing ideas glibly, depending more on anecdotes and less on well-reasoned and data-supported evidence. Unfortunately, it is just not possible to evaluate all programs. Over the past several years, the foundation has been experimenting with a standardized evaluation system for our initiatives that uses existing and newly collected data to document program activities and measure effectiveness. These data are fed back to the initiatives so that they can make appropriate changes in their operations. Since its inception four years ago, we have seen the effectiveness of our initiatives improve substantially. We are able to provide our trustees with detailed information about the initiatives and the broader community with information about their outcomes. The result is that we have greater confidence in the initiatives' achievements and appreciate the need for sustained support. Given the success of our initiative evaluation, we are now considering its use more broadly with our responsive grantmaking program.

The East Bay Community Foundation's board of trustees has long asked staff to provide data on the effectiveness of our grantmaking. As is the case with most philanthropic boards today, there is the sense that investments in communities must be accompanied by clear and direct evidence that these investments are having the impact intended and, if that impact is not being achieved, what the reasons might be. The evaluation system we have tested with our initiatives and are now instituting for our general grantmaking program will provide this information.

For our communities, there is no less of an expectation that we should be able to bear witness to our work by providing data on our effectiveness (or lack thereof). Glittering generalities about our efforts will no longer suffice when speaking to the media, government agencies, and community groups. Similarly, our new evaluation system will be able to disseminate this information to our service areas and beyond.

For The East Bay Community Foundation, the adoption of a combined strategy of monitoring, assessment, and evaluation of our grants and programs is necessary. As a community foundation with approximately $160 million in assets and a combined payout and advised fund distribution of approximately $15 million per year, we are not a large philanthropic organization, and we do not have the resources to evaluate all of our grants. However, we must be able to report to our donors, our grantees, our board, and the community on the results of the work we do. Most important, as a community foundation we must continually provide evidence of our work to a broad sector of the public. In this regard, we have taken the approach of combining information from our staff-monitoring reports, self-assessments by grantees, and evaluations of selected grants, initiatives, and programs. All of these are arrayed against our Community Investment Matrix, which not only looks at grants and operating programs but also provides an overview, through an evaluative lens, of how each of these is or is not fulfilling the goals, objectives, and outcomes of our Community Investment Guidelines. With the launching of our expanded evaluation system, we plan to document and report on our community investments more effectively.

I believe that the foundation's future depends on our ability to use our evaluation reports. This means that we are committed to learning from these reports and using them to make better grantmaking and program decisions, to understand the extent to which we are making progress on our organizational goals, and to report to our stakeholders and the broader community about our successes and failures.

This commitment will require that we learn to shift our priorities and revise our plans with knowledge gained from evaluation. Clearly, this side of the work may be the most difficult, as it requires the commitment of the staff, management, and board of the foundation to decide to make such changes. However, with evaluation results available we have found it easier to make clear and focused decisions about both the overall grantmaking operations and the direction of the foundation.

Over the past four years, we have come to understand the importance of this side of our evaluation work, and we have discovered that the overall work of the foundation has taken on a more deliberate and outcome-oriented course. This has produced greater clarity about the results of our work, along with a sense of accomplishment or, in some cases, the realization that we need to change certain important aspects.

Finally, by making sure that we use the evaluation results, our ongoing organizational development work both legitimates and formalizes the organizational learning process within the foundation. As a philanthropic organization, we continually strive to look beyond what is commonplace, to see how issues that continue to hobble our communities might be examined and addressed differently. In our case, we use evaluation to help us become more strategic and successful as community philanthropists. We make sure that as we dream about the future, we also use evaluation to help guide our dreams to more successful, better-understood realities.

PERSPECTIVE

Risa Lavizzo-Mourey

President and CEO, The Robert Wood Johnson Foundation

When I became CEO of The Robert Wood Johnson Foundation (RWJF), I took the helm of a philanthropy with a rich culture of evaluation and a long history of relying on the results of evaluations to inform grantmaking and build the knowledge necessary for replicating programs. The role evaluation plays at The Robert Wood Johnson Foundation is changing, but it is more central to the success of our programming than ever.

Why is that so? The Foundation has moved from a focus on individual grants or programs to an *Impact Framework* that groups programs into four grantmaking portfolios, each with distinguishing characteristics, time horizons, strategies, and objectives. Therefore, the new and exciting challenge for the Foundation's Research and Evaluation Group is to provide the information that will guide these portfolios of programs successfully toward their stated objectives. Evaluation joins smart strategy, deft implementation, and effective communication as the pillars of achieving results under our Impact Framework because it informs all three.

The Impact Framework

We chose the term *Impact Framework* because it makes the point that the goal is to create impact—to make a difference and achieve lasting results—through our grantmaking. The Impact Framework does *not* represent a radical change in our approach to philanthropy. Rather, it is an evolution of many of the principles that have been implicit in our grantmaking for years. In fact, in putting this framework together we actually reinforced our confidence in the basic direction of the Foundation's work and the areas we have supported. However, it does put greater emphasis on demonstrating results and driving toward social change, which is why evaluation is so critical. This new framework should help us overcome three problems: (1) tackling too many issues, (2) not being clear enough in advance about the outcomes we expect, and (3) not setting explicit targets for the dollar amounts of our investments or the timeframes for achieving objectives.

By making our approaches more explicit, more focused, and more measurable, we believe that we and our grantees will be better equipped to do what we set out to do together and to assess our progress along the way, making adjustments as needed. The assessment of progress, which will inform strategy adjustments and the balance among the portfolios, will be the direct result of portfolio-level evaluations.

We see the four portfolios in the new Impact Framework as analogous to mutual funds—with different purposes, performance measures, time horizons, and risk profiles. Our impact and progress toward our mission will depend, in part, on maintaining the appropriate balance across the portfolios. We expect that balance to shift from time to time, depending on such factors as the economy and the public policymaking climate.

The portfolios are named as follows: Targeted, Human Capital, Vulnerable Populations, and Pioneering. The Targeted portfolio is by far our largest. It is designed to help solve systemic problems in health and health care. In it are nine strategic objectives related to our goal areas—many fewer than in the past.

During the boom years of the 1990s, our growing assets enabled us to tackle many more problems. We developed thirty-six strategic objectives to guide our grantmaking. That is a lot, especially in these belt-tightening times, and since then we have carefully refined the objectives and winnowed the number. Each of the current nine objectives will have its own time horizon and specific, measurable outcomes. For example, within the Targeted portfolio, the objective for childhood obesity is, "To halt by 2015 the increase in prevalence of overweight among children." For health-care quality (still within the Targeted portfolio), the objective is, "By 2007, 25% of patients in the five diverse demonstration markets will report experiencing optimal care."

The second portfolio, Human Capital, seeks to make long-term investments to improve the current and future workforce in health and health care. Unfortunately, everywhere we turn the health-care workforce is wanting. The Human Capital portfolio will include new initiatives, as well as many of our longstanding signature programs such as Clinical Scholars, the Minority Medical Faculty Program, Health and Society Scholars, Innovators in Substance Abuse, and the Dental Pipeline. Our purpose is to attract, develop, and retain high-quality leadership and other aspects of a strong workforce to improve the nation's health and health care.

The third portfolio is designed to promote the health and health care of Vulnerable Populations. This portfolio incorporates many of our service programs, such as Faith in Action, which supports volunteers from local community faith congregations providing services to people in need. Also included are our Local Initiatives Funding Partners Program and the Experience Corps, which brings retirees into resource-strapped schools to nurture at-risk kids and help them learn.

Finally, we have a Pioneering portfolio that is designed to promote especially innovative, high-risk approaches to grantmaking. For the first time, we will create a specific set-aside for the kind of bold, high-risk exploration that philanthropies like ours ought to be pursuing. With this mix of portfolios, we can strike a balance between using our resources for emerging issues in health and health care and supporting our ongoing work; that is, we can be both strategic and opportunistic.

Performance Indicators

To foster both implementation and accountability for the strategies and to strengthen the Foundation's role as a learning organization, we borrowed a model from The Royce Mutual Funds in designing a basket of measurable indicators to monitor our results. The RWJF evaluation group has worked hand-in-hand with the program teams to develop eight to ten indicators for each objective within each of the four portfolios. The template is shown in Figure P.1.

Several features are worth highlighting. First, we established timeframes for the indicators—short, medium, and long term—that allow us to track the implementation of a strategy and better understand the interrelationships among programs. Short-term indicators may be process-oriented rather than outcome-oriented and may be tied to a single grant or project. In contrast, medium- and long-term indicators focus on outcomes and on groups or clusters of grants and projects. Second, in every case we assess the amount of control or influence that RWJF and the grantees have over the outcome in question and rate the control as low, medium, or high. In so doing, we acknowledge that many of the outcomes we and our grantees want to accomplish can be affected by factors beyond our control, which helps us learn about both the outcomes and the factors influencing them. Third, every indicator sets a measurable level for achievement of the outcomes as well as a target date. This is a new way of evaluating our progress toward addressing the most pressing problems in health and health care, and it is one that puts emphasis on the collective achievements of programs.

FIGURE P.1. RWJF'S MODEL FOR MONITORING PORTFOLIO RESULTS.

Strategic Objective or Purpose: Each portfolio or strategic team first briefly outlines its objective or purpose.

Current Context for Our Work: Then, a quick reminder is presented of problems being addressed and current environmental factors.

Strategy in Brief: A brief strategy statement outlines the logic behind related short-term, intermediate, and long-term indicators.

Target Budget Plan: Current and multi-year budget estimates are included, as well as the level of past spending.

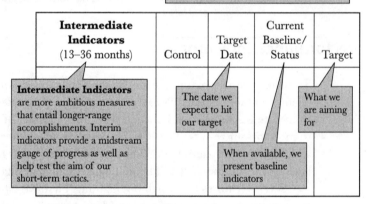

Short-Term Indicators (Over next 12 months)	Control	Target Date	Current Baseline/ Status	Target

Short-Term Indicators are benchmarks designed as annual checks on progress. Each has a target that is either measured by a numerical allowance, a "yes/no," or, in the case of activity indicators, a "completed/not completed" assessment.

Level of Control: Accompanying each indicator is staff's judgment about the level of control RWJF has to meet the target. High Control items (H) are measures staff can reasonably control "from our desks." Medium Control items (M) are those that staff do not directly control but hope to influence. And Low Control items (L) are those that are influenced by many factors other than our work but items that staff still hope to track.

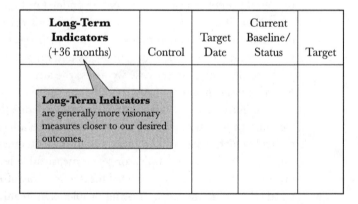

Intermediate Indicators (13–36 months)	Control	Target Date	Current Baseline/ Status	Target

Intermediate Indicators are more ambitious measures that entail longer-range accomplishments. Interim indicators provide a midstream gauge of progress as well as help test the aim of our short-term tactics.

The date we expect to hit our target

When available, we present baseline indicators

What we are aiming for

Long-Term Indicators (+36 months)	Control	Target Date	Current Baseline/ Status	Target

Long-Term Indicators are generally more visionary measures closer to our desired outcomes.

The Evaluation Group is charged with analyzing the data that will tell us how each portfolio is doing. In some cases, this will mean aggregating findings across grants or programs; in others, it will mean analyzing data from existing national or other datasets. And in a few cases, it will mean developing new datasets. For example, one of the long-term indicators in the Vulnerable Populations portfolio is the number of sites that continue after RWJF funding ends, which will require aggregating data across the programs in the portfolio. However, the Human Capital portfolio will rely more on the results of national surveys.

The results of individual program evaluations are still important, but they now are viewed as a cluster of assessments. Together with our new performance indicators, they will help us understand the impact of our funding strategies to address pressing problems such as smoking prevalence rates, obesity rates, and levels of public awareness about the consequences of being uninsured.

Program-Level Evaluation

In establishing portfolio-level performance indicators, we are not discounting the importance of program-level evaluation. However, we are shifting our rationale for doing evaluations and therefore the expectations of what they can offer. While portfolio-level evaluations focus on assessing meaningful and lasting impact, program-level evaluations provide for immediate feedback as we prepare to take risks on new approaches, leap into new areas, or make long-term commitments to a program. In these situations, the information gained by the Evaluation Group is invaluable. Without the findings of credible evaluations, any CEO and board of trustees would be much less willing to take risks. Having accurate, reliable information that can guide adjustments to programs is imperative, just as one needs a compass in uncharted terrain. For example, within the innovation-focused Pioneering portfolio, program-level evaluations will be essential as we enter new areas of grantmaking. Similarly, the program-level evaluations of Faith in Action, which uses interfaith coalitions to provide volunteers to serve homebound persons, have been instrumental in redesigning the program as it has moved through three phases of implementation since 1992.

Conclusion

As CEO, I depend on the products and wisdom provided by our evaluations, because we care deeply about addressing the most pressing health and health-care issues that this country faces. We seek to use every weapon in our arsenal to attack problems like covering the nation's millions of uninsured people, finding better ways to deal with chronic illness, reducing substance abuse, and improving the health of the most vulnerable among us.

We want to cultivate the range of views that can lead to sound solutions to those challenges. Equally important, we believe in funding programs that have measurable impact and that bring about timely, comprehensive, meaningful change—*measurable impact,* because we aim for care that reaches more Americans and helps us lead healthier lives, and *timely change,* because we expect our grantees to make a difference. And evaluation is integral to knowing whether we've indeed helped make that difference and to making our philanthropy more effective.

FOUNDATIONS
AND EVALUATION

PART ONE

UNDERSTANDING FOUNDATIONS AS A CONTEXT FOR EVALUATION

CHAPTER ONE

USING EVALUATION TO ADVANCE A FOUNDATION'S MISSION

Laura C. Leviton and Marian E. Bass

W hy should foundations and their grantees conduct evaluations? Evaluation should be done for a good reason; there are many good reasons and good uses for the results. In this chapter, we present several illustrations of the ways evaluation can be used in foundation-supported work. We want to capture the reader's imagination, express concretely what is possible to achieve, and point to some key conditions that we believe are necessary in order to conduct effective evaluations in the foundation context.

This chapter is intended for both the users and producers of evaluations. A precondition for useful foundation evaluations is that participants better understand their purpose. Participants include those who conduct the evaluations, the foundation staff members, as well as the grantees, who may themselves conduct evaluations or whose activities may be the subject of evaluation. Equally important, however, is for evaluation professionals to understand the distinctive context of foundation work. In the conclusion to the chapter, we summarize important features of the context, describe some potential uses of evaluation in the foundation context, and give specific recommendations for working within that context to improve evaluations.

The suggestions of Dana Phillips and Ernest House are gratefully acknowledged. Thomas Gilmore first suggested the material in Cases 8 and 9; William Bickel suggested the content in Case 2.

We make two basic points—emerging from two different perspectives—in the chapter:

1. *Looking inside a foundation,* useful evaluation depends on the organization's size, its culture, and the placement of responsibility and authority for evaluation.
2. *Looking outside a foundation,* evaluations will be better and more useful if they consider both the power and vulnerability of foundations and the predictable effects of foundations' power on grantees, evaluators, and the grantmakers themselves.

Two basic problems that must be confronted at the outset are that (1) most evaluations conducted for foundations are unsatisfactory (Patrizi, 2002), just as they are in the public sector, and (2) people bring preconceptions to the conduct and use of evaluations that are incorrect and often can harm the prospects for getting useful information. For example, grantees fear that they will be "evaluated"— and in poor practice, they sometimes are. Good practice is very different, as illustrated in this chapter. As a result of these problems, there is frequently tension and apprehension over the terms under which evaluations will be conducted, the ground rules of behavior, roles, and responsibilities, and the uses that might be made of the results. Foundation leadership, board members, staff, and grantees have frequently expressed disappointment over the value of evaluation results.

This situation is partly caused by confusion within philanthropy about the purposes for, and the likely consequences of, evaluation. People believe they understand what the word *evaluation* means, and often they do not. Even the trusted experts and veteran grant officers often get it wrong. Although the field of evaluation rests on decades of collective experience, in philanthropy both the users and producers of evaluation tend to be unfamiliar with some basic writings in the field. The result is that evaluations are often less useful than they might be, thus wasting time, resources, and valuable opportunities for learning. It is important to demystify the process and products of evaluation on behalf of the stakeholders (those with an interest in the program or its evaluation). It is important to identify the preconditions for getting useful information from evaluations.

An important product of evaluation's collective experience is summarized in the introductory chapter and helps to define what evaluation is really about. The Guiding Principles for Evaluators (see Exhibit I.1 in the Introduction), endorsed by the American Evaluation Association (AEA), is a key document that encompasses the wide-ranging approaches to be found in evaluation today. Both the users and producers of evaluation will benefit greatly from reading the principles in their entirety, either at the association's Web site (www.eval.org) or in any issue of *The American Journal of Evaluation.* The principles give stakeholders an idea of what to expect from good practice (Leviton, 2001). By reading and sharing the principles, evaluators and those who commission evaluation can often alleviate tension and prevent disappointment.

It is also important to define what we mean by the "use" of evaluations. Leviton and Hughes (1981) describe three general kinds of use that still hold up under scrutiny today: (1) *persuasive use* that argues for or against a policy or program, (2) *instrumental use* in identifiable decisions, and (3) *conceptual use* (such as the serious consideration of results in decision-making, enlightenment about program reality, or testing assumptions about the underlying problem). Foundation work gives its own imprint to these general types, as seen throughout this volume. At the end of this chapter, we point to some distinctive purposes for evaluation in philanthropy.

Looking Inside Foundations

Foundations vary in many ways that are important to evaluation; many are covered elsewhere in this volume. This chapter focuses on just three internal drivers: (1) foundation size, (2) foundation culture, and (3) the location of responsibility and authority for evaluation.

Foundation Size

A foundation's size refers to its assets, payout (dollar amount of grants issued each year), and staffing. About 350 foundations pay out $10 million per year or more, but only 29 of these gave more than $100 million in grants in 2001 (Foundation Center, 2004). The amount of the payout often affects the number of staff a foundation can maintain to manage its grantmaking, as well as their degree of specialization within program areas and technical support functions such as evaluation. Other features also affect the degree of grant officers' involvement with evaluation: they may award and oversee all grants, or they may operate through a variety of intermediary, "re-granting" organizations (Szanton, 2002). "Operating foundations" have staff who actually manage and implement programs.

High-Quality Evaluation Is Within Reach. The size of the payout does not have to affect the quality or usefulness of evaluation, but smaller foundations may believe that high-quality evaluation is simply beyond their reach. In truth, cost is an abiding issue among the stakeholders for evaluation of all kinds, whether it is conducted for government, for individual agencies and organizations, or for foundations. Decision makers often have no idea what an adequate study should cost.

However, cost is not the central issue for foundations in allocating evaluation resources. A more important issue is to select the most cost-effective approach, given the purpose of the evaluation. In other words, what are the real information needs of the intended audience, how important is the result, and what standard of evidence is required? High-quality evaluation does not necessarily mean high cost, given the many legitimate approaches available, and cost should be driven by decisions about what is a "good enough" standard of evidence for the purpose at hand (Rossi, Lipsey, and Freeman, 2004).

Chapter Seven outlines the challenges of resource allocation in more detail. Sometimes low-cost options may be highly appropriate to the purpose, as seen in Chapter Ten. At other times, however, it is essential for strategic purposes to invest more in the evaluation than in the program. As described in Case 1, the strategic aim of a foundation initiative can be lost, unless there is an appropriate evaluation focus. And evaluation should never be conducted *pro forma*, that is, just because someone believes it is supposed to be conducted. If evaluation is likely to be of poor quality, or if it has no purpose (for example, when foundation staff and program managers do not expect to use evaluation results in their decisions or thinking), then any evaluation is too expensive.

Case 1: Strategic Evaluation in Field Building

Program managers and advocates tend to view evaluation as taking away needed resources from programs. However, foundation officers sometimes value it because they recognize ways in which evaluation can help them build a field in line with the foundation's mission (Hirschhorn, Kelly, and Gilmore, 2002). Examples of *field building* include:

- Encouraging participation in the arts (The Wallace Foundation)
- Supporting research in health policy (The Robert Wood Johnson Foundation)
- Strengthening community leadership (The W. K. Kellogg Foundation)
- Creating the field of clinical epidemiology in less-developed countries (The Rockefeller Foundation)
- Building the capacity of youth development programs (The Edna McConnell Clark Foundation)

Individual programs may work together to build a field. For example, The Robert Wood Johnson Foundation (RWJF) funds several programs designed to improve the effectiveness of public health agencies, including leadership training, information infrastructure improvement, and advocacy and public awareness initiatives. Evaluation as part of a field-building strategy can work either at the level of individual programs or across various programs that are associated with building the field.

In 2003, funding for the evaluation of two national programs came into question at RWJF. In both cases, the grant officers said there was no point in funding a program if there was no funding for evaluation of the program. Grant officers of RWJF often believe that the evaluation of individual programs will help them build a field. They see strategic advantages for the national programs for which they have oversight. Evaluations aid the strategy by signaling the importance of the field being built, by informing funders of progress over time, and by assessing the value of the field to society.

The dynamics certainly are not perfect, but, often enough, both RWJF staff and grantees believe that evaluations can leverage important changes in a field of interest. This is the case whether the findings are positive, negative, or mixed. If the evaluation is positive, that is good publicity for the field. Because the evaluations are independent and generally of high quality, more confidence can be placed in the findings. If the evaluation is negative or mixed, then that becomes a basis for further learning in a field. It may not be pleasant, but it is the basis of a productive dialogue (for an example, see the description of the SUPPORT study in Chapter Six).

What Is Meant by the "Standard of Evidence"? A wide range of legitimate approaches is employed in evaluation today. Foundations have different program aims, and therefore they prefer different evaluation methods to give them the information they need. In the range of evaluation approaches, there is no single preferred method; there are simply appropriate and inappropriate methods to answer the question that is being posed. However, the legitimate evaluation approaches all use methods that have recognized standards of evidence—agreed-upon rules and criteria for the work—to which reputable evaluation practitioners adhere. The methods employed range from the quantitative analysis of so-called "hard outcomes" at one extreme (such as changes in the prevalence of a disease) to the qualitative, social-constructivist interpretation of a program's "story" at the other (such as stakeholder perceptions of participation in the arts). Foundation officers and grantees should be familiar with, and insist on, the standard of evidence for the methods that are to be used.

Much of the confusion regarding the choice of an evaluation approach centers on the use of cause-probing methods such as randomized experiments or quasi-experiments. These methods have had an illustrious, but uneven, history in demonstrating the worth of public policy and program approaches. Unfortunately, opinions about their use are often ill-informed. Some believe that no evaluation question is worth asking unless it involves a rigorous scientific assessment of outcomes. Yet in many cases a randomized experiment is premature or simply inappropriate to the situation, while other methods can help reduce uncertainty or keep an investment on course. Others believe that social experimentation is unethical and often overly negative about the true worth of social programs. Yet without social experimentation, foundations may help to advance programs and policies that remain unproven or eventually become discredited. These views of randomized experiments are all erroneous (Dennis, 1994). Field experimentation is one tool for the tool chest, to be used judiciously (see Chapter Twelve).

Size Can Affect Foundation Goals. Because of foundations' size, evaluations that address their goals will differ greatly in content, focus, structure, and consequences. The largest foundations often aspire to achieve societal change far beyond their actual payout. Evaluations for these foundations are often linked to effecting social change or to building a field. Staff of these foundations may be national or international experts in a field of work; their prestige derives, in part, from the funds they provide and their track record for achieving social change. Evaluation could either bolster or threaten their status in the field, with predictable consequences.

Other foundations have a local or regional mission, including most community and conversion foundations. Like the largest foundations, they fund worthy causes and may contribute to field building, but they are also important civic leaders. They often have local influence behind the scenes, far beyond the actual dollars they can provide. For these philanthropies, longstanding relationships with other organizations play an important role. Evaluation could affect those relationships by offering constructive or harmful criticism and by affecting nonprofits' bottom line, with predictable consequences.

The foundation community of Pittsburgh, Pennsylvania, offers a noteworthy illustration of philanthropy's civic role. Until the mergers of the 1980s, Pittsburgh had the third-largest concentration of corporate headquarters in the United States. Dating from the time of "robber barons" such as Andrew Carnegie and Henry Clay Frick, the wealth of the corporate leaders gave rise to significant private and corporate foundations, still among the largest in the country. Operating through the Allegheny Conference on Community Development, their civic leadership is celebrated for creating a far better quality of life in the region (for history and accomplishments visit www.accdpel.org). Evaluation played an important role in some of these improvements. In Case 2, the story of public education in Pittsburgh illustrates the power of foundations' civic leadership and the ways that evaluation can assist that leadership, but also people's ambivalence about foundations' power.

Case 2: Evaluation, Civic Leadership, and Philanthropic Power

Pittsburgh in the 1980s developed one of the finest urban school systems in the nation, thanks, in part, to the work of David Bergholz, associate director of the Allegheny Conference. Evaluation guided those improvements by determining the specific needs and providing information about "what works" in school improvement (Bickel and Cooley, 1986). However, philanthropy's role in this process was distinctly behind the scenes. More recently, the foundations' civic leadership and foundation-supported evaluation have been used in a very different way.

By 2002, the Pittsburgh school board had become notoriously dysfunctional, making the district almost impossible to administer. Three foundations had made grants to the school district to implement Literacy Plus, a program to increase the number of third-graders reading at grade level. However, foundation staff were concerned about implementation, so they required that the district meet specific performance measures. When these conditions went unmet, the foundations withdrew funding for the program. They did so publicly, as a rebuke to the school board.

This decision was controversial, because philanthropy so often chooses a discreet and private role. Grant Oliphant, associate director of The Heinz Endowments, explained that the decision "was influenced by our growing emphasis on evaluation and accountability. It also reflected our ongoing commitment to the strategic use of communications as a tool for effective grantmaking" (personal communication, December 2002).

In *H: The Magazine of the Heinz Endowments*, King and Oliphant note:

> Accountability has become almost a cliché in the philanthropic field. But there is a squeamishness that often sets in with foundations when accountability reaches this point, the painful moment at which funding to a valued grantee or cherished program may actually have to be withheld.
>
> "We must be that small, though significant, resource that can stay the course, for better or for worse . . . it is the requirement for being effectively at the table" David Bergholz, [now the] executive director of the George Gund Foundation in Cleveland, argued in a scathing critique of our action published in the *Post-Gazette*. . . . The problem with this sort of reasoning is that it makes a mockery of accountability. It suggests that foundations must continue to provide funding even when, despite their best efforts, a grantee has demonstrated an inability or unwillingness to abide by mutually agreed upon terms of behavior and performance. It's nothing more than a blank check for underperformance. Accountability is not accountability unless it has teeth. . . .
>
> There were some immediate positives. Overnight, the district's governance and leadership problems became headline news and gained the crisis status they so richly deserved. . . . Within days, Mayor Tom Murphy, who previously had kept a low profile on issues pertaining to the schools, announced the creation of a community-wide task force to examine the district's problems and recommend

solutions. . . . This was precisely the sort of community action we had hoped to spark through our decision, which is why all three foundations are funding the commission's work. The commission has no authority to implement its findings on its own. But it has a high-profile charter, membership and degree of public support that will make its work difficult to ignore (King and Oliphant, 2002, pp. 20 and 24).

Foundation Culture

Culture determines whether foundations attach importance to evaluative information and what kind of evaluation is preferred. Some believe that the standard of evidence should be as close to rigorous scientific method as possible; others rely on less formal, though systematic, methods of assessment. The culture also largely drives the kinds of uses to which evaluation will be put. (More discussion of the effects of foundation culture can be seen in Chapter Eight.)

Values and Expectations. A foundation's culture is defined by what its stakeholders value and expect. A foundation's internal stakeholders include the board of directors, senior management, grant officers, and, to a surprising extent, its grantees. For grantees, the boundary is often permeable and demonstrates the power of personal relationships. Foundations may ask trusted grantees or former grantees to sit on advisory committees or to author a white paper guiding grant initiatives. Grantees may be hired as grant officers; they may even be former grant officers. And sometimes they become foundation board members. In Case 3, we present an oral history of the emergence of an evaluator as a trusted advisor to a major foundation.

Case 3: The Rewards of Integrity

This is an oral history about how a researcher became an influential advisor to a foundation by sticking to the integrity of an evaluation. The incident must be anonymous. Most details are substantiated, but that is secondary to the role this incident plays in the foundation's culture. An anthropologist would say that it is part of the organization's "folklore" (or even a creation myth), to describe how and why the foundation supports evaluation. It also illustrates how "kinship" relations are formed in this type of elite organization (Weatherford, 1985).

In the 1980s, a large foundation created a national initiative that, over time, proved to be fatally flawed. A university-based evaluation team was hired at the outset of the program. Their report concluded that the program had no discernible effects and pointed to some very cogent and constructive reasons for the lack of effect.

The foundation had sought a highly placed, politically powerful advisory committee for the initiative. According to several parties, the chair of the committee threatened the evaluation team with political consequences if they released their conclusions—and one member of the evaluation team was coming up for tenure. The evaluation team defied the national advisory committee, presented the foundation with their original conclusions, and subsequently published their findings. There is some reason to believe, however, that the evaluation team may have lost a book contract due to political pressure on reviewers.

From the foundation's perspective, however, the committee's threat boomeranged. Far from having its intended effect, the threat against the evaluation team enhanced the team's credit in the foundation's eyes. The foundation officers, already unhappy with the way the program was going, knew they could trust these evaluators to tell the truth, courageously. Over the next decade, the foundation entrusted several other major evaluations to this team. The untenured evaluator received tenure, became a trusted foundation consultant, and eventually directed a prestigious fellowship program funded by the foundation.

Mission and Vision. Philanthropy is still an intensely personal activity, so the relationships among stakeholders matter a great deal in defining what is valued. The personal factor helps make the process more flexible and responsive, in contrast to the public sector. But at the same time, there are very few uniform procedures and rules for distributing funds, providing feedback to applicants, or wielding influence—a situation radically different from that of government funders (Downs, 1994). As seen in Chapter Six, the relative absence of procedures requires that individual grant officers develop their own ways to cope with the demands of stakeholders, with effects on evaluation.

Foundation staff are legally accountable only to the board of directors for the use of foundation funds, and the foundation is accountable only to the IRS to use the funds within legal requirements. Based on the work of certain commissions and national associations, there also exists some consensus about how foundation staff and boards of directors should comport themselves to avoid conflict of interest or abuse of power. Beyond these fundamentals, individual foundations have had to develop their own rules and traditions about fiduciary responsibility and duties.

The staff and board hold expectations about accountability and stewardship of both the financial resources and the foundation's reputation. Foundation staff make grants in line with what they conceive to be the foundation's mission, as well as a vision of the public interest. (Of course, visions of the public interest vary greatly across the political spectrum, and this spectrum is also represented in philanthropy.) The foundation's mission and the staff member's vision become central to conducting effective evaluation.

The foundation can often value both positive and negative findings, as long as they are constructive and in line with a shared definition of the mission and vision. For example, an evaluation that offers new knowledge to use in building a field would be deemed highly useful by some foundations (Hirschhorn, Kelly, and Gilmore, 2002). As seen in Cases 4 and 5, other foundations prize evaluation that permits grantees to improve their services or to make the case for funding to other grantmakers and public agencies.

Case 4: Effects of Evaluation on Subsequent Funding

The Local Initiatives Funding Partners program is especially revealing about how grantmakers respond to evaluation. Under this RWJF program, local organizations initiate health-related programs with support from a variety of philanthropic funders. RWJF then matches local support dollar-for-dollar. The funding partners range from the very largest community foundations in the country, such as The Cleveland Foundation, to small charities and individual donors that band together to seek an award. The median number of funding partners is five, and RWJF grants range in size from $50,000 to $500,000. Projects range from substance abuse prevention and treatment to health promotion and improved access to medical care. Mathematica Policy Research recently conducted a survey that followed the fate of projects after RWJF funding ended (Stevens, Peikes, and Patel, 2003). These included 120 projects that were funded from inception of the Local Initiatives Funding Partners program in 1986 through July 2001. Seventy-five percent of these projects survived and are in operation today. Of these, 61 percent obtained subsequent funding from other foundations, 59 percent from public revenues, 50 percent from individual donors, 42 percent from corporate donors, 35 percent from client fees or services, and 24 percent from United Way.

Among the surviving projects, evaluation may have been critical to subsequent funding; 92 percent had evaluated their activities, and 50 percent of surviving projects believed that a positive evaluation had been important to promoting their sustainability. These percentages may seem low to evaluation professionals, but they seem high indeed to many foundation staff and nonprofit organizations. These comments illustrate the organizations' view of evaluation:

Whether you are recruiting volunteers or asking for financial support, you need to sell benefits, not features.

The RWJF grant allowed us to prove that the . . . model works. We then took the finished product back to the government. Then it was a "no brainer" for them: they could choose between jailing drug offenders for $36,000 per year, or treating them more effectively in the community for less than $6,000.

Case 5: Evaluation in Social Enterprise Philanthropy

Nonprofit organizations can sometimes develop earned income streams, in addition to receiving private donations and grants from foundations and government sources. Earned income is helpful to the nonprofit mission as a way to (1) defray the cost of program operation, (2) promote more flexibility and fiscal health, and (3) help produce a "soft landing" once a grant ends. Social enterprise philanthropy (also termed *venture philanthropy*), aims to develop earned income strategies for nonprofit organizations in areas such as

- Helping them market and charge for their intellectual property
- Helping them create or expand a fee schedule for services
- Providing a low-cost loan or a program-related investment, or underwriting a loan obtained elsewhere

Even though a loan might carry risk, across a portfolio the foundation may see a "blended return on investment," consisting of debt repayment and interest, as well as the expected social benefits (Emerson, 2003).

Social enterprise philanthropy is more prevalent in the western United States, where foundations that were recently founded on high-technology fortunes find it an appealing model. Foundations of all sizes engage in social enterprise philanthropy, including The Pew Memorial Trusts, The Time-Warner Foundation, The UPS Foundation, and The Illinois Facilities Fund. More information is available from the Social Enterprise Alliance or from Grantmakers for Effective Organizations (www.geofunders.org). Descriptions of nonprofits that use a social enterprise model can be obtained from The Roberts Enterprise Development Fund (www.redf.org) and from Independent Sector (www.independentsector.org).

Several evaluation questions emerge about the social enterprise model. These include the following:

What is the "blended rate of return" that can be expected? Can the foundation's contribution go farther, dollar-for-dollar, in social enterprise organizations?

Will earned income streams defray the cost of a service, or is there increased overhead for social enterprise organizations, compared to other nonprofits?

What indicators of progress are reasonable in order to evaluate a social enterprise investment?

Are the chances for sustainability greater when this model is employed?

If social enterprise organizations and their missions and services are more likely to survive, then both the earned income stream and the sustained programs may be due to good management. However, if these organizations are more likely to disappear, then that presents a problem. Answers may determine the future of this idea.

Responsiveness. Foundation culture and perceived duty may also dictate the amount and style of responsiveness to grantees and grant applicants. Responsiveness means different things to different foundations, especially in evaluation, where there are legitimate differences in purpose and approach. Some large foundations take on a totally participatory or community-driven approach. Others have historically operated in a top-down approach, prizing independence of evaluation "to keep the process honest." These styles are contrasted in Case 6. At a minimum, though, responsiveness for foundation staff means that they must clearly convey what their mission and vision are, what they will fund, and what the "rules of engagement" are for grantees and for the fields that foundations support. Evaluation is important in conveying this information.

Case 6: Rules of Engagement

Evaluators and grantmakers will do well to clarify exactly what the rules of engagement are when an evaluation is conducted. One very important issue is whether the evaluation questions and methods will be participatory, or will be determined by outsiders on behalf of the funder. Contrast The Robert Wood Johnson Foundation (RWJF) with The W. K. Kellogg Foundation (WKKF). In 2001, WKKF was the eighth-largest and RWJF was the fourth-largest foundation in the United States by asset size (Foundation Center, 2003). RWJF espouses a view of evaluation that often (but not exclusively) relies on quantitative methods of social science. Moreover, the foundation values independent evaluation as a mechanism to ensure an honest answer. The process is seldom participatory, however, and the focus is less often on grantees' own program improvement than on building a field of health-related work, such as access to medical care, tobacco control, or addressing the nursing shortage (Hirschhorn, Kelly, and Gilmore, 2002). WKKF takes a radically different approach to evaluation: methods are more often qualitative; research questions are often set through a participatory process, and the products are more often conducive to "lessons learned" than to definitive statements about the causal effects of grantmaking (see www.wkkf.org). Doing evaluation that is even more participatory in some respects is the Group Health Community Foundation, of the Group Health Cooperative of Puget Sound at www.ghcfoundation.org. Other foundations may view evaluation as an audit or accountability mechanism, or purely as a performance-monitoring tool for managing a portfolio of grants.

Both the RWJF and WKKF approaches have advantages and disadvantages. A participatory model does not guarantee a useful or high-quality product, although it can and regularly does produce them. It takes an important set of skills to navigate a seemingly cumbersome process of consultation with community and program stakeholders and still produce a high-quality product. In the same way, an independent evaluation mandated from outside the programs themselves can often be threatening to those programs. It takes skill to gain the buy-in and cooperation of apprehensive program stakeholders. It also takes skill to show the client how consulting the stake-holders will help to craft a more meaningful question and gain more useful results. Evaluators' independence from the program does not mean ignorance of the program, does not mean a "black box" evaluation (one that only examines results, to the exclusion of attempting to understand the program), and does not mean oppression of program staff and clients. In truth, good-quality evaluations must somehow transcend these distinctions of "independent" and "participatory."

Responsibility and Authority for Evaluation

An effective evaluation function requires both authority from foundation leadership and a shared sense of responsibility, or buy-in, among foundation staff. We believe that some models of funding and organizing a large foundation's evaluation are superior to others. Eleanor Chelimsky (2001) agrees. She created what was arguably the most effective evaluation agency in the federal government for the U.S. General Accounting Office. In describing how foundation evaluation might be organized, she notes, "The point that needs to be made here, with some vigor, is that evaluation offices need independence, resources, strong staff, an agreed agenda for work, focused procedures and clear reporting channels among other things, if their products are to be objective, technically competent, relevant to foundation needs, and useful" (p. 26).

The Budget Process Dictates Authority over Evaluation. Independence of evaluation is strongly influenced by where the evaluation sits in the organization and, in particular, who controls the money. One model was in force at The Rockefeller Foundation beginning in 1990, when the foundation created a formal evaluation unit. The Central Evaluation Unit was established, reporting to a vice president. However, funding for evaluation was provided through the annual budget of each program division. The practical result was that each year, before each division submitted its budget for the coming year, the evaluation director would meet with each division director to determine which, if any, programs were ripe for evaluation for the coming year. They would then negotiate the selection of an appropriate evaluator. Final approval of programs subject to evaluation rested with the president of the foundation.

In this model, the evaluation director was weak relative to the division directors. She could encourage but could not compel the selection of a particular program for evaluation. Similarly, she could encourage or discourage the choice of evaluator, but with budgetary authority vested in the program rather than in the evaluation unit, she did not have the authority to make the final choice. Relationships were cordial and professional, but there was always a risk that the foundation's grant officers would strongly endorse an evaluator with inappropriate links to, or interest in, the program.

Typically, The Rockefeller Foundation's program director and the evaluation director were able to negotiate good choices of both programs and evaluators. On at least one occasion, however, the credibility of evaluation was placed in jeopardy. Evaluation staff were required to act with great tact and diplomacy in interactions with grant officers. This need was reinforced by the natural tendency of at least some grant officers to fear that an evaluation might encourage senior managers to terminate, or drastically alter, programs to which they had devoted many years and much determined effort. The evaluation director needed to establish that she could be trusted to work in the best interest, not only of the foundation but of its individual programs and staff members. With no budgetary authority, the evaluation director had instead to establish authority indirectly, via trust and influence.

The Robert Wood Johnson Foundation exemplifies a different organizational model for evaluation within large philanthropies. At RWJF, the Research and Evaluation Unit has its own vice president, who reports directly to the foundation president. Evaluation competes for funding along with other proposals and has the authority to select the programs to be evaluated, as well as the evaluators. Grant officers are consulted, but the final choice lies with the vice president for research and evaluation and with the president of the foundation.

Recommendation: Independent Authority but Shared Responsibility. In both models, the evaluative enterprise only becomes meaningful when the foundation's grant officers accept that evaluations are conducted for the right reasons:

- To discern the strengths of program design and implementation
- To discover weaknesses amenable to redress
- To improve both grantmaking and the implementation of program plans

Learning cannot be optimal, and sometimes it is not even possible, if grant officers suspect that the evaluators are "out to get them" or to kill their programs. Evaluation works best within foundations when both evaluation staff and foundation grant officers come to the relationship in a spirit of collaboration and mutual support. This collaboration sets an important tone for the programs being evaluated and the evaluators who carry out the work. We have observed that useful evaluations in philanthropy are neither independent nor subordinate to program; instead, they strive for the best characteristics of both models by an arrangement that shares responsibility for producing a useful product.

Looking Outside Foundations

Foundations respond to their environment as well. The important stakeholders outside the organization include grantees, government, and the public. Their responses dictate the way evaluation can be conducted, as well as the ways evaluation can demonstrate its value to foundations. Some of the most important external forces include foundations' power, their vulnerability to criticism, and grantee perceptions of evaluation in light of foundations' power.

Foundations' Power

Foundation staff often caution that their relationship with grantees is unequal; many do what they can to equalize it. One reason they do so is to make sure they are apprised of issues that are important to the success of a grant. As in other settings, information gets selectively filtered to those in power, yet conscientious stewardship requires the negative as well as the positive news. Effective program officers often realize that their status as a funder works to insulate them from negative program reality, thus necessitating the outside perspective that evaluation can offer. An illustration of the need for outside perspectives is seen in Case 7.

Case 7: Telling 'Em What They Want to Hear

Recently, an evaluator of our acquaintance who works in the arts attended a meeting of grantmakers and grantees on the East Coast. At that meeting, one of the grantees asked the grantmakers, "Do you people realize how often we are just putting stuff on paper that you want to hear so that we can get funding to do what we wanted to do in the first place?" The arts funders were astonished by this statement and insisted it never happened to them. The alternative explanation is that they were insulated from program reality.

Several kinds of philanthropic practice could redress this problem. Certainly, exercising due diligence before the fact could go a long way toward establishing that grantees will do the work in line with the proposal. Consistent monitoring by the grant officer might also keep the grantee on track—or at least keep the foundation officers in touch with what could and could not be accomplished. However, evaluation might also help put foundation officers in touch with this reality and perhaps ensure that funding was used as intended. Monitoring, making site visits, and observing products could all provide for accountability.

Program Side Effects. Foundations' power can produce both intended and un-intended consequences. Evaluation can play a useful role by documenting these consequences, especially the side effects of philanthropy's power that might be an-ticipated or controlled. Two examples illustrate how the power of philanthropy can produce these side effects, as seen in Cases 8 and 9.

Case 8: Evaluation of the Green Revolution

Rockefeller Foundation president Gordon Conway has written extensively about the Green Revolution, both its positive and negative effects (Conway and Ruttan, 1999). In 2003, Conway articulated what the foundation has learned from this experience and how it would incorporate that learning into a new approach to combat hunger in Africa. An important principle going forward is to involve communities, small farmers, and nongovernmental organizations in better formation of a "pro-poor" food policy.

> The first Green Revolution offered farmers new crop varieties that allowed them to improve their agricultural yields—to grow more wheat and rice per acre. . . . The call to action was the prediction of massive famine for India in the 1960s. . . .
>
> The Green Revolution has been criticized both rightly and wrongly, thought-fully and not. . . . It lowered food prices for everyone, including both urban and rural poor. This was important because the poor spend the highest propor-tion of their income on food. Prior to the Green Revolution, half of the popula-tion in the less developed countries did not get enough to eat; today that percentage has fallen to one-fifth. The Green Revolution also greatly increased employment in the rural non-farm economy and, while patterns varied, agri-cultural wages generally rose. Across Asia, the annual income per person rose several fold, and the number of poor people dropped rapidly. In 1975, six out of ten Asians lived in poverty; by 1993, it was only two out of ten East Asians and four out of ten South Asians.
>
> However, the Revolution had real failings. These failings—and I am using a very broad brush in this historical sketch—were both environmental and social. [The new crop varieties required more water, fertilizer, and pesticides and avoided the need for labor-intensive soil aeration, crop rotation, and working organic matter into the soil.] But these steps, we understand today, are key to long-term sustainability. The results of omitting them were soil erosion, nutrient depletion, falling water tables and salinization. . . . The seeds for the new varieties and the inputs required . . . were expensive, affordable mainly by the richer farmers (who by Western standards were still quite poor). The "rich" got richer and in some regions bought out the poor—to quote the critics, they "drove them off the land." . . . by the early 1970s many of the problems associated with the Green Revolution had been well documented and bet-ter understood. During the next two decades, governments in many parts of the world . . . put in place policies . . . to ensure that the Green Revolution might ben-

efit more of the poor. Village-level studies of the second-generation effects of the new technology in South India showed that small farmers had gained proportionally more income than large farmers, and the distribution of income improved. Nor, in most regions of India, did the disproportionate land distribution worsen. . . .

The world and the Rockefeller Foundation have changed considerably since the early Green Revolution days. We now understand the need to balance social and environmental concerns with getting new technologies right. . . . We are also trying to seize and develop the opportunities of globalization: *more transparency of process, more reporting of adverse effects in remote places, more informed criticism, and the possibility for faster and more precise course correction when the debate so indicates* (emphasis added; Conway, 2003, pp. 1–6).

Case 9: The Ford Foundation's Effort to Decentralize Governance of New York City Schools

This initiative worsened a growing rift between African Americans and Jews—groups whose historic solidarity promoted many civil rights achievements.

[In the late 1960s, the Ford Foundation was funding] experiments in structural change in public education, specifically the decentralization of the New York City school system. In 1967, McGeorge Bundy [president of The Ford Foundation] headed a panel appointed by Mayor Lindsay to make recommendations for school reform. Once the panel's report was published, the foundation gave support for two "demonstration districts" set up by the Board of Education in largely black areas, which in effect delegated authority over the schools in each district to newly formed community councils. The ensuing conflicts between the local councils, the Board of Education, and the teachers' union over questions of curricula and the right to hire and fire teachers led directly to the school strikes of 1968 and greatly exacerbated tensions between the black and Jewish communities. The role which the foundation, and Bundy in particular, had played in the whole affair drew great criticism. Albert Shanker, the head of the New York City teachers' union, even went on a nationwide speaking tour to warn other teachers' organizations of the threat to their position and power represented by "irresponsible intervention" of philanthropic organizations (Nielsen, 1972, p. 357).

One wonders whether prior consultation with the affected parties or formative evaluation early in the process would have apprised the foundation of the danger of side effects. From what we know, The Ford Foundation might not have changed its strategy. Yet the foundation's primary commitment was to the betterment of minorities. At least it would have known the potential tradeoffs for the civil rights movement, not to mention the public criticism this episode would bring down.

Revealing Flawed Assumptions. Evaluation is often highly useful when it reveals flawed assumptions (Leviton, 2003). A rather humble example is seen in Case 10. Testing assumptions can often help to preserve grant initiatives, make sure that money is well used, and preserve foundation reputations.

Why are such tests of assumptions necessary? Foundations often rely on a circle of elite experts they trust, and those elites often share assumptions about the world. These assumptions are occasionally wrong, or at least out of step with program stakeholders outside the circle. Philanthropy is not alone in this; erroneous but shared assumptions regularly cause both business and public policy mistakes (Allison and Zelikow, 1999; Mitroff, 1998). (This issue relates to the central point of Chapter Five: the benefits for philanthropy of being inclusive and listening to diverse voices when planning and making grants and when evaluating the consequences.)

Case 10: Engaging a Community's Leadership

In the early 1990s, the first author conducted evaluation for local funders, focused on a planning process to develop substance abuse services in three low-income, minority neighborhoods. The planning process was intended to be inclusive of community leadership in those neighborhoods. One of the neighborhoods had long been ignored by the city's power structure; it was the first time in a long time that the funders had sought this community's input on any topic whatsoever. However, the funders assumed they knew the community's leadership, and they clearly did not. An initial meeting erupted with resentment, as people shouted, "You don't even know who our real leadership is. Where are they? And why do you keep inviting people from [agency]—they don't represent us; they colonize us!"

The funders were greatly dismayed by this reaction. However, the evaluation put it in perspective for them. It pointed out that many good meetings in low-income communities can begin with residents' need to vent their frustration and hurt and to test whether the invitation to participate is made in good faith. The report also offered methods to better identify community leadership in the future. The process continued to be tense from time to time, but progress was made in planning for services, which are in place to this day. The evaluation report gave the funders some confidence to stick with the process in this neighborhood.

Philanthropy's Vulnerability

Foundations are vulnerable to criticism, whether deserved or not, both as a group and individually. Throughout the past century, both insiders and outsiders have called foundations elitist, overly privileged, unduly powerful, or sometimes simply wrongheaded (Brilliant, 2001; Cohen, 2002; Council on Foundations, 2003; Nielsen, 1972).

Consequences of Criticism. The justice of these criticisms is less important to our purposes than is the fact of foundations' vulnerability to damage to their reputations. The United States subsidizes foundations through favorable treatment under the tax law (Porter and Kramer, 1999). When foundations are criticized, this arrangement can be endangered. For example, in the early 1970s Congress created the Commission on Private Philanthropy and Public Needs "to clear the air after a string of scandals and reports of fiduciary misdeeds befouled the previously pristine reputation of American foundations in the late 1960s" (Cohen, 2002, p. ii; see also Brilliant, 2001). In 2003, the House of Representatives cited excessive executive compensation at one major foundation in proposing to exclude administration costs from the 5 percent IRS payout requirement. The bill did not pass but would have been a disaster for foundations that rely on in-house expertise and contract research to carry out their strategies (Foundation Center, 2004).

Foundation culture places great importance on the foundation's good name. It is difficult for outsiders to comprehend the importance of this consideration. Foundations rely on their "reputational" capital, as well as their financial resources, to shape programs and influence whole fields of endeavor. The good name of individual charities is difficult to come by and easy to lose. Foundation staff frequently allude to the fate of the United Way after its scandal of the early 1990s (Glaser, 1994; Sinclair, 2002). Charitable contributions to United Way increased only 6.9 percent between 1992 and 1996, although total private giving increased 24 percent during the same period (National Committee for Responsive Philanthropy, 1998).

Demonstration of Worth. Evaluation can provide important evidence of the value of philanthropy, helping to balance any criticism that a foundation might receive. Evaluation can demonstrate the worth of philanthropic activity in several ways, such as showing the value of a program design or intervention. However (and crucial to this discussion), evaluation is also valuable if it helps foundations avoid negative side effects and subsequent criticism through a midcourse correction (Chelimsky, 2001).

Grantees' View of the Evaluation Process

Although the focus of this chapter is on evaluation as perceived and planned within foundations, grantees will also benefit when evaluation has a sharper focus and a clearer purpose. Yet they will have understandable worries about a process that puts them in a position of relative weakness and potential loss of control.

Predictable Dysfunctions. Foundations' power translates into apprehension about evaluation among grantees. The need for trust and collaboration therefore carries over to the foundation's grantees and the evaluators who are commissioned to do the work. All too often, we see the same dysfunctional reactions to evaluation that are so common in other settings. We have seen defensive grantees damage themselves through misbehavior; we have also seen evaluators harm their ability to generate useful information by rigidity in thinking and by a disregard for the grantee's legitimate anxiety. These situations convey the impression that a foundation is being high-handed with grantees.

Interdependence of Evaluation and Program. Realistically, foundation evaluation often has to depend on the cooperation of the program. This can work to restore some of the power balance in the relationship and establish a business-like exchange agreement between the grantees and the evaluator. After all, grantee staff must be interviewed to get a sense of process. Program participants may need to be interviewed to assess effects of the program. Even when data collection does not have to rely on grantee cooperation (as in the case of existing datasets), fairness dictates that the evaluation should reflect an understanding of the program logic model or theory of change, as well as reported barriers and facilitators for program implementation and achievement of outcomes. Therefore, the grantees need to be kept involved over the course of the evaluation. Besides, people have the right to be kept apprised of something so important to their fate. Fairness (and the paper trail demonstrating fairness) often provides the best protection from future attacks on the process or the results.

Conclusion

Evaluations that consider both the internal and external context of foundations have a greater chance to be of good quality, relevant, and useful. Expectations about evaluation's purpose and the ways it might be used also affect usefulness. Examples throughout this chapter illustrate both the potential and the reality of useful evaluation.

The Foundation Context

Inside the foundation, we have argued for the importance of three features that drive evaluation choices:

1. Foundation *size* (assets, payout, and staffing), which
   - *Does not* necessarily affect the quality or usefulness of evaluation (see Chapters Eight and Ten)
   - *Does* influence evaluation's purpose, because large foundations often have different program goals from the smaller ones (Cases 1, 2)

- *Does* affect foundation staff and grantees' sensitivities about evaluation (Cases 2, 3, 10)
2. Foundation *culture* (shared values and expectations), which
   - Dictates whether evaluation is valued (see Chapters Three and Eight)
   - Values some approaches to evaluation over others (Cases 1, 3, 4, 6)
   - Prizes evaluation findings (positive or negative) that address the foundation's shared mission and the foundation staff member's vision of the public interest (Cases 1–5)
3. Location of *authority and responsibility* for the evaluation function, which
   - Affects the independence of evaluation from program (Chelimsky, 2001)
   - Requires trust and collegiality between foundation program and evaluation staff to ensure a meaningful evaluation (Cases 1, 3, 10)

Outside the foundation, we believe three important evaluation drivers include

1. Foundations' *power* in society, which
   - May insulate staff from on-the-ground reality so that evaluations can offer information about problems and opportunities (Cases 7–10)
   - May lead to unintended side effects of grantmaking—side effects that evaluation might detect at an early stage for midcourse correction (Cases 8, 9)
   - May lead to untested assumptions for which a countervailing evaluation perspective is helpful (Cases 7, 9, 10)
2. Foundations' vulnerability to criticism, which
   - Drives the need to demonstrate the value of grantmaking
   - May lead foundations to rely on evaluation to avoid public mistakes (Cases 8–10)
3. Grantee *perceptions of the evaluation process* (fear, extent of buy-in), which
   - Can assist or detract from the work (Cases 3, 6, 10)
   - Can lead to acceptance or attacks on results (Cases 3, 4, 6)
   - Can be managed through a fair and transparent process (Cases 6, 10)

Some Constructive Uses for Foundation-Sponsored Evaluation

Inside the foundation, evaluations might be used in any of the following ways:

- Exercising due diligence by foundation staff to gain information in advance about the potential effectiveness or worthiness of a proposal (Cases 4, 5, 9)
- Reducing uncertainty about the investment in a program or strategy (Cases 4, 5, 8, 10)
- Correcting funders' assumptions about a societal need, a program strategy, or the political climate for social change (Cases 7–10)

- Keeping the foundation staff accountable to the board for their choices of grantmaking strategies or program funding (Cases 1, 3, 5, 8)
- Providing a rationale for renewal of funding to the foundation's senior leadership and board (see Chapter Seven; Cases 1, 4, 10)

Outside the foundation, evaluations might be used in these ways:

- Keeping grantees accountable for performance (Cases 2, 3, 5, 7)
- Portraying the rationale for foundation choices to the rest of the world (Cases 1, 2, 8)
- Building a field of work (see Chapter Nine; Cases 1, 8)
- Affirming or disproving the value of a program intervention to encourage outsiders' attention and support (Cases 1, 2, 4, 8)
- "Fixing" the wayward investment (Cases 1, 2, 7, 8)
- Providing the rationale for renewal of funding to the foundation's staff (Case 4)

The Road to Better Foundation-Sponsored Evaluation

Most important, perhaps, is the potential that evaluation presents to elevate the debate about program investments and grant awards. Because philanthropy is still so intensely personal, evaluation properly conducted can depersonalize the process. This can be done through an appeal to altruism and duty—the higher motivations behind many foundation officers' choice to work in philanthropy. It can be especially effective when staff view program grants as portfolios of work for which they have fiduciary responsibility. Viewed in that light, both positive and negative evaluations become important information to those who manage those portfolios. The information can be used to advance a field through knowledge and program improvement. Just as a positive evaluation can validate a foundation's strategy for improving a field, a negative evaluation can steer its future activities toward newer and more productive activities.

References

Allison, G. T., & Zelikow, P. (1999). *Essence of decision: Explaining the Cuban missile crisis* (2nd ed.). Upper Saddle River, NJ: Pearson PTP.

Bickel, W., & Cooley, W. W. (1986). *Decision-oriented educational research* (Evaluation in Education and Human Services, no. 11). New York: Kluwer Academic Publishers.

Brilliant, E. L. (2001). *Private charity and public inquiry: A history of the Filer and Peterson Commissions.* Bloomington, IN: Indiana University Press.

Chelimsky, E. (2001). What evaluation could do to support foundations: A framework with nine component parts. *American Journal of Evaluation, 22,* 13–28.

Cohen, R. (2002). Introduction. In *The state of philanthropy, 2002.* Washington, DC: National Committee for Responsive Philanthropy (pp. iii–vii). Available at www.ncrp.org. Accessed June 17, 2003.

Conway, G. (2003, March 12). *From the green revolution to the biotechnology revolution: Food for poor people in the 21st century.* Woodrow Wilson International Center for Scholars Director's Forum. Available at www.rockfound.org/documents/566/Conway.pdf. Accessed July 22, 2003.

Conway, G., & Ruttan, V. W. (1999). *The doubly green revolution: Food for all in the twenty-first century.* Ithaca, NY: Comstock Publishing Association.

Council on Foundations. (2003). *Council on Foundations, Inc. records, 1949–1981.* New York: Rockefeller University. Available at www.rockefeller.edu/archive.ctr/council.html. Accessed June 18, 2003.

Dennis, M. L. (1994). Ethical and practical randomized field experiments. In J. S. Wholey, H. P. Hatry, and K. E. Newcomer (Eds.), *Handbook of practical program evaluation.* San Francisco: Jossey-Bass.

Downs, A. (1994). *Inside bureaucracy* (reissue ed.). Prospect Heights, IL: Waveland Press.

Emerson, J. (2003). *Total foundation asset management: Exploring elements of engagement within philanthropic practice.* Available at www.redf.org. Accessed May 20, 2003.

Foundation Center. (2004). *Top U.S. foundations by total giving.* Available at fdncenter.org/research/trends_analysis/top100giving.html. Accessed May 27, 2004.

Glaser, J. S. (1994). *An insider's account of the United Way scandal: What went wrong and why.* New York: Wiley.

Hirschhorn, L., Kelly, M., & Gilmore, T. N. (2002). *"Field" work in philanthropic strategy.* Contribution to the project, Improving the Practices of Philanthropy, supported by The Robert Wood Johnson Foundation, The Ewing Marion Kauffman Foundation, The John S. and James L. Knight Foundation, and The David and Lucile Packard Foundation. Philadelphia: Center for Applied Research.

King, M., & Oliphant, G. (2002). Tough love. *H: The Magazine of the Heinz Endowments, 2,* 10–25. Available at http://www.heinz.org. Accessed July 9, 2003.

Leviton, L. C. (2001). Building evaluation's collective capacity: American Evaluation Association presidential address. *American Journal of Evaluation, 22,* 1–12.

Leviton, L. C. (2003). Evaluation use: Advances, challenges, and applications. *American Journal of Evaluation, 24,* 525–535.

Leviton, L. C., & Hughes, E.F.X. (1981). Research on the utilization of evaluations: A review and synthesis. *Evaluation Review,* 1981, *5,* 525–547.

Mitroff, I. I. (1998). *Smart thinking for crazy times: The art of solving the right problems.* San Francisco: Berrett-Koehler.

National Committee for Responsive Philanthropy. (1998). *Charity in the workplace, 1997.* Washington, DC: Author. Available at www.ncrp.org/reports/charity97.htm. Accessed March 28, 2004.

Nielsen, W. A. (1972). *The big foundations.* New York: Columbia University Press.

Patrizi, P. (2002). *Briefing notes to the Evaluation II Roundtable.* Presented at the meeting of the Grantmakers Evaluation Network, Council on Foundations, Washington, DC, April 4, 2002.

Porter, M. E., & Kramer, M. R. (1999). Philanthropy's new agenda: Creating value. *Harvard Business Review, 77,* 121–130.

Rossi, P. H., Lipsey, M. W., & Freeman, H. L. (2004). *Evaluation: A systematic approach* (7th ed.). Thousand Oaks, CA: Sage.

Sinclair, M. (2002, March 1). William Aramony is back on the streets. Parsippany, NJ: *The NonProfit Times*. Available at www.nptimes.com/Mar02/npt2.html. Accessed April 15, 2003.

Stevens, B., Peikes, D., & Patel, S. (2003). Preliminary findings from the survey "When the Funding Stops." Princeton, NJ: Mathematica Policy Research. Manuscript submitted for publication.

Szanton, P. (2002). *Toward more effective use of intermediaries.* A contribution to the project, Improving the Practices of Philanthropy, supported by The Robert Wood Johnson Foundation, The Ewing Marion Kauffman Foundation, The John S. and James L. Knight Foundation, and The David and Lucile Packard Foundation. Philadelphia: Center for Applied Research.

Weatherford, J. M. (1985). *Tribes on the Hill: The U.S. Congress—Rituals and realities* (Rev. ed.). New York: Bergin and Garvey.

CHAPTER TWO

A HISTORICAL PERSPECTIVE ON EVALUATION IN FOUNDATIONS

Peter Dobkin Hall

W hy would foundations want or need to subject themselves to evaluation— a procedure that even its proponents concede is expensive and time consuming and that its critics argue yields results of questionable value? This chapter offers an answer to that question by reviewing what foundation decision makers have said and done over the past half century as they have tried to assess the impact of their efforts to serve the public, to bring about social change, and to justify the existence of private philanthropy to an often skeptical public.

The history of philanthropy offers useful lessons to contemporary decision makers in foundations. Insulated from market pressures and most other forms of accountability, officers, directors, and managers are prone to believe themselves free of the past as well. This historical review of the uses of evaluation by foundations suggests that if today's philanthropic leaders wish to avoid repeating the past, they would do well to learn from it.

Writing in 1987, management scholars Rosabeth Moss Kanter and David V. Summers framed the essentially problematic nature of evaluation in nonprofit settings. They wrote:

I am grateful to Lisa Berlinger, Eleanor Brilliant, Erna Gelles, Laura Leviton, Robert Long, Georgia W. McDaniel, Mark Moore, Andrew Morris, Michael O'Neill, Mark Rosenman, Carol H. Weiss, and Robert Wineburg, who shared their thoughts and their experiences about the development of evaluation research.

Nonprofit organizations have defined themselves not around their financial returns, but around their mission, or the services they offer. And services, of course, are notoriously intangible and difficult to measure. The clients receiving them and the professionals delivering them may make very different judgments about their quality, and donors may hold still another standard. And "doing good" is a matter of social values about which there may be little or no consensus. It is this factor, the centrality of social values over financial values, that complicates measurement for nonprofit organizations. (p. 154)

As ownerless organizations with fluid goals, unclear technologies, and multiple constituencies, the possibility of devising satisfactory ways of evaluating the performance of nonprofits seems difficult if not impossible. Invariably, as Peter Drucker wrote in 1968, any measurement of organizational performance is a value judgment:

It may sound plausible to measure the effectiveness of a mental hospital by how well its beds—a scarce and expensive commodity—are utilized. Yet a study of the mental hospitals of the Veterans Administration brought out that this yardstick leads to mental patients being kept in the hospital—which, therapeutically, is about the worst thing that can be done to them. Clearly, however, lack of utilization, that is, empty beds, would also not be the right yardstick. How then does one measure whether a mental hospital is doing a good job within the wretched limits of our knowledge of mental disease? (Drucker, 1968, pp. 196–197)

These difficulties are compounded by the fact that, as ownerless organizations, it is unclear to whom the accountability inherent in evaluation is due. Is it to donors—to demonstrate the efficient and effective use of their contributions or faithful implementation of their intentions? To clients—to vouch for quality of service? To trustees and directors—to show the competence of managers? To government agencies and other institutional funders—to give evidence of the effectiveness of the organization's programs? To the general public—to prove the value of the subsidy offered through tax exemption and deductibility of donations? Each of these constituencies, as Kanter and Summers suggest, is likely to prefer a different performance standard. And none, except an organization's governing board (which *is* the organization in a legal sense) and the attorney general (who represents the interests of the public) has legal standing to demand accountability. In contrast, stockholders, customers, voters, and legislators can demand—and in some instances have the authority and legal standing to require—accountability from business firms and government agencies.

If nonprofits are generically difficult to evaluate, grantmaking foundations pose the knottiest problems of all. Often framed to serve broad purposes, like The Rockefeller Foundation's mandate to "serve mankind," their trustees have enormous discretion to define and change their goals and purposes (Fosdick, 1952, p. 22). Unlike universities and hospitals, foundations are not engaged in selling goods and services of any kind, so there are no clients or customers to whom they must be accountable. And because they are not in competition with other firms, they have no obligation to offer themselves or their activities for comparison with other grantmakers. Because foundations' main business is managing their endowments and distributing its income, they seek support neither from individual donors, other grantmakers, or government agencies; nor, for that reason, do they have any obligation to account to them except with regard to compliance with tax, regulatory, and fiduciary obligations.

Although in many instances foundations are established by individuals and families, donors cannot hold their creations to account for the use of their gifts. Once a charitable gift is completed, donors have no legal standing to demand that their wishes be followed. Although donors can seek to increase the likelihood that the foundations they establish remain faithful to their wishes by serving on their boards and appointing as trustees family members and representatives, the law discourages donor control by subjecting such entities to more searching regulatory scrutiny and by reducing the tax benefits that accrue from charitable gifts made under such conditions. In any event, no matter how carefully donors may proceed in their efforts to ensure fidelity to their intentions, foundations are generally perpetuities and, with the passage of time and the procession of generations, there is no assurance that a donor's descendants will remain faithful to his or her original intentions.

Businesses exist to fulfill their charter purposes and to maximize returns to investors. Government agencies exist to fulfill the legislative mandates on which they were founded. Nonprofit producers of goods and services exist to fulfill their missions. All of these entities, depending on the industry in which they are located, are likely to be subject to different professional or industry standards. For example, all hospitals, whether public, proprietary, or nonprofit, must be licensed and must operate in accordance with pertinent government regulations. But most grantmaking foundations operate under no comparable public or private constraints. Beyond compliance to a generic set of fiduciary and regulatory obligations, they are free to define their goals and purposes as they see fit, with no substantive accountability to anyone.

This chapter reviews the recent history of philanthropy in order to explore the reasons why foundations have used evaluation, the ways in which it has been used, and the extent to which these efforts have been judged successful. I suggest first that the willingness of foundations to use evaluation techniques stems from the political milieu of the decades following World War II—an era in which an increasingly tax-sensitive public was given to episodic outbursts of concern about loopholes available to wealthy individuals and institutions. Second, I explore the peculiarities of foundations as complex organizations, pointing to the function of evaluation in settings in which decisions are made under conditions of ambiguity. Third, I examine the use of evaluation research by foundations and the view of foundation leaders about its usefulness. I hope that addressing these issues will help practitioners understand both the limits of evaluation and the social and political forces at work inside and outside the world of grantmaking—forces that have driven episodic demands for organizational accountability.

Foundations Under Fire, 1953–1969

Foundations were virtually unregulated before the 1950s. Because there were so few of them and because they were tax-exempt, the IRS took little interest in them. This made them especially attractive to tax advisers and estate planners in the years following World War II, as tax rates on individuals and corporations increased. After 1945, the number of foundations skyrocketed. Suspecting that many were established for tax-avoidance rather than charitable purposes, it was not long before congressional investigators turned their attention to foundations and other exempt entities. Even though foundations emerged unscathed from two congressional investigations in the early 1950s, farsighted foundation leaders feared they would be subject to further scrutiny.

Chief among these were officials of The Russell Sage Foundation. Founded in 1907, Sage was the first of the modern grantmaking foundations. Although it operated under a broad mandate to devote its resources to "the improvement of social and living conditions in the United States of America," by the 1940s it had become particularly interested in tracking the development of philanthropy and the proliferation of foundations. It sponsored the first directories of foundations (the ancestors of today's standard compendium, *The Foundation Directory*), the first of which appeared in 1920. Beginning in 1946, it initiated a series of major analytic publications identifying foundation trends and practices. Sage organized the 1956 Princeton Conference on the History of Philanthropy, which sought to stimulate scholarly interest in organized charity and philanthropy (Russell Sage Foundation, 1956). It was a leader in the effort to establish the Foundation Center, an enterprise devoted to collecting and disseminating information about foundations. The Foundation Center began issuing *The Foundation Directory* in 1960 and initiated publication of the periodical, *Foundation News* (which is now published as *Foundation News and Commentary* by the Council on Foundations; see Hall, 1992).

Clearly, Sage had more in mind than disinterested information gathering and analysis of foundations. Its concern with promoting transparency, accountability, and best practices as defenses against abuses and public exposure was evident from the contents of the earliest issues of *Foundation News*.

The efforts of Sage and a handful of other major grantmakers could not stem the public's growing skepticism about the value of foundations and its suspicion of the motives of their founders and executives. Through the 1960s, Congress and the U.S. Treasury Department focused attention on questionable foundation practices and priorities. Congressional hostility culminated in the hearings held by the House Ways and Means Committee and the Senate Finance Committee on the 1969 Tax Reform Act, which imposed reporting requirements, limitations on donor control and excess business holdings, and provisions requiring that foundations annually pay out a specified percentage of their annual revenues.

Some philanthropic leaders, notably John D. Rockefeller III, shared Congress's doubts about the practices and performance of foundations. While the Tax Reform Act was still being debated, he convened a national task force—the Commission on Foundations and Private Philanthropy, chaired by industrialist Pete Peterson—to study "all relevant matters bearing on foundations and private philanthropy" in order to make "long term policy recommendations" (Commission on Foundations and Private Philanthropy, 1970, p. 7). Among the questions the commission addressed was one of the most fundamental: "Do foundations have advantages over other means for promoting the general welfare?" (p. 117).

Although the commission did not find it possible to make a cost-benefit analysis of tax revenues foregone by government versus the social benefits produced by foundations, it did suggest that these benefits and their cost could be assessed both quantitatively and qualitatively. Among its final recommendations, it included a section on the "evaluation of programs—government and non-government," which suggested the value of "impartial appraisals" not only of government policies and programs, but also of other institutions, including foundations (Commission on Foundations and Private Philanthropy, 1970, pp. 129–130). In addition to the concrete benefit that such assessments would produce for program planners and policymakers, "periodical appraisals" of foundation performance, "shared with the American public . . . would help reduce some of the mystery from foundation activities and convey a sensitivity to the public that had not always been present" (pp. 130–131).

Though the commission's report had no impact on the substance of the Tax Reform Act and little discernible influence on foundations themselves, it undoubtedly encouraged the staff at Sage to begin investigating the potential of evaluation techniques and their applicability to foundations and their activities. As an institution whose primary focus was social welfare policy and which worked more closely with academic social scientists than most other grant-makers, Sage was uniquely well situated to tap into the emerging field of evaluation research (Glenn, Brandt, and Andrews, 1947; Hammack and Wheeler, 1994).

The Origins of Evaluation Research in Foundations

Evaluation of one kind or another had a historic association with social reform movements. By the mid-nineteenth century, public health advocates and physicians promoting "moral treatment" of the mentally ill used statistical methods to demonstrate the efficacy of the interventions they espoused. The Civil War era reports of the United States Sanitary Commission—the private body to which government had entrusted responsibility for military sanitation and relief—were replete with statistics vindicating the value of professionally administered programs. In the decades following the war, state charities commissions and private charity-organization societies used statistics to target problems and prove the economic and social benefits of "scientific philanthropy"—charitable activity directed to mitigating the root causes of social problems rather than merely providing relief to their victims (Frederickson, 1965; Lagemann, 2000).

As a product of the effort to reform private charity and government social welfare policy, The Russell Sage Foundation, over the course of the twentieth century, promoted this approach to identifying and addressing social problems. So, in the wake of the passage of the 1969 Tax Reform Act and the publication of the report of the Peterson Commission, it is hardly surprising that it should be the first foundation to give serious attention to evaluation. In 1973, sociologist Orville G. Brim Jr., who served as president of the foundation from 1964 to 1972, contributed a forthright essay titled, "Do We Know What We Are Doing?" to an edited volume, *The Future of Foundations*, published by the American Assembly, one of the era's most prestigious public policy forums (Heimann, 1973). In it, he not only sharply criticized foundations for the uninformed quality of their decision making and their isolation from the realities of public life but also provided a detailed account of Sage's own development and use of evaluation. These were framed by a reiteration of the foundation's overall concern with the future of foundation philanthropy. Brim (1973) wrote,

> The public, through its institutions, has a stake in the success or failure of foundations. The Tax Reform Act of 1969 challenged foundations to defend their position as contributors to pluralism, socially and politically, in a way distinguished from those activities of government and business. (p. 220)

Noting that over the previous two decades there had been "substantial expressions of public interest as to whether the public was getting its money's worth from the tax exemption granted to private foundations," Brim argued that "knowledge gained from evaluation" would have "more than just personal interest to foundation administrators." It might "help them to sustain the institution in American life" (p. 220).

Brim set forth five categories of information that might serve those purposes: (1) assessments of the success or failure of specific projects by foundation executives, grant recipients, and affected constituencies, (2) administrative comparisons of similar projects, (3) interprogram comparisons intended to assess areas of activity for foundation program planners, (4) comparisons of foundations in terms of their relative success in targeting problems and dealing with them effectively, and (5) comparisons of foundations' goals and activities with "those of other institutions, public and private, pursing the public good" (p. 222).

Brim went on to give an overview of the basic concepts of evaluation research as they existed at the time. He wrote,

> Evaluation research is the application of social research to provide the administrator with accurate information on the consequences of his action. The main aim is to measure the benefits received from the program, particularly with respect to objectives that have been set by the program, and to relate these to the cost incurred. More specifically, evaluative research must determine the extent to which a program achieves its goals, the relative impact of key program variables, and the role of the program itself versus external variables or influences. (1973, p. 226)

Citing Edward A. Suchman, whose pioneering monograph, *Evaluative Research* (1967), Sage had funded and published, Brim distinguished the "impressionistic evaluative procedures" used by administrators, politicians, and journalists" from "hard-headed" and "specific" assessments based on

> (1) extensive examination of objectives of a program (including underlying assumptions); (2) development of measurable criteria specifically related to these objectives; (3) establishment of controlled situations to determine the extent to which these objectives and negative side effects are achieved. (pp. 226–227)

Before turning to Sage's evaluation efforts, Brim gave his own assessment of the "state of foundation evaluations." Noting the "continuing exhortation" from both within and without the foundation field for evaluation, he found that there was little real interest in or understanding of formal evaluation. "The administrators of foundations seem trapped in foundation lore about how decisions should be made," he wrote. "Much of the traditional wisdom consists of unexamined maxims which have come to be rather comfortable substitutes for hard-headed evaluative information" (p. 228). He called attention to the handful of serious evaluation efforts: "Suchman & Ricker's study of the Maurice Falk Medical Fund, Eugene Struckoff's study of the New Haven Foundation, Winston Franklin's evaluation of the Kettering Foundation, and evaluations of specific programs at the Rockefeller, Sloan, Ford, and Markle foundations" (p. 230).

The major evaluation initiative undertaken by Sage was a year-long analysis of its projects over the past decade. Led by an outsider—CUNY sociology professor Lindsey Churchill (an ex-Sage staffer), assisted by Brim and two other foundation employees—the effort evaluated 110 research projects, 11 research and training programs, 10 fellowship programs, 16 dissemination projects (support for publications and conferences), and support for 15 visiting scholars. Data considered included documentary information about projects and grant recipients from foundation files and a survey of project directors in which they were asked to assess the impact of their own Sage-funded projects. As Brim describes it, the study seems to have raised more questions than it answered. The evaluators came up with nicely quantified ratings, but they weren't sure what they meant:

> If we find no strong positive or negative correlations between the various measures of success and the characteristics of projects and methods of operation, then we must consider at least three instructive reasons for the lack of findings. First, the cause may lie in unreliable or invalid ratings of success. Second, we may not have in our battery of potential predictors the truly significant factors that influence differential success of outcomes—we may not have the information in our records, and we did not think to ask for it. Or, third, perhaps both the ratings of success and the predictive factors are satisfactory and the reason there is no significant relationship between project outcome and our antecedent predictive characteristics of the project or administration is that success and failure are much too dependent on chance factors, that is, a number of unsystematically distributed effects on the course of a given program that cannot be anticipated. We can speculate about what this would imply for guidelines of "rational" foundation management. (p. 238)

It was one thing, as Brim discovered, to charge into evaluating complex settings and organizations with "hard-headed" and "specific" outcome-focused assumptions. It was quite another thing, regardless of how quantifiable the results, to come up with meaningful or reliable findings that could provide any real guidance to foundation decision makers.

Although Brim concluded his essay by endorsing continuing development of evaluation in foundation settings and with a long list of ways foundations could inform themselves about their work and how the public perceived it, his failure to demonstrate persuasively that evaluation could be applied effectively to foundation activities may account for why the second major national panel on nonprofits—the Filer Commission (the 1974–1979 Commission on Private Philanthropy and Public Needs, also organized at the behest of John D. Rockefeller III)—had very little to say about the subject and why evaluation was not docketed as a major concern of academically based nonprofits research that began to emerge after 1978 (Commission on Private Philanthropy and Public Needs, 1975, 1977; Brewster, Lindbloom, and Simon, 1975). It appears that by reframing foundations as part of a more inclusive domain of organizations—the "nonprofit sector"—grantmakers had enfolded themselves in the warm blanket of public approval enjoyed by other charities (see Karl, 1987). Having done so, foundations no longer felt the need to prove their right to exist.

The Great Society, the Conservative Revolution, and the Growth of Evaluation Research

The real impetus for the development of evaluation research came from two sources: (1) government and (2) the social and behavioral sciences. The social sciences had always seen themselves as informing social and economic reform efforts, identifying problems, and offering solutions. As the scope and scale of government grew after World War II, academics endeavored to expand the application of their expertise to new domains of policy and practice. As they did so, interest grew in developing ways of planning and evaluating government interventions. During the 1960s, the federal government committed itself to major social initiatives intended to eradicate poverty. At the urging of social and policy scholars, a number of these mandated evaluation and allocated funding to pay for it. Major Great Society legislation, including the Economic Opportunity Act of 1964 and the Elementary and Secondary Education Act of 1965, both required and provided funding for evaluation. According to Brim (1973), "federal expenditures for evaluation research in fiscal 1970 provided approximately $45 to $50 million in the general areas of social welfare and social services, housing, education, etc., with the largest portion being expended by the Department of Health, Education, and Welfare" (p. 239).

The establishment of publications like *Evaluation: A Forum for Human Services Decision-Makers* in 1972 affirm the fact that the public, not the private sector, was the real source of energy and innovation in evaluation research. The magazine

was produced by the Minneapolis Medical Research Foundation, with funds from
the National Institute of Mental Health. Its first issue featured a lead article by
Minnesota senator Walter Mondale titled "Social Accounting, Evaluation, and
the Future of Human Services" and an interview with Nixon administration
Health, Education, and Welfare secretary Elliot Richardson. In its lead editorial,
"What Is Evaluation Good For?" the journal's editor, Susan Salasin, set forth its
belief in the possibilities of evaluation. She wrote:

> In every article or discussion about evaluation these days, one question, implic-
> itly or explicitly, gets raised. "What good is it?" Some decry the current meth-
> ods available for use, others bemoan the fact that findings are not utilized, and
> still others recoil from the insights evaluations have provided regarding the in-
> adequacy of human service programs. (Salasin, 1972, p. 2)

More fundamental than the question of the effectiveness of evaluation, she
argued, was the question of our expectations of the procedure.

> If instead we try to ask ourselves what evaluation has given us, aside from a
> lack of answers, we can see a new role for evaluation. Instead of talking about
> what evaluation doesn't do, we can talk about what it does do. The experiences
> reported herein seem to indicate that evaluation does lead to a discovery of
> what some of the problems with human service programs are. Evaluation does
> highlight the fact that we think we can accomplish more for people than we
> can, in fact, accomplish. Viewed from this perspective, evaluation is a valuable
> and effective tool that can help sense out the problems in our programs, and
> keep us honest in making promises to people about how we can help.

In defining *evaluation* "as a tool for problem identification and realistic sight-set-
ting" and as "a social movement dedicated to finding out how well we are doing with
our human services programs, and discovering better ways of doing," Salasin was
clearly endeavoring to embrace evaluation as an instrument for maintaining public
commitment to human services. In doing so, *Evaluation* seemed to clearly place itself
in the service of welfare state liberalism. At the same time, her editorial suggests that
because of the huge political and financial stakes involved in how evaluation was used,
by whom, and for what purposes, the field and its methods were bound to develop,
not in the disinterested remoteness of the ivory tower but in the politically charged
and turbulent environment of an America that was becoming increasingly polarized
over what, if anything, the public owed to its young, poor, and disabled citizens.

Problematic findings, contested methodology, and political conflict do not appear to have slowed the growth of evaluation research. The continuing expansion

of the field was signaled by the establishment of two new journals in 1978: *Evaluation and Program Planning: An International Journal* and *Evaluation Quarterly* (later changed to *Evaluation Review*).

The lead article in the first issue of *Evaluation Quarterly*, written by Peter Rossi, one of the rising stars of American sociology, was an assessment of the state of evaluation research that assessed the major evaluation efforts of the previous decade (Rossi and Wright, 1977). It concluded that although some evaluation efforts exemplified best practice, most fell far short. "The current state of the art is, on the average, considerably below the level illustrated here" (p. 1). By the 1980s, evaluation research had clearly established itself as a credible enterprise. Despite continuing disagreement over objectives, concepts, and methods, it had moved from the margins of applied social science to full institutionalization (if not legitimacy), with its own academic journals, courses, and training programs. As this occurred, it began to attract the attention of foundation executives and trade associations.

Pioneers in Foundation Evaluation, 1972–1980

There can be no doubting the impact of The Robert Wood Johnson Foundation's commitment to evaluation on nonprofits' growing interest in the field during the 1980s. Established by General Robert Wood Johnson, head of the medical supply giant Johnson & Johnson, the foundation, when it began operating in 1972, was the second largest in the United States (Nielsen, 1985; Rogers, 1987). The foundation's trustees were given broad discretion to define its mission and programs. Approaching the responsibilities of philanthropy from a business perspective, they determined "that the Johnson Foundation should be 'productive': that it have clear goals and priorities, meet its deadlines, show results, and stay out of trouble" (Nielsen, 1985, p. 123). Working with a staff of physicians and health policy experts headed by David Rogers, they committed themselves to an activist, reform-oriented agenda. Rather than conventional funding of hospital construction and medical research and education, it would identify and seek to solve such policy problems as the availability of primary health care and the more equitable delivery of health care (p. 124). This orientation to "field trial" policy interventions was coupled with a commitment to "objective, third-party evaluations of the results" of these interventions (p. 125).

An account of Johnson's use of evaluation research was the subject of the first article in *Evaluation and Program Planning* to address the use of evaluation research by foundations—an article coauthored by foundation president David Rogers, staffers Linda Aiken and Robert Blendon, and University of California,

Los Angeles, sociologist Howard E. Freeman. The article took pains to distinguish what Robert Wood Johnson was doing from "'evaluation' as the term is typically used in the foundation world" (Aiken, Blendon, Rogers, and Freeman, 1980, p. 120). "Many of the larger foundations 'evaluate' their grants," they wrote.

> In this sense, evaluation is commonly employed to describe the general process of determining how well a foundation-funded project was implemented by a grant recipient. Although such an assessment implies an explicit and rational basis for judging the "worth" of an effort, it usually does not involve the marshalling of objective facts and evidence to impartially document whether the project improved the lives of people or the performance of an organization in carrying out its mission and reaching its objectives. Without being pejorative, they are usually impressionistic judgments based on unsystematic information about what went on during the period of the grant. (p. 120)

In contrast, Robert Wood Johnson's approach involved "the use of social research procedures, including systematic collection of factual data and use of appropriate analytical methods to arrive at a reproducible conclusion from which a decision can be made regarding success or failure in implementation and outcome of a particular program" (p. 121). These efforts had two foci: (1) the extent of the problems it is addressing (who is affected, to what extent, and for how long) and (2) using monitoring and impact studies on the extent to which projects significantly affect health-care problems in measurable ways.

Because there were no reliable data on problems relating to access to health care, the foundation began its work by supporting a series of baseline studies that sought to measure "the extent to which persons in the United States were experiencing problems in gaining access to desired medical care and to what degree this was attributable to the absence of health resources or to imbalances in the mix of physician specialists and other health-care providers" (p. 122). These would serve as the yardsticks for assessing the impact of foundation programs.

Although The Robert Wood Johnson Foundation remained strongly committed to evaluation, reporting that it had more than twenty such efforts under way as of 1980, it was also candid about the problematic nature of the enterprise. Rogers and his coauthors wrote:

> As our evaluation program has evolved, the reasons such studies are rarely undertaken by foundations has become increasingly evident to us. The answer to the question: Should a private foundation make major investments to "evaluate" their programs? is not as clear as the Peterson Commission report might suggest. Evaluations are expensive and require extraordinary care in their design and implementation if one is to answer generally significant questions.

The tools used in assessment of complex programs involving many people and institutions are imperfect. Data collection is enormously time-consuming, and such studies require continuing attention and patience to keep them on track. (Aiken and others, 1980, p. 127)

Because the cost of a multisite evaluation often exceeded $1 million, such efforts were clearly beyond the funding capacity of most foundations at a time when only 50 of the nation's 21,000 grantmakers had annual expenditures exceeding $4 million. "Thus," they concluded, "the cost of just one major independent evaluation study of three- or four-grant projects exceeds the grant-making capacity of 95% of the nation's private foundations" (p. 127). Evaluation efforts also required "trained research staff who spend their time almost exclusively on the design and monitoring of such programs"—at a time when only 2 percent of foundations had professional staffs. Finally, unlike Johnson's programs, which were designed to produce measurable outcomes, most foundation initiatives were "difficult to evaluate objectively" (p. 128). Although concluding that evaluation had served it well, the article closed by declaring that the costs of evaluation were "likely to be prohibitive for 99% of the nation's foundations" (p. 128).

The Limits of Evaluation

Looking back on his accomplishments as president of The Robert Wood Johnson Foundation on his retirement in 1987, David Rogers affirmed his belief in the value of evaluation in an article in *Foundation News*—a magazine published by the Council on Foundations, the national grantmakers' trade association. Rather than suggesting that evaluation had produced reliable assessments of the impact of its programs and projects, Rogers indicated that its major contribution was organizational. By focusing on the outcome of grants rather than on the process by which "we, or our grantees, might get there," evaluation permitted the foundation's staff—a "diverse lot of individuals of widely differing value systems and political persuasions"—to agree on its "major programmatic thrust" (Rogers, 1987, p. 49). This revealing admission illuminates an aspect of evaluation that few evaluation researchers at the time were willing to acknowledge: that rather than producing "objective" measurements of the impact of foundation interventions, its primary value was to reduce uncertainty and disagreement within grantmaking organizations.

Carol H. Weiss, the Columbia University–based evaluation research pioneer, had called attention to this issue as early as 1973 in a cautionary article in *Evaluation* titled "Where Politics and Evaluation Research Meet." While "evaluation research is a rational enterprise," she wrote that it "takes place in a political context"

(Weiss 1973b, p. 37). She went on to outline the three major ways in which politics "intruded" on evaluation. First, she suggested, "the policies and programs with which evaluation deals are the creatures of political decisions—proposed, defined, debated, enacted, and funded through political processes." Second, because evaluation was undertaken to inform decision making by political actors, findings inevitably had political consequences. "Third," she argued, "by its very nature, [evaluation] makes implicit political statements about such issues as the problematic nature of some programs and the unchallengeability of others, the legitimacy of program goals and program strategies, the utility of strategies of incremental reform, and even the appropriate role of the social scientist in policy and program formation" (p. 37).

To be "creative and strategically useful," Weiss contended, the evaluator must be sensitive to the "politics of evaluation research," including "the interests and motivations of other actors in the system, the roles that he himself is consciously or inadvertently playing," and the "limitations and possibilities for putting the results to work" (p. 38). Weiss was keenly aware of the likelihood that, in these political settings, evaluation might have little to do with the ostensible goal of measuring the success or failure of programs. Policymakers' decisions, she wrote, are "rooted in all the complexities of the democratic decision-making process." For this reason, how well a program is doing may be less important than whether a program "fits well with prevailing values, if it satisfies voters, or if it pays off political debts" (p. 40). Because of this, she noted, evaluation studies seemed to have little noticeable effect on the making and remaking of public policy.

The one situation in which evaluation research seemed most likely to affect decisions was when the researcher accepted the values, assumptions, and objectives of the decision maker. "This means, obviously," Weiss noted, "that decisionmakers heed and use results that come out the way they want them to." This suggested, as David Rogers would later conclude in weighing the impact of the Johnson Foundation's efforts, that evaluation had more to do with organizations' political and psychological equilibrium than with objective measurements of impact. The very willingness of social scientists to evaluate programs, she observed, "gives an aura of legitimacy to the enterprise" (p. 41).

Ultimately, Weiss concluded, "for the social scientist who wants to contribute to the improvement of social programming, there may be more effective routes at this point than through evaluation research"—most particularly, "research on the social processes and institutional structures that sustain the problems of society and closer social science involvement in the application of that research" (p. 45).

Given the evident shortcomings of evaluation research, particularly as it applied to foundations, it is curious that, by the mid-1980s, interest in the subject began to intensify. If publications are any evidence, evaluators themselves had shown little interest in foundations since the Russell Sage and Robert Wood Johnson initiatives of the early 1970s. But in 1981, Nick L. Smith of the Northwest Regional Educational Laboratory published the results of a National Institute of Education study of foundation support of evaluation. At the same time, articles on evaluation began appearing with increasing frequency in foundation trade publications and in nonprofit scholarly journals.

The Smith article, which appeared in *Evaluation Review* in the spring of 1985, began by calling attention to the fact that "resources usually available for evaluation have begun to dwindle" as the federal government, now in the full grips of the conservative revolution, was "encouraging increased private sector support for social programs. Evaluation researchers are looking more widely for financial support," he noted, "and are asking whether foundations might be a source of evaluation funds" (Smith, 1981, p. 215). With federal funds drying up, evaluation researchers were looking for new markets and, Smith suggested, "foundations are a multi-billion dollar a year enterprise with vast potential for contributing to the improvement of evaluation methods and practice" (p. 216).

Although Smith offered his readers a good overview of the types and sizes of foundations and the kinds of evaluations they had used, he curiously omitted any reference to the caveats that David Rogers and his colleagues from Robert Wood Johnson had issued five years earlier in their assessment of the foundation's own evaluation efforts. The emphasis in the article was clearly on the opportunities that foundation evaluation offered, not the obstacles it presented, including, most notably, the small number of foundations that could afford to support evaluation research, the small number of staffed foundations, and the problems of evaluating outcomes that eluded quantification.

Of the nation's 450 major foundations, Smith found only 205 evaluation grants awarded by 76 grantmakers. Most of these were by a handful of foundations: Ford (22), the Lilly Endowment (14), Kellogg (12), Robert Wood Johnson (9), The Cleveland Foundation (8), Charles Stewart Mott (6), and Markle (6). The mean size of awards from each of the foundations ranged from a high of $338,026 for the nine Robert Wood Johnson grants to a low of $34,793 for the eight awards by The Cleveland Foundation. Evaluation grants and contracts went overwhelmingly to research universities, though one consulting firm—Television Audience Assessment—was noted as a major awardee.

Smith's findings were not particularly encouraging. He noted that, relative to the resources available, foundation use of evaluation research was minimal and that most of the evaluation that had been done had produced only internal documents, not any material that was publicly available. (This reinforces the notion that foundations used evaluation to address internal conflicts rather than to generate public support for their work.) Smith's article ended with an epilogue instructing potential applicants for foundation support on how to do grants research and how to approach foundations. "It takes effort," he noted, "to match the interests of an evaluation researcher with the proper foundation."

Within months of the publication of the Smith article in *Evaluation Review,* a major feature on evaluation appeared in *Foundation News,* the bimonthly magazine of the Council on Foundations (Butt, 1985). The article, written by Martha Butt of the Northwest Area Foundation, offered an enthusiastic endorsement and detailed overview of the types and uses of evaluation. She recommended the use of independent consultants who could provide "the highly valuable characteristics of objectivity, autonomy, and credibility" (p. 29). Although the piece included cautionary sidebars on the limitations of evaluation, such as Robert Bothwell's urging that funders consider grantees as partners, not second-class citizens, in philanthropic endeavors, the thrust of the article was positive. It was clearly an effort to build a market for evaluation researchers in the foundation world. A high-visibility endorsement of evaluation by the Northwest Area Foundation, one of the most respected and innovative regional grantmakers, was bound to have a national impact.

The Ubiquity of Evaluation

By the late 1980s, evaluation was becoming ubiquitous in the nonprofit world. It was energetically promoted by the major philanthropy trade groups, the Council on Foundations, and Independent Sector, which published evaluation resource guides and hortatory memoranda and ran evaluation sessions at their annual meetings. Nearly every year after 1987, *Foundation News* featured at least one major article on evaluation, and the industry press—*Nonprofit World* (published by the practitioner-oriented Nonprofit Management Association), the *Chronicle of Philanthropy, Philanthropy,* and *Nonprofit Times*—among them ran a total of twenty-one articles on evaluation between 1987 and 2002. The nonprofit scholarly journals—*Nonprofit and Voluntary Sector Quarterly, Nonprofit Management and Leadership,* and *Voluntas,* which had ignored evaluation before 1990, began publishing on the subject. Between 1995 and 2002, fifteen articles on evaluation appeared in these journals, most of them by scholars who had not previously written about evaluation. Articles on evaluation in trade and scholarly publications touched on virtually every industry in which nonprofits operated—the arts and culture, education, health care, and human services.

Why did interest in evaluation grow so rapidly in the 1990s? Had the shortcomings of evaluation been overcome by significant improvements in technique? Had there been a transformation in some fundamental aspect of the nonprofit sector that led organizations to embrace a problematic and expensive activity that it had once generally scorned? Or were there forces at work involving the internal dynamics of nonprofits as organizations and the changing composition of the nonprofit sector?

It may be that all three of these factors have helped to encourage foundations and other nonprofits to accept evaluation as a part of their work. Carol Weiss believes that evaluation has come a long way from the unquestioning faith in the value of quantifiable measures and experimental methods expressed by such pioneers as Edward Suchman in the 1960s. She believes that current evaluation methods address qualitative issues far more effectively. Certainly, her own contributions to a richly contextualized approach to evaluation and her role in helping evaluators appreciate the complexity of complex organizations have helped the field progress. The ability to focus on qualitative issues undoubtedly made evaluation more user-friendly, as did the expansion in the range of types of evaluation (Alie and Seita, 1997, pp. 40–49).

Undoubtedly, two major trends in the nonprofit sector helped to promote the acceptance of evaluation research—or at least the rhetoric of evaluation. One was the huge increase in the number of new foundations established during the 1990s. As Foundation Center president and former Carnegie Corporation executive Sara Engelhardt pointed out in an interview, half the foundations in existence today have been created within the past twenty years (Saidel, 2002, p. 489). The proliferation of foundations brought large numbers of donors and trustees, most of them from the results-oriented world of high-tech business, into the world of philanthropy. They expected, realistically or not, to see the results of their generosity. Another factor was the professionalization of nonprofit management, in particular the training of managers in schools of business and public administration, many of which offered courses on evaluation as part of their curricula. Professionally trained managers understood the reassurance donors and boards were likely to find in the rhetoric, if not the reality, of evaluation.

Whether there was any real substance to this evaluation activity is far from clear. Engelhardt says:

> Many foundations fall into a trap when they decide they want to do evaluation. They aren't really serious about what it would take and what it would mean, but they feel the pressure to do it. They feel they're helping the grantee by doing it. I don't think that's helpful. In fact, in the [mid-1980s], I was chairing the Council on Foundations Research Committee, and its foundation members wanted help in how to do evaluation, so we decided to do an evaluation handbook. It would take good evaluation models from foundations and get them out

there. So we made a call for evaluations that foundations thought had been helpful. We got the worst, unbelievable things, like counting how many proposals they got and worse. It was clear to us that there was not a very high understanding of what evaluation was, what it would take, and what good evaluation might tell you. (Saidel, 2002, p. 493)

Certainly, *Nonprofit World*'s 1997 survey, "Who's Using Evaluation," did not suggest that things had improved much since the mid-1980s. The article defined "formal evaluation" as "the systematic investigation of the worth or merit of an object; for example, a program, project, or grant proposal" (Alie and Seita, 1997, p. 41). This approach relied on such data as written reports, site visits, indirect contacts, financial reports, numbers of clients served, accreditation and licensing, and assessment of management practices—a far cry from the kind of hard data that Brim of Russell Sage and Rogers of Robert Wood Johnson seem to have had in mind.

Engelhardt herself, looking back on thirty years of watching foundations trying to use evaluation, remained skeptical of its value. She saw internal pressure from foundation boards as having played an important role in prompting grantmakers to use evaluation:

On the larger-staffed foundations, often the trustees were not in the field of philanthropy; they were in business or some other areas, and they too needed to understand what is success, often again because you don't see the huge leverage, the huge outcomes that you might have seen before. Several foundations began experimenting even then [in the 1970s] with evaluation and discovered the hard truth that you don't often find out anything useful, except that you bet on a good or a bad person to run the program. Usually, the success or failure couldn't be pinned on the strategy but had more to do with some other things, and often it cost more to study the results of a project, to get some really good useful information, than the project itself cost. And they found evaluations were often not used very faithfully, even if they did give you some answers, because people didn't trust them. (Saidel, 1992, p. 492)

Although she thought that interest in evaluation had subsided, she noted the upsurge of attention it was receiving in the late 1990s, which she viewed (incorrectly in my view) as "actually coming from the new research in the evaluation field, external to foundations and external to the specific research programs that they're supporting" (p. 492). She continued:

My own view is that evaluation as part of the grantmaking cycle and process has still not been perfected in a way that makes it terribly useful. Every renewal request, every renewal grant entails some kind of evaluation. Someone is making a value judgment about whether it worked and how and why, and often making adjustments to the strategy or the staffing or whatever they think will make it better. It's not as though there's no evaluation, but I think we're still faced with some resource issues and some timeliness issues about the degree to which you can use evaluation effectively to operate a grant program. (p. 492)

Engelhardt reiterated a view that had been voiced as early as the 1970s by Carol Weiss: "Evaluation is not meant to inform grantmaking so much as to help the organization" (Weiss, 1973a; Saidel, 2002, p. 492). More to the point, as Engelhardt described it, evaluation, as used by major foundations like Kellogg and Lilly, appeared to be more geared to aligning grantor-grantee expectations and to protecting foundation staff from board pressure than to yielding measurable results regarding outcome and impact.

In 1998, the findings of a Kellogg Foundation–commissioned study of the use of evaluation by twenty-one grantmakers confirmed the notion that evaluation may have had more to do with maintaining organizational equilibrium than with assessing impact (Patrizi and McMullan, 1999). According to the study, the increased importance of evaluation since the mid-1990s "in most cases reflects rising concern among foundation board members about accountability and outcomes" (p. 30). Participants in the study identified five important purposes for evaluation: (1) improving grantee practice, (2) improving foundation practice, (3) providing additional feedback to foundation board members, (4) understanding how grantmaking affects public policy, and (5) gaining insight toward best practices—purposes that Patrizi and McMullan (the researchers conducting the study) considered problematic. "The wide range of purposes in the 'top five' raises significant questions about the ability of evaluations to meet successfully the broad array of demands placed on them" (p. 32).

Curiously, Patrizi and McMullan report that "management is minimally involved in evaluation," though staff were interested in it as a way of helping them monitor grants in their portfolios. Although they found lip service given to evaluation as a way of improving grantee practice, they could discover little in the way of substance. "We say we want to improve grantee practice and learning," reported one foundation evaluation director, "but we're unwilling to pay for some of the things that might help, like data systems or research, since we're not going to use them ourselves" (p. 33). Although the study concluded with a lukewarm endorsement of evaluation, it offered far more detailed descriptions of its shortcomings. Several of their respondents "questioned whether learning from the past was valued when every indication from management and the board was that only the future mattered to them" (p. 35).

The skepticism Patrizi and McMullan found among foundation professionals was widely echoed in other studies and commentaries. Minneapolis Foundation president Emmett Carson, writing under the title "Grantmakers in Search of
a Holy Grail," affirmed that "evaluation can work when applied to social programs that require 'counting' success," such as new units of affordable housing or
numbers of children inoculated. "It had serious limitations," he believed, "when
considering people both as the input and the output" (Carson, 2000a, p. 25). In
any event, he believed the inherent ambiguity of evaluation results limited their
usefulness. Evaluation researcher Vic Murray, writing in the journal *New Directions
for Philanthropic Fundraising*, was optimistic about the potential of evaluation to
improve the performance of nonprofits. But in assessing the question of whether
evaluation, as practiced, could yield the kinds of useable knowledge the various
nonprofit constituencies desired, he had to conclude "not yet" (Murray, 2001, p.
40). "It appears," he wrote, "that there is still a long way to go before there will be
a tried and tested evaluation system that can be applied by most nonprofit organizations to reveal a valid picture of how well they are performing" (p. 48).

Skepticism Regarding Evaluation

What explains the proliferation of program evaluation in the foundation world in
the face of widespread skepticism about its value? One reason is certainly that
the most energetic promoters of evaluation research in foundations were the three
most generous funders of nonprofits research during the 1990s—Atlantic Philanthropic Service, The Lilly Endowment, and The W. K. Kellogg Foundation. The
sheer weight of their influence on the associations of nonprofits researchers and
their capacity to incentivize areas in which they wanted research done assured that
evaluation would receive attention from the scholarly community.

Another factor is the extraordinary growth in the number and size of foundations. During the 1990s, the number of foundations increased by nearly 50 percent, and their assets nearly quadrupled. Unlike earlier foundations, which were
concentrated in the Northeast and Upper Midwest, the new foundations were
more likely to be found in areas of the Southeast and West that had less well-developed professional cultures of grantmaking. As the national philanthropy trade
associations—the Council on Foundations, Independent Sector, National Center for Nonprofit Boards, the National Society of Fund-Raising Executives, and
others—made particular efforts to reach out to new foundations, officers and directors of new philanthropies were, through the course of the 1990s, ever more
likely to be exposed to information about evaluation. (In the course of the 1990s,
the major nonscholarly philanthropy periodicals published more than thirty ar-

ticles on evaluation, most of them after 1995.) Learning on the job, the cohorts of new "philanthropoids" were eager to respond to pressures from results-oriented donors and trustees by demonstrating their knowledge of such "best practices" as evaluation.

Is evaluation, as practiced by foundations today, any more than conventional wisdom cloaked in a rhetoric of organizational rationality? The same conditions prevail that Brim identified in his 1973 essay on evaluation: foundations continue to be institutionally isolated by the lack of accountability to external stakeholders—or, as Brim put it, "they don't know whether they are doing what they think they are doing—or whether what they are doing makes any difference to anyone or not. Institutional isolation breeds narcissism and illusory feelings of power, and separates administrators from the frontiers of thought" (Brim, 1973, p. 223). There is still "no readily accessible hard-headed impersonal way to evaluate the performance of foundation administrators. There are no performance statistics . . . no bottom line showing profit or loss" (p. 223). The best contemporary evaluation can do is raise subjective standards, based on the aligned expectations of grantmakers, grantees, and relevant stakeholders about purpose and process. Though foundation executives and trustees are not as "socially encapsulated" as they were thirty years ago—boards are no longer overwhelmingly white, male, and Protestant—to say this is a little like saying that Harvard is no longer an elite institution because it recruits most of its students from public rather than private schools, as it did half a century ago. Foundation executives are no more likely to "deal in truth in exchanges with their primary constituency—the grant applicants" than they were in Brim's time. Because few efforts have been made to address—or even study—the problematic "social relations of philanthropy," as Susan Ostrander (1995) calls them, foundation officers are unlikely to hear criticism from grantees (including, of course, evaluators, a substantial number of whom do their work under foundation grants and contracts). Finally, then as now, "foundations lack natural enemies in our society" (Brim, 1973, p. 224). They have no competitors. They are not regularly or systematically monitored by journalists, public agencies, or trade associations.

Conclusion

In weighing the usefulness of contemporary evaluation research in foundations, it is also worth recalling the caveats offered by Robert Wood Johnson Foundation president David Rogers and his associates two decades ago. On the basis of their experience, evaluation was more costly than most foundations could afford and of problematic value unless, as was the case with Johnson, projects were planned to produce evaluable outcomes. Although there are certainly more foundations that can afford evaluation than in the mid-1980s, they still remain a tiny minority. Even though a few foundations may, like Johnson, design their projects to be evaluable, most do not.

It may well be that the broad skepticism about the usefulness of evaluation research is based on two sets of fundamental misconceptions—the first about what foundations are and why they exist, the second about what constitutes useful evaluation outcomes.

It is a common misconception that foundations are primarily committed to pursuing instrumental ends, to maximizing the efficient use of funds to bring about particular results. Whereas some grantmakers (Robert Wood Johnson, for example) may view their work instrumentally, many others are likely to be dedicated to expressive purposes—propagating values rather than solving problems or changing society (for example, The Hershey Trust and The Barnes Foundation). The conception of foundation charity as a results-oriented enterprise intended to produce measurable social change is barely a century old. And even in its twentieth-century heyday, "scientific" philanthropy, framed by instrumental purposes, has constituted only a small portion of the funds given by Americans for charitable purposes (the vast majority has been devoted to expressive activities, primarily religious ones). Because foundations are so diverse, varying not only in size and scope of ambitions but in purpose, it is a mistake to assume that evaluation methods appropriate to instrumentally oriented grantmakers are going to be useful to expressively oriented ones.

Since the 1960s, evaluation methods have accommodated themselves to the increasing complexity and diversity of foundations. As this has happened, the reliance on scientific method, as espoused by Suchman and Brim, has been supplanted by more nuanced understandings not only of the ways in which evaluation can be done but of the variety of purposes it may serve. Whereas the instrumentally oriented might dismiss evaluation methods whose major outcome is building consensus within an organization, few organizational researchers (or managers) would doubt the value of broadly shared purposes and commitment. Similarly, whereas the instrumentally oriented might question the value of evaluation that accommodates the possibility that the goals of an intervention or program might change over time, as engagement with problems reshapes understandings of how to best address them, the practical reality is that an organization that fails to recognize such shifts would be remiss in its responsibilities.

In place of the simple tool envisioned by the pioneers of evaluation research in foundations, a set of methods that could be applied, regardless of the many goals to which grantmakers were dedicated, today we have a toolbox containing a wide range of methods and techniques. These can be applied to different kinds of organizations and programs and for a wide variety of purposes. These are crafted to serve the needs of the constituencies within and beyond foundations, each of which has its own set of concerns about the effectiveness of grantmaking.

Inevitably, the increasing range of available tools presents its own challenges, the greatest of which includes knowing which best serve the purposes intended and the possibilities, as well as the limitations, of each. As this study suggests, the use of evaluation has been too often accompanied by unrealistically high expectations of the usefulness of the knowledge it would produce and too often used to seek answers to unanswerable questions. If historical perspective serves no other purpose, it can encourage practitioners to approach the evaluation task with a measure of humility.

References

Aikin, L. H., Blendon, R. J., Rogers, D. E., & Freeman, H. E. (1980). Evaluating a private foundation's health program. *Evaluation and Program Planning 3,* 119–129.

Alie, R. E., & Seita, J. R. (1997). Who's using evaluation and how: New study gives insight. *Nonprofit World, 5*(5), 40–49.

Brewster, K., Lindbloom, E. C., & Simon, J. G. (1975). "Proposal for a study of independent institutions." Unpublished grant proposal, Yale University, New Haven.

Brilliant, E. L. (2000). *Private charity and public inquiry: A history of the Filer and Peterson commissions.* Bloomington: Indiana University Press.

Brim, O. G., Jr. (1973). Do we know what we are doing? In F. F. Heimann (Ed.), *The future of foundations.* Englewood Cliffs, NJ: Prentice Hall.

Butt, M. G. (1985). Getting to know you. *Foundation News and Commentary, 26,* 26–35.

Carson, E. (2000a). Grantmakers in search of a holy grail. *Foundation News and Commentary, 41,* 24–26.

Carson, E. (2000b). On foundations and outcome evaluation. *Nonprofit and Voluntary Sector Quarterly, 29,* 479–481.

Commission on Foundations and Private Philanthropy. (1970). *Foundations, private giving, and public policy: Report and recommendations of the Commission on Foundations and Private Philanthropy.* Chicago: University of Chicago Press.

Commission on Private Philanthropy and Public Needs. (1975). *Giving in America: Toward a stronger voluntary sector.* Report of the Commission on Private Philanthropy and Public Needs. Washington, DC: U.S. Department of the Treasury.

Commission on Private Philanthropy and Public Needs. (1977). *Research papers* (Vols. 1–6). Washington, DC: U.S. Department of the Treasury.

Drucker, P. (1968). *The age of discontinuity.* New York: Harper & Row.

Fine, A. H., Colette, E. T., Coghlan, A. T. (2000). Program evaluation practice in the nonprofit sector. *Nonprofit management and leadership, 10,* 331–339.

Fosdick, R. B. (1952). *The story of the Rockefeller Foundation.* New York: Harper & Row.

Frederickson, G. M. (1965). *The inner civil war: Northern intellectuals and the crisis of the union.* New York: Harper & Row.

Glasrud, B. (2000). So it's 2000—Now what? *Nonprofit World, 18,* 16–18.

Glenn, J. M., Brandt, L., & Andrews, F. E. (1947). *Russell Sage Foundation, 1907–1946.* New York: Russell Sage Foundation.

Guba, E. G., & Lincoln, Y. S. (1989). *Fourth generation evaluation.* Thousand Oaks, CA: Sage.

Hall, P. D. (1992). *Inventing the nonprofit sector and other essays on philanthropy, voluntarism, and nonprofit organizations.* Baltimore: Johns Hopkins University Press.

Hammack, D. C., & Wheeler, S. (1994). *Social science in the making: Essays on the Russell Sage Foundation, 1907–1972.* New York: Russell Sage Foundation.

Heimann, F. F. (1973). *The future of foundations.* Englewood Cliffs, NJ: Prentice Hall.

Kanter, R. M., & Summers, D. V. (1987). Doing well while doing good: Dilemmas of performance measurement in nonprofit organizations and the need for a multiple-constituency approach. In W. W. Powell (Ed.), *The nonprofit sector: A research handbook.* New Haven: Yale University Press.

Karl, B. D. (1987). Nonprofit institutions. *Science, 236,* 984–985.

Lagemann, E. C. (2000). *An elusive science: The troubling history of education research.* Chicago: University of Chicago Press.

Murray, V. (2001). The state of evaluation tools and systems for nonprofit organizations. *New Directions for Philanthropic Fundraising, 31,* 39–49.

Nielsen, W. A. (1972). *The big foundations.* New York: Columbia University Press.

Nielsen, W. A. (1985). *The golden donors: A new anatomy of the great foundations.* New York: E. P. Dutton.

Ostrander, S. A. (1995). *Money for change: Social movement philanthropy at Haymarket People's Fund.* Philadelphia: Temple University Press.

Patrizi, P., & McMullan, B. J. (1999, May-June). Realizing the potential of program evaluation: A new study looks at how 21 foundations "do" evaluation. *Foundation News and Commentary,* pp. 30–35.

Rogers, D. E. (1987). On building a foundation. *Foundation News, 28,* 48–51.

Rossi, P. H., & Wright, S. R. (1977). Evaluation research: An assessment of theory, practice, and politics. *Evaluation Quarterly, 1,* 5–51.

Russell Sage Foundation. (1956). *Report of the Princeton conference on the history of philanthropy in the United States.* New York: Russell Sage Foundation.

Saidel, J. (2002). Interview: Sara L. Engelhardt of the Foundation Center. *Nonprofit Management and Leadership, 12,* 485–498.

Salasin, S. (1972). What is evaluation good for? *Evaluation, 1,* 2.

Smith, N. L. (1981). Classic 1960s articles in educational evaluation. *Evaluation and Program Planning, 4,* 177–183.

Suchman, E. A. (1967). *Evaluative research: Principles and practice in public service and social action programs.* New York: Russell Sage Foundation.

Three funders: Process or outcome? (1996). *Foundation News and Commentary, 37,* 46–48.

To the reader. (1978). *Evaluation and Program Planning, 1,* iii.

Weiss, C. H. (1973a). Between the cup and the lip. . . . *Evaluation, 1*(2), 49–55.

Weiss, C. H. (1973b). Where politics and evaluation research meet. *Evaluation, 1*(3), 37–45.

CHAPTER THREE

FOUNDATIONS AND EVALUATION AS UNEASY PARTNERS IN LEARNING

Mark R. Kramer and William E. Bickel

B y our estimate, based on an informal sampling of evaluation budgets, U.S. foundations spend well over $100 million each year on the evaluation of the programs they fund. The results ought to be immensely valuable, demonstrating the contribution that foundations make to our society, identifying powerful new approaches for social change, shaping future grantmaking decisions, and highlighting effective nonprofit organizations. Generating and sharing this knowledge should strengthen the role of foundations as social innovators and learning organizations, undertaking well-informed experiments in social change, and teaching others the lessons they have learned.

Regrettably, reality falls far short of this ideal. Foundations have long struggled with the question of how to use evaluation to improve performance and to assess impact, whether their own or that of their grantees. Well-intentioned foundation staff search for answers to the "evaluation dilemma"—hoping to find consultants, software, or some methodology that will give them a way to gauge the social impact of their work and a knowledge base to inform others. Yet the answer remains elusive. Despite the resources consumed, few evaluations appear to produce significant changes in the behavior of foundations, other funders, or grantees (Patrizi, 2002; Bickel, Millett, and Nelson, 2002; Easterling and Csuti,

Sections of this chapter build on prior research and analyses in Bickel, Millett, and Nelson, 2002.

1999; Snow, 1996). Similarly, few foundations seem to have discovered how to use evaluation results consistently to foster organizational learning (Knickman, 2000).

First, a note about terminology will be helpful: we use the term *evaluation* broadly to include a wide range of analytical and information-gathering activities to support program and strategy development and improvement, decision making, and the measurement of outcomes and impact.

Constraints on Evaluation

Why has the effective use of evaluation by foundations proved to be so difficult? Foundation staff point to the lack of "good" evaluators and the difficulty of understanding ponderous evaluation reports that come in long after key decision points have passed. Evaluators, in turn, criticize foundations for having unrealistic expectations about the impact of their grants or the types of conclusions that evaluation studies can support, along with a reluctance to confront bad news or change behavior. Our research suggests that both sets of complaints have some merit, but neither is the real obstacle.

The problem, we suggest, is neither with foundation staff nor with evaluators but with a much larger set of systemic, organizational, and cultural constraints that undermine the effective use of evaluation and deter organizational learning. Neither the good intentions nor the hard work of foundation staff and evaluators will be sufficient to realize the potential that evaluation can bring to philanthropy until these barriers are candidly recognized and overcome.

This chapter sketches out several of these barriers. Some are inherent in the field of philanthropy and the culture that infuses foundation staff and professional evaluators alike. Others result from the organizational and decision-making structures typical of foundations, as well as practical aspects of contemporary evaluation practice. The perspectives in this chapter are intended to help foundation executives and trustees create an environment that is conducive to the more effective use of evaluation in their foundations and to help professional evaluators understand and anticipate some of the barriers they may face in working with foundations.

We conclude with a few thoughts about how constructive change might begin, along with indications that some of these changes are already emerging in practice. In our judgment, strong leadership, with a commitment to improving effectiveness on the part of foundations, will be required if a more meaningful role for evaluation and organizational learning is to be developed in philanthropy.

Observations on Current Practice

Foundations have a set of privileges unlike any other institutions in our society (Freund, 1996; Wisely, 1993). Their considerable autonomy from political or market forces enables them to take chances with their grantmaking that other institutions cannot. They have the time to carefully research initiatives before funding them, draw on world-class expertise, fund unpopular causes, or think about the long term by sustaining their programs for decades.

However, this very freedom presents significant challenges. Without having to satisfy customers, investors, voters, or any other empowered stakeholders, foundations lack any consistent external feedback about their performance. Evaluation reports are one of the few reliable and objective measures of how well a foundation performs. Over time, the careful evaluation of grants should enable foundations to improve the accuracy and effectiveness of their grantmaking decisions, clarify their strategies, and increase the success of the programs they fund. For foundations, therefore, evaluation provides an essential base of knowledge for organizational learning.

In fact, evaluation serves three separate functions in philanthropy:

1. *Accountability.* Evaluation satisfies the fiduciary responsibility of a foundation to oversee the use of its money and to ensure that grant funds were spent according to its terms. Evaluation, therefore, provides the evidence for both grantee and foundation accountability.
2. *Learning.* A foundation can strengthen its ongoing strategy and program design by understanding what has worked in the past and what has not. Evaluation can contribute to learning by distilling important lessons from past efforts and building a knowledge base for future action.
3. *Knowledge sharing.* The dissemination of results, both positive and negative, is a way of informing the field as a whole, letting other foundations, nonprofits, or government agencies benefit from the foundation's learning and experience to improve the effectiveness of their own funding decisions.

These three aspects of evaluation are increasingly powerful, although they are also increasingly rare in practice. Accountability for the use of funds is the most common form of evaluation but contributes little to the learning of the foundation or the broader field. Learning within the foundation is more valuable, though less common, and knowledge sharing with the field is critically important, though least common of all. According to one theory, advancing knowledge and practice by testing new and potentially more effective ways to address social problems and *then* communicating these results to influence the behavior of other funders is the most powerful role that foundations can play in our society (Porter and Kramer, 1999). This theory puts the effective use of evaluation and the sharing of results at the core of foundation effectiveness.

Yet with some notable exceptions (see Backer, 1999), the role of evaluation in support of effective philanthropy is all too often a matter of discussion and assertion by its proponents rather than a reflection of actual practice (Patrizi, 2002; Wisely, 2002; Bickel, 1996). Although data are quite limited, it seems that the vast majority of the more than 60,000 foundations in the United States do not conduct formal evaluations at all. This is not surprising, considering that only about 3,000 have any paid staff, and most of those have only one or two employees. Fewer than 40 foundations have full-time evaluation officers (Patrizi, 2002). Even among the 225 largest U.S. foundations (those most able to afford professional evaluations), roughly one-third evaluate less than 10 percent of their grants, and the majority evaluate less than 50 percent (Center for Effective Philanthropy, 2002, p. 9). It was estimated "in 1993 that it was unlikely that more than 100 U.S. foundation and corporate giving programs were pursuing serious or sustained evaluation of their own programs or of grantee projects" (Walling, 1997, p. 16). This situation does not seem to have changed appreciably in the past decade (Wisely, 2002; Grantmakers for Effective Organizations, 1998). Indeed, with assets falling and renewed pressure on foundations to expend more of their resources on grants, any short-term growth in evaluation expenditures seems unlikely (Lipman and Wilhelm, 2003).

The term *evaluation* itself, as used within the foundation field, encompasses such a wide range of practices—from a brief grantee report on the use of funds to a multi-million-dollar academic study of impact using carefully chosen treatment and control groups—that it is difficult to discuss without clearer definition. The most common form of evaluation is the simplest: a brief self-report by the grantee at the conclusion of a grant, describing how the funds were used, what was accomplished, and often setting the stage for a subsequent grant request (Snow, 1996; McNelis and Bickel, 1996; McNelis, Bickel, and Connors-Gilmore, 1996). In some cases, such a subjective report may offer the opportunity for thoughtful self-examination by the grantee in a way that will contribute to both the foundation's and the grantee's learning.[1] In most cases, however, the pressures of time and the need

---

1. See *Creating a Culture of Inquiry* (Hernandez and Visher, 2001), for an example of a foundation (The James Irvine Foundation) making a commitment to enhance the capacity of its grantees to conduct and use evaluation. See also Draper (2000) and Backer and Bare (2000), for discussions of the issue of capacity building in nonprofits and what some foundations are doing in this regard.

for additional funding tend to undermine the quality and reliability of these self-reports. Without objective verification, there is a risk that such a limited form of evaluation may not even serve the minimal function of accountability.

Note that we are not arguing that all grants need to have expensive external evaluations. But some assessment of the results of a grant is essential if any organizational learning is to result from its implementation. Moreover, what is known about current practice suggests that even "strategic grants"—those most crucial to a foundation's strategy and holding the greatest potential for knowledge production—go largely unexamined along with the rest (Center for Effective Philanthropy, 2002).

At the other end of the spectrum from foundations that rely on brief grantee self-reports are those that conduct highly sophisticated evaluations using external evaluators to document implementation processes, to assess the effectiveness of a grant program, or to test the theory of change on which it relies. These latter studies are more thorough and objective, yet they occur only rarely.

Even among the largest foundations that commit substantial resources to professional evaluation, recent research suggests that the purpose of evaluation is often ill defined, and evaluations are frequently conducted in an organizational limbo (Patrizi, 2002; Chelimsky, 2001). Studies of evaluation staff within foundations have found that they typically have limited authority and an ambiguous mandate (Patrizi, 2002; Chelimsky, 2001). Often they report to the Vice President of Program rather than to the CEO or board directly. This can create an uncomfortable tension when the results of evaluation cast a negative light on the projects chosen by program staff. Indeed, evaluation officers complain, at times, of being the unwelcome guest in the program department (Patrizi and McMullan, 2000).

Similarly, the fees of external evaluators often come from program budgets controlled by the program officers. Typically, the evaluator is hired by, and the final report is directed to, the program officer who approved the grant in the first place, creating a potential conflict of interest. These reports may not be circulated more widely within or outside the foundation unless the program officer chooses to do so. As a result, the knowledge produced is not shared consistently.

As one commentator notes, "When evaluation in and for foundations is assessed, the picture is dismal. Frequently, even when foundations do evaluations, evaluation reports are not used by program staff to inform grantmaking decisions" (Hunter and Kaye, 2001, p. 1; see also Wisely, 2002; Bickel, Millett, and Nelson, 2002; Bickel, 1996). Other evidence suggests that evaluation reports are used even less often by foundation boards in approving grants or setting strategy (Center for Effective Philanthropy, 2002).

In short, despite the widely acknowledged importance of evaluation and the substantial resources expended, there is little documented evidence that evaluation, as practiced by many foundations today, effectively serves any of these three objectives of accountability, learning, and knowledge sharing.

Why does so much effort result in so little useful learning? It is not because of any lack in the intelligence, hard work, or commitment of foundation staff and evaluators. Rather, the nature of foundations and the larger context in which they operate raise serious obstacles to effective organizational learning and the constructive use of evaluation. Different but equally profound challenges exist within the evaluation community and in the relationship to its foundation clients. These barriers are not insurmountable, but they must be understood before they can be overcome.

Foundation-Side Barriers to Learning

Three systemic barriers are particularly powerful on the foundation side (Bickel, Millett, and Nelson, 2002). The first is that the field gives too little attention to performance and results, which has the effect of undercutting internal and external pressures to improve. Second, the positive feedback that comes from acts of philanthropy tends to strongly reinforce the status quo, thus discouraging change and inflating expectations. Third, foundation boards often lack the expertise, time, and motivation to impose strict standards of accountability.

Inattention to Performance and Results. As noted earlier, foundations have no external accountability to empowered stakeholders. Their privileged tax status depends only on distributing an appropriate percentage of assets to 501(c)(3) organizations each year and on the avoidance of self-dealing that would result in economic benefits for the donor or board members. Although foundations in recent years have come under increased scrutiny, knowledgeable observers see the criticism as not having "reached anything like a crisis stage" (Chelimsky, 2001, p. 17). In the absence of external performance standards for the field, foundations face no imperative to improve but instead are left to their own devices as to what criteria to set, if any, for effectiveness and learning in their work.

In practice, the only commonly accepted performance benchmarks for foundations are investment returns and the ratio of administrative expenses to grants (Center for Effective Philanthropy, 2002). Unfortunately, neither investment performance nor administrative expense ratios are indicative of the social impact achieved by a foundation's grantmaking. The lack of attention to performance measurement in philanthropy is a critical barrier to foundations' use of evaluation, and the lack of demand has retarded the development of effective performance-measurement tools.

In fact, the degree to which the performance of foundations can ever be measured or compared is the subject of hot controversy in the field today. Opponents would argue that the measurement hurdles are nearly insurmountable and that imperfect measurement might lead to a narrowing of foundation agendas or to disseminating misleading information to the public. Proponents, including one of the authors, insist that comparative performance standards can be developed and are essential to foundation effectiveness (see Exhibit 3.1). Both sides can agree, however, that most foundations, at present, have little basis on which to judge their own performance and no compelling need to do so.

EXHIBIT 3.1. THE NECESSITY OF COMPARATIVE PERFORMANCE MEASURES (by Mark Kramer).

I would go further than my coauthor by insisting that the creation of performance standards for the field is essential to increasing effectiveness and enabling learning. The classical approach to evaluation, which is concerned with the social impact of a single grant, cannot be stretched to encompass the measurement of all grants and all foundations against some common metric and, therefore, there is strong objection among many evaluators and foundation leaders to the idea that comparative performance measures are possible.

However, foundations are in the business of making choices about which projects to fund and which to decline. The quality of their performance depends not on whether a single grant achieved impact but on whether they are consistently choosing well, and comparative benchmarks can be developed to shed light on whether one foundation is consistently creating greater value than another. These measures may not always rise to the level of scientific rigor, but they can offer reliable guidance to management and the potential for constructive learning among foundations. Through the research of the Center for Effective Philanthropy, such measures are being created around the quality of service that foundations provide to grantees and around indicators of value creation, such as the thoroughness of the foundation's selection process, the degree of leverage achieved, the helpfulness of nonmonetary assistance provided to grantees, and the foundation's overall impact on thought and practice within its field. (See, for example, a grantee perception report at www.effectivephilanthropy.org and Porter and Kramer, 1999, for a discussion of the ways foundations create value.)

Our research suggests that foundation executives and board members pay far more attention to performance measures that can be compared or benchmarked (Center for Effective Philanthropy, February 2002). Investment performance and administrative expense ratios, for example, are carefully monitored, in part, because a foundation's performance can be compared to the norm and judged as either better

**EXHIBIT 3.1. THE NECESSITY
OF COMPARATIVE PERFORMANCE MEASURES (by Mark Kramer).**
(continued)

or worse, thereby creating greater pressure to perform well and greater opportunities for learning from the data. Knowing, for example, that an investment portfolio earned a 5 percent return is informative, but one cannot say whether the investment adviser's performance is good or poor without a benchmark to compare against. In short, without objective performance standards, one cannot judge performance, and without judging performance, it is very difficult to learn how to improve.

The evaluation results of individual grants are much like the investment adviser's returns taken in isolation, that is, one cannot tell exactly what lesson is to be learned from a single program evaluation or, at times, even from a comprehensive set of evaluations at a single foundation. For example, an evaluation officer for The Robert Wood Johnson Foundation once estimated that roughly two-thirds of their grants achieved the desired results, but he had no basis on which to say whether or not this proportion was better or worse than other foundations (*New York Times,* Giving Supplement, November 2001).

Evaluation, to be sure, can provide accountability and some degree of learning in distinguishing between more or less successful outcomes of past grants. But even the criteria for what is considered a successful outcome tend to vary from one evaluation to the next. Often different evaluations of similar programs cannot be meaningfully compared, as each funder or grantee develops its own set of desired outcomes or performance standards. Many practitioners in philanthropy view this independence as a major virtue. There is a strong and systemic bias throughout the nonprofit sector that resists comparisons in performance. But the ability of foundations to wring the greatest learning from evaluations, to increase their effectiveness over time, and to share meaningful information with each other, is severely limited when each grantee, each evaluation, and each foundation stands unique and alone.

Positive Reinforcement and Inflated Expectations. A learning organization must be predisposed toward ongoing change and evolution. Even without clear ways to measure performance, people naturally experiment with new approaches when they confront criticism or corrective feedback. The problem for foundations, however, is that virtually all the feedback they get is positive, deeply undermining any motivation to change. Wisely (2002, p. 5) writes of this cultural phenomenon: "The power and wealth of private foundations often prevents them from getting good criticism. People are reluctant to speak truth to power and risk favor they need or desire."

Grantees and others who might hope to become grantees are understandably wary of any criticism that might discourage future funding. Board members, often related by family, social, or business ties, have no desire to offend each other, and foundation staff certainly do not want to offend the board. Most of the participants in the grant-application and approval process, therefore, prefer to build up goodwill in order to gain support for projects they favor, rather than raise criticisms that might lead to dissension. Even the media, which occasionally zero in on scandal or abuse, find it hard to be critical of giving away money to good causes. This tendency toward constant positive feedback serves to reinforce existing foundation practices, whether good or bad, and thereby discourages learning or change.

In such an environment, the penalties for honesty can be severe. Negative evaluation results stand out starkly from the background of positive reinforcement and are likely to be thoroughly unwelcome. The uncritical environment of success orientation also encourages inflated expectations about the results a grant might achieve. Grantees, anxious to promote the importance of their projects, naturally tend to overpromise, and any grant applicant or program officer who chooses to be more realistic may lose out in the competition for limited grant dollars.

This tendency toward overstating the likely impact of a grant has severe consequences for evaluation. Suppose, for example, that a foundation sends out an unrealistic request for proposals that would produce major change from a modest short-term grant. Rather than challenge the foundation's premises and be eliminated from consideration, prospective grantees are far more likely to overstate what they hope to accomplish in hopes of qualifying for the grant. The program officer may then use these overstatements to help convince the board to fund this grant instead of competing alternatives. By now, the evaluation is already in serious trouble. If the evaluator hopes to get hired, he or she is hard-pressed to tell the grantee, program officer, and board that what they have all agreed to is unrealistic. And, having acquiesced to their premise of what can be achieved at the outset, the final evaluation will find it difficult to retreat from these assumptions. Nor can the grantee, hoping for renewed support, willingly admit to failure. Everyone involved is caught in the same trap of wanting to affirm the ambitions and, ultimately, the success of the initial proposal, however unrealistic.

In practice, this inflated economy works smoothly and will continue to do so, as long as there is a tacit understanding that no one will really measure the results or that the evaluation, years later, will not affect either the grantee's funding or the program officer's status. Alternatively, if every major grant were routinely evaluated or if all grantees gave candid feedback and accurate projections of impact, the process would work far better and foundations would have the information they need for useful organizational learning. Barring such a shift in practice, evaluators working on realistic assessments of results confront a culture of positive reinforcement that works strongly against incentives to change.

Weak Governance. Beyond the minimal legal requirements of the tax code noted earlier, there is only one source of foundation accountability: the board of trustees (we use the term *board* to refer to the governing body, whether composed of trustees or directors). Board members could demand excellent performance, rigorously assess progress toward the foundation's goals, and bring the expertise needed to accurately calibrate expected outcomes or critique grantmaking decisions and strategies. They could hold staff accountable for learning from results and improving over time. If boards routinely played this role, organizational learning and evaluation would become essential to the job performance of every foundation executive and program officer. We have seen this in practice, but rarely.

Recent corporate scandals have highlighted the limited effectiveness of board oversight, even for public companies in which performance standards and legal responsibilities are reasonably well defined and backed up by the constant threat of shareholder litigation. By comparison, the obligations and risks of foundation boards are far fewer, the qualifications of board members more ambiguous, and the incentives for being attentive more attenuated than those of their corporate peers.

Few data have been gathered on the composition and practices of foundation boards. Our own research suggests that foundation board members do not always bring significant expertise in nonprofit management, in the fields that the foundation funds, or in foundation work. Lacking such knowledge, the board may be hard-pressed to judge the performance of program staff or grantees. Often unaware of what other foundations do, they may be easily satisfied with whatever grantees propose or staff suggest. Inexperience about the complex social problems being addressed may leave them demanding too little or, alternatively, entirely too much from their grants. Lack of sophistication about social change and evaluation processes may lead to unrealistic expectations about how quickly or conclusively one can expect to document impact.

The structure of board meetings tends to involve lengthy dockets of proposed grants, with little opportunity to discuss them; when there is professional staff involved, there is a strong tendency to rubber-stamp staff recommendations. With the constant pressure of completing the current grant-selection cycle before requests start to build up for the next docket, there is simply no time to independently evaluate the program staff's judgment, and past performance is of little moment.

These problems are often compounded by the lack of time that board members set aside for foundation responsibilities. As generally busy and important people, they rarely make time to become knowledgeable about the field, visit grantees, review the results of past grantmaking decisions, or read evaluation reports. As others have observed of nonprofit boards generally, there often can be relatively "little personal accountability . . . and as a result individual board members may not bring themselves fully to the task of governance" (Taylor, Chait, and Holland, 1996, quoted in Klusman, 2003, p. 40). The board's inattention to past results or organizational learning undercuts incentives the staff might have to be attentive to these issues themselves (see Letts, Ryan, and Grossman, 1998, and Trice Gray, 1997, for discussions of the nonprofit board's role in creating a culture of performance).

In short, the system in which foundation boards, staff, and grantees find themselves offers little reason to pay attention to performance or confront shortcomings. The system instead reinforces the comfort and safety of preserving the status quo, avoiding the risks inherent in evaluation and the pressures for ongoing change that might lead to organizational learning. Like the reforms currently being put forth in the private sector for corporate boards, foundation boards need to become more active and informed, exercising their oversight responsibilities less in theory and more in practice (Center for Effective Philanthropy, 2004).

Cultural and Organizational Barriers

In addition to these systemic barriers, a range of cultural and organizational characteristics within foundations can further discourage organizational learning and the effective use of evaluation. One is the "culture of good intentions."

The Culture of Good Intentions. Throughout much of the nonprofit sector, there is a tension between the passionate commitment to caring for others and the need to objectively measure performance. Motivated by a "culture of service," foundations and grantees alike are driven by a vision of helping others, even against great odds (Letts, Ryan, and Grossman, 1999). This is a major strength of the nonprofit sector but one that presents certain challenges.

It seems almost contrary to the spirit of philanthropy to turn down passionate and dedicated grantees who are sincerely trying to help others merely because they haven't fully achieved their desired objectives. It is even harder to fault donors who are giving away money or nonprofit staff who work long, stressful hours for minimal compensation, just because they aren't working as efficiently as they might. Yet passion and sincerity are not the same as effective management and positive outcomes. If grantmaking decisions are influenced solely by good intentions, not results, then this inevitably creates a tension around the use of evaluation, which is, after all, primarily about improving capacity and learning from the measurement of results. This tension is one of the key cultural barriers that resists the use of past evaluation results to influence future grantmaking decisions.

We are describing an extreme picture, of course. No one would ever say that results do not matter. But the field of philanthropy walks a fine line between analysis and sentiment. It seems too hard-hearted to take a more analytical approach to an activity like grantmaking that is so deeply rooted in a sense of vision, empathy, and good intentions. However, foundations want to use their resources to achieve the greatest possible impact, and this requires a realistic assessment of their effectiveness. The result of this tension is ambivalence about the merit and utility of evaluation and a constant readiness to overlook shortcomings in performance.

The magnitude of social problems and the scarcity of resources with which most nonprofits operate are also often cited to explain why one cannot expect more consistent results in philanthropy. Grantees, the argument goes, lack the capacity to operate at the level we expect of for-profit organizations, and no one can seriously be expected to make significant progress on the intractable problems they address. Yet evaluation is inescapably an investigation of effectiveness and performance, and what can be learned from these. If good intentions, a lack of resources, or recognition of the magnitude of the problem blocks a realistic examination of results (including the role of the grantee in achieving them), then evaluation loses its purpose.

This culture of good intentions undercuts not only learning from evaluation but the potential for sharing knowledge as well. Foundations recognize the vulnerability of their grantees and often decide not to publicly release negative evaluation results that could threaten a grantee's survival. (The foundation, of course, may also wish to preserve its good name by avoiding the embarrassment of publicly acknowledging a failed grant.) This practice of withholding negative evaluation reports is, however, a sure indication of a culture that risks excusing poor performance by failing to share and learn from its disappointments. The result, unfortunately, undermines the use of evaluation to influence future grantmaking and to advance knowledge and practice throughout the sector. Keeping evaluations confidential also slows the development of evaluation as a field by shielding methodologies and practitioners from scrutiny by other evaluators.

In fairness, grantees have much at stake when evaluation results are made known to other funders. The foundation's intention to make evaluation results public should be made clear from the beginning, and the grantee should be engaged in the evaluation as learning partner, whether the news is good or bad. But the valuable role that evaluation could play in improving programs and in advancing the field cannot be reliably fulfilled if shortfalls are concealed and only positive results are shared.

Passion and the valuing of service are laudable values in the social reform arena. We see attention to organizational capacity, effectiveness, and learning as making passion more powerful and service more valuable. What is needed is the will to marry passion with reflective practice and, ultimately, a commitment to improved performance.

Professional Autonomy. Foundations are often compared to universities in their pursuit of knowledge and experimentation, and it is no accident that a significant number of foundation executives and CEOs are former university presidents or administrators. Academic administration, however, is a very different training ground than other kinds of management. Faculty members have considerable autonomy and, within their fields of expertise, are typically judged only by their peers. This "hands-off" management approach is often transferred to the foundation, resulting in an organizational culture that confers nearly complete autonomy on program staff to devise strategies, formulate initiatives, and recommend grants for approval with little independent verification, accountability, or oversight.

This culture of autonomy is accentuated by program staff drawn from a wide variety of backgrounds, with little opportunity for education or training in their new responsibilities. Unlike other professions or trades, foundation staffs often do not share a common base of expertise or culture (Orosz, 2002). This strongly encourages a sense that there are no right or wrong answers in philanthropy. Everyone helps in his or her own way, and the performance of one program officer cannot be compared to that of another or judged in any meaningful way.

Even at the highest levels, job performance is rarely tied to concrete results. Interviews with CEOs from many of the largest U.S. foundations, conducted by the Center for Effective Philanthropy (2002, p. 11), found

> a wide range of variation about whether and how the board evaluated CEO performance. In some cases, the board and CEO agree on written objectives at the start of the year, and the CEO reports on progress made against each one. In other cases, CEOs confessed that there was no formal evaluation process at all: the board was satisfied if it had a general sense that "things were going OK."

Few foundations tie performance reviews or compensation to achieving programmatic and learning objectives. The evaluation of past grants, therefore, may have little meaningful impact on a foundation executive's or program officer's future career, confirming their freedom from accountability and undercutting any need to use evaluation. In such an environment, internal politics and favoritism tend to fill the void left by the absence of more objective measures of performance or achievement, further complicating the work of an evaluator who has a foundation as a client.

Tyranny of the Grant-Selection Cycle and Administrative Expense Ratios. The average large foundation makes four hundred grants per year, although some make upwards of two thousand (Center for Effective Philanthropy, 2002). The number of grants considered and investigated is, of course, substantially larger than the number approved.

At the same time, foundations strongly value the lowest possible expenditures for overhead, investments in research, management infrastructure, or evaluation (Letts, Ryan, and Grossman, 1999). Unable to assess social impact, boards give disproportionate weight to minimizing administrative expenses in the unfounded belief that a larger percentage of payout going into grants means greater effectiveness. This attitude may derive from the broader field of nonprofit management, in which charities are often rated on the ratio of administrative and fundraising expenses to program expenditures. Program officers themselves often come from this background, having previously worked in nonprofits (Bickel, 1996). Used to scarce resources, they value program dollars above all and would prefer to minimize the resources devoted to evaluation (Letts, Ryan, and Grossman, 1999).

Foundations, of course, have the freedom to adopt whatever operating style they would like. However, the choice to combine a large volume of grants with a small operating budget inevitably results in a constant sense of pressure to handle the work as expeditiously as possible. Staff and boards alike barely manage to complete one grant-selection cycle before the next docket starts to build up. This keeps program staff and boards on a constant forward-looking treadmill. There is simply no time to review past performance or distill lessons learned.

Yet the process of learning requires time for reflection and collegial sharing of perspectives that is at odds with such constant pressure. Systematic knowledge-capture processes require substantial financial investments. By underinvesting in these resources, foundations discourage their use. As a result, neither the board, CEO, nor staff has the time to review, share, and learn from evaluations that the foundation commissions.

Even if they had the time, the results might no longer be relevant to the current grant docket. Many foundations tend to shift their funding frequently, rarely staying with a program for more than one to three years. Evaluation results inevitably come more than a year, often many years, after the grant was approved. By then, most foundations have moved on to other programs or sometimes even other fields. As a result, the learning from an evaluation that could improve the effectiveness of future funding decisions is often irrelevant to the foundation's current grantmaking.

Taken together, the cultural bias favoring good intentions over rigorously measured results, the autonomy of staff, a lack of meaningful performance reviews that include evidence about results and learning, the limited administrative budgets, and the constant press of new grants in frequently changing fields create an organizational structure that fights against the time, money, or incentives for disciplined evaluation and ongoing organizational learning.

Evaluation-Side Barriers

Thus far, the discussion has focused on foundation characteristics that hinder the use of evaluation to support learning and foundation effectiveness. Here we consider how certain structural and cultural characteristics within the field of evaluation and its current state of practice also undermine the contribution that evaluation could make.

A Diverse and Changing Field

We noted earlier that the term *evaluation* can refer to widely different kinds of activities from effective practices reviews and needs assessments, to informal grantee self-reports, to substantial studies by professional evaluators. We now focus on the latter category of program and policy evaluation by professional evaluators. Even at this end of the spectrum, however, there is a tremendous diversity of practices and approaches.

The diversity of practice has steadily increased over the past twenty years. Theories, models, and techniques of evaluation are multiplying, even as debates intensify about what the future and mission of the profession are, who belongs in it, and whether evaluation could even be considered a profession (Smith, 2001; Worthen, 1999). This intellectual ferment, coupled with a lack of solid research about current practice, makes it difficult to firmly characterize the field, much less to know with confidence who conducts evaluation and what training, if any, those practitioners have. Unlike other professions and academic disciplines, no particular set of qualifications is needed to become an evaluator.

The limited data available suggest that a majority of people who are employed as evaluators hold advanced degrees, mostly in the social sciences (Kistler, 2002). Few seem to have formal training in program evaluation. They ply their trade within and from a variety of organizational and independent settings; roughly one-third are college- or university-based, another third work in the nonprofit or private sectors, and the rest hold positions in various local, state, and federal or public agencies (Kistler, 2002). Many (probably most) are part-timers. Those in academic positions devote only 30 percent of their time to evaluation, compared to 60 percent of the field-based evaluators' time (Modarresi, Newman, and Abolafia, 2001, p. 8).

The fault line between academic-based and field-based evaluators is significant, as is true in other fields. Academics take the lead in published research and theorizing about evaluation strategy, methods, and mission, whereas the vast majority of evaluations are actually carried out by nonacademic practitioners (Modarresi, Newman, and Abolafia, 2001). Cross-fertilization between the two groups is largely undefined and undocumented.

The part-time practice of evaluation and the academic-practitioner dichotomy reflect another key characteristic: the boundaries for entering evaluation practice are quite permeable. No formal certification requirements exist, although the possibility is currently generating considerable debate among prominent leaders within the field. When polled, most practicing evaluators predictably opposed certification (Worthen, 1999). As one leader in the field put it, the reality is that many "evaluators" are "self-anointed" or find themselves given the role by organizational circumstance (Sanders, 2002).

This permeability of entry means that foundations encounter tremendous variability in approach and qualifications when they retain evaluators. One cannot assume that a given evaluation has met any particular professional standard; therefore, one cannot consistently rely on the results. (This difficulty is not unique to evaluation but applies to research generally. However, when research is published, it becomes accessible for scrutiny; little evaluation research is published.) Even the task of identifying an adequately qualified evaluator can be daunting to foundation staff, who generally lack training in evaluation themselves. Combined with the tendency of foundations to minimize expenses and so economize on evaluation costs, one might question whether foundations are sufficiently attentive to evaluation designs and evaluator qualifications.

The variability in the field also reduces the ease of comparability between different evaluations. Even within the very small proportion of grants subject to professional evaluation, the purpose of the evaluation, the kind of information collected, the validity and accuracy of the data, the assumptions made, and the conclusions that can reliably be drawn are dramatically different from one study to the next. As a result, the utility and cumulative learning that could occur across different evaluations of similar projects is far more difficult to assess.

Beyond issues of training and credentialing and the nature of the evaluative product, the field is rife with debate, at least among the academic evaluation community, about the core purposes that evaluation should fulfill in society and for the clients and organizations it serves. Among the more common purposes held for evaluation by leaders in the field are accountability, judgment of merit and worth, organizational learning, program improvement, knowledge production, and social empowerment of disadvantaged stakeholder populations. All of these functions, and more, are legitimate uses of evaluation.

Not only the purposes but the methodologies of evaluation have proliferated in the past two decades, since Lee Cronbach and Associates (1980) published their call for a reform of program evaluation. Reflecting the applied social sciences as a whole, Greene (2001, p. 399) describes

> [a] fantastic . . . diversification of our methods . . . now [embracing] ever-more precise estimates of error variance for multivariate analyses alongside procedures for narrative analysis of participant observation field notes [and] . . . alternative forms of representation for presenting our findings (e.g., stories, poems, public forums, fictional documentaries).

Although new methods and new ways of interpreting social and human behavior have grown in legitimacy, as has the use of multiple forms of data in research and evaluation designs, these developments too often are not reflected in actual practice (for new developments, see Greene and McClintock, 1991; Greene, 2001). Social science and evaluation preparation programs are slow to revise their curricula, and many clients are unaware of alternative paradigms and methodologies.

Similarly, there have been positive developments in the field recently regarding the promulgation of "program evaluation standards" to address a wide range of methodological and ethical issues (Joint Committee on Standards for Educational Evaluation, 1994) and "guiding principles for evaluators" (Shadish, Newman, Scheirer, and Wye, 1995). However, the extent to which such standards have influenced daily practice is unknown.

This tremendous ferment in the field in terms of mission and strategy, the growing variety of methods, the permeability of professional boundaries, and the diversity of those who call themselves evaluators all offer foundations a wide range of tools to enhance effectiveness, capture learning, and bring the voices of disadvantaged stakeholders into policy deliberations. This same degree of diversity, however, has serious drawbacks. The range of purposes, methodologies, and qualifications is so broad that to say a grant has been "evaluated," without a fuller elaboration, carries very little consistent meaning, thus diminishing the credibility of evaluation results and the ability of other foundations to learn from them.

Comfort in Traditional Roles

Traditionally, the evaluator was asked to assess the merit of the program being examined after some period of operation. (Indeed, many in the field argue that this is the essence of evaluation; anything else, although potentially useful, is something other than evaluation [see Scriven, 1991]). The framing questions typically were, "Is the program achieving its objectives?" or "What impact is the program attaining?" External evaluators were expected to maintain a distance from the program in order to increase their objectivity.

In contrast to this traditional role, new approaches place a greater emphasis on the use of evaluation results (see Patton, 1997). Evaluators are integrated early into the program's development, helping to explicate program theory, conducting evaluability assessments, and analyzing implementation processes. These "nontraditional" functions for evaluation are viewed as ways of strengthening the program's *potential* for impact, taking place well before outcomes and impact can be assessed. Under this approach, the evaluator is expected to play an important role in distilling lessons learned and in the active dissemination of those lessons. Here closeness to the program is prized; the evaluation process is seen as an integral component of program development and implementation.

More recently, the utilization approach has been taken one step further by making *organizational development* central to the role (Patton, 1997). In this case, the evaluation process is an integral component in the way the grantee conducts business; its central function is to support continuous learning to shape future organizational strategy and action.

Evaluation is increasingly being asked to take on roles within foundations themselves that parallel some of the aforementioned developments in the field, thus contributing to strategic planning, program design, and knowledge capture. Many innovative practices have emerged in recent years that link the work of internal evaluation officers to program development, knowledge production, communication, and dissemination functions within the foundation (Backer, 1999).

Our point here is two-fold. First, as evaluators move from traditional roles into new responsibilities for strengthening the organizational capacity of grantees and guiding the strategy of foundations, an entirely new set of skills is required. Evaluators have begun to take on the work of management consultants, strategic planners, and facilitators of organizational change, without necessarily bringing any training or experience in these new fields. Second, and precisely because many evaluators have no training in these areas, they are often reluctant to fully take on these broader consulting roles, even when they are expected to do so. Instead, evaluators tend to be most comfortable working within the parameters of their traditional role of assessing outcomes and judging merit and do not always realize the full potential of assisting the grantee and foundation in other ways.

This is not to say that the traditional role of evaluation is inappropriate to foundation work, nor do we suggest that foundations should refrain from helping their grantees increase organizational capacity or including evaluation experts in their strategy development. The question is whether evaluators are comfortable with and adequately prepared to fulfill all of these functions at the same time.

Evaluation Defined by Those It Serves. Evaluators typically work at the behest of clients and stakeholders. Although perhaps independent in "soul," evaluators are rarely independent in action. In the United States and around the world, our practice of program evaluation is shaped, not by the discipline of our profession but by the corporate and accountability notions of our clients and program managers. "We are a service profession," says Stake (2001, p. 349).

The literature is replete with discussions of the nuances that attend client-evaluator relationships and the inherent risk of co-optation, whether conscious or otherwise. This asymmetrical power relationship between the evaluator and client is intensified when the client is a foundation. Foundations often choose to tackle "messy social problems" with complex program strategies, limited funds, and untested theories of change. In most cases, the evaluator is not engaged until a project has already been chosen and funded, at which point there is very little opportunity to rethink basic assumptions or redefine expected outcomes. Under these circumstances, rigorous evaluation designs (what many evaluators are best trained to execute) will frequently and predictably produce "no effect" findings. As a result, the evaluation process can be quite painful and can risk wasting precious resources.

The incentives for evaluators to become willing collaborators in flawed social programming are similar to those operating between foundations and grantees generally. It is difficult to tell a potential funder that his or her program ideas are unfounded, that much more research needs to be done before going forward in order to tighten the link between resources, activities, outcomes, and goals, or that the outcomes promised to the board in securing approval for the program are unlikely to be realized. Above all, the foundation is the customer and, potentially, a repeat customer. If the evaluator is to be hired, he or she has every incentive to accept, rather than challenge, the foundation and the grantee's promised outcomes.

Evaluation of Projects Instead of Strategies. As we have noted, most evaluation that is supported by foundations focuses on the grantee (Snow, 1996; McNelis and Bickel, 1996; Patrizi and McMullan, 1998). With some notable exceptions (for example, The Robert Wood Johnson Foundation, The Pew Charitable Trusts, and The Charles and Helen Schwab Foundation, to name just a few), program evaluators are typically asked to assess the impact of individual projects. This is a good fit for many evaluators; that is what they have been trained to do. But few individual projects are likely to achieve substantial change in the broad social issues that foundations address. Social problems are highly interdependent, and the impact of a program that tackles one of them, even successfully, may be offset by other variables. It becomes extremely difficult then for a single pilot project ever to demonstrate sufficient efficacy to be replicated or expanded. And, more broadly, limiting evaluations to individual projects can undercut the organization's capacity to learn about interactions between social problems and to build cumulative knowledge. Equally important, by focusing on the grantee, the foundation's program strategy and its own effectiveness remain largely unexamined.

Both the foundation and evaluation communities share culpability here. It is much easier to focus on grantees' work than one's own, and the field of evaluation is only beginning to develop practical measures for assessing program strategy and foundation mission. Cluster evaluation designs offer some assistance, but they are often complex, time consuming, expensive, unwieldy, and difficult to implement (W. K. Kellogg Foundation, 1994.) Recent interest in "meta-evaluation," as a way of accumulating knowledge across individual evaluations (see Weiss, 1998, pp. 236–244), offers an interesting avenue to build knowledge from individual evaluations. But again, there must be institutional interest and technical capacity to do it.

In sum, we see much promise in the growing diversification of methods and potential roles for evaluators. Many of these newer developments match the informational and learning requirements we see as essential to creating greater effectiveness in philanthropy. The challenge rests on both sides of the interaction: (1) more evaluators need to be trained in broader arrays of methods in order to meet the emergent standards of the field, and (2) they need to become comfortable working on organizational processes and strategy development. Foundations, for their part, need to be aware of the growing possibilities of evaluation so they can become more discerning clients—clients who set the right expectations and hire the right evaluators with the right skills for each assignment.

Surmounting the Barriers

We contend that the many substantial challenges confronting both foundations and the field of evaluation are surmountable. Change must happen on both sides for a new paradigm to emerge. However, we believe that the initial opportunity for change lies primarily with the leadership of foundations.

Foundations, after all, are the clients and are in a stronger position to influence evaluators than vice versa. They have substantial resources at hand to fund the development of new methods or to standardize existing ones. Equally important, foundations are increasingly concerned with ways to increase their effectiveness and therefore have an incentive to bring about change. For example, the foundation affinity group, Grantmakers for Effective Organizations, has found in a recent membership survey that its members are as interested in promoting "funder effectiveness" as they are in grantee effectiveness. As noted earlier, organizations like the Center for Effective Philanthropy have begun to compile comparative data on foundation performance, based, among other sources, on surveying thousands of grantees to create comparative performance benchmarks around dozens of indicators—a first step toward better performance standards for the field (see the Grantee Perception Report on-line at www.effectivephilanthropy.org).

For foundations to lead the change, however, boards and CEOs must go much further, making foundation performance, learning, and effectiveness their highest priorities. As long as good intentions count equally or more than results, job performance is taken for granted, and external feedback is always good, evaluation cannot be effectively conducted and improvements in practice will not occur. Simply put, boards must set expectations and hold senior management accountable for meeting them. If foundation boards do not assert their authority, no external or internal forces can replace it.

Within the foundation, the CEO must use time, money, and performance reviews to demonstrate that learning from the evaluation of past results is valued. Without the support of the board, such priorities might well endanger his or her job.

If boards are to play this critical role, they must become more engaged and better informed. Overpromising, whether by program staff to gain board approval, grantees to persuade program officers, or evaluators to get hired, undermines the entire system. Transparency, consistency, and realism in decision making must be reinforced at all levels throughout the organization.

Failure must be tolerated a reasonable proportion of the time, without penalizing grantees or staff for their candor. However, failure without learning and improvement cannot be accepted practice. Foundations must track their own progress over time if they are to become learning organizations. If there is no improvement, then most likely there has been no learning of practical value.

These measures won't automatically lead to new solutions for persistent and complex social problems, but they should lead to increasingly powerful knowledge about effective practices and, with application over time, greater social impact by the most successful foundations.

Evaluation can play a crucial role in supporting such a shift by being integrated into organizational planning and grantmaking processes, thus helping to create a realistic base for learning, and by evaluating the results of strategy implementation. All evaluation results, good or bad, should be made publicly available to be reviewed by peers and inform other funders.

Staffs need the time, resources, and incentive to examine past results, reflect on them, and educate board members about the consequences of their decisions.

And foundation staffs must be expanded to include those with expertise in management, organizational change, and knowledge capture if foundations are serious about using those tools to become more effective. They also need to become knowledgeable about the many new developments taking place in the field of evaluation and be prepared to contribute to the development of that field and the training of evaluators (see Greene, 2001; Greene and McClintock, 1991). This means that boards may need to willingly accept higher administrative expense ratios if the results justify them.

Such profound changes may sound utopian. But there are already examples of foundations that have begun to take some of these steps. The Robert Wood Johnson Foundation has, over the past decade, developed a rich combination of foundation performance measures that accomplish many of these goals. Both board and staff have deep medical expertise that supports informed decision making within the foundation's focus area of health, and evaluation results for all programs (good or bad) are publicly available on the foundation's Web site. Similarly, the Hewlett Foundation has made the results of its Grantee Perception Report public on its Web site.

The Pew Charitable Trusts and The Lumina Foundation engage evaluation staff in the initial planning and design of program initiatives to be sure that the goals program staff pick are both measurable and achievable. Every staff member's performance, from the CEO on down, is judged annually on progress toward his or her program goals, and annual bonuses are awarded accordingly.

These developments are not limited to the largest foundations. The Woods Fund in Chicago, with an annual grant budget of $4 million, and The Rockdale Foundation in Atlanta, with a budget half that size, both have similarly detailed goal-setting and evaluation processes in place. What these exemplars have in common is neither a different pool of evaluators nor a sophisticated computer system to capture knowledge, but strong management, appropriate staff expertise, and, above all, a board that is determined to demonstrate results. These foundations track performance at multiple levels and encourage organizational learning through clear performance incentives. They have had to systematically examine and revise every policy, attitude, and tradition within their foundations, embracing a willingness to change in order to overcome the constant positive reinforcement and culture of good intentions that so entrenches the rest of the field.

For its part, the evaluation community needs to continue to define alternative ways of evaluating and supporting the implementation of sound programs and strategies, as well as assessing their impact. The development of program evaluation standards—taking into account the multiple roles that evaluation can play—will be an important component of field reform (see Sanders and The Joint Committee on Standards for Educational Evaluation, 1994; Stufflebeam, 2001).

Greater consistency and depth in the preparation of evaluators are essential. Foundations can help shape the emergent field of evaluation directly by funding new training programs for evaluators and indirectly by hiring well-qualified evaluators and funding innovative evaluation projects that create demonstrable value. The field of evaluation is currently in sufficient flux to make this a propitious moment for significant reform. Using evaluation effectively for foundation learning is, in the end, neither about finding the newest and best evaluation methodology nor building complex knowledge-capture systems. It is about overcoming the systemic, cultural, and organizational barriers in both fields. This means that no quick and easy answer is waiting to be discovered to resolve the many serious challenges we have discussed. There is only the slow and disciplined work of gradual improvement within foundation management and within the evaluation field. The reward for this effort, however, would be a more effective use of foundation resources, a healthier evaluation profession, and a strengthened nonprofit sector.

References

Backer, T. E. (1999, November). *Innovation in context: New foundation approaches to evaluation, collaboration, and best practices.* Miami, FL: Knight Foundation.

Backer, T. E., & Bare, J. (2000, September-October). Going to the next level. *Foundation News and Commentary, 41*(5), 38–40.

Bickel, W. E. (1996). *Program director perspectives on the use of evaluation: A case study.* Indianapolis: Lilly Endowment.

Bickel, W. E., Millett, R., & Nelson, C. A. (2002, March-April). Challenges to the role of evaluation in supporting organizational learning in foundations. *Foundation News and Commentary.*

Center for Effective Philanthropy. (2002, February). *Toward a common language: Listening to foundation CEOs and other experts talk about performance measurement in philanthropy.* Available at www.effectivephilanthropy.org.

Center for Effective Philanthropy. (2002, August). *Indicators of effectiveness: Understanding and improving foundation performance.* Available at www.effectivephilanthropy.org.

Center for Effective Philanthropy. (2004). *Foundation governance: The CEO viewpoint.* Available at www.effectivephilanthropy.org.

Chelimsky, E. (2001). What evaluation could do to support foundations: A framework with nine component parts. *American Journal of Evaluation, 22*(1), 13–28.

Cronbach, L., & Associates. (1980). *Toward reform of program evaluation.* San Francisco: Jossey-Bass.

Draper, L. (2000, September-October). "Do" capacity building. *Foundation News and Commentary, 41*(5), 32–36.

Easterling, D., & Csuti, N. B. (1999). Using evaluation to improve grant making: What's good for the goose is good for the gander. Denver, CO: The Colorado Trust.

Foundation Center. (2002). *Foundation giving trends.* New York: Author.

Freund, G. (1996). *Narcissism and philanthropy.* New York: Viking Press.

Grantmakers for Effective Organizations. (1998, October). *Grantmakers for effective organizations: Inaugural conference report.* San Francisco: James Irvine Foundation.

Greene, J. C. (2001). Evaluation extrapolations. *American Journal of Evaluation, 22*(3), 397–402.

Greene, J. C., & McClintock, C. (1991, Winter). The evolution of evaluation methodology. *Theory into Practice, 30*(1), 13–21.

Hernandez, G., & Visher, M. G. (2001). *Creating a culture of inquiry.* San Francisco: The James Irvine Foundation.

Hunter, D.E.K., & Kaye, J. W. (2001, November). *Evaluation as a core element of institution building at the Edna McConnell Clark Foundation.* Paper presented at the annual conference of the American Evaluation Association, St. Louis, MO.

Joint Committee on Standards for Educational Evaluation. (1994). *The program evaluation standards: How to assess evaluations of educational programs.* Thousand Oaks, CA: Sage.

Kistler, S. (Nov. 11, 2002). Personal communication. Washington, D.C.

Klusman, J. E. (2003, May/June). Bringing personal accountability on board. *Foundation News and Commentary, 44*(3), 40–41.

Knickman, J. (2000). How the pursuit of evaluation and organizational effectiveness can change the life of our foundations. In *High performance organizations: Linking evaluation and effectiveness.* Grantmakers Evaluation Network-Grantmakers for Effective Organizations, Washington, DC: Council on Foundations.

Letts, C. W., Ryan, W. P., & Grossman, A. (1999). *High performance non-profit organizations: Managing upstream for greater impact.* New York: Wiley.

Lipman, H., & Wilhelm, I. (2003, May 29). Pressing foundations to give more. The *Chronicle of Philanthropy, 15*(16), 7, 10–11.

McNelis, R. H., & Bickel, W. E. (1996). Building formal knowledge bases: Understanding evaluation use in the foundation community. *Evaluation Practice, 17*(1), 19–41.

McNelis, R. H., Bickel, W. E., & Connors-Gilmore, M. (1996). *A national survey of small and mid-sized foundations: The role of evaluation.* Pittsburgh: Learning Research and Development Center, University of Pittsburgh.

Modarresi, S., Newman, D. L., & Abolafia, M. Y. (2001, February). Academic evaluators versus practitioners: Alternative experiences of professionalism. *Evaluation and Program Planning, 24*(1), 1–11.

New York Times. Giving Supplement, November 2001.

Orosz, J. J. (2002, October). *Terra incognita: Poorly understood challenges and trade-offs of managing private foundations.* Speech delivered at Georgetown University on October 4, 2002, Center for the Study of Voluntary Organizations and Service, Waldemar A. Neilson Issues in Philanthropy Seminar Series. Available at http://csvos.georgetown.edu/NeilsenTranscripts/Orosz.pdf.

Patrizi, P. (2002, April 4). *Briefing notes to the Evaluation II Roundtable.* Presented at the Grantmakers' Evaluation Network meeting, Council on Foundations, Washington, DC.

Patrizi, P., & McMullan, B. (1998, December). *Evaluation in foundations.* A report prepared for the W. K. Kellogg Foundation, Battle Creek, MI.

Patrizi, P., & McMullan, B. (1999). Evaluation in foundations: The unrealized potential. *Foundation News and Commentary, 40*(3), 30–35.

Patrizi, P., & McMullan, B. (2000, August). *Meeting proceedings: Evaluation Roundtable.* Washington, DC: The W. K. Kellogg and Robert Wood Johnson Foundations.

Patton, M. Q. (1997). *Utilization-focused evaluation: The new century text* (3rd ed.). Thousand Oaks, CA.: Sage.

Pauly, E. (2000, June 26). *Using evaluation to strengthen foundations' effectiveness.* Paper presented at the International Foundation Symposium 2000, Gutersloh, Germany. New York: Wallace–Readers' Digest Funds.

Porter, M. E., & Kramer, M. R. (1999). Philanthropy's new agenda: Creating value. *Harvard Business Review, 77,* 121–130.

Preskill, H., & Torres, R. (1999). *Evaluative inquiry for learning in organizations.* Thousand Oaks, CA: Sage.

Sanders, J. (2002, November 12). Personal communication. Washington, DC.

Sanders, J., & The Joint Committee on Standards for Educational Evaluation. (1994). *The program evaluation standards.* Thousand Oaks, CA: Sage.

Scriven, M. (1991). *Evaluation thesaurus.* Thousand Oaks, CA: Sage.

Shadish, W. R., Newman, D. L., Scheirer, M. A., & Wye, C. (Eds.). (1995). *Guiding principles for evaluators.* New Directions for Program Evaluation, no. 66. San Francisco: Jossey-Bass.

Shulha, L. M., & Cousins, J. B. (1997). Evaluation use: Theory, research, and practice since 1986. *Evaluation Practice, 18*(3), 195–208.

Smith, M. F. (2001). Evaluation: Preview of the future #2. *American Journal of Evaluation, 22*(3), 281–300.

Snow, P. (1996). Moving beyond the boundaries: Rethinking the role of evaluation in foundations. Paper presented at the annual conference of the American Evaluation Association, Atlanta, GA.

Stake, R. E. (2001). A problematic heading. *American Journal of Evaluation, 22*(3), 281–300.

Stufflebeam, D. L. (2001). Interdisciplinary Ph.D. programming in evaluation. *American Journal of Evaluation, 22*(3), 445–455.

Taylor, B. E., Chait, R. P., & Holland, T. P. (1996). The new work of the nonprofit board. *Harvard Business Review, 74*(5), 36–43.

Trice Gray, S., and Associates (1997). *Evaluation with power.* San Francisco: Jossey-Bass.

Walling, W. (1997). Are foundations effective? Who knows? *Foundation News and Commentary, 38*(4), Washington, DC: Council on Foundations.

Weiss, C. (1998). *Evaluation* (2nd ed.). Upper Saddle River, NJ: Prentice Hall.

Wisely, D. S. (1993). *Reflections on a foundation's relationship to its public legacies and lessons for the Lilly Endowment.* Indianapolis, IN: Lilly Endowment.

Wisely, D. S. (2002). *Parting thoughts on foundation evaluation.* Indianapolis, IN: Lilly Endowment.

W. K. Kellogg Foundation (1994). *Improving cluster evaluation: Some areas for consideration.* Battle Creek, MI: W. K. Kellogg Foundation.

Worthen, B. R. (1999, Fall). Critical challenges confronting the certification of evaluators. *American Journal of Evaluation, 20*(3), 533–556.

CHAPTER FOUR

BUILDING STRONG
FOUNDATION-GRANTEE RELATIONSHIPS

Michael Quinn Patton, John Bare,
and Deborah G. Bonnet

The following case describing an evaluation of a summer camp program reveals the ease with which evaluators get tangled up in the complexities and deceits of foundation-grantee relationships.

Figuring Out Relationships: A Case of Mismatched Expectations

The program for kids was held at a school-based summer camp located in the school district's lower-income neighborhoods. At the time of funding, the grantee emphasized that the program was about fun, learning, and positive youth development and that its effects might carry over into enhanced student performance during the subsequent school year.

The foundation wanted to test that theory. Only one board member thought that continued support should hinge on evidence of academic outcomes, and he understood his position to be a minority one. The other foundation board and staff members, like the outside evaluators, were just curious: "Wouldn't it be cool to find that these few weeks in the summer are actually turning kids on to learning, even in regular school?"

The school superintendent went along: "Of course, we should evaluate on academic achievement—tests scores, attendance, grades. Let's do it all!" But when the evaluation plan was presented to teachers and principals, they balked. They could hardly believe that the foundation and their evaluation accomplices were taking their proposal rhetoric literally! "Creating lifelong learners." "Cultivating enthusiasm for math." "Wiping out truancy and teen-age pregnancy." They had included those outcomes as possibilities—as icing on the cake—but they hadn't expected that such lofty goals would actually become the focus of an evaluation. How could the foundation possibly be so naïve?

Naïve or not, the achievement evaluation proceeded, along with a number of other evaluation components that came to happier endings. The endings were not happy enough, though, to overcome the results that teachers had predicted. There was no discernible effect on school performance whatsoever, unless you were inclined to interpret a bit too simplistically, in which case you'd conclude that the program actually did harm.

The discussions of how to interpret and publicly report the evaluation's findings were animated. The stakes had risen. The seemingly innocuous idea of just exploring the possibility of academic outcomes had become, from the grantees' perspective, a summative evaluation, at least if the findings were reported publicly. The level of fear is suggested by the comment of one school employee to the evaluator and foundation staff, speculating on the negative publicity that would ensue from a public report: "Your innocent intentions don't matter. If the press gets hold of this, we're dead meat." Over the following months, the foundation managed to rebuild a productive relationship with the school district, even to the point of making good use of the other evaluation findings. Other, similar situations have turned out less well.

Thus it falls to evaluators to help foundations and grantees figure out the right kind of relationship for a given situation. In that regard, we begin the chapter with a typology of foundation-grantee relationships, followed by a discussion of some of the relationship challenges that are often encountered. Next, we discuss how foundations' methods of operating can create tensions in relationships with grantees. Special emphasis is given to ways in which evaluation can harm funder-grantee relationships. We end by presenting a promising strategy for enhancing foundation-grantee communications and effectiveness: the technique of risk analysis.

Types of Foundation-Grantee Relationships

Different kinds of foundation-grantee relationships typically involve different kinds of evaluation approaches and issues. The relationship categories discussed next offer a framework for considering how variations in these relationships affect evaluation. In particular, we focus on how the foundation-grantee relationship, at least with respect to evaluation, can change when a foundation plays an active role in bringing about social, economic, and policy change. The categories range, in order, from more passive to more active.

Cooperative, Businesslike Relationships

For many foundations, the relationship with grantees is very passive or businesslike. The foundation provides financial support for a specific proposal, and the grantee is funded to implement the proposal. The grant agreement specifies basic accountability reporting requirements, usually quarterly or annually, and a final summary report. Grantees are responsible for managing any evaluation within the scope and terms of the grant itself.

On occasion, for a large grant the foundation may commission an external evaluation. The foundation's relationship with the external evaluator is much like that with grantees—very businesslike. This relationship prevails most often when the foundation defines itself as primarily a grantmaker. That self-definition leads the foundation to focus on managing grants efficiently. Evaluation is part of that routine management.

Collaborative Relationships

Here, the foundation offers not only financial assets but staff expertise and a commitment to facilitating connections among key players in the sector. The foundation plays a convening role in bringing actors together, treating a group of grantees as an investment cluster. The foundation's "cluster evaluator" may help coordinate grant evaluations, provide technical assistance to local evaluators, facilitate development of common instrumentation across grantees, and aggregate individual grant evaluations to glean cumulative outcomes and lessons learned for the entire collaborative cluster. The cluster evaluator may provide advice to the foundation about managing collaboration, enhancing networking, and convening among grantees. The cluster evaluator may also investigate the quality of foundation-grantee relationships.

This collaborative relationship prevails most often when the foundation defines itself not just as a grantmaker but as an investor actively facilitating the change process through collaboration with grantees. A foundation's self-definition as a collaborative grantmaker leads the foundation to focus on facilitating connections and synergies among grantees, with evaluation used to monitor collaborative processes, provide feedback along the way, and, in some cases, become part of the connective tissue of the collaboration. In other words, evaluators can become part of the collaborative effort.

An example is the Kellogg Foundation's Grassroots Leadership Program. Over several years, more than twenty communities participated in the program, each with its own local evaluation. Kellogg's cluster evaluation team coordinated the local evaluations and organized an annual networking conference among grantees in which Kellogg staff participated. The evaluators came to be viewed as key participants in the collaboration effort itself and played an especially important role in conceptualizing and defining the nature and outcomes of the collaboration.

Partnering Relationships

In some cases, a foundation may choose to move from collaboration to partnership. This typically involves substantial funds and long-term commitments to grantees in support of mutually developed and shared goals to bring about substantial change. In these cases, foundation staff and grantees design the grant together, work closely during implementation, use evaluation to adapt the implementation over time, and share accountability for results. Several funders may partner together, as well as work in partnership with multiple grantees.

The Northwest Area Foundation exemplifies this approach. The foundation no longer accepts requests for grants. Rather, the foundation is forming partnerships with select communities to develop long-term solutions to poverty. Once both the community and the foundation agree on a plan, they enter into a partnership agreement in which the foundation funds a significant part of the implementation costs, helps leverage additional funds, and dedicates staff to continuing full-time work on the partnership.

Evaluation begins with establishing baseline data on key community indicators and continues by providing monitoring data—process and outcomes data about specific initiatives, and, ultimately, summative data about reduction in poverty. The evaluators report to and serve *both* the foundation and the community, and the evaluation plays the role of helping keep the strategic initiatives focused on poverty reduction.

Birthing and Parenting Relationships

A foundation may create and endow a new entity when moving into an undeveloped area of work or into an arena that cuts across existing organizations. In such circumstances, evaluation becomes part of the organizational development process, helping the new entity create internal evaluation processes. This includes supporting the development of policies regarding external evaluation and facilitating the creation of a learning culture within and throughout the new entity. Organizational effectiveness and sustainability become special evaluation issues. Sharing evaluative information becomes part of the relationship between the foundation and the new entity, much as school evaluative information flows between a teacher and parents during a school conference.

The McKnight Foundation in Minnesota exemplifies this approach. It has created and endowed a housing alliance that cuts across the borders (and barriers) of the Twin Cities of Minneapolis and St. Paul. During the farm crisis in Minnesota in the 1980s, McKnight created and endowed "Initiative Funds" in six regions throughout the state, each with its own mission, board of directors, and staff. In each case, external evaluators played an organizational development role, helping to assess capacity-building needs, providing technical assistance, creating internal evaluation procedures and external evaluation policies, and supplying organizational effectiveness data as both parent and offspring negotiated the nature of their ongoing and future relationships.

Operating Foundations

Operating foundations represent yet another variation on the funder-grantee relationship, one that is particularly close. The proximity presents special challenges. Operating foundations provide direct services and implement programs within the foundation structure. Sometimes an entire foundation is an operating foundation; in other instances, the operating program is a specific component within a larger foundation structure.

For example, the Blandin Community Leadership Program conducts leadership training within The Blandin Foundation, which also engages in traditional grantmaking. When the operating program resides within a larger foundation structure, the operating program is a grantee. The relationship between that grantee (the operating foundation) and the funding foundation can be unusually personal. In such cases, the evaluation function may provide some distance between the two entities. This ensures that independent and fair performance assessments flow back and forth. Evaluation provides a kind of mediating role.

Developmental Evaluation Relationships

In some cases, the evaluator role can be interdependent with foundation-grantee roles, as in developmental evaluation. *Developmental Evaluation* (Patton, 1994) refers to long-term relationships that evaluators may have with foundation staff and grantees when they are all engaged together in ongoing program or organizational development. The evaluator becomes part of the design team. All team members, working together, interpret evaluation findings and apply results to the next stage of development.

Developmentally oriented programs pursue the sometimes vague notion of ongoing social change. They eschew clear, specific, and measurable goals up-front because clarity, specificity, and measurability are limiting. They've identified an issue or problem and want to explore potential solutions, but they realize that where they end up will be different for different participants in the process.

The process often includes elements of *participatory evaluation*, for example, engaging foundation staff and grantees in setting goals and monitoring goal attainment, but those goals aren't fixed. They're milestones for assessing progress, subject to change as learning occurs. As the evaluation unfolds, program designers observe where they end up. They discuss what's possible and what's desirable and make adjustments accordingly.

An example is the Blandin Community Leadership Program, an operating program within The Blandin Foundation that is committed to supporting change aimed at healthy communities throughout Minnesota. The three external evaluators for the program became part of a design team that included a sociologist, a couple of psychologists, a communications specialist, some adult educators, the foundation's grantmaking program officers, and the operating foundation's program staff. All design team members had a range of expertise and experiences.

The relationship lasted more than six years and involved different evaluation approaches each year. During that time, the evaluators engaged in participant observation, conducted several different surveys, undertook field observations, gathered data through telephone interviews, generated case studies of individuals and communities, did cost analyses, helped with theory-of-change conceptualizations, facilitated futuring exercises, and supported training program participants to do their own evaluations. Each year, the program changed in significant ways, and new evaluation questions emerged. Program goals and strategies evolved. The evaluation evolved. No final report was ever written, as the program continues to evolve.

Challenges in Developing Useful Foundation-Grantee Relationships

Developing honest and open foundation-grantee relationships can be a rocky process. There are potential and real conflicts embedded in all the relationships we've described—conflicts born of differing rewards, incentives, interests, and risks. In the sections that follow, we explore some of the strains that can emerge in foundation-grantee relationships.

Barriers to Open Relationships in the Grant Development and Approval Process

Guarded relationships develop during the grant application process. Foundation staff learn to avoid making promises, lest they create funding expectations prior to final approval. Grantees learn to listen carefully and parrot back what they believe funders want to hear. This relationship is often experienced as "a game of rhetorical persuasion where the rules regarding honesty and candor are suspended or subtly altered, just as they are in poker" (Hooker, 1987, p. 129). Or the foundation-grantee relationship can be described as a dance in which the funder leads and the prospective grantee follows.

Patton observed a foundation-grantee negotiation for a large grant to enhance the training of agricultural extension agents. The grant proposal focused on knowledge and behavior changes among extension agents. The funder insisted that, in order to get board approval, the proposal would have to include a 10 percent increase in farmer incomes annually. The grantee shyly noted that (1) a 10 percent income increase annually seemed awfully high, and (2) the grant's proposed outcomes focused on the results of extension training. Any subsequent increases in farmer income would only occur after the grant period, when the trained extension agents worked with farmers. The funder's response was, "Our new president is outcomes-driven. I can't take this to my president and board without showing a substantial impact on farmers' incomes." So the grantee added the dubious "increase in farmer income" result (outcome). The grantee's explanation was to invoke the time-honored golden rule: "He who has the gold makes the rules."

In another case, a proposal to provide technology resources to low-income families as an experiment in community organizing met with board resistance. The board insisted that the project add job outcomes for the families receiving the assistance. A foundation board certainly has the power to ask for such changes but should only do so as part of a rethinking of the fit between the outcomes and the proposed strategies. This practice illustrates the power dynamics of foundation-grantee relationships and the ways in which the power inequities can affect both the proposed outcomes and the ultimate evaluation findings.

Effects of Initial Contacts

Applicants with considerable experience and good connections may start out talking to a foundation trustee or president. Grant applicants entering the process through high-level contacts may feel immune to evaluation. When a foundation president hands off a favorite idea to a junior staff member for follow-through, the impression may be given (accurately, in some cases) that the proposal will get privileged consideration, including exemption from evaluation.

Another way an applicant may enter the process is through a foundation-designated point of contact. Foundations may simplify the application process by providing one point of contact that remains stable over time. As this staff member forms a relationship with nonprofit organizations, there is a chance to increase levels of trust and thereby arrive at the kind of candor needed to make evaluation meaningful. If an applicant's contact is continually changing, however, it may increase frustration and diminish the usefulness of planning phases.

Evaluation as a Tool for Compliance

With foundations trained to keep their eyes on the grant horizon, grant recipients' reports and evaluations are notoriously underused. One of grantees' most common complaints is that they dutifully submit reports to foundations and wait in vain for feedback. Then grantees fail to take reporting seriously. Prompting from program officers and threats of delayed grant payments create an impression that the reports are somehow urgently needed by the foundation. In fact, reporting is usually a compliance function. Few foundations, in our experience, have mechanisms and processes for systematically harvesting wisdom from grantees' reports.

Foundations are so driven by proposal review and payout that few have time or incentives for dealing with the back-end processes of learning from evaluation. It's not that evaluations aren't required and commissioned. It's that the results aren't used. Evaluation becomes a compliance function—Did the evaluation report get submitted?—rather than a learning function. Many foundations have incorporated the rhetoric of learning into their grantmaking and evaluations, but our experience suggests that few have mechanisms for using evaluation findings in new grant decisions.

Foundations' operating structures usually provide little incentive for staff to report negative findings to their boards. There is incentive for staff to stay focused on the next round of grants, not to spend time reviewing old and unfortunate history. Of course, program officers are encouraged to share success stories and anecdotes—the kind of positive results that fill the pages of foundations' annual reports. Rare are the annual reports that disclose and discuss failures. All of this feeds cynicism and reduces the likelihood of honest dialogue about what works and doesn't work.

Frustration Over Small and Matching Grants

Small planning or pilot grants are common tools for foundations testing new relationships before making a major financial commitment. However, these small grants have proven especially frustrating for grantees when, at the close of the initial process, it becomes clear that the foundation is not prepared to entertain a full proposal in a timely manner (Backer and Bare, 2002).

Foundation grants that require recipients to raise dollars to match all or some of the award have implications for foundation-grantee relationships. On the positive side, the matching requirement can help grantees raise additional funds.

However, if grantees cannot meet the requirement, the condition may trigger problems for the organization and foundation. Planned activities may be shelved. The relationship with the foundation may sour. Fundraising may cause grantees to neglect other responsibilities. For a foundation that believes the match is necessary for the strategy to succeed, the condition can protect foundation dollars. Yet a foundation with too many unpaid matching grants on its books may find it difficult to meet payout requirements.

Power and Consensus

Consider the case of a community foundation working with an inner-city community to set up a committee to advise on grants. After the local committee put in long hours to develop review procedures for community grants, the committee members came to resent being second-guessed by "the suits" in the foundation board room. The foundation's ten-year commitment to the community was endangered. Eventually, the community foundation resolved the crisis by devolving decision-making authority to the community but demanding more accountability.

In community-based planning, shared decision making by foundation staff, community stakeholders, and grantees can enhance effectiveness. Beierle's analysis of many cases reveals that stakeholder involvement results in higher-quality decisions (Beierle, 2002). Further, the more intensive the process, the more value stakeholders add. The most intensive efforts in Beierle's review "involved negotiations and mediations in which participants—usually formally representing interest groups—formulated consensual agreements that would bind their organizations to particular courses of action" (p. 743). These findings support the call for an emphasis on deeper engagement in new, community-based models (Heath, Bradshaw, and Lee, 2002).

Difficulty of Capacity-Building Initiatives

Poor progress on the capacity-building component of a grant may jeopardize the nonprofit organization's overall relationship with the foundation. Learning one troubling thing about a nonprofit may influence a foundation's view of the entire organization. Likewise, nonprofits coordinating multiple strategies for a single foundation may find all of the different projects put in jeopardy if there is an unpleasant experience with just one of them. Grantees may be so anxious to receive funding that they agree to most any capacity-building condition in order to receive the project support. When this happens, the grantee's disinterest in the capacity work is almost certain to emerge after the project dollars arrive. When it does, it may cause the foundation to lose trust in its partner.

Complications from Public Communications

The degree to which a foundation draws public attention to its social change efforts can complicate grantee relationships. Recently, a large foundation ran into unexpected hazards when making high-profile announcements about a cluster of grants. Several small nonprofits were upset because the awards were announced in a manner that made it appear they each had received substantial grants. In fact, the award was actually a collection of relatively small grants to be divided up among several organizations within the collaboration. Further, the intermediary organization charged with passing along grant funds to smaller partners was perceived as a barrier preventing the small organizations from developing relationships with the foundation. These issues would have emerged under any circumstances, but the foundation's highly public announcements made things more complicated and damaged the relationships, which in turn slowed progress on evaluation planning.

Confusion About Guidelines

Grantees are often confused by guidelines that seem clear to the foundation. One example is the widespread policy of limiting grant renewals, even if the grant is successful. From the grantee's perspective, the foundation's unwillingness to make case-by-case decisions about the merits of a proposed grant renewal is an excuse for not making a real decision. This can impair trust. It can also lead the grantee to reframe the project in some "innovative" package, simply for the purpose of disguising a continuation grant as a new project.

We hear a great many complaints about foundations' unrealistic expectations concerning sustainability, especially when grant support runs only one to three years. Governments aren't picking up new programs anymore. Foundations seldom want to fund another foundation's success; they want their own projects. In the current climate, most nonprofit organizations are cutting back. Under these conditions, evaluators can help foundations and grantees align their expectations regarding sustainability.

A different kind of grantee complaint emerges from multifunder collaborations. Grantees find it especially taxing when each foundation requires different data in different formats. Grantees are often reluctant to complain openly about the onerous nature of this lack of coordination among funders for fear of alienating a funder and losing support. But in private, we often hear from grantees about funders unable to collaborate among themselves to coordinate reporting requirements, schedules, and frameworks.

Ways Evaluation Can Promote Change and Improve Relationships

Foundations can enhance evaluation use by clarifying decisions regarding who will use evaluative information and for what purposes (Patton, 1997). One of The John S. and James L. Knight Foundation's partners, in its initiative to reduce youth violence and promote youth development, demonstrated how evidence can be used for making real-time program adjustments. The foundation planned for grantees to be responsible for their own evaluations and provided them with technical assistance. The grantees were to be the primary users of their own evaluation information.

However, a grantee expanding an in-school alternative education program serving youth at risk of school failure found that empirical evidence on math and English achievement gains did not live up to the positive reports from youth, parents, teachers, and principals. So the program made changes. It adjusted its target population to focus on the at-risk youth most likely to improve their school performance. It moved away from a focus on homework help and brought in teachers licensed in math and English to teach the subject matter. Most important, the program began working to identify short-term outcomes closer in proximity to the intervention.

All of this occurred during the Knight Foundation's three-year grant. The foundation did not provide a second round of funding to assist with the new changes, so there was no additional benefit or reward for the approach taken. A foundation could send stronger signals by providing additional grant support to grant recipients that distinguish themselves in terms of candor, learning, and use of evidence. This requires foundations to reward experimenters who honestly report problems and propose remedies, not just those who report that things worked well.

Ways Evaluation Can Harm Relationships

In deciding whether to undertake an evaluation, foundations and grantees must weigh the potential benefits against the potential negative side effects. Several potential side effects are discussed next.

• *Evaluation can tell funders more than they want to know and surface issues they'd rather not face.* For a number of years, a large, rich suburban church paid for a program run by a small, poor urban church for the benefit of its inner-city neighborhood. Thinking it was the responsible thing to do after so many years and so many dollars, the big church commissioned an evaluation. The findings were mostly favorable. "Just one thing," noted the evaluator in her final briefing. "It turns out this program has an exorbitant cost per participant. I understand that you don't expect God's work to be cheap, but all it would take to bring this price down from scandalous to merely generous would be to beat the bushes a little to keep enrollment up to capacity. It's not like the need isn't out there."

Jaws dropped. It was hard to say who was more astounded. The little church was embarrassed and defensive, but it was the big church's trustees who took the evaluator by surprise. Efficiency wasn't on their minds at all. Maximizing returns on their philanthropic investments wasn't, either. They were working from the charity model of philanthropy, and all they wanted to hear was that their grants were doing good. So far, they'd managed to smooth over the paternalism underlying the congregations' relationship. The evaluation had put the notion of accountability right on the table. Neither side knew what to do.

• *Evaluation can tell foundation leaders more than the program officers want them to know.* In one case, a hands-on program officer persistently favored even the frailest of grassroots efforts if he viewed them as helpful to kids. His downfall was that he favored evaluation as well. Although this officer was usually able to shepherd grantees through the foundation's routine scrutiny, finding evaluators who are willing and able to join the conspiracy proved to be a challenge. Evaluators continually pointed to weaknesses—things like cockroaches in the facilities, flaky accounting, loosely screened staff—that the foundation's leaders had a hard time looking past. The program officer found himself needing to balance his quest for knowledge against the trusting relationships he had cultivated deep down in the trenches.

• *Evaluation can insulate foundation staff from grant recipients.* Especially in foundations that adopt a "lean and mean" staffing strategy, lines blur between grant monitoring and external evaluation. Staff may lose touch. At the end of a long evaluation interview, one grant recipient offered this final remark: "Yes, there's something else I'd like to say to the foundation! This is the ninth consultant you've sent my way in under three years. Next time, come yourself!"

• *The evaluation burden can make a grant cost more than it's worth.* The CEO of a human services agency put it succinctly: "Yeah, these foundations, you know how they are. Their idea of 'leveraging' is to cover 8 percent of your budget, then think they get to run your operation however strikes their fancy." This too often includes foundation-imposed evaluation mandates, sometimes unfunded.

The United Way push for outcome reporting, for example, caught many agencies off guard. In several communities, United Way jumped on the bandwagon before they themselves knew how to do performance measurement. They ended up offering their agencies technical assistance to build evaluation capacity, which met the needs of only some agencies. Even then, agencies were often expected to produce outcome data before the internal capacity was built and without supplemental funding to cover data collection and other hard costs. The approach created resentment toward evaluation and reporting, as well as toward United Way.

• *A cluster evaluation can make grantees feel like "data points," which, in fact, they sometimes are.* In cross-site or cluster evaluations, each project's contact with the evaluator may consist of no more than a single site visit. Administrative data available from the funder are all it takes to round the picture out for the purpose the evaluation is to accomplish. But that can leave grantees on edge. One cluster evaluator reports hearing from grantees, "Are you *sure* that's all you need from us?" Between the lines the grantee is saying: "You mean you're going to report on us to our funder, based on nothing more than *that?*" The challenge is to find a way of explaining that the evaluation isn't designed to draw conclusions about individual projects. At the least, referring to people and their grant as "data points" isn't helpful to relationship building.

• *Evaluation consultants are often seen as representing the foundation.* It happens all the time when an evaluator visits grantees. He explains very carefully that he is not a foundation employee, just a consultant hired for an assignment. The host listens, nods his head, then turns around and introduces the evaluator: "Please join me in welcoming Dr. Smith, from our very generous sponsor, the XYZ Foundation. He's here today to evaluate us."

Our advice for foundations: Don't hire a consultant you wouldn't want mistaken for your vice president. Make sure anyone you send out gets briefed on your culture and etiquette. A pioneer in foundation evaluation learned this lesson early when the foundation hired a talented scholar with impeccable credentials for one of its first evaluation assignments. As a New Yorker, she didn't give a second thought to taking a limousine from the airport. It hadn't occurred to her that the Holiday Inn might be the only hotel in the county she was visiting or that no limousine had ever been seen there before. It made a splash when she pulled up to the high school in a chauffeured stretch—but not quite the impression the foundation had in mind.

• *Heavy-handed funders get in the way of good evaluation.* When foundations place nonessential burdens on grant recipients, the relationship suffers, and evaluation loses out. An evaluator complained that one foundation's grantees were the whiniest she'd ever encountered. A half-hour telephone interview was more than some would graciously give. Things came into focus, though, when she learned that the foundation required all grantees to submit periodic financial reports for their whole organization (not just grant funds) in a uniform format the foundation had concocted. Grant recipients were to map their own revenue and expense categories onto the foundation's—essentially, keep two sets of books. There was no explanation as to how the foundation would use this information.

• *Evaluators can be useful as translators, but they can also get in the way of much-needed direct communication between foundations and grantees.* On the other end of the continuum is the problem of treading too lightly. One foundation is so timid about interfering that grantees (and more so, applicants) cling to any clue as to the foundation's preferences. The grantees may view the evaluator as someone on the inside who can help explain the workings of this mysterious black box. Some evaluators are comfortable playing that role, and some aren't; still others overplay it to enhance their own status.

• *Evaluators can be compared to axe murderers.* Some funders use evaluation as a ruse for justifying decisions already made. Rather than the foundation owning a decision to walk away from a grant, an evaluation is designed in such a way as to guarantee negative findings. Then the evaluation bears the burden of what, from the grantee's perspective, is an unfair decision. Lore among professional evaluators about the dangers of being used as program axe murderers has evaluators on the watch for such misuses, but that doesn't always keep it from happening, especially with less experienced evaluators.

Enhancing Foundation-Grantee Communications and Effectiveness Through Risk Analysis

Introducing the notion of risk into foundation-grantee relationships is a way of acknowledging that things seldom turn out as planned. There are plenty of adages to remind us that human endeavors carry risks: "Even the best laid plans. . . ." "Many a slip twixt cup and lip." "Nothing entertains God more than watching humans plan."

Risk analysis may help foundations and grantees become more realistic and honest about the challenges of attaining stated outcomes. Without a more candid

approach to identifying and addressing potential hazards, foundations may per-
petuate the "sham" of foundations asking grant recipients to achieve grant outcomes "with wholly inadequate resources and tools" (Schorr, 1999, p. 42).
Foundations must either be willing to "expect less from limited investments or to
invest more to operate at the level of intensity that is necessary to achieve promised
results" (p. 42). Risk analysis begins with an assessment of the consequences of
what's most likely to go wrong, as foundations and grantees address the following questions:

- What can go wrong?
- What is the likelihood that it would go wrong?
- What are the consequences, and how bad would they be?

Longstaff, Haimes, and Sledge (2002, p. 4) define *risk analysis* as "an antici-
patory disciplined process, proactive rather than reactive. It is holistic in that it addresses all plausible scenarios, rather than simply managing convenient common
problems." Addressing risks at the outset of the grant development process can
make contingency planning the basis for foundation-grantee interaction, pushing
foundation staff and grantees to figure out how they might respond when hazards
materialize. This places a premium on using "high-quality" lessons to advance
learning and problem solving (Patton, 2001, p. 333).

The William and Flora Hewlett Foundation is one of the few foundations that
attempts a public explanation about its concept of risk:

> A considerable part of the Hewlett Foundation's grants budget is devoted to
> relatively risky investments that have the potential for high social returns. A
> "risky" investment in this sense is one where the desired outcome—for exam-
> ple, restoring an endangered ecosystem or improving the lives of disadvantaged
> youth—is by no means assured. Responsible risk taking requires specifying the
> intended outcomes and measures of success and monitoring progress during
> the implementation of a grant. There are other forms of risk as well—for ex-
> ample, the risk to the Foundation's reputation when it supports a controversial
> project, or the possibility of a well-intentioned philanthropic initiative causing
> unintended harms—that can be mitigated only by watchfulness and good judg-
> ment. (William and Flora Hewlett Foundation, 2001, p. 9)

Because it is impossible and impractical to consider every potential surprise,
risk analysis should enable foundations and grantees to agree on interim check-in
points. These moments should allow foundations and grantees to hold real-life ex-

periences up against their planning lens to see how actual events compare to what was anticipated.

When foundations' commitment to learning fails to live up to their rhetoric favoring innovative ventures, the notion of risk will take on a "stigma" that causes program staff to steer clear (Kunreuther, 2002). We've all heard foundation presidents and boards say to staff and grantees: "Be innovative. Take risks. Just make sure you succeed." Staff and grantees react by avoiding risk. And since fomenting genuine social change is among the riskiest of strategies, fear of failure is likely to trump the call for innovation, resulting in safer, more predictable efforts—ultimately yielding less social change, less experimentation, and less learning.

Scenario Planning

In traditional risk calculations (the probability of an occurrence multiplied by the severity of the consequences associated with the hazard), risk analysts have always considered easy-to-measure variables such as dollar costs, health effects, and the loss of life. These days, they have added in the kind of variables that influence foundation-grantee relationships:

> Rather than basing one's choices simply on the likelihood and consequences of different events, as normative models of decision making suggest one do, individuals are also influenced in their choices by emotional factors such as fear, worry and love. (Kunreuther, 2002, p. 659)

Foundation-grantee relationships can be illuminated by inquiring into risk. In the financial sector, investors agree to commit funds for a specified duration in the hope of realizing a dollar return that falls within an acceptable range. There is typically a correlation between risk and reward. Patton (2002) developed a training exercise to help foundation staff and trustees take up the subject of risk directly. In teaching these sessions, Patton presents risk in a way familiar to foundation staff, grantees, or trustees by asking them to fit various types of grants into the same categories chief investment officers use to diversify foundations' portfolios. For example, participants in the exercise are asked to identify the equivalent of a Blue Chip grant (one to a well-established, highly reputable grantee with a long and successful track record). Then they are asked to identify other kinds of grants similar to different types of investments, for example, small cap stocks, value stocks, venture capital, and bonds. As participants discuss the results, they come to see that the relationship between risk and return, which is well documented in the financial world, also holds in the grantmaking world. This exercise provides a way of opening up the risk-return dialogue so that trustees and staff can think about how much risk they can tolerate in relation to the kinds of effects they aspire to achieve.

Evaluating Types of Risk

In foundation-grantee conversations about risk, it's helpful to break the "what can go wrong?" question into three interdependent categories: (1) idea risk, (2) implementation risk, and (3) evidence risk (Bare, 2002).

- *Idea risk:* How clear, well-tested, and logical is the intervention idea?
- *Implementation risk:* What are the challenges to implementing the idea?
- *Evidence risk:* How difficult will it be to evaluate the idea's effectiveness or its implementation?

This is an elaboration of a longstanding distinction between theory failure and implementation failure. A theory—a grant idea or strategy—cannot be judged unless it is implemented with some fidelity. Good ideas can be rejected as ineffective when, in fact, they never get a fair test. Untangling idea risk and implementation risk is essential for foundations interested in improving their learning. In some cases, more conceptual work is needed to improve the theory of action. In others, more technical assistance is needed to help grantees execute. Considering evidence risk helps foundations and grantees get clear with each other about what can, should, and will be evaluated.

Exhibit 4.1 presents a list of factors that can affect each type of risk. Developed by the program staff of The John S. and James L. Knight Foundation, the list offers, in common language, several foundation-grantee discussions of potential hazards.

In the Knight Foundation's initiative to reduce youth violence and promote youth development, most grantees ran into hazards not accounted for in the grant proposal. A cumbersome purchasing process delayed one grantee's launch nearly a year. Another program was slowed by a common difficulty: not all of the local partners shared the same enthusiasm for the project. A program with support from multiple foundations had to change its design when the largest funder pulled out. At one site, a building that was intended to house part of the programming fell into serious disrepair. Leaders at another program became so immersed in creating an information-management system that they eventually became overwhelmed by the magnitude of their own database. They were not sure how to use the resource. If the foundation had included risk analysis as part of the grant development process, potential remedies might have been at hand.

EXHIBIT 4.1. RISK FACTORS.

Environmental turbulence: The conditions in which the foundation is working may be changing, due to instability within a given community or the fluid nature of a public issue.

Needs of the target population: Individuals, families, and neighborhoods with severe or multiple needs present foundations with greater challenges. Ongoing unmet needs may overwhelm gains.

Time horizon: Foundations find it difficult to pinpoint the time needed to produce desired changes. When foundations are impatient, they may miss opportunities. In other cases, pressures may cause them to support a nonperforming investment past the point at which adjustments might have worked.

Implementer's history: An organization's track record is no guarantee of future performance, but it is one element for foundations to consider.

Size of the investment: Foundation investments that carry large price tags or put the foundation's reputation on the line raise the prospect of special hazards.

Clarity of the logic model: Ambiguity regarding the desired outcomes and the proposed theory of action mean that different stakeholders are able to proceed under different assumptions. This makes it difficult to make adjustments when things get off track, given that there may be no consensus as to what "off track" means.

Sustainability: A question foundations often ask is, What happens when our funding ends? Failing to agree on a strategy for sustaining the program can cause hard feelings when a foundation and grantee part ways.

Degree of controversy: Hot-button issues draw enough attention that foundations and grant recipients find it hard to work through problems and give ideas a fair test. Further, stakeholders are more likely to base decisions on values, not on program results documented through evaluation.

Complexity: Cumbersome investments and programs are more troublesome than elegant ones. Everyone likes to understand where the money is going and how the activities are associated with the desired outcomes.

Leadership: Leadership issues represent an entire field of study. Foundations must understand the formal and informal influence individuals exert over a program's design, implementation, and sustainability.

EXHIBIT 4.1. RISK FACTORS. *(continued)*

Novelty of the idea: New concepts bring their own types of problems. Foundations must attend to the special needs of untested ideas.

Nature of capacity needed: Foundations must always ask the question, Capacity for what? Capacity checklists are everywhere these days, but it requires careful thinking to understand the capacities needed for a particular mission.

Visibility of the effort: Programs that have the benefit of a quiet trial-and-error process may get a better test than programs for which every decision is part of a public debate.

Partners' relationships: Collaborations can be difficult to sustain through the staff and program changes that inevitably occur.

Number and nature of foundation investors: The greater the number of foundations involved, the more directions in which nonprofit organizations may be pulled.

Degree of consensus on advisory committees: Many foundations use advisory groups to increase their technical knowledge or their understanding of complex communities. These devices bring with them their own challenges, especially if buy-in and contributions must be sustained as roles change over time.

Degree of politicization: Situations that already are highly charged require foundations to make use of political skills instead of relying solely on the usual technical or grantsmanship skills.

Potential for negative side effects: The consequences of foundation efforts may include outcomes other than "no effect" or "positive effects." Foundations may support programs that cause harm, and foundations' own strategies have the potential to damage individuals, families, or communities.

Rifle-shot approach versus natural variation: Rarely does a single approach work identically for all populations in all situations at all moments in time. It diminishes risk to match subgroups with solutions that suit them.

Depth of knowledge base: Foundations working in areas where there is little practical or research experience run into challenges. Similarly, foundations that do not make use of existing knowledge may repeat mistakes.

Hidden assumptions: Foundations fail to be explicit about different scenarios and various programmatic options when they fail to recognize and test their assumptions.

Source: This list was developed by the John S. and James L. Knight Foundation. Printed with permission.

Conclusion

In this chapter, we've reviewed a number of ways in which foundation-grantee relationships can be strained at various points in the grantmaking process. Evaluation can be a particular source of strain and tension because it raises the stakes and evokes natural fears about being judged and found wanting. Clear and ongoing communications can alleviate some, but not all, of these fears. One focus we've suggested for strengthening honest, evaluative conversations between foundation staff and grantees is careful and ongoing risk analysis that promotes candor, shared learning, and contingency planning.

References

Backer, T. E., & Bare, J. (2002, March-April). Looking before leaping. *Foundation News & Commentary, 43*(2), 49–53.

Bare, J. (2002). Risk. *Evaluation Exchange, 8*(2), 9, 18.

Beierle, T. C. (2002). The quality of stakeholder-based decisions. *Risk Analysis, 22*(4), 739–750.

Heath, R. L., Bradshaw, J., & Lee, J. (2002). Community relationship building: Local leadership in the risk communication infrastructure. *Journal of Public Relations Research, 14*(4), 317–353.

Hooker, M. (1987, Spring). Moral values and private philanthropy. *Social Philosophy and Policy, 4*(2), 128–141.

Kunreuther, H. (2002). Risk and risk management in an uncertain world. *Risk Analysis, 22*(4), 655–664.

Longstaff, T. A., Haimes, Y. Y., & Sledge, C. (2002). Are we forgetting the risks of COTS products in wireless communications? *Risk Analysis, 22*(1), 1–6.

Patton, M. Q. (1994). Developmental evaluation. *Evaluation Practice, 15*(3), 347–358.

Patton, M. Q. (1997). *Utilization-focused evaluation: The new century text* (3rd ed.). Thousand Oaks, CA: Sage.

Patton, M. Q. (2001). Evaluation, knowledge management, best practices, and high quality lessons learned. *American Journal of Evaluation, 22*(3), 329–336.

Patton, M. Q. (2002). Teaching and training with metaphors. *American Journal of Evaluation, 23*(1), 93–98.

Schorr, L. (1999, September). Changing the rules: The key to expanding what works. *The Chronicle of Philanthropy, 11*(22), 42–43.

William and Flora Hewlett Foundation. (2001). *The Hewlett Foundation's approach to philanthropy.* Menlo Park, CA: Author.

CHAPTER FIVE

EVALUATION AS A DEMOCRATIZING PRACTICE

Jennifer C. Greene, Ricardo A. Millett,
and Rodney K. Hopson

Brief snapshots of program initiatives in three hypothetical foundations anchor this presentation of a democratizing vision for evaluation in philanthropy. In this vision, evaluation serves to promote philanthropic programs that meaningfully redress inequities and injustices in our social system and holds philanthropy accountable for doing the same. After opening with these snapshots, the discussion returns to them several times to illustrate both the conceptual and practical arguments being advanced. In the conceptual arguments, the case for an explicitly democratic approach to evaluation is developed. The case is also made for evaluation that serves educational aims by seeking not simple answers to questions about a few program outcomes but rather better understanding of the complexities of social interventions in their varied contexts. Challenges to foundation leadership in promoting this democratic and learning-oriented approach to evaluation are then offered—challenges that recount the uneven historical legacy of American philanthropy in addressing social issues of race, class, and equality. In the latter half of the chapter, three principles of practice are offered for this democratic and educational vision of evaluation, along with illustrative strategies and guidelines for each.

Foundation Snapshots: The Large City Foundation, the Historic American Foundation, and the Local Community Foundation

Snapshot 1: The visionary new leadership of the Large City Foundation recently committed unparalleled resources to help the city address the problem of the "ghettoization" of the poor in public housing. Too many poor people—far too many of whom are people of color—live in these cloistered high-rise factories of despair and hopelessness, where drugs, crime, family dysfunction, and unemployment find fertile ground to breed and replicate their devastating effects from generation to generation. In a bold transformative initiative, the Large City Foundation has allocated significant grants to the city, to nonprofit organizations, and to other community-based stakeholders working in public housing. With these funds, grantees are challenged to find effective ways to identify and build sustainable alternatives to public housing ghettos and to engage in a citywide relocation process for the city's public housing tenants—a process that would also enable these tenants to learn to live in newly integrated neighborhoods, to get relevant employment training, and to become self-sufficient. The new leaders of the foundation wonder, "What kinds of programs are likely to be most successful in achieving these objectives? What approaches are most likely to meaningfully catalyze public housing tenants to take advantage of these new housing opportunities, to garner support by others, and to realize the dream of decent housing for all city residents?"

Snapshot 2: The Historic American Foundation has long dedicated significant resources to improving health-care access and quality care in the country (and indeed around the world). The last two decades in the United States have been a nightmare for this foundation, given the exponential growth in health-care costs, the takeover of many community-based clinics by large HMOs, and the loss of too many clinicians to other locations and other careers. To interrupt and possibly reverse these trends, five years ago the Historic American Foundation initiated an innovative educational program for U.S. health-care practitioners of all ranks and previous training and experience. In exchange for a seven-year commitment to practice health care in urban and rural neighborhoods of greatest need—neighborhoods of the poor, again too many of whom are people of color—the foundation fully funds two to four years of medical education that is individually tailored to the learner and fully equips and maintains health clinics as sites of both training and employment. Given the significant costs of this program, the leadership of the Historic American Foundation wants to know, "Is this innovative, individually tailored medical education program working to reverse the exodus of qualified medical personnel from communities of greatest need? Are broader structural changes in our nation's health-care system needed, in addition to or instead of this effort? What is the quality of the medical education being provided? What aspects of the program need improvement or redirection?"

Snapshot 3: The Local Community Foundation is committed to honoring a recent bequest to provide adequate food on a sustainable basis for *all* members of the community. "The tragedies of hunger and malnutrition are unconscionable in our beloved community and must be fought until they are vanquished," stipulated the conditions of the bequest. The Local Community Foundation is currently engaged in an experimental four-year partnership with a local religious coalition, which has long fed the hungry through soup kitchens and emergency food packages, as one approach to creating a long-term, adequate food supply and distribution system in the community. Foundation leaders and board members are wondering, "How well is this partnership going? Is it a good idea? What are community perceptions of The Local Community Foundation and its work in the sustainable food sector? Is this just business as usual, or is it in some important way, business as unusual?"

Envisioning an Educative and Democratizing Evaluation Practice

The questions in the foundation snapshots about the potential of these foundations' creative initiatives to effect significant and sustainable changes in people's lives are all evaluation questions. At root, the questions address the likely value and worthiness of these foundations' endeavors to make life better for a given group of people and thus to improve our collective social life. Evaluation has a long tradition of contributing to social betterment through empirically based judgments about the viability and benefits of social innovations. As part of this tradition, the evaluation community has developed many conceptual tools and practical methods of gathering, analyzing, and interpreting data.

Our methods are diverse; they include familiar quantitative surveys and comparative designs, alongside qualitative life history interviews and case study designs. *But* evaluation is not simply a matter of method and design. It is also, inherently and fundamentally, a matter of politics and values. This is because evaluation is *politically* located in social contexts; it is both shaped by the political relationships and power dynamics that characterize a given context and, in turn, influences the contours and future character of these relationships

(House and Howe, 1999). So the critical questions become not only which evaluation approaches and methods should be used in a given context but which political positions and whose values should be advanced in the social practice of evaluation.

In the snapshots, for example, how can evaluation meaningfully address legitimate questions about the attainment of desired changes in people's lives, as identified by program visionaries and developers, *as well as* critical questions about the people's lives in and of themselves—about how and why they lack adequate housing, medical care, and food; about what is needed to redress these injustices; and, specifically, about what a particular program offers that could make a meaningful difference in people's daily lives. These are all compelling and valid demands on evaluation. They are demands that are fully entangled with the complex relationships of power and privilege that characterize our contemporary society. And thus the evaluation enterprise is as well.

Given these entanglements, we disclaim any possibility of positioning evaluation in some politically neutral, detached, disengaged space. Rather, we aim in this chapter to position evaluation within its honored tradition of policy education and political enlightenment. Even more important, we aim to stretch this tradition toward democratic ideals. We do so by initially re-emphasizing the educative vision of evaluation; then we extend this vision to a democratic one in which evaluation challenges of privilege, power, and authority can be mitigated by meaningful participation, voice, and engagement on the part of program beneficiaries and their communities. We next argue that foundations are vitally important vehicles for realizing this educative and democratizing vision of evaluation. And finally, we translate these conceptual arguments into practice by offering key principles and concrete strategies for conducting educative, democratizing evaluations of foundation programs.

Evaluation as Education

In the tradition of evaluation as education, empirical data are used to enlighten and educate interested decision makers, program developers, media journalists, and citizenry about the nitty-gritty realities of our persistent social problems and the daily lived experiences of people caught in their web. The late Lee Cronbach, along with Carol Weiss, was a lifetime advocate for the educational potential of evaluation to contribute to our understanding of social problems and how best to address them. The "ninety-five evaluation theses" figuratively nailed to the wall in Cronbach and Associates' classic 1980 proclamation, *Toward Reform of Program Evaluation*, include the following (pp. 2–11):

- The evaluator is an educator; his [or her] success is to be judged by what others learn.
- Program evaluation is a process by which society learns about itself.
- Program evaluation should contribute to enlightened discussion of alternative plans for social action.

Our vision of evaluation is an educative one, consistent with the noble aspirations of Cronbach and Weiss, whereby evaluation helps society to better understand its social problems and to craft better plans for social change.

In an educative evaluation of The Large City Foundation's bold housing initiative (Shapshot 1), for example, interested audiences could learn about what it is like to live in "the projects" (perhaps through descriptions of the daily lives of selected tenants), or about housing choices currently available to the city's poor, or about how this current initiative is similar to past ones—whether "same old, same old" or a meaningfully different plan for social action.

Democratic Values in Evaluation

We also stretch this educative vision along two explicitly democratic pathways, aiming for evaluation studies that are both educative *and* democratizing. Along the first such pathway, we broadly embrace democratic ideals of equity, fairness, and social justice as the explicit value commitments of our evaluation approach, in consonance with other contemporary evaluation theorists and practitioners (Hood, 1998; Hopson, 2001; House and Howe, 1999; MacDonald, 1978; Mertens, 1999; Whitmore, 1998). Although democracy and evaluation are not strangers, open value commitments remain rare events in evaluation practice (Greene, 1997a). To explicitly embrace such democratic values implies the intentional *inclusion* of all legitimate stakeholder perspectives and stances, for this is democratically fair and just. To so do also implies significant *participation* by stakeholders in the evaluation process, as one step toward redressing past and continuing inequities. And in particular, to serve democratic ideals in evaluation further implies serious *engagement* with the challenges of contemporary difference and diversity in today's society, for a genuine acceptance of difference is fundamental to democratic justice in the United States in this new millennium.

A democratizing evaluation of The Historic American Foundation's health education initiative (Snapshot 2), for example, would seek both statistics and stories about well-being and illness in communities underserved by our health-care system; an inclusive evaluation practice situates board members and health-care experts alongside recent immigrants with chronic diseases and mothers whose only physician is the city hospital's emergency room.

The Use of Authentic Knowledge

Along our second democratic extension of the educative tradition of evaluation, we intentionally give preference to the daily lives, experiences, and standpoints of the people who are the intended beneficiaries of the program being evaluated. We emphasize these not to silence other standpoints but rather to juxtapose, in creative tension, diverse yet equally legitimate ways of experiencing and knowing about the world. We assume that program beneficiaries are authors of their own life stories, even under stark economic and political legacies of scarcity and discrimination, but that their stories are too rarely written and even more rarely listened to. We assume, in particular, that people who are the intended beneficiaries of social interventions have valuable self-understanding, are knowledgeable about their own lives, and aspire to a better life but are rarely consulted when interventions directed toward this better life are being created or designed. Indeed, our educative and democratizing vision of evaluation can serve in an important way to test and to challenge the assumptions on which policy initiatives are envisioned and program interventions developed.

We believe evaluation can do so by generating *authentic knowledge* about our social problems and programs—knowledge that is not only grounded in and thus credibly represents the daily lives of those the program is designed to serve but also privileges the experiences and perspectives of participants' daily lives. *Conventional evaluative knowledge* offers an understanding of how well participants respond to a given social or educational program. *Authentic knowledge* offers an understanding of how well a program responds to the nitty-gritty realities of participants' daily lives. Both kinds of knowledge are themselves multiplistic, for diversity exists within all walks of life. Both kinds of knowledge are valuable, and both are needed. But, to date, authentic knowledge has been scarce. We believe the private foundation community in the United States is exceptionally well positioned to engage in a democratizing evaluation practice, with the specific aim of generating and legitimizing authentic knowledge. Absent the authentic, legitimized voices of the poor, the marginalized, the discriminated-against, we fear our social policies will continue to be misguided at best, and our evaluations will miss the point or, worse, serve the function of legitimizing the status quo.

In an evaluation of The Local Community Foundation's partnership to provide adequate food for all community residents (Snapshot 3), authentic knowledge would illuminate the experiences of those who have been hungry in this community, including the meanings of hunger to them and their choices of what, when, or even whether to eat. This knowledge would be respected as important, accepted as credible, and, in fact, serve as a key basis for judging the effectiveness of the foundation's efforts to abolish hunger in this community.

Knowledge and Power in Evaluation

To position evaluation as a democratizing social practice is to explicitly take up issues of power and privilege in contemporary American society. In our democratizing conceptualization of evaluation, issues of power and privilege are firmly embedded in the kinds of evaluation results expected or the kinds of evaluative knowledge claims to be generated. We again disavow the possibility of neutral, value-free knowledge claims and instead seek evaluative knowledge that is itself liberating in both form and substance.

This view of knowledge, or of what can be learned from an evaluation, rests on the assumption that social reality is, to a significant extent, socially constructed and reflects, in important ways, the cultural, political, and historical location of the knower as well as of the known. We further argue that, on a more fundamental level, there is a pervasive socialization process in our society that creates and legitimizes a dominant social reality. Historically molded, this dominant social reality includes a class system of economic privilege, which is anchored in a permanent "underclass," filled mostly with poor people of color—people born into institutionalized structures of racism and discrimination that even our most noble and idealistic social policies have failed to dismantle. Societal institutions then, as implementers of the existing social order, function largely to maintain and sustain it. Challenges by the less advantaged to change the order and the very definition of "advantaged and less advantaged" are uncommon events. This is because the socially constructed definitions of who is "deserving" of privilege and advantage and who is not have become so ingrained that most people unconsciously and unthinkingly act in ways that maintain the existing social order. Not only the privileged but the poor and disadvantaged behave in ways that, more often than not, are accepting of their societal status. It is in this manner that a collective social consciousness evolves over time that legitimizes and normalizes class and, by extension, racial differences; at the extreme, it normalizes the superiority of one class and race over another.

It is not an exaggeration to believe that evaluation has a liberating role to play in extricating society from this particular social construction of privilege and advantage. Given that evaluation inevitably advances certain values and interests and not others, it can either maintain and reinforce the existing system, or it can serve to challenge, disrupt, and strive to change the existing social order to one that is more equitable and just, more democratic. And one of the most important ways that evaluation can serve democratizing values is by generating and legitimizing multiple alternative constructions of reality, for instance, through diverse stories about people's daily experiences in different societal contexts and through varied judgments, arising from these different experiential contexts, about the quality and effectiveness of particular social policies and programs. Evaluation, that is, can generate knowledge that is fundamentally multicultural (Kirkhart, 1995), beneficial (Hilliard, 2002), and authentic (Millett, 2002).

Foundations as Leaders in Educative, Democratizing Evaluation

Martin Luther King Jr. once said, "Philanthropy is commendable, but it must not cause the philanthropist to overlook the circumstances of economic injustice that made philanthropy necessary" (often attributed to King but unconfirmed quotation).

We believe the philanthropic world is uniquely well positioned to actively and energetically promote an educative, democratizing vision of evaluation. We offer two main justifications for this stance. First, contemporary philanthropy, in general, embraces a broad social change agenda yet is relatively free from political allegiances that entrap and constrain its policy and financial decisions. More than any other social institution, foundations are suitably positioned to experiment with ways of reducing social disparities and inequalities. At minimum, foundations have a societal mandate and responsibility to contribute to the "public good," given their status as public trusts. Susan Wisely of the Lilly Endowment argues the following:

> Private foundations, whose work is largely unencumbered by the pressures of public opinion, must make a special effort to consider perspectives that differ from their own. Evaluation offers an opportunity to ask not only whether a program has made a difference, but also how wisely and well that difference accords with varying ideas of "the public good." (Wisely, 2002, p. 162)

Wisely further argues that foundations' hybrid mix of private funds to be used for public commitments raises special opportunities for them to be public centers of learning as means of fulfilling their obligations to improve the common good. By extension, we argue that to realize the common good requires the removal of systemic barriers to full societal participation for those historically and permanently relegated to an inferior societal status and that evaluation can play an educational and catalytic role in this process. With an educative, democratizing approach to evaluation, foundations can embrace a responsibility to legitimize and provide a space for the less advantaged in our society to tell their own stories, to educate others about life on the margins. With this evaluation approach, foundations can become centers of public learning about our persistent social problems and how best to address them, and thereby help to identify, highlight, and enact strategies to re-move institutionalized barriers to full political, economic, and social equity for those on the margins (see Bickel, Millett, and Nelson, 2002).

Second, the foundation community, like all others, can likely benefit from self-reflection on its own history of combating injustice and inequity in our society, and, concomitantly, consideration of a bold and intentional redirection of this his-torical course. Foundations, again like every other institution in our society, have an uneven legacy with respect to seriously engaging our nation's fractures of class, race, and ethnicity.

It is precisely this legacy that Mark Dowie (2001) addresses in a critique of philanthropy in the mid-twentieth century. Dowie's work documents how the "tim-ing and structure of notable philanthropic initiatives intended to ameliorate na-tional and international challenges . . . have had the effect, sometimes intentionally, of slowing down rather than accelerating progress" (p. xxviii). This *drag-anchor phil-anthropy*—a term coined after the device carried aboard sailboats to slow the boat's movement and counteract effects of strong winds, has served a dual and para-doxical function. Although preventing the larger vehicle from being blown off course (or shipwrecked in the worst case), the drag-anchor is also counterpro-ductive—slowing forward progress, sometimes considerably. Dowie's work focuses on the counterproductive character of drag-anchor philanthropy within founda-tion investments in civil rights and other social movements of the 1950s to the 1980s. Observing this phenomenon, former Ford Foundation program officer and Stern Family Fund executive director David Hunter, in a 1975 address to the annual meeting of the Council on Foundations, chided foundations for not being "close enough to critical and fundamental issues of our society . . . [and for being] too distant from the controversies that pervade our public discourse" (Hunter, 1975, cited in Dowie, 2001, p. 206). Our call for foundation self-reflection about their contributions to justice and equity in our society echoes Hunter's critique and Dowie's troubling record of drag-anchor philanthropy.

In an earlier and equally provocative argument, John Stanfield's work on phil-anthropy and Jim Crow in American social science (Stanfield, 1985) reveals a past that must be acknowledged and confronted if foundations are to continue their leadership in social betterment and democracy. Stanfield researched the role of financiers in the production of scientific knowledge about racial inequalities during the first half of the twentieth century. His research suggests that some fi-nanciers were part of a "fraternally oriented social circle" that actively supported and contributed to a Jim Crow societal structure.

Philanthropists and the administrators of their foundations constructed an elite status culture, which produced knowledge as a means of social control. They were not merely passive gatekeepers of knowledge waiting for ambitious re-searchers to submit their research proposals. More often than not (and contrary to the claims of official foundation histories), philanthropists and foundation of-ficers had their own ideas about the world and sought accommodating benefi-ciaries to carry them out. (Stanfield, 1985, p. 7)

In Stanfield's examination of the historical intersections of philanthropy, Jim Crow, and social-scientific knowledge production about racial inequalities, he was not suggesting (nor are we) that all foundations were blatantly and consciously racist. These were clearly few in number. Yet even the vast majority that were not racist often contributed to, undoubtedly without intention, the construction of a prejudicial reality "about race and the normative separation of the races in a rigid caste order" (1985, p. 8).

To illustrate and substantiate this argument, Stanfield examined the case of Booker T. Washington. Stanfield observed that many people of that time per-ceived Booker T. Washington as an important spokesperson for African Ameri-cans due to his fundraising prowess in establishing and funding industrial education in the South. And many did not recognize, then or even now, that Washington was sought as an "accommodating beneficiary" in contrast to oth-ers (such as Ida B. Wells, W.E.B. DuBois, and Marcus Garvey) who had more radical thoughts about the place of African descendants in the American society. To not understand that Washington's agenda was part and parcel of the agenda of Northern elites and Southern liberals would be naïve, considering the social context of the time, argued Stanfield.

It was not problematic for national magazine and newspaper editors, philan-thropists, and southern liberals to support effects like Booker T. Washington's edu-cational philosophy, which were tailored to the rural South and discouraged blacks from migrating north. It was easy and convenient for northern elites to have pater-nalistic and biological attitudes about blacks as a southern problem while ignoring small black populations in their own communities. (Stanfield, 1985, p. 7)

And as Dowie (2001) further reminds us, during the heyday of civil rights, de-spite the push by organizations such as the Congress of Racial Equality (CORE) and the Student Nonviolent Coordinating Committee (SNCC) to encourage uni-versal suffrage rights at the time, these organizations were perceived as radical and were "left out in the cold by these [mainstream] foundations, which routinely aban-doned organizations that projected black power sentiments" (p. 208).

In short, the many good intentions of the philanthropic community in times past may well have been undermined by "drag anchors" that were embedded in the very design of the intended good works—embedded in a few cases on purpose but in most cases from the more subtle, de facto, institutionalized racism inherent in the larger society. And foundation leaders may have had particular difficulty seeing this because philanthropists are society's elite. They are society's successful entrepreneurs—people who hold considerable power and reap significant benefits from the system as it currently is. They are thus more vulnerable to "overlooking the circumstances of economic injustice that made [their] philanthropy necessary" in the first place (from Martin Luther King Jr.), because such circumstances are so very foreign to their lives and their positions of political and especially economic power in the world. Our self-reflective challenge to foundations, as leaders of contemporary agendas for democratizing social change, is to ensure that their work advances the interests of justice and equity, even when such work is *not* in the interests of wealthy and elite institutions.

Back to the opening snapshots: with this vision for educative and democratizing evaluation, The Large City Foundation would put in the foreground the standpoints of public housing tenants in generating understanding and judgments about what kinds of innovative housing alternatives are likely to make a difference and how those housing alternatives need to be institutionally and politically legitimized. The Historic American Foundation would visit the communities of the health clinics it has funded and learn from residents about the character and quality of medical care available to them and how their lives are better supported, or not, by these health-care institutions and practitioners. And The Local Community Foundation would want to know about the experiences of hunger from those who had been hungry, or if and how their program is meaningfully alleviating those experiences of hunger, or if and how the program is contributing to further inequality and dependence.

Democracy, Knowledge, and Evaluation

In its most ideal participatory form, democracy is about equity of voice and power and about caring for those on the margins of society. Democratizing social and educational programs are thus fundamentally designed to redress historical imbalances of access, resources, opportunities, privileges, and power. This is commonly the social change agenda of foundations' investments in social programs. An educative, democratizing approach to evaluating such investments, then, seeks to understand how well such historical imbalances have been redressed, especially from the standpoints of those on the margins.

In short, we are promoting evaluation in philanthropy as an educative and democratizing practice through which society can learn about itself, particularly about the character of our persistent social problems *from the lived experiences of those who continue to suffer their injustices.* With this kind of authentic knowledge, in tandem with explicit commitments to democratic ideals, foundations can assert leadership in legitimizing and promulgating efforts at social change that disrupt the prevailing social order, that is, the current construction of social reality. Such efforts can lift the veil of commonly understood characterizations of the less advantaged as less deserving than others and offer them a genuine opportunity to influence the vision and design of interventions that are thereby more likely to impart important and sustainable social change. This is evaluation with a conscience and a commitment to action. It speaks to a new generation of philanthropy, where charities have had to face challenges to their effectiveness in a post-9/11 context, as well as to a new generation of programs that enable Americans to truly engage with diversity and accept difference, both in their back yards and around the globe (Greene, 2002).

Educative, Democratizing Evaluation in Practice: Core Principles

We now turn to a discussion of how to enact this educative and democratizing vision of evaluation in practice. Our discussion centers around three interconnected major principles. We present and then elaborate each principle with illustrative guidelines, strategies, and examples from practice. We invite and welcome dialogue about our principles and about other ways to transform them into practice.

Principle 1

Educative, democratizing evaluations of foundation programs are intentionally and meaningfully engaged with, not detached from, the moral, political, and value dimensions of the social contexts being evaluated.

The argument in this chapter is premised on the stance that the social practice of evaluation is neither neutral nor benign. Rather, through the entanglement of knowledge and method with values and politics, evaluation inevitably advances certain worldviews and interests and not others. We further assert, along with many other contemporary social philosophers and critics (see, for example, Schwandt, 1989), that not only is it not possible for evaluative knowledge to be value-free, it is not desirable. A significant problem with Westernized social and political life today, argue these critics, is precisely the primacy of technological, rationalistic thinking that is intentionally stripped of its moral, ethical, and political dimensions. We have endless electronic gadgets and wondrous new inventions every day, but we have lost our moral compass and thus our moral pathway. To find our way again, we must recognize that our enduring social problems are not only technical problems that can be solved with new scientific knowledge and creative engineering; these are also challenges of the heart and the soul, of our most cherished values of equity and justice, of our collective commitment to the public good. To help find our way again, evaluation must fully engage with these challenges, values, and commitments, and evaluators must be positioned as scientific citizens, as stewards of the public good. And foundations can assuredly lead the way.

Principle 2

Educative, democratizing evaluations of foundation programs embrace liberatory or emancipatory frameworks for legitimizing multiple and diverse constructions of social reality. They must strive, not for a new hegemony or even for consensus but for an acceptance and understanding of diversity as intrinsically valuable to meaningful human action and democratic vitality.

We must begin to have some hard conversations about race and class, as well as about privilege and advantage. Our society is not the meritocracy it has long aspired to be. A few people, born into "disadvantaged" societal strata, make it out and are successful by varied standards of success. But most never have the chance. And it is *not* their fault! Blame-the-victim and deficit models for social change have radically misunderstood the ways in which opportunity in contemporary society is structured less by individual aspiration than by family history, neighborhood schooling, community safety, employment prospects—and thus by class and race.

Frameworks for science, for knowledge, for action that acknowledge these realities *and find them insupportable*, must be embraced as guides for foundation evaluation practice. With such frameworks, foundation evaluation would *begin with* a critical questioning of assumptions and stances. What does this particular policy or program initiative assume about the lives of people it is intended to affect? Where do such assumptions come from? Have the people who are the intended beneficiaries been active contributors to this initiative? In what ways are their "theories of change" represented in the initiative? In what way is the initiative responsive to context and respectful of diversity? To what extent does the initiative endeavor to change the system and not (just) the people?

There are many inquiry frameworks that would be consonant with this evaluation principle. Again, the point is not to advance any particular framework but to advance a critical, questioning stance. Possibly consonant frameworks include social constructionism (as briefly described earlier in this chapter), the critical urban ethnography of social researchers such as Michelle Fine and Lois Weis (Fine, Weis, Weseen, and Wong, 2000), the emancipatory evaluation framework of Donna Mertens (1998, 1999), and the culturally responsive evaluation approaches of Henry Frierson, Stafford Hood, Ricardo Millett, and Rodney Hopson (Hood, 1998; Hopson, 1999; Millet, 2002).

Principle 3

Educative, democratizing evaluations of foundation programs are accountable to social justice and equity; the evaluations are to be judged by how well they advance these democratic ideals.

Meta-evaluation is the evaluation of evaluations, seeking to assess the merit and worth or the value of a given evaluation study. Criteria for judging the value of evaluations remain contested but characteristically focus on methodological quality and the utility or relevance of the work conducted. The evaluation standards of the Joint Committee, for example, include utility, accuracy, feasibility, and propriety (Joint Committee on Standards for Educational Evaluation, 1981). But, by whatever criteria, meta-evaluation that goes beyond methodological wrangling is an uncommon event, especially on the public stage. There are some wonderful exceptions, notably the late Eleanor Farrar and Ernie House's critique of AIR's (American Institutes of Research) evaluation of Jesse Jackson's Push-Excel program (Farrar and House, 1983) and Bob Stake's moving critique of how evaluation "quieted the reforms" envisioned by the Cities-in-Schools Program (Stake, 1986). These are wonderful exceptions, precisely because they struggle with the question, To whom is the evaluator most importantly accountable?

With this third principle of educative, democratizing evaluation, we assert that evaluators should be accountable primarily to the ideals of equity and social justice and thus to the people whose lives fall short of these ideals. The evaluation community does recognize that its responsibilities often extend beyond a given client to the "general welfare and public good." But recognition does not equal support or action. Herein, we offer a call to action, and we again encourage foundations to lead the way. Some practical elaboration of each of these principles, with examples, follows.

An Engaged Evaluation Practice

Historically, evaluators have sought distance and objectivity in their work. Yet distance does not ensure relevance or utility of the evaluation. Rather, "influence comes from engagement, not detachment" (Cronbach and Associates, 1980, p. 53).

We next offer some practical strategies that can help evaluators to actively engage in the social contexts being evaluated, particularly with the often messy and complex political and value dimensions of these contexts. These strategies are written as possible guidelines for foundation evaluators.

• *Publicly acknowledge democratic value commitments.* Openly acknowledge and explicitly define for that particular context the democratic values and ideals that are framing and steering the evaluation. Publicly locate the evaluation as one that is mainly value-engaged rather than one that is seeking causal knowledge or trying to inform policy or program decisions, to improve an organization, or to render a holistic understanding of that context (Greene, 2000). These other evaluation purposes may well be served by this evaluation, but its primary purpose is democratization. And the specific meanings of democratization in that context must be engaged and articulated.

• *Be inclusive; legitimize voice.* Include the perspectives and value stances of all legitimate stakeholders in the evaluation. Provide a space for diverse stakeholders to voice their understandings, experiences, and perspectives on the program being evaluated *and* on the social conditions that gave rise to this social program. To guarantee fairness in this inclusiveness, special efforts must be taken to ensure that the experiences and stances of the least advantaged are equitably represented and respectfully heard. Such efforts may include holding separate discussions about concerns and interests for each stakeholder group (Guba and Lincoln, 1989), making sure that the least advantaged stakeholders make up the majority in all cross-stakeholder discussions about evaluation priorities (Mathison, 1996), using more literate or well-spoken advocates to speak with and for the least advantaged in evaluative discussions (House and Howe, 1999), and providing for less advantaged stakeholders advance coaching and opportunities to practice articulating and advancing their own perspectives (MacNeil, 2002). Inclusiveness and voice can be realized or enacted both in the processes used to design, implement, and interpret the evaluation *and* in the technical methods or tools of the evaluator. Many qualitative methods, for example, explicitly seek diversity and contextuality of understanding.

• *Feature portraits and stories of participants and the world they live in.* As just noted, qualitative methods can be especially valuable in illuminating and giving "voice" to the perspectives of program beneficiaries. Ethnographic methods in particular can generate rich and deep portraits and narrative understandings of program participants' daily experiences in specific social, economic, and cultural contexts (Agar, 2000). With Hopson's notions of the "ethnoevaluator" (Hopson, 2002), these portraits and narratives can further illuminate the contributions and connections of philanthropic program initiatives to participants' daily lives.

• *Use participatory evaluation processes.* Beyond inclusiveness and voice, design an evaluation process that incorporates active and meaningful stakeholder participation, especially in evaluative decisions related to what questions will be addressed and what follow-up actions are implied by the evaluation findings (Greene, 1997b). Participation can take the form of an evaluation advisory board with decision authority, an evaluation team composed of diverse stakeholders with responsibility for implementing the evaluation (Whitmore, 1998), periodic public forums in which diverse stakeholders are involved and in which issues surfacing in the evaluation are publicly aired and discussed and the evaluation is redirected as appropriate (Greene, Bowen, and Goodyear, 1997). The evaluation can also include discrete evaluation activities that are meaningfully participatory, for example, a village sample survey or a discussion of interim evaluation findings. Ana Coghlan (1998), for example, conducted a variety of such participatory activities within her overall nonparticipatory evaluation of an AIDS education program in Uganda.

• *Conduct an explicit values inquiry.* Mark, Henry, and Julnes (2000) offer a systematic process of empirical inquiry into diverse stakeholder values related to the program being evaluated as one way of ensuring that values are explicitly surfaced and engaged as part of an evaluation process. Using surveys, interviews, or even electronic data-gathering techniques, evaluators can take the "value pulse" of a context and incorporate these findings into the rest of the evaluative process. Henry's work in values inquiry related to a statewide evaluation of the Georgia Pre-K educational initiative is exemplary in this regard (Henry, 2002).

To return again to the snapshots that opened this chapter, how could an evaluator be engaged with the moral, political, and value dimensions of The Large City Foundation's bold initiative to replace ghettoized public housing developments with decent, affordable, and sustainable housing alternatives for the city's poor? As one illustration, this evaluator could constitute an evaluation advisory board, made up of representatives from the foundation, the city housing authority, community advocacy groups (for example, for tenants' rights), public housing tenants, urban and community development experts, and practitioners. Tenants could constitute the majority of the members on this advisory board. The board could be empowered with critical decision-making authority for the evaluation—an authority implemented via regular meetings in which the evaluator presents for discussion *and* action-decisions important substantive issues, preliminary evaluation plans, draft evaluation methods or instruments, ongoing findings and results, and possible directions for policy and action. Diversity of experience, perspective, and values would be expected to surface during board discussions and interactions. Issues surely to be contested in such a context are the meanings of racial integration, the importance of and influences on property values, and the desired residential character of urban neighborhoods. The board's overall mission would be to seek the most democratic (equitable, just, fair) stances and actions on such issues in this particular context. Meetings of the advisory board would be facilitated by a highly skilled group facilitator under a set of guidelines for interaction agreed to by all at the outset. Meetings would be held in or near public housing, so tenants and advocates could easily attend. As needed, child care, meals, and transportation would be provided for board members. All board meetings, associated costs, and the actual work time of board members would be paid for by the evaluation budget.

A Critical Evaluation Practice: Toward Acceptance of Diversity

With our second principle of educative, democratizing evaluation practice, we are advancing the adoption of a critical framework for evaluation as a catalyst for *engaging with the differences* that are critical today in public debates about public issues—differences of perspective, experience, values, and political ideology, *and* differences of privilege, power, prestige, and possibility. As discussed previously, meaningful engagement with difference rests on a legitimization of *authentic knowledge,* that is, knowledge about social problems and programs of interest that is grounded in the daily lives of those the program is designed to serve. Authentic knowledge and other forms of knowledge are all to be respected in this evaluation practice. Here are some ideas for enacting this principle.

• *Model respectful, reciprocal interactions with others and acceptance of difference in the evaluation process itself.* Use the evaluation practice to establish relationships and interactions in the evaluation that are themselves open and accepting of diversity and difference. Evaluation is a social practice; it takes place in the messy, contingent, unpredictable world of human action and interaction and therefore inevitably partakes of the relationships of that everyday world. In fundamental ways, these relationships help to constitute the very knowledge that is generated in evaluation—our results, our findings, our judgments of program quality. Hence, what is taught and learned in evaluation is not just information about the program but also information about relationships, particularly about the normative and political dimensions of relationships—notably, trust, reciprocity, and caring and respect, tolerance, and acceptance (Greene, 2003). Evaluators can expressly seek to interact with various program stakeholders and to develop relationships that model norms of acceptance and reciprocity and an ethic of respect for difference.
• *Include "visiting" activities as part of the evaluation process and design.* To enact an evaluation as a site for engendering better understanding of others different from ourselves and deeper acceptance of such differences, an evaluator may well in-

vent creative ways in which stakeholders can "visit" with one another. "Visiting," says Hannah Arendt, is grounded in the assumption that difference is not a threat to social life. Instead, the web of human diversity is viewed as a prerequisite for meaningful, defensible, good action and sound judgment (Biesta, 2001). Moreover, to use this web of human diversity as enabling of meaningful action and judgment, to develop an appreciation for and understanding of the viewpoints of others, Arendt advocates "visiting" and "listening well" to others. Arendt's notions of visiting, as presented by others, include the following:

> Visiting involves constructing stories of an event from each of the plurality of perspectives that might have an interest in telling it and imagining how I would respond as a character in a story very different from my own. (Biesta, 2001, p. 397)

> Visiting involves carefully listening to the perspectives of others because [in the words of Arendt, 1968], "the more people's standpoints I have present in my mind while I am pondering a given issue . . . the better I can [judge and act]." (Coulter and Wiens, 2002, p. 18)

> Visiting is therefore *not* to see through the eyes of someone else, but to see *with your own eyes* from a position that is not your own . . . in a story very different from [your] own. (Biesta, 2001, p. 398)

Visiting activities in an evaluation could include key stakeholder interviews of one another, one stakeholder "shadowing" or following after another as she or he goes about daily life, or observational visits to the "other side of town" by various stakeholders—to cultural events, sports activities, or to the corner café or local bar. Visitors could report on their visits to gatherings of stakeholders, perhaps through narrative or video or performance modes, followed by facilitated discussions of what was learned anew. Many other ideas for "visiting" can well be created and tailored to specific contexts.

• *Use a "search conference" process as part of evaluation planning, implementation, or both.* A search conference (Emery and Purser, 1996) is a facilitated group process for reflections on relevant (group, program, or organizational) history and sharing of views on current practice and changes needed therein. Search conferences intentionally embrace diversity as a cornerstone of contemporary life and use processes that meaningfully engage with difference without striving for consensus or agreement.

• *Use "dialogues" as part of the evaluation process.* From the work of Gadamer, Bahktin, and others, "dialogue" is understood as a form of verbal interaction with others, where the intent is to better understand the viewpoints of the other through putting one's own preconceptions at risk (Schwandt, 2002). In other words, dialogues are a particular form of respectful, caring communication in which participants are open to learning about others *and* about themselves. In evaluation, dialogues can take place at many different points in the process, including planning, implementation, and sharing of results (Abma, 2001a). For example, Tineke Abma (2001b) has used "story workshops" as dialogic engagements with difference. In these workshops, results from an evaluation study (specifically, results that offer contrasting and divergent understandings of a program) are captured in brief narrative stories and then shared with service professionals in other settings as catalysts for meaningful discussion and dialogue.

• *Use program theories or logic models as ways to explicate and engage varied program assumptions, value stances, and political commitments among diverse stakeholders.* Fundamental to seriously respecting difference is to understand and to have the safe space to challenge diverse assumptions about the nature of the social problem being addressed and the program designed to address it. Articulating the theory or logic of the program from diverse perspectives—what problem is being addressed, what is the cause of this problem, why it is that these activities are likely to meaningfully address this cause, what outcomes can be expected—is an important vehicle for engaging with difference. Particularly in the educative, democratizing form of evaluation being advanced herein, engaging with diverse program logics may be an especially powerful way to meaningfully engage with and foster acceptance of difference. Strategies for and approaches to program theory articulation are plentiful (see United Way [1996]; W. K. Kellogg Foundation [2000]; Rogers, Hacsi, Petrosino, and Huebner [2000]; and Weiss [1998], among others). Critical to this idea is the importance of engaging not only the question of how and why this program responds to people's lives but the question of how and why people's lives make sense of and room for this program—or why they do not.

Returning again to our opening snapshots, how might an evaluator craft her or his practice so as to foster an acceptance and understanding of diversity as intrinsically valuable to meaningful human action and democratic vitality, within an evaluation of The Historic American Foundation's initiative to retain, even attract, qualified medical practitioners to communities of greatest need? Part of this evaluation process could involve the development, exchange, and dialogue about program theories, constructed from diverse stakeholder perspectives. And part of the process of program theory development could involve visiting, such that stakeholders participate in developing the program theories of each other. That is, a resident of a community in need of better medical care could visit a stakeholder who resides in a community with adequate medical care and learn about what it is like to get health care in this other community. And vice versa. Each stakeholder could report on the chain of conditions, assumptions, activities, and outcomes (the program theory) that characterizes the health-care services in the community of the other. Dialogue about these different program theories and their applicability to the foundation program being evaluated could then productively ensue.

An Accountable Evaluation Practice

Finally, what are some practical strategies for enacting our third principle of educative, democratizing evaluation practice—that of judging evaluation itself by how well it advances democratic ideals of equity and social justice?

• *Incorporate meta-evaluation as an important part of the evaluation process.* With rare exceptions (Scriven, 1991; Stake, 1986), meta-evaluation—an evaluation of the evaluation being conducted—is not routinely included as part of evaluation practice. Evaluators often encourage accountability, self-reflection, and critique on the part of others but less frequently engage in such activities themselves. With meta-evaluation, evaluators can engage in thoughtful self-critique themselves. With meta-evaluation expressly conducted on criteria of equity and justice, evaluators can advance democratizing aims.

• *Encourage reflexivity and self-critique, especially in foundation sponsors and leaders.* A key component of a meta-evaluative process can be an opportunity for foundation sponsors and leaders to critique their own program priorities and concomitant evaluation requirements from the perspective of how well these promote greater equity and justice in this particular context. All persons of privilege in this society are vulnerable to continued complicity in prejudicial policies and discriminatory practices. An evaluation process that insists on reflexivity and self-critique is one response to such vulnerability. This could be accomplished in writing as in reflective journals, in conversation, or in other forums or genres.

• *Promote evaluation capacity building in stressed neighborhoods, with people disadvantaged by the current system, so that they can become the evaluators.* Evaluation is not inherently the province of the white, educated liberal. Enhancing the capacity of those targeted by foundation social interventions to conduct evaluation themselves or to be significant partners with outsiders in evaluation is another way to promote democratically rooted judgments of evaluation quality. This could be a key leverage point of democratic evaluation, in that it goes beyond participation to enable participants to conduct their own evaluations, based on their own criteria of quality, in the present and in the future.

One final return to our snapshots: How can the evaluator of The Local Community Foundation's effort to address hunger in that community be accountable to democratic ideals of equity and justice? A key idea here is to conduct or commission or enable a meta-evaluation using as core criteria the democratic ideals of justice and equity. The key question to be addressed in such a meta-evaluation is, How well did this evaluation enhance or contribute to greater equity and justice in this context? Multiple and diverse stakeholders could participate in such a meta-evaluation (thus enhancing their own evaluation capacity), perhaps facilitated by an outsider. Reflective dialogues about the quality of the evaluation could well complement dialogues about the quality of the foundation's hunger initiative itself, forming an even stronger conjuncture of democratizing engagements and actions.

Conclusion

The most powerful means we have for effecting long-term meaningful change in society is education. With enhanced knowledge, skills, and self-awareness, people can become active, self-sufficient agents in their own lives and contributing, caring citizens in their communities. American philanthropy has long been a leader in advancing education in the service of social change. With the vision of evaluation we have presented herein, American philanthropy can strengthen this tradition of leadership by committing to a process of assessment and critique that is itself fundamentally educative in the service of democratic ideals.

References

Abma, T. A. (Guest Ed.) (2001a). Dialogue in evaluation (special issue). *Evaluation, 7*(2).

Abma, T. A. (2001b). Evaluating palliative care: Facilitating reflexive dialogues about an ambiguous concept. *Medicine, Health Care, and Philosophy, 4,* 261–276.

Agar, M. H. (2000). Border lessons: Linguistic "rich points" and evaluative understanding. In R. K. Hopson (Ed.), *How and why language matters in evaluation.* New Directions for Evaluation, no. 86. San Francisco: Jossey-Bass.

Bickel, W., Millett, R. A., & Nelson, C. A. (2002, March-April). The civic mandate to learn. *Foundation News and Commentary, 43*(2), 42–46.

Biesta, G.J.J. (2001). How difficult should education be? *Educational Theory, 51*(4), 385–400.

Coghlan, A. T. (1998). *Empowerment-oriented evaluation: Incorporating participatory evaluation methods to empower Ugandan communities to prevent HIV/AIDS.* Unpublished dissertation, Department of Human Service Studies, Cornell University, Ithaca, NY.

Coulter, D., & Wiens, J. R. (2002). Educational judgment: Linking the actor and the spectator. *Educational Researcher, 31*(4), 15–25.

Cronbach, L. J., & Associates. (1980). *Toward reform of program evaluation.* San Francisco: Jossey-Bass.

Dowie, M. (2001). *American foundations: An investigative history.* Cambridge, MA: MIT Press.

Emery, M., & Purser, R. E. (1996). *The Search Conference: A powerful method for planning organizational change and community action.* San Francisco: Jossey-Bass.

Farrar, E., & House, E. R. (1983). The evaluation of Push/Excel: A case study. In A. S. Bryk (Ed.), *Stakeholder-based evaluation.* New Directions for Program Evaluation, no. 17. San Francisco: Jossey-Bass.

Fine, M., Weis, L., Weseen, S., & Wong, L. (2000). For whom? Qualitative research, representations, and social responsibilities. In N. K. Denzin & Y. S. Lincoln (Eds.), *Handbook of qualitative research* (2nd ed., pp. 107–131). Thousand Oaks, CA: Sage.

Greene, J. C. (1997a). Evaluation as advocacy. *Evaluation Practice, 18,* 25–35.

Greene, J. C. (1997b). Participatory evaluation. In L. Mabry (Ed.), *Evaluation and the postmodern dilemma: Advances in program evaluation* (Vol. 3, pp. 171–189). Greenwich, CT: JAI Press.

Greene, J. C. (2000). Understanding social programs through evaluation. In N. K. Denzin & Y. S. Lincoln (Eds.), *Handbook of qualitative research* (2nd ed., pp. 981–999). Thousand Oaks, CA: Sage.

Greene, J. C. (2003, January). *The educative potential of educational evaluation.* Keynote address presented at the *Primer Congreso de Evaluacion, Universidad Autonoma de Nuevo Leon* (First Evaluation Conference, The Autonomous University of Nuevo Leon), Monterrey, Mexico.

Greene, J. C., Bowen, K., & Goodyear, L. (1997, June). *LGBT resource office program review, final report.* Cornell University, Ithaca, NY.

Greene, S. G. (2002, September 5). In disaster's wake: Charities missed opportunities to win confidence, experts say. *Chronicle of Philanthropy,* pp. 4–11.

Guba, E. G., & Lincoln, Y. S. (1989). *Fourth generation evaluation.* Thousand Oaks, CA: Sage.

Henry, G. T. (2002). Choosing criteria to judge program success. *Evaluation, 8*(2), 182–204.

Hilliard, A. (2002, April). *Beneficial educational research: Assumptions, paradigms, definitions.* Paper presented at the annual meeting of the American Educational Research Association, New Orleans.

Hood, S. (1998). *Responsive evaluation Amistad style: Perspectives of one African-American evaluator.* Paper presented at the Robert E. Stake Symposium on Educational Evaluation. Champaign, IL: University of Illinois.

Hopson, R. K. (1999). Minority issues in evaluation revisited: Reconceptualizing and creating opportunities for institutional change. *American Journal of Evaluation, 20,* 445–451.

Hopson, R. K. (2001). Global and local conversations on culture, diversity, and social justice in evaluation: Issues to consider in a 9/11 era. *American Journal of Evaluation, 22*(3), 375–380.

Hopson, R. K. (2002). Making (more) room at the evaluation table for ethnography: Contributions to the responsive constructivist generation. In K. E. Ryan & T. A. Schwandt (Eds.), *Exploring evaluator role and identity.* Westport, CT: Information Age.

House, E. R., & Howe, K. R. (1999). *Values in evaluation and social research.* Thousand Oaks, CA: Sage.

Hunter, D. (1975). *Plenary address.* Council on Foundations, Chicago.

Joint Committee on Standards for Educational Evaluation. (1981). *Standards for evaluations of educational programs, projects, and materials.* New York: McGraw-Hill.

Kirkhart, K. (1995). Seeking multicultural validity: A postcard from the road. *Evaluation Practice, 16,* 1–12.

MacDonald, B. (1978). *Democracy and evaluation.* Norwich: Centre for Applied Research in Education, University of East Anglia.

MacNeil, C. (2002). Evaluator as steward of citizen deliberation. *American Journal of Evaluation, 23,* 45–54.

Mark, M. M., Henry, G. T., & Julnes, G. (2000). *Evaluation: An integrated framework for understanding, guiding, and improving policies and programs.* San Francisco: Jossey-Bass.

Mathison, S. (1996, November). *The role of deliberation in evaluation.* Paper presented at the annual meeting of the American Evaluation Association, Atlanta.

Mertens, D. (1998). Research methods in education and psychology: Integrating diversity and qualitative approaches. Thousand Oaks, CA: Sage.

Mertens, D. (1999). Inclusive evaluation: Implications of transformation theory for evaluation. *American Journal of Evaluation, 20,* 1–14.

Millett, R. A. (2002, June). Missing voices: A personal perspective on diversity in program evaluation. *Non-Profit Quarterly Newsletter.*

Rogers, P. J., Hacsi, T. A., Petrosino, A., & Huebner, T. A. (Eds.). (2000). *Program theory in evaluation: Challenges and opportunities.* New Directions for Evaluation, no. 87. San Francisco: Jossey-Bass.

Schwandt, T. A. (1989). Recapturing moral discourse in evaluation. *Educational Researcher, 18*(8), 11–16, 34.

Schwandt, T. A. (2002). *Evaluation practice reconsidered.* New York: Peter Lang.

Scriven, M. (1991). *Evaluation thesaurus* (4th ed.). Thousand Oaks, CA: Sage.

Stake, R. E. (1986). *Quieting reform: Social science and social action in an urban youth program.* Urbana, IL: University of Illinois Press.

Stanfield, J. H. (1985). *Philanthropy and Jim Crow in American social science.* Westport, CT: Greenwood Press.

United Way of America. (1996). *Measuring program outcomes: A practical approach.* Alexandria, VA: Author.

W. K. Kellogg Foundation. (2000). *Logic model development guide.* Battle Creek, MI: Author.

Weiss, C. H. (1998). *Evaluation* (2nd ed.). Upper Saddle River, NJ: Prentice Hall.

Whitmore, E. (Ed.). (1998). *Understanding and practicing participatory evaluation.* New Directions for Evaluation, no. 80. San Francisco: Jossey-Bass.

Wisely, D. S. (2002). Parting thoughts on foundation evaluation. *American Journal of Evaluation, 23*(2), 159–164.

CHAPTER SIX

INTEGRATING EVALUATION INTO FOUNDATION ACTIVITY CYCLES

Laura C. Leviton and William E. Bickel

The utility of evaluation is greatly strengthened if evaluative processes are well integrated into fundamental organizational routines. In foundations, there are no more fundamental routines than those associated directly or indirectly with grantmaking. These routines occur in cycles—some as short as the life of an individual grant, others that are much longer term. Within these cycles, key decision points can be identified—points that are crucial "organizational moments" for evaluative input. By *evaluation*, we mean a wide range of information-generation activities (well beyond the traditional assessment of program impact) that can support decision processes and learning in organizations (for example, Cooley and Bickel, 1986; Patton, 1997; Preskill and Torres, 1999).

This chapter describes foundation cycles and how evaluations fit into the cycles; it is intended both for evaluators and foundation staff. Evaluators are usually unfamiliar with philanthropy's special cycles, yet they need to know how they affect the timeliness and relevance of evaluation findings. And foundations are idiosyncratic organizations. Although we believe these cycles typify foundation work, the organizations may experience the cycles in very different ways. For this reason, the chapter is aimed at foundation officers, as well as evaluators. Although foundation officers often recognize these cycles once they are described, the officers are usually less familiar with the various purposes of evaluation and how to ensure that evaluation findings are integrated into foundation operations.

Paying careful attention to cycles in philanthropy can help evaluators produce timely and relevant information that can be used in a range of decisions that are at the core of the foundation's work. Our basic assumption is that information in the forms of evaluation, other research and policy analysis, advocacy debates, and media attention can contribute to grantmakers' decisions in a variety of ways (Leviton and Boruch, 1983; Weiss and Bucuvalas, 1980; Patton, 1997).

First, we discuss the foundation context in terms of seven core cycles that structure the grantmaking process. We then describe how five of these affect foundation work and how evaluation can play a role. We then treat grant and program life cycles separately, posing key questions about the program that can structure the conduct and use of evaluation and illustrating with two examples. Finally, we describe how these various cycles create challenges and opportunities for conducting and using evaluation effectively.

The Context of Grantmaking: Seven Cycles

In some ways, the cycles of foundation work are similar to those of the U.S. Congress, with its cycles of appropriation and amendments of legislation (Redman, 2000). There is also a similarity to the work of federal bureaucracies, with their cycles of regulation, oversight, procurement, and block granting (Rich and Zaltman, 1978). Philanthropic cycles differ from the public sector cycles, however, in that there tend to be far fewer opportunities for diverse kinds of information to be considered in decision making. This limited access is due to the discretionary nature of foundations—what Susan Wisely, former director of evaluation for The Lilly Endowment, has described as "public in regard, private in operation" (Wisely, 1993, p. 1). After all, access to public officials is mandated by law and approved by tradition; citizens expect responsiveness, even when they are displeased with the amount of responsiveness to information they provide or concerns they express. In contrast, private foundation money belonged to individual donors, to be used as dictated in their bequests and as directed by appointed boards. Foundation staff turn to trusted experts and information sources for what they need, and they do so on their own schedule; the choice is always optional. Under these circumstances, providing timely and diverse information can be a challenge.

Following are seven organizational cycles that affect evaluation in foundations.

1. *Life cycle of an individual grant.* This cycle is obvious, as grants are usually short term (for example, one to five years), with a starting and ending date, fi-

nite budget, and specific requirements about the use of the funds. Even the longer-term grants, such as those to provide core support to a nonprofit organization, often exemplify a life cycle. Although the cycle is obvious, the dynamics underlying the cycle are less obvious. One of the strongest forces in philanthropy is the need to manage expectations about how long and how much funding will be provided.

2. *Program life cycles.* The program life cycle will receive special attention in the next section. This cycle is not always synonymous with a grant life cycle, although it can be. For example, a foundation might give a grant to a nonprofit organization's services for battered women—"the battered women's program." However, the nonprofit organization's program may predate the grant and may continue in existence after the grant ends. Thus programs can either reflect short-term or long-term (many-year) cycles. Also, *program* is a term that many of the larger foundations apply to their own multigrant initiatives. These programs may be implemented by a variety of different nonprofit organizations. For example, the Active for Life Program of The Robert Wood Johnson Foundation (RWJF) funds nine large nonprofit organizations to implement the program, as well as a social marketing effort by AARP. These multigrant programs may fund individual grants across more than one grant cycle, but they are often relatively short term (one to five years).

3. *The annual payout cycle.* Private foundations are driven by the requirement to donate at least 5 percent of assets each year or face tax consequences. The pressures involved in this cycle are rarely visible to outsiders.

4. *Business cycles.* Foundations' investment income rises and falls with business conditions. Therefore, the required payout is larger or smaller in a given year, which in turn affects the need to say no to proposals. These cycles are usually longer term, as in the case of the economic boom market of the 1990s.

5. *The life cycles of individual nonprofit organizations.* Foundation-funded programs are embedded in organizations, most of which are nonprofits, with varying capacity to do the required work and resiliency to environmental hits such as funding and de-funding. Although not a cycle of philanthropy as such, the life cycle of nonprofits radically affects the work and is underrecognized by funders and evaluators alike. Life cycles for organizations are often long term, although many startup organizations have only a short lifespan.

6. *Board voting cycles.* Foundation boards may meet several times a year. The board approves both the award of individual grants and the general direction and emphasis of foundations. Increasingly, boards are demanding evaluation results, or staff use those results in preparing for board presentations.

7. *Waxing and waning of foundation interests and initiatives.* These may change relatively suddenly, as with a change in strategic objectives, or they can occur over

decades, as foundation boards and staff turn over and foundations learn about what can and cannot be done with grant initiatives.

How Cycles Affect Foundation Behavior

The first two cycles—the life cycles of individual grants and programs—are an obvious focus for evaluation and will receive detailed attention later. Perhaps it will come as a surprise, however, that many foundations devote little ongoing attention to these two cycles. In fact, most foundations in the past viewed their role as providing the resources, without much monitoring or interference. For many, this is still the pattern. The remaining five cycles are less obvious to outsiders but often drive philanthropic practice and can be profoundly affected by evaluation. We therefore attend to them first.

The Payout

The annual payout determines how the big picture looks for philanthropies for the coming year. Each year, the leadership must determine priorities for funding or revisit those priorities, and they must develop budgets for each priority area. (To some degree, many foundations are also "responsive" in that they entertain proposals outside their primary focus. But even for this purpose, they need to develop budgets.)

The priority-setting process in a foundation might work as follows. Assume that education, the environment, and the arts are the focus of foundation giving. In the bequests that helped to create the foundation, part of its budget was earmarked for specific institutions and activities. The remainder could go to existing initiatives or to new initiatives and strategies that are championed by foundation staff or board members. The treasurer or financial officer estimates the likely payout necessary, and budgets are generated for each area of emphasis. As the year progresses, the financial officer may need to revise estimates, given the grantmaking activity to date and the financial performance of the foundation's assets. The overall direction of the foundation may be an issue for board discussion during one identifiable meeting each year, or such decisions may accrete across board meetings.

Evaluation and other forms of evidence might have impact on these decisions in several ways, if the timing is right. For example, the foundation finds about midway through the year that the payout must slow down. Which types of initiatives can cope with more gradual funding? Should renewals of program initiatives have to meet a higher bar for performance? Or what if the payout must increase?

Where should it increase? In other words, where is the leverage for change, where are the most pressing human needs, and where might additional resources lead to more robust implementation of program initiatives?

Business Cycles

The amount of the payout changes over a business cycle, but expectations about the payout radically affect the behavior of grantmakers and grantees alike. From 1980 to 2000, the assets of all active U.S. foundations grew from $48.2 billion to $486.1 billion and giving increased over eight-fold (Foundation Center, 2002). Grant applicants' expectations expanded with respect to the size of awards and the likelihood of a successful proposal. In addition, many foundations decided that additional staff had to be hired to make responsible decisions. After the economy entered a period of recession in 2000–01, however, these expectations changed. Both grantmakers and grantees experienced many more difficulties in maintaining programs, and in many cases the programs were not sustainable in their previous form.

A feature of philanthropic life is the need to say no to prospective grantees. In economic downturns, "no" must be the response even more often. Most applicants will have to be turned down for funding, and this part of the job is not fun for people who went into philanthropy to do good and make a difference. Also there are few defined rules to regulate this process, in stark contrast with public sector funding procedures. For this reason, foundation officers need to develop ways to cope with offering the disappointing news. This need goes a long way to explaining the arms-length relationship that foundation officers often maintain with grantees.

In general, the expansion of philanthropic assets was good for evaluation, as evaluation staff were hired along with other program officers. Boards began to demand more in the way of performance and results, and resources to answer their questions were more abundant than before. Although some board members, foundation officers, and grantees continued to voice the opinion that evaluation took needed resources away from programs (for example, Patrizi, 2002; Patrizi and McMullan, 1999), the sheer size of the available resources made this assertion less compelling. A culture of assessing results became instilled to a greater degree.

In periods of economic recession, it remains to be seen whether evaluation results will continue to be sought. On the one hand, resources are more limited; on the other, there is a continuing, some would argue even a heightened, need to bring a critical eye to the quality of philanthropic investments as competition intensifies over fewer resources. Evaluation results may provide grantmakers with coping mechanisms to help say no to grantees, by allowing them to speak from principle in their drive to critique proposals and to renew the most effective programs.

Life Cycle of Nonprofits

Boom-and-bust economics affect the health and well-being of nonprofit organizations as well. This is a matter of growing concern to foundation officers who must reduce funding overall in the unfavorable economic periods but who would like programs to be sustained within nonprofit organizations. However, doing so requires both resources and organizational capacity. Both tend to be lacking.

Foundations are well served when they understand the life cycle, and therefore the capacity, of the organizations they fund (Stevens, 2001). Nonprofit organizations are born, live, and die by their capacity to conduct their business. Capacity includes the service function but also includes, in a critical way, financial management, financial health, human resources, administration, and governance. Capacity varies considerably and has marked effects on organizations' ability to receive a grant and to carry out the work effectively.

Nonprofits tend to starve their administrative functions, diverting as many resources as possible to services or to "the mission" (Letts, Ryan, and Grossman, 1998). This tendency can affect fiscal health, making them highly dependent on one or two funders. Ideally, nonprofits should be able to absorb a grant and then sustain efforts after the grant ends. But foundation funding can inadvertently foster financial dependence if it reduces the organization's viability for funding from other sources. Nonprofits need diversified funding for flexibility, strategic planning, and, most critically, to survive environmental shocks (Tuckman and Chang, 1992).

Evaluators recognize that organizational capacity and life cycles provide important context, for example, in explaining a nonprofit's failure to implement a program as specified. However, evaluators seldom apply an organization development lens as part of evaluation itself. This might be done, for example, by offering early, formative evaluation advice on capacity needs as they affect performance or by helping the grantmaker generalize about the kinds of nonprofits that will succeed in implementing the program. Perhaps evaluators tend to ignore these issues because they often assume the organizations that get the grants will be resilient and capable. Even for many public sector organizations, that assumption is highly questionable (for example, in underfunded school districts and welfare offices). For foundation-funded nonprofits, it is often painfully and destructively fallacious to assume resiliency and capacity.

Board Voting Cycles

The board of directors for a philanthropy must approve all expenditures, either directly or by reviewing decisions made by staff members. For this reason, board meetings set the pace for other activities of a foundation. In some foundations the board meets quarterly. It can meet more or less often, depending on the extent of board involvement and the amount of money to be distributed. It should be clear that a lot of foundation officers' activity is geared to the timing of such meetings and that a great deal of preparation goes into the meetings themselves.

Evaluation findings may play an important role in some of these preparations. Foundation staff may begin their preparations for an important board presentation six months or a year in advance. Evaluation findings are more likely to be useful when they are available early in those preparations. Preliminary results, where appropriate, a series of reports, and periodic verbal briefings are all helpful in permitting a conceptual use of findings—conceptual use that can often frame the decisions to be made and the opportunities to be addressed. Conceptual use is often required so evaluations can play a later role in decision making or in the formation of philanthropic strategy (see Chapter One).

The complaint is frequently voiced that evaluations are not timely. Yet in the foundation context, timely information is less important for board meetings themselves than for the preparation for meetings. Government operates in much the same way, particularly in Congress. Evaluation findings offered during the initial preparations for a change in law are much more useful than they would be once the hearings start; people need time to digest their meaning (Leviton and Boruch, 1983; Leviton, 1987).

Waxing and Waning of Foundation Interests and Initiatives

Most foundations are careful to specify the areas in which they do and do not make grants. These areas change over time. The board of directors is charged with steering the foundation as a whole in terms of these special areas of grantmaking. Changes in these areas over time can result from turnover among board members and foundation officers. Changes can also be seen as the environment changes, for example, when government picks up the cost of addressing a need or when society changes so that the need is less compelling. In many cases, strategic planning can bring out changes in foundations' specific focus.

Increasingly, philanthropic boards rely on evaluation and other kinds of information to assist their strategic planning. Though often imperfect, research and evaluation can inform the board about knowledge gaps, service needs, and opportunities to leverage change in society. For example, a city's community foundation wanted to explore the extent to which it should be involved in programming for an aging population. An issue brief outlined some of the opportunities, needs, futures, and federal policies that were in operation, as a way of informing the process. Moreover, the issue brief described a portfolio of programs for an aging population—programs that had been funded by the foundation already, several of which had been evaluated favorably. The board voted to donate increased funds to address the needs of the aging population for quite a few years.

Once a focus has been selected, performance measurement can focus on the broad results of the investment focus (as opposed to evaluation of specific programs or grants). Such performance measurement can be carried out in several ways:

- By addressing the broad societal effects of a grantmaking area, such as improving people's access to medical care in the case of The Robert Wood Johnson Foundation
- By aggregating the results of evaluations across the funded programs within a grantmaking area, as in the case of The Pew Charitable Trusts (Rimel, 1999)
- By examining indicators of the degree to which key intermediate objectives of a grantmaking area have been achieved, as specified in a logic model or theory of change

A Closer Look at the Grant

For this discussion, we use the grant cycle to illustrate what is admittedly an idealized version of the numerous ways evaluative processes can support decision making about both individual grants and foundation programs with multiple grants. Figure 6.1 depicts a generic version of a program or grant cycle.

Observe that the cycle unfolds in three broad phases related to *planning, implementation,* and *postimplementation.* During each phase, typical activities are undertaken to varying degrees to move the process along. For example, the cycle begins in Phase I with the identification of a "problem" or area of interest—one that presumably fits within the overall mission of the foundation. From this grows a process for designing possible foundation "responses" to the issue.

These problem identification and strategy development activities vary considerably from foundation to foundation. The degree to which these are *collaborative* processes inside a foundation (as compared to ones undertaken by a single program officer), as well as the use and range of types of information that are brought to bear on a foundation's deliberations, are just two of the dimensions of variability across foundations. Moreover, people within organizations do not

FIGURE 6.1. THE PROGRAM OR GRANTMAKING CYCLE.

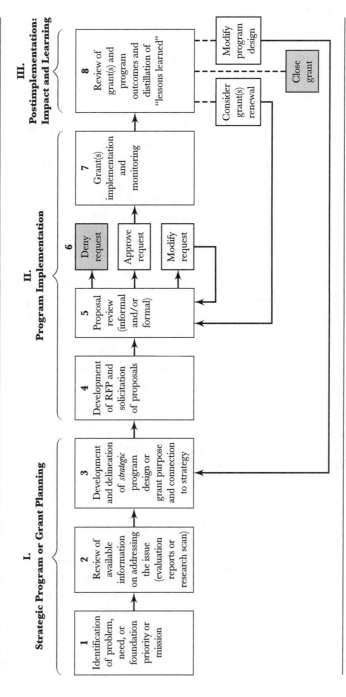

Source: Bickel, Post, and Nelson (2001), as cited in Oliphant (2002), pp. 28–34. Reproduced with permission.

necessarily think about planning, implementation, and assessment of results in an orderly fashion. Staff may anticipate questions that emerge later, challenge assumptions about implementation, or jump ahead to potential side effects of programs (Rich and Zaltman, 1978). For all those reasons, we would argue that it is especially important to offer a framework for orderly questioning and decision making. Without one, neither staff nor evaluators will have a context from which to understand the great diversity of foundation styles and activities.

There are key decision points at each of these phases of the grant cycle; theoretically, evaluative processes can make important contributions at each. One way of thinking about how evaluation can be integrated into the cycle is to imagine questions foundation staff might be reasonably expected to ask about the process along the way and then relate evaluation activities to these questions. Table 6.1 lays out the kinds of questions and evaluative actions that might be asked and conducted, respectively, across the several phases.

We do not mean to suggest that every foundation does, or even should attempt, to faithfully fulfill each of these idealized steps. Such a "hyper-rationalization" of the granting process belies the organizational realities of most foundations. Our goal is to demonstrate a reasonable relationship among the cycle stage, questions likely to be posed by foundation staff at each stage, and possible evaluative responses. We would contend that within strategic grantmaking cycles where major investments are at stake, an approach like this is an important element to support effective integration of evaluation into foundation grantmaking cycles. However, we also recognize that there are significant challenges to such integration and will discuss several of these shortly.

The Planning Phase and Subsequent Events in the RWJF-Funded Program, SUPPORT

We illustrate the first stage of the idealized cycle (Planning) with an RWJF program that contributed to stimulating a variety of initiatives on improving care at the end of life. The Study to Understand Prognoses and Preferences for Outcomes and Risks of Treatments (SUPPORT) was a two-phase multigrant program that first described health care for nine serious and life-threatening illnesses, then mounted a randomized patient-level experiment to determine whether intervention would improve care. Space does not permit a full description; details of SUPPORT are found in the foundation's *Anthology* (Lynn, 1997), and further information on end-of-life initiatives can be found at www.rwjf.org.

Returning to Phase I of Table 6.1, note that the phase is further broken down into three substeps or stages: (1) problem identification, (2) the grounding of strategy development in validated information, and (3) strategic design. At each of

TABLE 6.1. THE PROGRAM-GRANT CYCLE.

Phase I: Planning

Stage	Typical Questions	Possible Evaluative Activities
1. Identification of a problem, need, or priority for the foundation	• What are the pressing problems or needs that the foundation is uniquely positioned to influence? • To what extent do these problems or needs reflect core foundation priorities?	• Align foundation goals and program goals. • Conduct a needs assessment. • Assess foundation strengths (for example, policy context, special niche for foundation leverage possibilities, or intellectual capital).
2. Grounding of strategy development in validated information	• What do we already know about addressing the problem? • What has been done by others to address the problem? • What efforts have been successful or unsuccessful? Why? • What were the characteristics of the broader context in successful and unsuccessful endeavors? Which of these characteristics influenced the outcome of the program or grant?	• Summarize what we know that works and doesn't via scans of internal and field knowledge for commonly used indicators, potential barriers, effective strategies. • Identify readily available data sources on a targeted issue (for example, government statistics). • Consult with stakeholders, and get field leaders' perspectives on the problem and possible strategies.

TABLE 6.1. THE PROGRAM-GRANT CYCLE. *(continued)*

Stage	Typical Questions	Possible Evaluative Activities
3. Development and delineation of design	**Developing a theory of change:** • Based on our responses to item #1, how can we (foundation program staff) best influence this problem, given our unique position and expertise? • Given the scale of resources we have to commit, where can we best get traction on the targeted issue? • What do we know about the enablers of and barriers to the effective use of the identified approach? • Are there initiatives or plans for new initiatives (in other program areas within the foundation, from potential funding partners) that could be used to maximize the effects of this new program or grant? • What is the broader context in which these grants will be implemented? Are there policies, pressures, trends, or legislation that will influence the implementation or effectiveness of the grants? • Have we identified realistic, measurable goals and outcomes? (How will we know if this strategy is effective?) • Have we clearly described our theory of change? **Developing an action plan:** • Do we have a realistic timeline for achieving change? • What other nonmonetary resources or support might grantees need to achieve their goals? How will we address these needs? • Have we established milestones to monitor the progress of the program or grant? • Have we established a timeline for grant implementation, grant review, midcourse corrections, and strategy review? • Do we need a formal evaluation beyond what the grantee is being asked to do? What should the budget be? Should it be done in-house? Externally?	• Align program goals and strategic programs or grants. • Work with program staff to make the change theory explicit (goals, strategies, activities and grants, outcomes, impact, indicators, and targets). • Sketch out the preliminary scope of work and a budget for evaluation. • Develop key indicators of progress with regard to context, implementation, and success. • Conduct a preliminary assessment of relevant data access or conditions required by evaluation.

TABLE 6.1. THE PROGRAM-GRANT CYCLE. *(continued)*

Phase II: Program or Grant Implementation

Stage	Typical Questions	Possible Evaluative Activities
4. Development of Requests for Proposals (RFPs)	• Does the design of the program or grant demand additional (nonmonetary) support from the foundation? (For example, if the grant is foundation-driven, it may require professional development for the grantees.) • What are the characteristics of potential grantees that might heighten the level of success? • How can we best identify and recruit applicants for this grant? • What type of information do we need from applicants (about their context, organizational capacity, proposed activities, resource needs) to make a funding decision? • What messages do we want to convey to grantees about our expectations, both for their role in enacting the grant and specifically with regard to evaluation responsibilities (their own and in relation to external evaluation)? • What type of baseline information do we need from applicants at this stage to monitor progress if funding is awarded? • How will we manage the application-proposal process to maximize its utility? Will it be linked to existing reporting structures if funded? Will it be accessible, even if not funded, for retrospective analyses of foundation funding patterns? • How will responsibility for assessing progress be divided between the foundation and the grantee with respect to evaluation?	• Align program and individual grants (includes specification of how a grant advances strategy). • Develop RFP evaluation relationships and requirements. • Review overall RFP for its "evaluability." • Develop (or have in place) a data management system for proposal review, monitoring, and evaluation functions.

TABLE 6.1. THE PROGRAM-GRANT CYCLE. *(continued)*

Stage	Typical Questions	Possible Evaluative Activities
5. Proposal review	• What are the criteria for proposal review? • What do we already know about this grantee? • Who should be involved in the proposal review? • What approaches best facilitate assessment of potential grantees and their requests (for example, face-to-face meetings, site visits, reviews of past performances)?	• Develop proposal evaluation criteria. • Summarize internal and external past performance data on potential grantees. • Identify appropriate individuals and actions to support program staff in proposal review (for example, consultations with stakeholders, site visitations, review of evaluation sections of proposal).
6. Funding decision and grant agreement	• Which grantees have the most capacity to achieve the strategic goals? To fulfill evaluation requirements? • What specific support or conditions will individual grantees need to fulfill the goals (write into the grant agreement)?	• Review or realign indicators, based on plans of specific grantees selected. • Tailor the evaluation section of each grant agreement to capacity of specific grantees selected or specify capacity building necessary to evaluate work. • Craft the evaluation section of the grant agreement to clearly delineate expectations for data collection and reporting.
7. Grant implementation and monitoring	• What kind of information do we need from grantees during implementation to answer the broader questions we have about the effectiveness of the program (particularly our key indicators of context, implementation, and success)? • How often should we collect the information? • How should we collect information from grantees? • How should we store grantee information so that it is accessible and usable? • Who is responsible for the management of grantee information? • What are the implications of the data as we continue to implement these grants? • How will we provide formative feedback to grantees? • What opportunities are there for grantees to learn from each other through the evaluation process? • How might we share learning with evaluators connected with a program or grant (if an external evaluation is in place)?	• Develop or tailor grantee reporting templates. • Develop grantee reporting procedures, data-collection agreements. • Develop the foundation's data management process for grantee data, if necessary. • Survey work across grantees; synthesize emergent findings. • Develop a plan to continuously assess grantee needs for support or additional resources. • Develop a formal external or foundation-led evaluation plan.

TABLE 6.1. THE PROGRAM-GRANT CYCLE. *(continued)*

Phase III: Assessing Impact and Learning to Improve Program Design and Grantmaking

Stage	Typical Questions	Possible Evaluative Activities
8. Review of grant or program outcomes and distillation of lessons learned	• To what extent were the grantees able to actually implement their projects?	• Synthesize data on individual grantees within the program.
	• What progress was made by our grantees?	• Interpret cluster evaluation results, if applicable.
	• What contextual and organizational factors most helped or hindered grant implementation? Attainment of desired outcomes?	• Compare what is known in the field to foundation-generated knowledge.
	• What implications (if any) do the results from the program or grant have for the field? For future strategic grantmaking?	• Implement appropriate dissemination strategies (product creation and distribution) for "substantial" lessons learned about strategy, next steps, policy implications.

Source: Bickel, Post, and Nelson (2001), as cited in Oliphant (2002), pp. 28–34. Reproduced with permission.

these steps, there are potential evaluative actions that can inform the process. Some easily lie within the purview of foundation staff; some may require outside expertise, and others a combination of both. Evaluation planning of this type can accomplish the following:

- Encourage the elucidation of the logic model or program theory
- Force articulation of the initiative's objectives
- Bring attention to what is already known about an area
- Bring about the side-by-side preparation of initiative and evaluation

A program officer might reasonably ask a number of questions during the planning phase, as seen in Table 6.1. For example, under "problem identification" is listed the question, "What are the pressing problems or needs that the foundation is uniquely positioned to influence?" Useful activities to address this question include assessing foundation strengths, such as opportunities for leverage of change. For example, RWJF is known for having influence through provider education and health system improvement. When faced with the problem of care for patients with serious and life-threatening illness, the foundation turned to these tested strategies in SUPPORT.

At the "information-validation" stage shown in Table 6.1, one of the questions posed is, "What were the characteristics of the broader context in successful and unsuccessful endeavors?" Helpful activities include scanning the field for potential barriers and effective strategies, and identifying data sources on the targeted issue. In the case of SUPPORT, data from the descriptive phase provided important insights about predicting patient survival time and onset of serious functional disability. Insights were also provided about the primary issues in determining what would improve care for serious and life-threatening illness (such as providers' awareness of patients' wishes and the need to address the great pain that patients were experiencing).

As seen in Table 6.1, the development of a strategic design rests on these initial steps and is itself divisible into two further steps, developing a "theory of change" and an "action plan." Appropriate questions here include, for example, "What do we know about the enablers of and barriers to the effective use of the identified approach?" Useful evaluative activities include working with program staff to make change theory explicit. On the basis of planning data in SUPPORT, for example, staff determined that better provider awareness of patient wishes would be a key enabler of improvements. To accomplish this, the study focused on the training and commitment of nurses, who counseled patients and their families and determined their preferences, met with providers, developed contingency plans, and provided complete information to the patient care team.

In the development of an action plan, an illustrative question is, "Do we have a realistic timeline for achieving change?" Developing key indicators of progress constitutes a useful activity. The second phase of SUPPORT was a randomized experiment that assessed indicators of progress on several key variables. These included the timing of a "do not resuscitate" order, accord between patient and physician about this order, and, for those patients who expressed a wish not to be resuscitated, reduced time spent in an intensive care unit in a coma or on a ventilator.

A follow-up to the example offers several insights about foundation decision making. The randomized experiment indicated that the intervention had not improved any of the targeted problems reflected in these indicators. Although this was disappointing, it could not be said that the randomized experiment was premature in any way. In fact, the descriptive stage led to more detailed understanding of the problem and systematic planning for a well-developed intervention, tested in the second phase. Because the foundation had achieved documented benefits from similar intervention strategies in the past, it was puzzling why these benefits were not seen in the SUPPORT randomized experiment.

It is often assumed that a negative outcome will have a chilling effect on innovation. Yet this does not have to happen within foundations, and did not happen in the case of SUPPORT. The project identified the obstacles to the intervention's effectiveness in some detail, at the levels of the patient, provider, and health system. With these insights, RWJF became interested in attempting to change the entire field of end-of-life care—a broader and more challenging mission than the fairly focused SUPPORT program. The evaluation, as one of many sources of information, convinced the board and staff that the challenges were worth pursuing in a more aggressive way. Thus the SUPPORT evaluation had little impact on decisions about an individual program. However, it had profound effects on the waxing (and waning) of an entire foundation-supported field of work.

Among other things, this reaction to a negative evaluation may reassure grantees about how evaluation will be used at a foundation. It is equally instructive about the difference between entrepreneurial grantmakers and governmental decision makers. A negative evaluation of a government program leaves decision makers with limited options and a lot of angst over what can be done. In philanthropy—at least during the bull markets—a negative evaluation is a challenge to find the more powerful leverage points for change, particularly when implementation is understood. With pressure for a 5 percent payout behind them, foundation staff can become more entrepreneurial in addressing the targeted social change.

Evaluation Use in the Implementation and Learning Phases

The Heinz Endowments' Early Childhood Initiative (ECI) illustrates how evaluation can be integrated into the two later phases of Figure 6.1. The ECI completed its first year of operation in 1998, after two years of intensive planning. The basic goal of ECI was to "make Allegheny County [Pennsylvania] the first community in the country to make quality early learning programs broadly available to low-income children" (Oliphant and Root, 2002, p. 1). Building on substantial research, the foundation knew that the first few years of life were critical to a successful school career (analogous to Phase I, Stages 1 and 2, in Table 6.1). In a state that does not fund preschool or all-day kindergarten programs, the foundation saw an important role for its investment. With the initiative's success, it was hoped that the state could be influenced to change its policies on early education. The idea was to connect thousands of low-income children with high-quality early learning experiences.

The initiative was impressive in scope. With The Heinz Endowments' leadership, it involved numerous foundations, community organizations, business leaders, and thousands of children. It was resource-intensive, with $60 million to be invested from a variety of sources over a five-year period to create a network of eighty early childhood education facilities in the region's poorest neighborhoods (Table 6.1, Phase I, Stage 3). By late 2000, it was recognized from all sides that the program "had failed to reach its ambitious objectives," and a decision was reached by the foundations that it would be "ramped down" (Oliphant and Root, 2002, p. 1).

So far, the ECI story is not especially unusual; foundations often start out with high ambitions in difficult social programming contexts only to find a few years later that program goals are not being met. What makes ECI salient here are two facts. First, the foundation built into the initiative from the start a comprehensive program of research and evaluation based at Children's Hospital of Pittsburgh (Bagnato, 2002). The evaluation was designed to document the implementation process and to determine the viability of the model being tested and the outcomes achieved (Table 6.1, Phase I, Stage 3; Phase II, Stages 4–7).

Second, once the determination was made to terminate the initiative as originally conceived, the lead foundation made another decision: to commission the RAND Corporation to undertake a retrospective investigation of ECI. The goal of the RAND study was articulated by Teresa Heinz, board chairman, as "needing to know why" (2002, p. 5). The RAND Study, although funded by Heinz, was designed so that the community was, in effect, the client. "We felt everyone who had supported the program, or had participated in it, or just plain believed in it, had the same right as we did to know what really happened," said Max King, CEO of the Heinz Endowments (Oliphant, 2002, p. 5).

These two evaluative exercises represent a combined investment by the endowments of $1.8 million. The results of both studies have since been released to the community (Bagnato, 2002; Gill, Dembosky, and Caulkins, 2002; Table 6.1, Phase III, Stage 8).

In terms of our grant cycle evaluation table, these two studies speak to several of the kinds of questions typically addressed during the "implementation" and "learning" phases of the cycle (II and III, respectively, in Table 6.1), that is, the questions related to levels of implementation reached, results achieved, and lessons learned from the initiative that should be shared with others working on similar issues in the field. The outcomes study tracked results on forty indicators involving a range of social, early learning, and behavioral domains. Overall, the evaluators found that the small number of children (834, studied in Bagnato, 2002, as quoted in Oliphant, 2002, p. 6), who actually experienced quality programs as originally designed, showed significant progress on these indicators. Furthermore, impressive drops were recorded in referrals to special education.

The problem was that these impressive results were achieved in very few instances. The RAND study documented numerous challenges faced in the implementation of what was a very complicated program, both conceptually and structurally. These challenges included cumbersome organizational arrangements and lines of responsibility and communication, significant and unanticipated costs (ultimately three times the original cost proposed in the ECI business plan), and a continuing lack of state interest in providing new public sector support for early childhood initiatives, despite some early indications from the Ridge administration that this might be different (see Oliphant and Root, 2002, pp. 5–8.)

The details of what was found are less salient here than are the uses the foundation and community has and intends to make of them. Because of the perceived power of the intervention when fully implemented, funds have been forthcoming to support the continuation of two small demonstration sites. Dissemination of the results of both evaluations has been energetic to local, state, and national venues (Root, 2002; Gill, Dembosky, and Caulkins, 2002). The work continues to shape foundation strategy formulation vis–à–vis the state, as evidenced by efforts to bring state policymakers on board with the need for quality early childhood education for all Pennsylvanians (Heinz, 2002).

The ECI case nicely illustrates the integration of evaluation into a program cycle, as described in the previous section. Furthermore, it demonstrates the power of doing so. In the words of the foundation's board of trustees chairperson:

> Taken together, these studies tell us how we can be smarter in promoting early-learning programs, but also that we are absolutely right to make that our focus. . . . The lessons we uncovered are already being applied in our work around Pennsylvania, and by other innovators in early learning initiatives in other states around the country. (Heinz, 2002, p. 3)

How Grant Cycles Create Challenges and Opportunities for Evaluation

Using evaluation well in foundation decision making is a laudable goal. Yet past performance suggests that this is not easily done (for example, Patrizi, 2002; Bickel, Millett, and Nelson, 2002). The challenges to do so are many; some are rooted in the culture and structure of foundations, others in the way evaluation is typically practiced. Here we identify several *practical issues* that must be addressed that specifically hinder the integration of evaluation into the granting cycle routines of foundations. However, those same cycles also permit opportunities for evaluations to be conducted and used.

Challenge 1: The Need to Recognize the Cycles

Usually, the "insider" (staff) to philanthropy is in a better position to recognize the cycles and therefore attempt to sequence evaluative activity and results in time for specific decision points. Even the most politically perceptive evaluator will sometimes fail to identify these cycles and often does not have the access to give timely suggestions. Yet sometimes the insider cannot identify the cycles either, because of the idiosyncratic processes in a foundation, or cannot recognize or take advantage of the opportunities. Working closely with foundation staff to make cycles transparent, well in advance, is a necessary strategy to building an effective evaluation process. Of course, even close working relationships between foundation staffs and evaluators can be defeated by the rush of work and the amount of discretion that foundation staffs have over decisions.

Challenge 2: Circumstances and Timing of Organizational Learning

When staff are preparing for board presentations, they can become advocates of the program idea and consequently may overpromise what the program can deliver. As long ago as 1972, Carol Weiss (in Weiss, 1997) described similar problems in the public sector. In philanthropy, it makes sense to discover where in the cycle there is room for genuine learning from evaluation. We would maintain that the optimum time for learning is when board authorizations for the program are somewhat distant—on either side. At the same time, when board attention is looming, it certainly does manage to attract the attention of busy staff.

A recent program of RWJF illustrates the challenges. Release of authorized funding for the remaining eighteen months of the grant was contingent on a favorable qualitative evaluation of progress. The evaluation was favorable, and the funds were released, so one might conclude that the results contributed to a decision about the program. However, the more interesting use of evaluation came several months later. The evaluator was well known for building organizations similar to the grantee organization. Due to largely extraneous events, the grantee organization had reached a "teachable moment," when grantee staff actively solicited advice from the evaluator about how to improve quality control and retain their best professional staff. The teachable moment would have been impossible even a few months previously, due to apprehension about the release of funds.

Challenge 3: Unwarranted Expectations for Evaluation

Although we are proponents of evaluation being integrated into granting cycles, we recognize that even sophisticated consumers of evaluation (and evaluators) can sometimes have expectations about evaluation that are unrealistic, for example, when findings should become available, what impact they might have, or how large a role they might have. This applies to the foundation staff member, board member, and evaluator as much as to members of Congress or new officials in bureaucracy.

Complex social programs take time to implement well; seeking "results and impact" prematurely are consistent errors in the field. In some cases, even with well-specified program theory and careful evaluation designs, it will be difficult to sort out causation from correlation in outcomes. This simple truism is often underestimated in the "selling" of a program (or for that matter an evaluation). One often is forced to settle for varying degrees of "knowledge" about grants. Grant Oliphant (2002) describes The Ewing Marion Kaufmann Foundation's apt approach to this issue.

> It is essentially a hierarchy of certainty, with "proven" impact, which denotes scientific knowledge, at the top of the hierarchy and "plausible impact," denoting a justified assumption, at the bottom. (Blissful ignorance presumably is the implicit sub-basement of the hierarchy!) Kaufmann is attempting to move its programs and grantees from the "plausible quality" level up to the middle, "demonstrated quality" level. What this will actually mean from a process and data-collection standpoint remains to be seen, but the essential notion—that we can accept a level of learning below absolute certainty and profit mightily from it—is extremely valuable. (p. 3)

Challenge 4: Fear of the Go/No-Go Decision

The stereotype is that evaluation findings will enter deliberations about a program and that decisions to continue or discontinue funding will ride on the answers. An incredible amount of dysfunction results from this stereotype—predictable misbehavior on the part of program managers, evaluators, and funders alike. Yet the stereotype is seldom true in government, and our experience to date suggests that it is seldom true for foundations. Even when evaluations contribute to identifiable decisions, it is very seldom in the "go/no-go" manner that people seem to expect. Very seldom have we seen programs die on the basis of a negative evaluation; neither is a glowing evaluation the sole consideration in program survival.

Programs seldom live or die on the basis of evaluation alone for three reasons. First, it has long been established that evaluations can be used but are usually only *one* contributing source of information in decision processes (Leviton and Boruch, 1983). Along with political considerations and individual preferences, information can contribute to decision making, whether through long-term enlightenment of decision makers (Weiss and Bucuvalas, 1980), directly through action (Leviton and Boruch, 1983), or through legitimation of advocacy positions that were arrived at for other reasons (Leviton and Hughes, 1981). Second, powerful constituencies often protect programs. Foundations have constituencies, even though they may take a different form from those of government. With staff and board turnover, foundation constituencies may be more changeable, but it is the turnover that may put the programs at risk, not the evaluation findings. Third, the expectation that an evaluation will be used for specific decisions presumes that the evaluation findings are of a quality and definitiveness that would merit such a high degree of influence. In truth, most evaluations are highly flawed and unsatisfactory, as they are looking for program effects in very messy and complex contexts where causality is difficult to determine.

Fear of de-funding a program takes on substantially greater proportions in nonprofits than in the public sector. Because many nonprofits are not financially diversified, de-funding can mean ruin or at least painful layoffs. Public institutions may be underfunded, but at least there are predictable cash flows from governmental sources. Moreover, the stakeholders for public institutions such as school districts generally hold substantial clout with governments. Can the same be said of nonprofit organizations? In general, it will require substantial work from foundation staff to alleviate concerns about evaluation when they are groundless.

Conclusion

We began this discussion with two important assumptions. First, evaluation processes can play an important role in supporting effectiveness in philanthropy. Second, to fulfill this role, evaluation needs to be integrated into the fundamental work routines of foundations.

The practical implication of this work is that both evaluators and foundation officers will be more effective when they identify and tailor evaluations to the core cycles of foundations. Each cycle offers key decision points, wherein evaluative information can be brought to bear on the deliberative work of a foundation. Using a "questions–evaluative responses" framework, we sought to illustrate how this interactive relationship between decision processes and evaluation can work. It requires staffs and evaluators who are planful and nimble, and foundation cultures and boards of trustees that are committed to using information to advance the work of the organization.

We recognize that the challenges are many. Further, we have an ample sense of modesty about how dominant a role evaluation can (or even should) play in foundation life cycles. Be that as it may, we are convinced that evaluation is an important tool in supporting effectiveness in philanthropy. A crucial element in using evaluation processes to support philanthropy wisely rests with an understanding of how foundations work and finding practical ways to integrate evaluation into the core life cycles of these special organizations.

References

Bagnato, S. (2002). *Quality early learning—key to early school success: A first-phase program evaluation research report for Pittsburgh's early childhood initiative (ECI)*. Pittsburgh, PA: Children's Hospital of Pittsburgh, SPECS Evaluation Research Team.

Bickel, W. E., Millett, R., & Nelson, C. A. (2002). *Challenges to the role of evaluation in supporting organizational learning in foundations*. Available at http//www.foundationsnews.org/webextra/learningweb.htm. Washington, DC: Council on Foundations.

Bickel, W. E., Post, J., & Nelson, C. A. (2001, May). *Supporting organizational learning in the initiative/grant-making cycles*. Pittsburgh. PA: University of Pittsburgh, Evaluation Coordination Project, Learning Research and Development Center.

Cooley, W. W., & Bickel, W. E. (1986). *Decision-oriented educational research*. Boston: Kluwer-Nijoff Publishing.

Foundation Center. (2002). Profile of the funding community: How much have foundations grown and why is that important? *Foundations Today Tutorial*. Available at http://fdncenter.org/learn/classroom/ft_tutorial/ftt_part1_q2.html. Accessed February 20, 2003.

Gill, B. P., Dembosky, J. W., & Caulkins, J. P. (2002). *A noble bet in early care and education*. Pittsburgh, PA: Rand Corporation.

Heinz, T. (2002, Spring). To our readers. In *E*, p. 3. Pittsburgh, PA: Heinz Endowments.

Letts, C. W., Ryan, W. P., & Grossman, A. (1998). *High performance nonprofit organizations: Managing upstream for greater impact*. New York: Wiley.

Leviton, L. C. (1987). Changes in law as leverage points for policy research. *American Behavioral Scientist, 30*, 632–643.

Leviton, L. C., & Boruch, R. F. (1983). Contributions of evaluation to education programs and policy. *Evaluation Review, 7*, 563–598.

Leviton, L. C., & Hughes, E.F.X. (1981). Research on the utilization of evaluations: A review and synthesis. *Evaluation Review, 5*, 525–547.

Lynn, J. (1997). Unexpected returns: Insights from SUPPORT. In S. L. Isaacs & J. R. Knickman (Eds.), *To improve health and health care*. San Francisco: Jossey-Bass.

Oliphant, G. (2002, March). *Evaluation at the Heinz Endowments: A position paper for internal review*. Pittsburgh, PA: Heinz Endowments.

Oliphant, G., & Root, D. (2002). *Pittsburgh's noble bet*. Pittsburgh, PA: Heinz Endowments.

Patrizi, P. (2002, April, 4). *Briefing notes to the Evaluation II Roundtable*. Presented at the Grantmakers' Evaluation Network Meeting, Council on Foundations, Washington, DC.

Patrizi, P., & McMullan, B. (1999). Evaluation in foundations: The unrealized potential. *Foundation News and Commentary, 30*, 32–35.

Patton, M. Q. (1997). *Utilization-focused evaluation: The new century text* (3rd ed.). Thousand Oaks, CA.: Sage.

Preskill, H., & Torres, R. (1999). *Evaluative inquiry for learning in organizations*. Thousand Oaks, CA: Sage.

Redman, E. (2000). *The dance of legislation* (Rev. ed.). Seattle: University of Washington Press.

Rich, R. F., & Zaltman, G. (1978). Toward a theory of planned social change: Alternate perspectives and ideas. *Evaluation and Change,* 41–47.

Rimel, R. W. (1999). Strategic philanthropy: Pew's approach to matching needs with resources. *Health Affairs, 18,* 228–233.

Root, D. (2002, Spring). Early childhood learning: The national scene. In *E,* pp. 33–37. Pittsburgh, PA: Heinz Endowments.

Stevens, S. K. (2001). *Nonprofit lifecycles: Stage-based wisdom for nonprofit capacity.* Long Lake, MN: Stagewise Enterprises.

Tuckman, H. P., & Chang, C. F. (1992). Nonprofit equity: A behavioural model and its policy implications. *Journal of Policy Analysis and Management, 11,* 76–87.

Weiss, C. H. (1997). Evaluation (2nd ed.). New York: Prentice Hall.

Weiss, C. H., & Bucuvalas, M. J. (1980). *Social science research and decision-making.* New York: Columbia University Press.

Wisely, D. S. (1993). *Reflections on a foundation's relationship to its public legacies and lessons for the Lilly Endowment.* Indianapolis, IN: Lilly Endowment.

PART TWO

BUILDING CAPACITY
FOR EVALUATION PRACTICE

CHAPTER SEVEN

MAKING JUDGMENTS ABOUT WHAT TO EVALUATE AND HOW INTENSELY

Melvin M. Mark and William L. Beery

In principle, a foundation might be able to evaluate everything systematically. Each grant, each initiative, every aspect of the grantmaking process, the foundation itself—all of these could be systematically evaluated. At the other extreme, a foundation could forgo all systematic evaluation. In practice, we argue, foundations can and should make systematic judgments about *what* to evaluate. Additional judgments should be made about *how intensely* to evaluate those things the foundation has decided to evaluate systematically. In short, this chapter is designed to help foundation staff and boards do the work of deciding whether and how intensely to evaluate the foundation's efforts.

Of course, less systematic, *informal* evaluation may occur for everything a foundation does, based, for example, on program officers' observations of grantees. Indeed, some form of evaluation, however informal, presumably informs all the decisions made within a foundation. Like the rest of this book, our focus is on the deliberate and thoughtful use of systematic forms of evaluation. And for most foundations, *systematic* evaluation, with well-planned data collection,

Work on this chapter was supported, in part, by a grant from The David and Lucile Packard Foundation and a grant from The National Science Foundation (REC-02311859) to Melvin M. Mark. We thank Victor Kuo and numerous staff members at the foundation for their assistance and Marc Braverman, Rodney Hopson, Laura Leviton, and Emil Posavac for their helpful comments on a previous draft.

isn't feasible for everything all the time, at least not at a high level of intensity. Resources are limited. Evaluation can be costly. Choices must be made.

Those choices can and often are made without formal procedures—by happenstance, by best professional judgment of program officers, by intuition, or by tradition. However, when foundations create explicit processes for making decisions about what to evaluate at what level of intensity, important benefits should follow. For instance, thinking systematically about the allocation of evaluation resources should help the foundation achieve the kind of evaluative thinking advocated in this volume. One theme of this book is that using evaluation-based information and evaluative thinking throughout the planning and grantmaking process will lead to more effective foundations. In this chapter, we expand on this theme to suggest that, for foundations to truly achieve an evaluative frame of mind, they need to think evaluatively about *how they spend their evaluation dollars.*

Foundations need to consider explicitly which of the work they fund should be evaluated and at what level of intensity. Doing this will not, of course, guarantee that foundations always make optimal decisions. But on the whole, by making such judgments thoughtfully, foundations will be more likely to bring about the potential benefits of evaluation.

The Pieces of the Process

In general terms, to implement the kind of systematic approach to evaluation planning we advocate in this chapter, several interrelated questions must be answered. First, do decisions about what to evaluate (and how intensely) focus on the individual grant, or a component of the grant, or some kind of strategically or geographically defined cluster of grants, or the strategic initiative or line of work, or the grantmaking process itself? Second, what is the menu of typical options for evaluation for the foundation? For example, will some grants be allowed to proceed without formal evaluation, whereas others are required to collect data on outputs, that is, on the services delivered? Or will output information alone be expected for some grantees, output and outcome data for others, and, for yet others, comparative designs intended to tease out the grant's impact? Third, what procedures are used to decide which grants (or initiatives) fall into the different levels of intensity on the foundation's menu of evaluation options? In subsequent sections, each of these questions is addressed in turn. First, we turn to a more fundamental question: Why is it worthwhile for a foundation to develop an explicit process for making judgments about what to evaluate?

Why an Explicit Strategic Evaluation Planning Process Is Desirable

Foundations, of course, already fund evaluations. Foundations decide which grants (or initiatives or clusters) to evaluate and which not. And many foundations already fund evaluations that vary in terms of intensity, from contact monitoring to randomized trials. Why, then, is it a good idea to move beyond current procedures and develop more explicit processes for allocating evaluation resources?

Table 7.1 summarizes some of the key problems that are likely to arise without a clear and relatively systematic process for making decisions about the intensity of evaluation. As Table 7.1 shows, there are several reasons to have a sensible, explicit process for deciding what to evaluate more and less extensively. More generally, some of the key reasons include:

- Providing greater objectivity and transparency, thereby clarifying for program officers, the board, grantees, and others what gets evaluated, how intensely, and why
- Linking evaluation decisions more closely to foundation mission and to the potential payoff for intensive evaluation
- Making evaluative thinking routine in program officers' considerations of proposals and funding decisions
- Enhancing the prospect of learning from evaluation, both for parties within and external to the foundation

More generally, the choice of what gets evaluated and at what level of intensity constrains the potential benefits of evaluation. For example, if grantee-provided services are not evaluated in terms of their effectiveness, other potential funders, public policymakers, and the public will not be able to learn whether the services are working. If grantees' services are not evaluated in terms of processes and implementation, no one would know what groups receive them and what the challenges to effective implementation are. What gets learned as a result of evaluation and what gets changed following evaluation are, obviously, limited by *what gets evaluated.*

Another likely benefit of more explicit planning for evaluation resource allocation involves moving away from a cookie-cutter, one-size-fits-all view of evaluation. Many funding programs, in the foundation world and elsewhere, require the same evaluation activities of all grantees, big or small (for example, some set of performance indicators). Many funding programs also mandate proportionately equal spending on evaluation, that is, a set percentage of the grant budget

TABLE 7.1. CONSEQUENCES OF UNSYSTEMATIC VERSUS SYSTEMATIC DECISION MAKING ABOUT EVALUATION LEVEL.

Without Careful Discussion	With Careful Discussion
Decisions to evaluate intensely may be idiosyncratic or "accidental."	Decisions should be more consensual and thoughtful.
Decisions to evaluate intensely are not as likely to be tied to the strategic mission of the foundation.	Decisions should be better tied to strategic mission.
Foundation staff and grantees are more likely to feel evaluation is arbitrary.	Decisions should be more transparent, better understood.
Evaluation activities may be cookie-cutter, one-size-fits-all types.	Evaluation resources are more likely to be allocated so as to maximize potential payoff.
It is not as easy to communicate reasons for evaluation to the board.	Rationales for evaluation are more easily communicated.
The likelihood of evaluation paying off in ways important to the foundation is reduced.	Evaluation is more likely to pay off.

(say, 3 or 5 percent) must go to evaluation. But a common mandate for evaluation activities and proportionately equal evaluation budgeting simply may not make sense. Grantees have different capacity for evaluation. Some grants provide more opportunity for learning or otherwise supporting the mission of the foundation than others. If a foundation moves toward the kind of process we describe in this chapter, the result should be more thoughtful decisions about how to allocate resources to evaluation.

Yet another, rather general reason exists for adopting the proposed planning process. It is easy to see that a foundation's mission should influence decisions about what to evaluate, and how intensely. But the opposite may also be true. A foundation's portfolio of evaluation activity may influence the foundation's mission—real and perceived—as well as its image in the public and among more specialized audiences (for example, grantees or the foundation world). Consider, for example, Denis Prager's distinction between grants as charitable donations and grants as investment in social change (Prager, 1999). Or consider Thomas David's similar distinction between responsive grantmaking, which focuses more on doing good in the immediate context, and proactive grantmaking, which focuses more on testing interventions that might be implemented on a larger scale (David, 1999). If a foundation decides to rigorously evaluate most of its grant portfolio, it probably will be seen, at least by some audiences, as mostly doing proactive grant-making as an investment in social change. Alternatively, if a foundation decides not to evaluate any of its grantee activities extensively, it may instead be seen more as a reactive grantmaker treating grants as charitable donations. In short, the judgments a foundation makes about what to evaluate, and at what level of intensity, may help to define the foundation and its image. This is perhaps especially true if the evaluations that are conducted are publicly disseminated. But even if they are not, the evaluation choices a foundation makes are likely to affect its image, at least for its grantees.

In addition to the reasons summarized in Table 7.1, another argument for adopting the proposed planning procedures is that the incremental costs of doing so are small. Admittedly, additional staff time may be required in carrying out the process, at least initially. However, some staff time is already required to make decisions about what level of evaluation to use, if any. The additional time for the proposed process should not be significant. Indeed, by regularizing the process, the allocation of evaluation resources may actually become more efficient in the long run. And the potential payoff is notable, if for no other reason than that it should help move forward dialogue about evaluation within the foundation.

For foundations relatively new to the use of evaluation, the issues discussed in this chapter may not be the first evaluation-related issues to deal with. Setting up a process for the systematic allocation of evaluation resources is important but may be more feasible after a foundation has a certain level of experience with evaluation. Of course, some foundations may pursue a less deliberate allocation of evaluation resources—following hunches, allowing program officers great flexibility, focusing on grantmaking, and not worrying too much about evaluation. However, weighing the pluses and the minuses should lead most foundations to move in the direction of a more systematic process for making decisions about how to allocate funding for evaluation.

What to Focus on in the Planning Process

When deciding not to evaluate one "thing," to evaluate another extensively, and to evaluate yet another at an intermediate level, what are the "things" that a foundation's staff, and perhaps the board and stakeholders, are discussing? Using a term popularized among evaluators by Michael Scriven, the question is, What is the "evaluand"? We present several options here and suggest this is a topic worthy of *explicit* attention within a foundation.

Foundations award grants. Grantees then engage in various activities within the scope of a grant. Thus the most obvious focus for strategic evaluation planning is probably the grant and the set of activities funded under it. Note, however, that grants can vary dramatically. Some grants support a relatively simple endeavor, with one agency offering a single kind of service. Other grants support a complex community development or community health improvement initiative, with multiple parties engaging not only in service provision but in administration, technical assistance, long-range planning, and training. A single grant can also be part of a larger endeavor, a strategic initiative, or a line of work. A grant may be one component of several grants that have been strategically designed to address a single problem or set of interrelated problems. Alternatively, a grant from one foundation may be part of a larger endeavor supported by several funding sources. As a result, there are a variety of alternatives for the focal unit for evaluation. These include the following:

• *The grant.* This is the most obvious focus of discussion during the planning process, in part because it is the level at which much of the action within the foundation takes place. But this is not always the best choice.

• *A subcomponent of a single grant.* For example, a grant might fund several kinds of services in Boys & Girls Clubs, and an evaluation might focus only on after-school services for younger children.

• *A cross-grant evaluation of similar activities.* For instance, a foundation may fund several different grantees who provide after-school services for young children; these after-school services, provided by multiple grantees, might be examined in a single evaluation.

• *A cross-grant evaluation of different activities that are designed to achieve similar outcomes.* As an example, a foundation may provide funding to some grantees for after-school services and to other grantees for certain kinds of in-school services; an evaluation might compare these alternative approaches, both designed to reduce delinquency and increase school attendance.

• *A location-based cluster of grants.* A foundation might fund several grantees to undertake different kinds of activity in a community, all directed toward the same outcome. For instance, one organization may provide after-school services, another may help enroll families with young children in the state's Children's Health Insurance Program, and yet another may offer violence reduction interventions in the school—all designed toward the general goal of increasing young people's health and well-being. An evaluation might focus on the effect of the *overlapping set of services* funded under the different grants. This category includes complex community-based interventions, with multiple grants to different organizations.

• *The strategic initiative or line of work.* More complex packages of foundation funding sometimes are labeled formally as "initiatives" or "lines of work." For example, several large health foundations have made significant investments in initiatives, particularly in the area of health improvement through community partnerships. Examples include The Turning Point Initiative (The W. K. Kellogg Foundation and The Robert Wood Johnson Foundation), The Health Improvement Initiative (The California Wellness Foundation), The Partnership for the Public's Health (The California Endowment), and Making Connections (The Annie E. Casey Foundation).

Other grant-related possibilities also exist, including activities that are funded in conjunction with another foundation or funding agency.

In short, although evaluation and evaluation planning can focus on the individual grant, evaluation resource allocation can instead focus on components of a grant or on various kinds of packages of multiple grants. Alternatively, evaluation can focus on the entire foundation itself or on various *functions* within the foundation. For example, functions such as the grantmaking process, general management, and accounting systems could be evaluated. Because this book focuses on foundations as a lever of social change, we generally set aside these more administrative functions, which, though important, are in a sense simply the mechanisms by which the foundation does its business. Instead, we focus on evaluation related to grants and the activities grantees carry out.

To flesh out the issue of whether the strategic evaluation planning process should focus on the grant, initiative, or something else, we next provide an example and then briefly discuss several general considerations that may affect this choice.

Example: The Packard Foundation

As this chapter was being prepared, The David and Lucile Packard Foundation was considering implementation of a foundationwide process for general evaluation planning. This process would include procedures for determining what to evaluate and at what level of intensity.

At Packard, the expectation is that virtually every grant is to be evaluated *in some way*, if evaluation is defined broadly to include monitoring against goals and objectives. In many cases, the evaluation is low-cost, with the grantee reporting back on its success in achieving the desired outputs and outcomes, perhaps with observations added by the program officer. In other cases, the evaluation will be relatively expensive, perhaps even with a randomized experimental or other comparison-group design, and with a third-party evaluator. Several intermediate options also exist, corresponding to different levels of evaluation intensity. It appears, then, that planning for the general allocation of evaluation resources at Packard will center on the question of *how intensely* to evaluate the various activities its grants fund.

At this broad level of planning, Packard intends to focus not on the individual grant but on the line of work, which generally involves numerous grants, collectively targeted toward similar or complementary outcomes. An important line of work addresses significant strategic goals of the foundation, or at least one of its programs, and generally shares some important features:

- Shared *outcomes* (for example, increasing children's health insurance coverage, preserving biodiversity in the Western Pacific, or teaching youth about the arts)
- Shared or complementary *activities*—services, delivery modes, methods—across grants (for example, mass media campaigns, grassroots mobilization, or research)
- Shared or complementary *mechanisms,* or change processes, even if these are triggered by different kinds of activities (for example, multiple grants thought to work by fostering organizational capacity or by enhancing individual empowerment)

Examples of lines of work at Packard include the Conserving California Landscapes Initiative (CCLI), Preschool for All, Population Future Leaders, and the School Arts Program. A line of work at Packard appears similar to what other foundations might call an initiative. Although general evaluation planning at Packard will usually focus on the line of work, in select cases it may also focus on the individual grant, presumably large-budget grants that are central to a program's mission. (These individual grants would presumably stand out in terms of the full set of criteria described in the next section.) Even when the planning process centers on the line of work (or other cluster), it may subsequently be necessary to select specific grants for inclusion in the evaluation. For instance, in Packard's CCLI evaluation, described later in the chapter, a purposive sample of CCLI grants was chosen for more intensive evaluation.

General Considerations

As noted, general decisions about evaluation funding at Packard would typically focus on the line of work. What would work best at other foundations? There are several considerations we believe might be taken into account as a foundation considers whether to focus on grants, initiatives, or something else in the process of allocating evaluation resources.

    • *A focus on grants and grantee activities.* Although systematic evaluation attention to functions within the foundation (for example, grantmaking procedures or management) is desirable, for the most part strategic evaluation planning will probably deal with the grant or with component activities within the individual grant, initiatives, or some other meaningful clustering of grants. These are the recurring instruments through which the foundation achieves, or fails to achieve, its goals, objectives, and mission. They are also likely to be the place of action where the learning potential of evaluation is greatest.

• *The size of grant portfolios.* If a foundation makes literally thousands of grants in a year, unless it makes a large commitment to evaluation, including substantial internal evaluation staffing, it is probably overwhelming to make strategic evaluation decisions at the level of the individual grant. Instead, the initiative, or a strategic or geographic cluster of grants, is probably more feasible as a unit of decision making for the allocation of evaluation resources.

• *The nature and degree of strategic grouping of grantee activities.* Initiatives or clusters of multiple grants are generally more sensible as a focus of discussion in allocating evaluation resources, to the extent that the foundation plans, makes funding decisions, and seeks to learn in terms of these groupings. For example, do high-level decisions about grant funding allocations center on the initiative or on some other clustering of grants grouped by location, desired outcome, or activity? In addition, discussion focused on groupings of multiple grants will usually be more sensible the more "tightly coupled" their activities are (that is, clusters of grants will be less interesting in the case of "block grant" style funding than for truly strategic packages of grants).

• *The possible inclusion of "by exception" rules.* As in the Packard example, a foundation may identify a *typical* focus of discussion, along with the exceptional circumstances under which a *different* focus will be examined. For example, a foundation might generally focus on strategic initiatives but make exceptions for big, important single grants. Another foundation might typically focus on the grant but have guidelines about when it will make decisions about a component of a grant.

• *Possible "off-the-table" rules.* At some foundations, a few grants may be sacred cows. For example, these might be grants made to an organization with which the foundation's founder had a special relationship. Or they may be grants to an organization in the community that, for whatever reason, the foundation will continue to fund no matter what. In such cases, any evaluation funding may focus on program improvement. Depending on the menu of evaluation options the foundation has, pragmatism may dictate that these special grants be excluded from serious consideration during the process of allocating evaluation resources.

From the preceding considerations, a few tentative guidelines can be offered about what to focus on in strategic evaluation planning. In general, foundations with a larger grant portfolio are more likely to attend to the initiative or other cluster. To figure out whether some grouping of grants makes sense, one should examine the strategic grantmaking the foundation makes or the responsive grant-making programs the foundation has: Are there important groupings that staff talk about and that are used in funding and other decisions? Including "by exception" and "off-the-table" rules may be important, at least for some foundations. The individual grant might be a safe default option as a place to start, unless the initiative or some other clustering seems obvious. What's most important, though, is that a foundation thinks through what works for it.

A Menu of Evaluation Options to Define Levels of Intensity

For most foundations, there is likely to be a range of evaluation alternatives that vary in terms of complexity, expense, and labor-intensiveness. The details of the acceptable range of choices will vary from one foundation to another. For example, for some foundations, especially some larger ones, the most complex, expensive, and labor-intensive forms of evaluation may include causal assessments of the effects of an intervention, perhaps through experimental or quasi-experimental methods, carried out by a third-party independent evaluator (see Chapter Twelve). For these foundations, the high-intensity end of the menu of evaluation options can be characterized in terms of methods that seek to answer causal questions about the impact of the grantee activities and to minimize bias in the resulting answers. The lower end of intensity for such foundations may consist of monitoring done by the grantee, who is asked to report on outputs.

But these are not the only possible menu options a foundation might have. For another foundation, the lower end of intensity may consist of routine financial reports, and the high end may involve frequent stakeholder forums or other attempts to generate democratic deliberation (House and Howe, 1999), with external consultant facilitators. Here the high-intensity end of the menu can be characterized as an extensive, facilitated, participatory approach to evaluation. For yet another foundation, a relatively intense evaluation might involve the construction by specialists of a well-designed performance measurement system, with indicators of demonstrated reliability and validity, while a low-intensity evaluation may involve grantee reports on whatever performance indicators they can readily identify.

Although foundations may vary in terms of the options they consider, within a given foundation, more intense evaluations probably will have:

- A larger budget for evaluation
- Greater involvement from foundation staff (especially from evaluation staff, if such exist)

- Greater likelihood of a third-party evaluator
- More complex negotiations and oversight regarding evaluation
- More design features intended to minimize various forms of bias in the evaluation

We have not tried to lay out a single menu of evaluation options, in part because a single chapter cannot satisfactorily identify all the varied menu options and all the reasons some options might be preferred to others (relevant discussions are given throughout this volume).

Each foundation's menu should be designed to match the kind of questions it wants to answer through evaluation. For example, some foundations want a portion of their evaluations to provide reasonably convincing evidence about the efficacy of the programs they fund, so that others might be persuaded to adopt the programs if they prove effective. Such a foundation should have causal methods, such as randomized trials and quasi-experiments, on the high-intensity portion of its menu. However, another foundation might have different reasons for undertaking evaluation. For example, it might want to have evaluation methods that program managers can use as a guide (Wholey, 2003) and that can also indicate whether social conditions related to the foundation's mission are getting better or worse. Such a foundation might have, on the high-intensity end of its evaluation menu, high-quality performance indicator systems, with indicators both at the program and the community level. Again, the menu should reflect the kind of questions the foundation hopes to address through evaluation.

Our concept of evaluation intensity thus can apply across organizations with different approaches to evaluation (and to a single foundation that changes its approach to evaluation over time). All we assume is that there are two or more options, varying in intensity, on the foundation's evaluation menu. This is consistent with Melton, Slater, and Constantine's suggestion (Chapter Ten) that foundations should develop a "two-tiered" evaluation strategy. Taking that idea a step further, foundations may decide to have finer gradations of evaluation intensity. Importantly, the existence of a menu of typical evaluation approaches need not forestall all creativity or experimentation in evaluation design. The menu should be subject to change, and new evaluation options may be tried out. Indeed, one of the high-intensity evaluation options could be to have a relatively high-budget evaluation, with *all* details of designs to be developed with the evaluator, grantee, program participants, and any other important stakeholder groups.

Implicit in the idea of an evaluation menu, with options of varying levels of intensity, is the previously discussed notion that one size of evaluation does not fit all the work a foundation funds. But this leads to an important question: How should a foundation make judgments that one grant (or initiative) should have a more intense evaluation, whereas another should have a less intense evaluation?

What Criteria to Use in the Planning Process

In this section, we discuss several factors that might be taken into consideration by a foundation as it makes judgments about what to evaluate and how intensely. Foundations vary substantially in the way they approach this judgment task. Some foundations have thus far avoided decisions about how to match grants (or initiatives or clusters) to more and less intense evaluation options *by carrying out little if any systematic evaluation!* Others rely on a routine formula, with a set percentage of each grant's budget marked for evaluation, at least for key funding streams; the implicit rationale is that one size, proportionately, fits all. Yet other foundations rely on a kind of happenstance, largely involving whether the program officer is interested in pushing for more intense evaluation, along with the occasional grantee who seeks intense evaluation.

In contrast, a select set of foundations apparently engage in relatively thorough discussions about how to allocate evaluation resources. As more foundations move in this direction, they should consider how to structure the conversation within the foundation about the process for matching foundation-funded work to the different levels of intensity on the evaluation menu. As a step in this direction, this section contains a set of possible criteria, drawn from several sources, including the literature on portfolio management in research and development (for example, Cooper, Edgett, and Kleinschmidt, 2001). An explicit set of criteria can greatly enhance discussions about strategic evaluation decisions. At the same time, we acknowledge the limits to rational planning of evaluation resource allocation. As in any endeavor, being lucky or appropriately opportunistic can be as important as having a good, reasoned plan. But luck and effective opportunism are more likely when one has planned well.

The following are several criteria that, we suggest, can be used in making strategic evaluation decisions.

• *Investment.* Put simply, what are the costs and opportunity costs for a given grant, kind of activity, or initiative?

• *Potential learning.* How likely does it seem that an evaluation, and in particular a high-intensity evaluation, will increase learning that will, in turn, influence the beliefs and behaviors of various parties, including the grantee, foundation staff, the foundation board, or others? For example, will evaluation likely help determine whether the foundation continues funding this kind of grantee activity?

• *Potential leveraging.* To what extent may evaluation, especially high-intensity evaluation, stimulate other funding sources, whether local, state, or federal government, or other foundations? If, for example, an evaluation finds a demonstration program to be effective, does it seem likely that this will help shake loose funding to implement the program elsewhere?

• *Mission centrality.* Are the funded activities central to the mission of the foundation (or of the program area within the foundation)? In general, high-intensity evaluation may be more warranted for activities closest to the core of the foundation's mission.

• *Potential for partnerships to support or expand the evaluation.* In some instances, potential partners might help fund an evaluation or increase its scope by evaluating similar activities. Evaluation, and higher-intensity evaluation, may be more reasonable when such a partnership is possible.

• *Past evidence.* To what extent is there a compelling research base already answering the potential evaluation questions (for example, demonstrating the effectiveness of the funded activities)? In general, the more compelling the existing research base, the less sense it makes to invest large amounts of evaluation resources to answer that question. (However, other evaluation questions—for example, about implementation—may remain important.)

• *Uniqueness.* To what extent are the funded activities unique, as opposed to commonplace? There may be more room to make a difference if the activities are not commonplace. Uniqueness may be a key criterion for "risk capital" or especially innovative grants.

• *Plausibility of grantee's rationale.* To what extent is there a clear, compelling rationale indicating how the activities should be effective? In program evaluation language, is there a plausible program theory? Without a compelling rationale, it may make little sense to invest in high-intensity evaluation and may instead make sense to revise the program or further probe the program theory.

• *Evaluation capacity and feasibility.* How practical is it to evaluate these activities? Is there a pool of evaluation specialists with the relevant skills? Are there ready-to-use evaluation methods and instruments? High-intensity evaluation may not be sensible if evaluation capacity is lacking (unless funding is adequate to help build capacity).

• *Consistency with grantee and stakeholder concerns.* The foundation is only one of many stakeholders in the evaluation of its grants. Decisions about the evaluation intensity and approach should consider and respect the views of these multiple stakeholders.

These criteria, we believe, should not be treated like parts of a mathematical equation. One criterion may outweigh another for a given initiative. For example, low-budget grants may still call for high-intensity evaluation, if they are mission central and offer strong learning potential.

In addition, the criteria could be combined into larger subgroups, some of which may be more important to one foundation than to another. Consider two possible groupings of the criteria. First, for a foundation trying to use its grants and evaluations as a lever to influence others, the most important criteria might be potential learning, potential leveraging, uniqueness, past evidence, and perhaps potential partnering. This set of criteria might be especially important when, as may be increasingly common, the foundation sees *evaluation itself as a change strategy.* That is, in addition to the other ways that foundations may strive to help create social betterment, such as funding direct services or media campaigns, a foundation may be drawn to a grant or initiative precisely because evaluation itself may help bring about social change (for example, by helping to persuade the government or other funders to support a new kind of service). A second grouping of criteria makes more sense when evaluation is intended primarily for audiences internal to the foundation, such as the board. Under these conditions, mission centrality and investment may be relatively more important criteria.

As these two examples suggest, different foundations may reasonably use different criteria in making strategic evaluation decisions. At larger foundations, program areas within the foundation may have their own criteria as well.

How should a foundation decide which criteria to use? Put simply, we think it is vital to openly consider which criteria are to be emphasized in strategic evaluation planning. The preceding list should prove a good place to start the discussion. Are some of these criteria less relevant for the foundation? Are a few of them key? Are there important criteria for the foundation that are not listed here? Which criteria seemed to be important in past decisions about what got evaluated at greater or lesser intensity? Looking at a few case studies from within the foundation can be a good way to help make the discussion concrete and to help sort out which criteria foundation staff and the board see as most important.

In addition, a decision is needed about whether to use the same set of criteria for the sequential decisions about *whether* to evaluate and (if so) *how intensely* to evaluate. The simplest procedure is to use the same set of criteria for both decisions, but this is not necessary. For example, mission centrality and investment might be the criteria used in deciding whether to evaluate. For instance, all grants above a certain dollar cutoff might be evaluated, except for those that were made for special relationship or donor reasons and are less central to the foundation's mission. Next, potential learning and leveraging might serve as the key criteria in judgments about how intensely to evaluate, with uniqueness, past evidence, and evaluation capacity and feasibility as secondary criteria. Whatever sets of criteria emerge from initial discussion, they should be tried out and then modified if needed.

In addition to helping create a more thoughtful and systematic allocation of evaluation resources and responsibilities, the process of selecting criteria should help generate a foundationwide discussion about what foundation staff and the board hope to get out of evaluation.

The Processes of Making Strategic Evaluation Decisions

Having a set of criteria is important but not enough. Also needed is a process for judging the grants (or initiatives or other clusters) in terms of the criteria. In this section, we briefly discuss some key aspects of the process through which a foundation makes strategic evaluation decisions. For ease of presentation, in this section we assume that discussion about allocating evaluation resources will focus on the initiative.

In one sense, the needed procedures are relatively straightforward. Each initiative, current and prospective, should be considered in terms of the criteria the foundation has decided to use. An initiative that "scores" relatively high on the criteria should receive relatively intense evaluation. However, several questions need to be considered in developing a decision-making process:

• *Who is at the table?* A number of parties might be involved in strategic evaluation planning. These include senior leadership of the foundation, all foundation officers, board members, representatives of grantees, and the clients served by grantees. Current plans at Packard involve an initial round of deliberation within each of the foundation's three program areas. Although not required, input from grantees and clients would be considered. A second round of deliberation would take place among senior leadership and, for particularly significant evaluation efforts (for example, high investment or mission centrality), deliberation within the board. Greene, Millett, and Hopson (Chapter Five) make a case for broad inclusiveness in all evaluation activities. There are several ways this could occur, including consultation prior to the decision-making process in the foundation or consultation afterward but prior to any further evaluation planning. When involving clients or other stakeholder groups, one should think about how to obtain input that is representative of the group (and not simply the idiosyncratic views of a few).

• *How formal is the process?* Our sense is that most foundations would prefer a less formal process, using the criteria as a basis for framing *discussion* about the initiatives at a work meeting rather than using a formal system with rating forms and formulas to combine ratings. More formal techniques could serve as a fallback in case discussion gets stalled.

• *Is there a single decision or multiple overlapping decisions?* The process could be divided into two decisions: (1) which lines of work shall be evaluated, and (2) for those lines that will be evaluated, which ones will be evaluated more, or less, intensely. Alternatively, these two decisions could be made simultaneously, with both informed by the foundation's chosen criteria. Or, as is the case at Packard, a decision could be made in advance that every line of work will be evaluated at some level, which means that the decision process boils down to the question of intensity.

• *What is the cycle for decision making?* Is this a periodic, perhaps annual, process that provides the blueprint for evaluation activities for the coming year? Or is it a continuing process, beginning each time an inquiry about funding or a new grant application comes in or a new initiative is developed? Perhaps the most important consideration is that the evaluation planning cycle needs to be sensibly aligned with the grantmaking cycle (see Chapter Six), which at most foundations needs to be in sync with the board meeting cycle.

• *How does one deal with the various agendas that may be at the table?* What steps should be taken to try to ensure that honest and open deliberations take place, given, for instance, that different initiatives may be shepherded by different program officers and may be of interest to different board members? It may help to have a facilitator who is sensitive to the various agendas but not seen as an advocate of one or another. A member of the foundation's evaluation staff might be a suitable facilitator. Presumably, this person should be open in the sense of advocating quality evaluation, with levels of intensity and methods that fit the questions and offer the best potential for evaluation to contribute to learning and to social betterment.

In short, a process needs to be developed whereby judgments are made, using the selected criteria, about how intensely (if at all) to evaluate which work. Depending on the culture of the foundation, this can be relatively straightforward and involve open discussion added to regularly scheduled staff meetings. Or it can be relatively formal, with a special meeting, rating cards, and explicit decisions about which criteria are "must-haves" and which are "nice additions." In either case, decisions are needed about several issues: who will be at the table, whether to combine or separate decisions about what to evaluate and about how intensely, what the decision-making cycle is, and how best to deal with the various agendas at the table.

Bringing It All Together: An Example

In this section, we examine a real-life example to illustrate several aspects of the process of making judgments about what to evaluate and at what level of intensity, focusing on use of the criteria. The David and Lucile Packard Foundation's CCLI was announced in March 1998 as a five-year, $175-million line of work. The purpose of CCLI was to "conserve large expanses of open space, farmlands, and wildlife habitat in three California regions—the Central Coast, the Central Valley, and the Sierra Nevada—and to develop supportive organizations and policies" (David and Lucile Packard Foundation, 2000, 2003). The initiative consisted of a number of strategies that have been translated into CCLI-supported activities:

- Transactions, including both direct purchases and the acquisition of easements
- Policy and planning, by making grants to organizations that work on land-use practices and policies
- Capacity building of nonprofit conservation groups
- Restoration and stewardship, that is, grants to restore and ensure quality long-term management of a high-priority resource
- Public education to increase interest in the preservation of open lands

There has also been a focus on leveraging by stimulating contributions from others, whether foundations, government bodies, nonprofit organizations, or individuals.

The general evaluation planning for CCLI took place before the proposed process for strategic evaluation planning at the Packard Foundation was developed. Nevertheless, it illustrates many aspects of the potential planning process.

Recall that the Packard Foundation has tentatively decided to focus on lines of work in its evaluation planning process. In addition, the foundation's plan is to initiate the planning process within each of the three programs within the foundation (Children, Families, and Communities; Population; and Conservation and Science—the latter having been formed in 2002, after CCLI was implemented, with the merger of the Conservation and Science programs). Thus discussion of CCLI as a possible focus of evaluation would have started within what is now the Conservation and Science Program. Conservation and Science staff clearly would have identified CCLI as a major *line of work*. The initiative was designed with a specific, coherent set of intended outcomes. Multiple kinds of activities (for example, transactions, restoration, and capacity building) were included, but were included specifically to create a menu of options to test while trying to maximize effectiveness.

If CCLI had been judged relative to the criteria presented earlier, the conclusion almost certainly would have been that a relatively intensive evaluation was warranted. Consider this claim in terms of each criterion. The level of *investment* was substantial, with expenditures of $175 million budgeted at the beginning of the planned five-year initiative. CCLI was also very *mission central* for the Conservation and Science Program and for the foundation more generally, as the program's mission includes efforts to "ensure a healthy future for all life by conserving critical natural systems, addressing key threats to the systems, and providing scientific information and training that will enhance their conservation." CCLI was a key effort to help achieve these ends in California. Given the high level of investment and high mission centrality, it was important for the foundation to determine whether the CCLI approach was effective and to try to assess which of its strategies, alone or in combination, work best.

Leveraging was explicitly part of the design of CCLI. Key examples of leveraging emerged during the initiative. For example, special funding from the state of California was made available during the initiative to share in the purchase of open spaces in the state. The criterion of *learning* was also important, with the emphasis on learning that could influence both the foundation and others. This is evident in numerous foundation statements about CCLI, such as "create a model for replication elsewhere" and "advance the state of the art." The potential for CCLI to generate learning that could influence others' actions was also noted by Bruce Babbitt, former Secretary of the Interior, who said, "Down the road, it will be much easier for government agencies to put money into landscape-level projects and restoration practices that have been proven thanks to these kinds of philanthropic investments." (The statement is available on the Packard Foundation Web site: http://www.packard.org/index.cgi?page=ccli.)

As this quote also implies, although the general notion of transactions as a way to enhance conservation is not new, the specific configuration of CCLI appears to be *unique*. For example, the "transaction mix," including the package of other CCLI components that could be combined with transactions, was not common elsewhere. In addition, CCLI in part emphasized "innovative transactions," including the acquisition of water rights or other easements that fostered conservation and compatible uses.

In short, when CCLI is examined in terms of most of the criteria presented earlier, it seems to warrant a relatively intensive evaluation. In fact, with input from the Conservation and Science Program, the Packard Foundation's Department of Evaluation and Learning Services (ELS), and others, CCLI was initially slated for a comparative, quasi-experimental evaluation designed to assess the impact of the initiative, with a third-party evaluator. At this point in the process, however, another criterion came into play. Concerns arose with respect to *evaluation capacity and feasibility*, specifically in terms of the feasibility of a comparative, quasi-experimental evaluation. CCLI sites had been chosen precisely because of their special characteristics, including perceived likelihood of success. As a consequence, it would have been difficult after the fact to select comparison sites that were truly comparable. In addition, given the many potentially important variables, both environmental and social, plus the absence of strong theory, questions existed about the feasibility of creating matched comparison sites or of adjusting statistically for the relevant factors.

Given these difficulties, another consideration that should influence evaluation planning, that is, the *incremental value of a more intense evaluation,* also became important. In light of the difficulties of constructing a good comparison group, it seemed that the investment in a comparative, quasi-experimental evaluation would not be justified, relative to the expected payoff. At the same time, CCLI remained a key line of work, highly important in terms of such criteria as investment, mission centrality, leveraging, and learning. As a result, the decision was made to alter the intensity of the evaluation by dropping the comparison group.

This decision involved extensive discussion among Conservation and Science Program staff, ELS staff, and the evaluator, as well as some input from executive management and discussion with the board committee overseeing Conservation and Science work. If the general evaluation planning process currently under consideration at the Packard Foundation had been in place at the time, some of the discussion would presumably have taken place within Program Leadership—a group that includes senior members of all program areas, as well as top foundation staff. In part, the rationale for this broader participation is that major evaluations are significant investments that benefit from wider discussion.

Conclusion

Some form of evaluation, however informal and unsystematic, presumably informs the decisions made within a foundation. This chapter, like the rest of this book, focuses on the deliberate and thoughtful use of systematic forms of evaluation. And, like the book as a whole, we see substantial benefits for foundations if they use evaluation-based information and evaluative thinking throughout the planning and grantmaking process, including goal setting, agreement on indicators, design of methods, data collection, and analysis, as well as the reporting of results to important audiences. We have tried to extend this theme by laying out a form of evaluative thinking that can be used to help allocate evaluation resources and responsibilities.

We have suggested that foundations would be well served by going through an explicit process for making decisions about what should be evaluated systematically and at what level of intensity. Unless foundation leadership and staff think carefully about these issues, decisions about whether something is rigorously evaluated may occur by happenstance or by the personal preference of a single staff member. To the extent that such decisions are idiosyncratic, foundation and grantee staff may be more likely to see demands for evaluation as arbitrary. In addition, if more explicit and thoughtful decisions are made about what to evaluate, this should make it easier to communicate to the foundation board and others about how evaluation is a sensible activity for the foundation. More generally, thoughtful, explicit, and transparent judgment processes about what to evaluate should increase the likelihood that evaluation contributes to the mission of the foundation.

We have discussed three key questions that confront a foundation as it makes judgments about what level of evaluation intensity (if any) to use. First, *what will be the subject of strategic evaluation planning*—grants, components of grants, initiatives, or something else? In short, we expect that among foundations with a large and strategically driven grant portfolio, discussion is likely to center around the initiative or some other meaningful clustering of grants. Other foundations may be more likely to focus on grants or components of grants.

Second, *what kinds of criteria or considerations should be considered in strategic evaluation planning?* We have offered a set of criteria that a foundation could use as a starting point in selecting its own criteria. These include mission centrality, investment, potential leveraging, potential learning, uniqueness, past evidence, potential for partnering, plausible rationale, evaluation capacity and feasibility, and consistency with grantee and stakeholder concerns.

Third, *what procedures might be used in making such judgments?* We have suggested that many foundations will do well with open-ended discussion of the work they fund, relative to their chosen criteria. Certain aspects of the process, such as who is at the table and what the decision-making cycle is, must also be worked out.

Foundations must make decisions—important decisions—on an ongoing basis. Chief among these is how to allocate the foundation's resources—what kind of work to fund. As is illustrated throughout this book, evaluation can contribute to such decisions. Evaluation can also contribute to the choices that grantees make, for example, whether to keep delivering services in the same way or to make changes. In some instances, evaluation can influence the decisions of others, such as decisions by other foundations and local, state, and federal governments about whether to fund some new program. Informal evaluation (based, for example, on hunches, experience, or observations, whether many or few) can be the basis for all these decisions. Or more formal, systematic evaluation can be used to help support decision making. Because resources are scarce, it is important to make decisions well, using quality information.

But there's a catch. Systematic evaluation costs money and generally costs more, the more intensive the evaluation methods. And the more that's spent on evaluation, the less the foundation can spend on other things. All this has led us to suggest procedures that can be used to decide, in a thoughtful, systematic, and potentially transparent way, what to evaluate and what to evaluate most intensely. The automatic allocation of resources for intense, systematic evaluation of everything is no more defensible than doing no systematic evaluation at all. Evaluative thinking should apply widely, including to the task of allocating evaluation resources and responsibilities.

References

Cooper, R. G., Edgett, S. J., & Kleinschmidt, E. J. (2001). *Portfolio management for new products* (2nd ed.). Cambridge, MA: Perseus.

David, T. (1999). *Reflections on strategic grantmaking.* Woodland Hills, CA: The California Wellness Foundation.

David and Lucile Packard Foundation. (2000). *Conserving California Landscapes: Midterm report.* Los Altos, CA: Author.

David and Lucile Packard Foundation. (2003). *Conserving California Landscapes: Five-year report.* Los Altos, CA: Author.

House, E., & Howe, K. (1999). *Values in evaluation and social research.* Thousand Oaks, CA: Sage.

Prager, D. (1999). *Raising the value of philanthropy: A synthesis of informal interviews with foundation executives and observers of philanthropy.* Washington, DC: Grantmakers in Health/Strategic Consulting Services.

Wholey, J. S. (2003). Improving performance and accountability: Responding to emerging management challenges. In S. I. Donaldson & M. Scriven (eds.), *Evaluating social programs and problems: Visions for the new millennium* (pp. 43–62). Hillsdale, NJ: Erlbaum.

CHAPTER EIGHT

ADAPTING EVALUATION TO ACCOMMODATE FOUNDATIONS' STRUCTURAL AND CULTURAL CHARACTERISTICS

Ross F. Conner, Victor Kuo, Marli S. Melton, and Ricardo A. Millett

There are many issues to consider and questions to answer before implementing evaluation within a foundation. What resources does evaluation require? What exactly should be evaluated? How will evaluation fit within the culture and context of a particular foundation? Who should be involved in setting the evaluation agenda for a foundation? What factors facilitate or hinder the implementation of evaluation? What are possible challenges to a smooth, productive evaluation experience? This chapter answers these questions, drawing on the coauthors' collective experience in foundation-based evaluation. The material in this chapter will help readers understand the importance of four dimensions of foundations that are relevant to the conduct of evaluation. These dimensions are described, and their implications for successfully planning, implementing, using, and benefiting from evaluation are discussed.

The factors that affect evaluation are both internal to a foundation and external to it (Bickel, Nelson, and Millett, 2002; Preskill and Torres, 1999). Although there are important external factors, our focus here is on internal factors that influence evaluation-related decisions and activities within most foundations. The four dimensions fit into two general categories—structural factors and cultural factors—which can be outlined as follows:

The authors are grateful to several outside reviewers for comments on earlier versions of this chapter.

1. Structural Factors
   - *Resource level* relates to the foundation's fiscal and financial aspects, as well as its administrative and personnel characteristics
   - *The focus of evaluation* involves considerations about what should be evaluated; it usually centers on whether individual projects, general initiatives, or overall foundation activities are to be the primary concern
2. Cultural Factors
   - *Organizational climate* refers to the understanding among foundation staff and board about the purpose of evaluation and its anticipated outcomes
   - *Diversity of stakeholders* involved in the foundation's work refers to the audiences for evaluation planning, implementation, and outcomes

In the next sections, we describe and illustrate all four of these dimensions in more detail and discuss the implications for implementing evaluation.

Structural Factors

Both of the structural factors we discuss allow for wide variability across foundations and result in distinctive differences among them.

Resource Level

The United States has more than 60,000 foundations, which in 2001 granted about $30 billion (Foundation Center, 2003). These foundations vary widely in their asset base, their programmatic focus, the size of grants they make, and the number of staff they employ. A foundation's ability to carry out evaluation is perhaps most significantly affected by its overall asset size; consequently, we divide our discussion between (1) evaluation within large foundations and (2) evaluation within small or medium-size foundations.

Large Foundations. In 2001, there were about 1,120 large foundations (2 percent of the total number of foundations) with assets of $50 million or more (Foundation Center, 2003). These are the foundations most people think of when they hear the word *foundation*. This top 2 percent distributed more than half of all grant dollars. If the ordinary foundation annual payout policy is used (5 percent of the endowment), the smallest of these "large" foundations (those with assets of $50 million) each distributed $2.5 million and the largest distributed well over $100 million each.

The level of grantmaking by these larger foundations has implications for the number and type of evaluations they can conduct. Generally, more financial resources are required to implement complex evaluation designs, such as true experiments and quasi-experiments, or designs that require a long time period, such as longitudinal studies. In 2000, the average dollar amount for a program evaluation grant was slightly under $250,000 (Foundation Center, 2002), making the purchase of complex evaluations well beyond the reach of small and of some medium-size foundations.

Among this group of large foundations, most employ full-time staff, with a median staffing level of seven and an average of more than twenty people (Atienza, 2002). If we assume that a foundation's operating budget is approximately 10 percent of its payout (Lipman and Wilhelm, 2003), then large foundations have significant resources ($250,000 to over $10 million), some of which could be used to hire additional evaluation-focused staff and consultants. Researchers estimate, however, that fewer than twenty of the largest foundations (about .02 percent) have director-level staff dedicated to evaluation (Patrizi and McMullan, 1998). Consequently, the capacity of all large foundations to implement evaluation, as measured solely by the presence of dedicated evaluation staff, appears limited.

The number of dedicated staff, however, tells only part of the story, because it is mainly the competencies evaluation staff members offer that ultimately enable the implementation of evaluation activities. Most large foundations have evaluation-focused staff that perform two different oversight roles. The first role is working with program staff and evaluation consultants to plan and manage particular evaluation projects. Evaluation staff have the technical knowledge about evaluation models and methodological approaches that is needed to determine what evaluation designs are best suited for given programs, what they are likely to cost, and how adjustments can best be made during implementation (Kuo and Henry, 2002). The second role is monitoring grant expenditures across grants and analyzing, in a general way, whether program benefits occurred.

In addition to these roles, evaluation staff can enhance the capacity of foundations to implement and use evaluation. They can assist in establishing well-defined grant programs that can be evaluated, and they can work with communications and policy staff to synthesize, manage, and use knowledge produced from completed evaluation projects (Preskill and Torres, 1999).

Larger foundations can also build evaluation into other aspects of their grant-making. They often have long-term relationships with some grantees and invest in their organizational capacity. Foundations with this perspective may train grantees to conduct and use evaluation as an internal management tool to improve program outcomes. Large foundations can build in funding for evaluation as part of key grants, with the evaluation performed (or at least managed) by the grantees themselves.

The grantees and a large foundation may also work together on the evaluation. This is especially true when the foundation is supporting several related projects, possibly in different locations. For example, each grantee may conduct or contract for an evaluation of its own activities, whereas the foundation conducts or contracts for an evaluation of the grants program or the project as a whole, with perhaps the added task of ensuring some level of consistent evaluation at the individual sites. Although this sounds relatively simple, capturing the learning both from the individual grant sites and across the whole project often requires a sophisticated and sensitive evaluation plan.

In spite of their available resources, many large foundations perform relatively little grant evaluation because they are focused primarily on "getting the money out the door for good causes." This is particularly true of a new, expanding category of large foundations composed primarily of donor-advised funds. Often operated by nonprofit affiliates of commercial investment companies, mutual fund companies, or banks, these foundations may operate primarily as fundraising, investing, and charitable check-writing entities for the many small donor-advised funds. The donors to these component funds, who recommend the grants themselves, rely on annual reports, newsletters, and other publications from the grantee organizations to gauge grant results rather than use information gleaned from formal evaluation. Thus these very large foundations, which may have hundreds of millions of dollars in assets and distribute tens of millions in grants, tend to operate more like a collection of very small foundations. Because many of these donor-advised funds are relatively new, their experience with grantmaking, much less with evaluation, is limited. As they mature and gain more experience with grantmaking and with the differences among promised, perceived, and documented outcomes, they may develop an interest in promoting evaluation to their donors. Donor advisers with an interest in evaluation can build an evaluation requirement into their grants and may find some of the ideas about evaluation at small and medium-size foundations useful.

Small and Medium-Size Foundations. We define *small foundations* as those with assets under $10 million; in 2002, there were more than fifty thousand of them (Foundation Center, 2003). With grant budgets of about $400,000 to $500,000 a year, they face the choice of making a few significant grants annually or spreading their funds to more projects in smaller grants. Over 90 percent of small foundations do not employ staff, relying instead on volunteers (usually board members) to do all the foundation's work; the remainder may employ one or two people, frequently part-time. Additional administrative resources dedicated to foundation activities are very limited, if they exist at all.

There are approximately three thousand medium-size foundations, with assets ranging from $10 million to $50 million—about 6 percent of the total number of foundations. The nation's more than six hundred community foundations are concentrated in this foundation group. The average staffing level for these foundations is two people, and their administrative resources and systems vary widely. To the extent that a foundation's assets approach $50 million, with a resulting annual payout of approximately $2.5 million, evaluation can begin to play a more prominent role. This occurs not only because there are financial and staff resources that can be devoted to evaluation but because grant reporting often becomes a significant issue.

With few, if any, staff and limited resources, most small and medium-size foundations need to spend evaluation funds carefully. Self-reported expenditure (sometimes called *program input*) information and process-focused information may be the extent of evaluation activities that are possible on small grants. Grantees can also be asked to provide outcome information, but without extra funds, technical assistance, or outside consultants, the information would likely be limited because it is the rare grantee organization that already does evaluation as a regular part of its activities. Alternatively, funders with limited resources but similar interests can consider cofunding evaluations to leverage grantee resources for more comprehensive evaluations, including input, process, and outcomes data.

Although small and medium-size foundations need to be realistic in asking for complex evaluations, they may be surprised at the amount of information grantees can make available. Grantees frequently receive funds from several different sources and may already be collecting evaluation information for another funder. This information may serve the foundation's interests or, with some additions, may provide an even more complete report. The periodic communications between grantees and foundations, which now are frequently submitted electronically, can include evaluation-focused information. Using foundation-generated templates that relate to the foundation's interests and the grantee's goals, small and medium-size foundations can ask grantees to complete and submit electronic files with evaluative information.

All foundations, even small ones, can improve their own capacity to monitor and analyze some or all of their grants, undertaking the same kind of capacity building that foundations often ask their grantees to do. Even if small and medium-size foundations only evaluate a few of their most significant grants, this can help them decide where additional resources might make an even greater difference for the next funding cycle. There are some short-term evaluation training workshops and classes specifically developed for foundation staff. (More information is available from The Evaluator's Institute, on-line at www.evaluatorsinstitute.org.) Up-to-date computers, software, and the training to use both are now readily available and affordable, both for foundations and grantees. (See Chapter Ten for other ideas.)

Although larger foundations can afford to do more evaluations and can do them in more depth, all foundations can learn more about the issues that are important to them if they encourage grantees to include some level of grant evaluation as a regular part of their activities. Foundations can invest funds to build grantees' capacity to conduct in-house evaluations. This can be done by sponsoring workshops on evaluation so that grantees can think through the logic models that underlie their programs and devise techniques to track progress and to monitor short-term and longer-term outcomes at reasonable cost. Even investing in additional training about some aspect of evaluation, such as interview techniques, can help boost capacity and morale among grantees. In this way, foundations can leverage their resources to foster more evaluation activity among grantees.

Focus of Evaluation

The second important structural factor is the focus of evaluation—what is to be evaluated. If evaluation is to be implemented, foundations and their partners must identify what ought to be evaluated, because this determines the scope and purpose of the evaluation effort. Evaluation may be focused on a variety of activities and at a variety of levels: individual projects, groups of projects, entire program areas, the foundation as a whole, grantee organizations, grantmaking strategies, geographic regions, or targeted populations. We now describe some of the common evaluation foci for foundations, the advantages and disadvantages of each, and how those responsible for the evaluation function within foundations might consider selecting a focus for their evaluation efforts. Note that evaluation foci are described here as unique types, but foundations are likely to have multiple foci, making the situation more complex in actual practice.

Projects. Most foundation grantmaking supports *projects,* that is, single grants to single organizations to carry out activities to achieve a set of outcomes. *Outcomes* here are defined as changes in the status or condition of an entity such as an individual, organization, system, or geographic region. Outcomes for these projects may be identified and proposed by the grantee organization, or they may be identified by the foundation. Foundations' desired outcomes are often outlined in grantmaking guidelines or broadly defined in their mission or historical character. In other cases, grantee organizations and foundation staff may work in partnership to develop and agree on a set of outcomes, which can then serve as the basis for evaluation activities.

Initiatives. An *initiative* is a collection of grant activities involving more than one grantee organization and aimed at achieving a common set of outcomes. Initiatives are also called clusters of projects, lines of work, and subprograms. Initiatives may involve multiple strategies, span multiple years, involve multiple geographic regions, engage multiple grantees, operate at multiple levels of organizational entities, and involve millions of dollars in grants. As the term implies, initiatives are frequently driven by the foundation and reflect foundation interests in becoming strategic investors. Some philanthropic initiatives specify programmatic outcomes at the beginning and also articulate, at the outset, the interventions and activities to be employed to achieve those outcomes.

To illustrate how an initiative might be designed, consider the hypothetical example of a youth initiative. A foundation could make multiple and similar grants to different community-based youth organizations to raise student achievement. These grantee organizations would all employ a similar youth-mentoring model with a desired set of outcomes, specifically increases in student test scores. In this example, all grantees adopt the desired outcomes and use the same set of program activities. In another youth initiative case, different grantees might have the same set of outcomes (for example, increases in test scores) but use different program activities (for example, mentoring, tutoring, or self-esteem building).

Evaluation at the initiative level involves specifying the commonalities of an initiative, in outcomes as well as in program activities. Initiatives that have a common set of outcomes enable the evaluator to aggregate results for the initiative as a whole. Initiatives that have disparate outcomes present challenges for the evaluator in identifying overall results.

The concept of evaluating a collection of projects within philanthropy is more than a decade old. In 1988, Ronald Richards, director of evaluation for The W. K. Kellogg Foundation, developed the label "cluster evaluation" (Sanders, 1997). The Kellogg Foundation continues to use this approach, now emphasizing systemic and policy-change outcomes, as well as the process for identifying common themes in retrospect, after grants have been made (W. K. Kellogg Foundation, 1998). The Pew Charitable Trusts use the term *cluster review* and commissioned their first review in the early 1990s. Cluster reviews are prospective; evaluations are conducted on a set of grants pursuing a collective goal articulated at the outset (Pew Charitable Trusts, 2001; Snow and Baxter, 2002).

The Foundation as a Whole. Evaluations focused on the foundation as a whole have constituted, in recent years, a mixed bag of evaluative activities. Some foundations have focused on evaluating "customer service" elements of the grantmaking process. They have hired consultants to survey grantees' experiences working with program officers to measure responsiveness, collaboration, respectfulness, and timeliness. Other foundations have refined their overall grantmaking portfolios such that most, if not all, of their grantmaking focuses on a few select outcome indicators. By focusing their programmatic goals, they have made it possible to evaluate the programmatic achievements of the foundation as a whole. Many other foundations continue to hold multiple program goals, making aggregation impossible. Finally, senior management within foundations has historically focused on evaluating the foundation's administrative efficiency, typically measured as the ratio of administrative costs to dollars granted. This type of analysis is less relevant to program evaluation.

Strategies. The term *strategy* has been used in various ways within the foundation world. Here it is defined as the general approach of activities employed to achieve program outcomes. Strategies are the "how," and program outcomes are the "what" of grants. Some examples of strategies include grassroots organizing (to achieve community improvements) and direct services (to achieve health improvements). This conceptualization may also include "cross-cutting" strategies or programs. Strategies are not necessarily restricted to a program area such as education or the arts but may be generic and used across various program areas. Complex grantmaking portfolios may use multiple strategies in parallel or in sequence.

Evaluating strategies can be challenging because similar strategies may be employed across projects, initiatives, and program areas in different ways. Consequently, intended program outcomes may be very dissimilar, and aggregating results may not make sense. The classic problem of comparing apples to oranges arises, unless we are able to specify and track similar types of results across areas. Even if we are able to track similar outcomes, can we be sure that similar strategies contributed to the outcomes in similar ways in each area? In the simplest case, if causal evaluation designs are used in individual evaluations within these multiple program areas, and if all outcome indicators exhibit a positive trend, one might be justified in claiming the virtue of the strategy. Evaluating strategies typically requires significant resources and a complex coordination of efforts.

Geographic Regions and Targeted Populations. Grants focused on geographic regions are sometimes referred to as "place-based"; examples include grantmaking within the city of the foundation's founder or within select neighborhoods, cities, counties, states, regions, or countries. Examples of targeted populations (or special populations) are youth or people with AIDS. Evaluating geographic regions or targeted populations poses a challenge similar to that of evaluating strategies. Both tasks require the identification of a variety of outcome indicators (for instance, of economics, health, education, the environment, and civic participation) that reflect the overall well-being associated with a physical location or a group of individuals. An example is the commissioning of agencies to track statistical trends.

Selecting a Focus for Foundation Evaluation Efforts. Given the variety of possible foci for evaluation activities and the advantages and disadvantages associated with each one, what factors (in addition to resource level, discussed in the previous section) should a foundation consider in selecting a focus for evaluation? Perhaps the most important is the foundation's philosophical approach toward its relationship with grantees. Some foundations have developed a proactive stance toward identifying program goals, whereas others have chosen to be much more responsive to community needs (David, 1999). In the former case, evaluation efforts are likely to be focused at the initiative level; in the latter, they are likely to be focused at the project level or on elements of customer service of the foundation as a whole.

Another factor to consider is the developmental stage or maturity of the foundation's program areas. Program areas that are emerging or that are experimental, with the intent of identifying innovative programs, will probably select an evaluation focus at the project level. Other areas that are long established, have positive individual project results, and are being more broadly implemented might be selected for initiative-level evaluation. Still other program areas that are conceptualized by geographic region or target population may dictate more comprehensive, overarching evaluation approaches.

Finally, the evaluability of the programs must be weighed. Whatever the philosophy of the foundation, program goals and activities need to be articulated in a way that permits evaluation to take place. Specifying program outcomes is perhaps the first step in making foundation efforts evaluable. This specification may be initiated by foundation program staff alone, or foundation staff in conjunction with outside experts or grantees. However they are arrived at, having agreed-upon outcomes is essential for launching evaluation work.

A key step that follows is to specify the strategy or set of activities to be employed in achieving those outcomes. Foundations have begun to represent these activities in graphic forms such as logic models, theories of change, logframes, outcome chains, and causal models. Within the evaluation community, these forms are generally known as the program theory. By specifying how one expects to achieve program goals, the evaluator has a greater likelihood of knowing what to measure and what to judge.

Cultural Factors

As noted earlier, the cultural factors we discuss are the organizational climate pertaining to evaluation and the diversity of the foundation's stakeholders.

Organizational Climate Regarding the Purpose of Evaluation

Although there are many different aspects of organizational climate, in relationship to evaluation we want to focus on one particular aspect: the understanding about evaluation's general purpose. Foundations tend toward one of two perspectives on this matter: (1) evaluation is mainly for accountability, or (2) evaluation is mainly for improvement and learning. Each of these is explained next, along with the implications for evaluation.

An Accountability Climate. Foundations with an accountability perspective want evaluative information on what activities were planned, what activities occurred, and what was spent. These kinds of questions are motivated by an interest in tracking what grantees proposed to do, what they actually did, and how much they spent to achieve their proposed goals. We characterize them as accountability questions because the main interest is in having an accounting of the activities that occurred compared with the activities that were proposed for a specific budget. The goal is an overall positive or negative assessment of achievement, followed by consequences and actions. If the assessment is positive, the program may receive supplemental funds. If the assessment is negative, the program may be de-funded or, in rare cases, sanctioned or fined.

This perspective is particularly common among some foundation board members, and this is understandable, given the fiduciary responsibilities associated with their role. They are authorizing funds to groups and organizations to undertake activities in line with their proposals and budgets, and they want to know whether these activities occurred. Foundation program staff members also can have this perspective, in part because of requests from board members for information of this type or because they feel accountable for the portion of foundation funds that they administer.

Answering questions from an accountability perspective tends to involve input- and process-monitoring evaluation approaches. Monitoring inputs and processes (or activities, as these are known in many programs) requires an evaluator to develop a system for recording inputs and activities, either by those undertaking the activities or by an evaluator observing the activities. This system might involve a computerized or a paper form, which is regularly completed and submitted.

The wide use of computers makes the computerized form a more likely choice and a more cost-effective one as well. Assuming that the information entered is accurate and complete, the evaluation analysis is a straightforward tally of what was recorded, with a comparison to what was proposed. A list of expenditures completes the report. A report of this type provides an accounting of what happened and with what costs but not necessarily of why it happened or what could have happened differently to make the activities more effective or cost-efficient.

Those working within an accountability perspective use evaluation findings to assess and judge a grantee's performance, with special consequences for non- or underperformance. A foundation using this perspective needs to be aware of how those being evaluated in this way will likely react to a requirement for evaluation. Because of the focus on judgment and the consequences of negative findings, those being evaluated will tend not to present an unbiased report of expenditures and activities but instead will concentrate heavily on positive findings. Objective evaluation, particularly if conducted by outsiders, is threatening because it might expose deficiencies. This organizational climate is created because grantees know that reporting negative findings could result in penalties and possible loss of funding, as well as in lessened chances for future grants. This climate fosters, often inadvertently, an adversarial relationship between funder and grantee, with the funder in the role of skeptical judge and the grantee in the role of "positives-only" reporter. It is important to understand that the climate is generating this outcome, not the action of dishonest individuals. In view of the accounting context and the pressures within it, it is understandable that grantees would focus on the positives, which will be rewarded or at least cause no change, and avoid the negatives, which will be penalized. Even if the grantee's planned activities and expenditures are well defined and very clear from the outset (qualities that might characterize the replication of a previously tested and well-refined program), the contextual pressure will still be present and cause a focus only on expected, positive outcomes.

An Improvement and Learning Climate. If "What happened?" encapsulates the first organizational climate perspective on the purpose of evaluation, then "Why did it happen—or not happen?" encapsulates the second perspective—the "improvement and learning" perspective. Foundations with this perspective are more concerned with questions about why things did or did not occur, what explains these differences, and what could be changed to result in better outcomes and more extensive impact. This perspective is similar to that of a *learning organization*— Peter Senge's term for a group "where people continually expand their capacity to create the results they truly desire, where new and expansive patterns of thinking are nurtured, where collective aspiration is set free, and where people are continually learning to see the whole together" (Senge, 1990, p. 3). Preskill and Torres (1999) share this perspective and apply it specifically to evaluative inquiry.

Foundations with an improvement-learning perspective, compared to an accountability perspective, are more interested in ultimate results and how best to achieve them. They are also interested in the process of moving toward these results and in learning about both successes and failures along the way, and, in the latter case, in trying again to improve the process to achieve long-term effects.

The evaluation methods required to answer questions about impact are summative approaches, with longitudinal pre- and postprogram assessments of changes and, in some cases, with comparison groups or control groups included. Compared with the input- and process-monitoring approaches associated with the accountability perspective described earlier, these summative approaches require more time and resources, in terms of both personnel and activities. The staff of a typical foundation-funded program frequently do not have the expertise to undertake evaluations of this type, so outside assistance frequently must be brought in and supported for the duration of the program. In addition, summative measurements, such as pre- and postprogram surveys or interviews, are labor-intensive, both to collect and to analyze.

Those working within an improvement-learning perspective use evaluation findings to improve a grantee's performance, realizing that the successful realization of project goals is an iterative process, with some successes and some failures along the way but with learning occurring throughout. Successes are valued, but there are not sanctions for failures if they result in new learning that is incorporated into program changes. The organizational climate related to evaluation that results from this perspective is one that values both positive and negative outcomes and fosters program changes and refinements to improve outcomes. In this evaluation climate, grantees are more open to discovering and sharing both positive and negative outcomes. In addition, a grantee's primary focus is making an impact on the problem or issue, using information along the way to adjust the means to do this more effectively. Evaluation information is a valued commodity in this climate, because it provides a way to know which program components are working and which need changing.

Comparison of the Two Climates. In addition to differences between the accountability and the improvement-learning perspectives in the types of evaluation approaches typically used, there are differences in several other characteristics of the evaluation process. Accountability-perspective evaluations frequently put project staff on the defensive, because staff members feel they are being put to a test that they will either pass or fail. This inadvertently engenders an "us-versus-them" attitude among the project staff, with "them" being both the foundation and the evaluator, particularly if she or he comes from the outside. In contrast, those involved in evaluations within an improvement-learning climate work as partners over the course of the evaluation. This, however, requires time and regular attention from all the partners. The two perspectives also differ on their ultimate ends for the evaluation. Accountability-perspective evaluation concludes with an assessment of whether a grantee did what it proposed to do and for the original cost. Improvement-learning-perspective evaluation concludes with an assessment of the grantee's success in making an impact on the problem or issue, regardless of the match between the proposed and actual activities.

Although we have presented these two perspectives on evaluation's purpose as discrete, they can both exist in a foundation, particularly in large ones. The board may tend toward one perspective, for example, and the operating staff may tend toward the other, or the operating staff may be split in their tendencies. Or these two perspectives can be present in the same person, with one perspective foremost on some projects and the other foremost on other projects. We do not believe that a foundation can or should take only one overall perspective. Instead, for the particular project, program, or initiative that is to be evaluated, it is important to make the perspectives explicit and conscious so that people can resolve differences in the importance of each perspective and, within a perspective, resolve differences in the depth and comprehensiveness of the answers sought.

Although evaluation can answer questions in great depth related to both perspectives, it is expensive and time consuming to do so and therefore not advisable for every foundation project, program, or initiative. In a particular instance, it is best to decide on the relative importance of the two perspectives and then decide how definitive the answers need to be. With this knowledge, the evaluator can decide between simpler, less costly evaluations and complex, more resource-intensive evaluations. From the accountability perspective, a simple tracking of inputs and activities may be sufficient for many projects; a thorough and rigorous tracking of all inputs and documenting of all activities would be done for only the most important or most costly projects. From the improvement-learning perspective, a limited summative assessment may provide enough information about outcomes to fulfill the evaluation information needs for many projects or programs. However, where the evaluation questions are focused on linking causes with effects, the most sophisticated evaluation designs and measures need to be used.

Diversity of Stakeholders

The second cultural factor we outlined earlier is the diversity of stakeholders. Evaluation is undertaken to answer questions about a program, initiative, or area, and these questions can come from a variety of stakeholders. Different stakeholders can have different evaluation questions, and one evaluation plan may not be able to produce answers to all these questions. Consequently, priorities have to be identified among these diverse stakeholders and their questions before evaluation can proceed. At the outset of evaluation planning, therefore, it is critical to identify the primary stakeholders and their most important evaluation questions and, depending on resources and interest, to identify secondary stakeholders and their questions as well. At a minimum, primary stakeholders include the foundation program officer and the head of the grantee program, but the set is often much larger and will vary from project to project. Foundation-funded programs typically have two general groups of stakeholders to consider: (1) those inside the foundation and (2) those outside.

Stakeholders Inside the Foundation. Although foundations vary in staffing levels and responsibilities, there are two general groups of stakeholders within a foundation: (1) those who make overall funding decisions and (2) those who carry out the decisions. The first group includes the board and the executive staff; the second consists of the operational staff, including program officers. In large foundations, these groups may be large and can be divided into smaller subgroups; in small and medium-size foundations, these groups will be small—possibly the same person acting in several roles. For ease of discussion, we refer to the former group as *board members* and the latter as *program officers,* although we recognize that this simplifies the situation within any particular foundation, especially for small and medium-size foundations. The important distinction is between those who make general, overarching decisions about funding and those who oversee the operation and outcomes of grants; we encourage the reader to substitute the appropriate labels for his or her foundation.

The group of foundation stakeholders who make overall funding decisions (the "board member" group) may or may not be among the group of primary stakeholders for a particular evaluation. In some cases, these stakeholders are interested only in allocating resources and may be content to have others, such as program officers, focus on the operational aspects of foundation funding, including evaluation. In these cases, the views of these individuals do not need to be included in the set of evaluation concerns and questions. In other cases, however, the board members may have a strong interest in evaluation questions related to process (for example, Who participated?) and outcomes (for example, What changes occurred? What effects is our support responsible for?). These questions can focus on individual programs or on sets of programs or initiatives. If board members have definite evaluation questions that they want answered, these need to be made explicit at the outset. In addition, board members must understand that other stakeholders inside and outside the foundation will have other questions, and they should indicate their willingness to have those questions included in the set of primary evaluation questions, realizing that more questions will require more resources. Initially, this will be challenging for board members, but over time they will understand the implications (in terms of time and resources) of considering different types of evaluation questions from different stakeholders. If board members want their questions to be addressed, no matter what other questions are considered, then other stakeholders inside and outside the foundation need to understand this from the outset. Grantees, for example, should be told what the board's questions are and agree that, as a condition of accepting the foundation's funds, these questions will be addressed. Ideally, the questions would be set out in the request for proposals so that, from the outset, grantees understand the context in which they are operating if they receive funding.

The second group of foundation stakeholders to consider is those who carry out the operations of the foundation, such as program officers. In most cases, these individuals will have questions about a project or initiative, and their questions should be considered as primary. For a particular project, their questions may focus on process or outcomes and are usually guided by the grantee's proposed goals, objectives, and activities. As with board members' questions, program officer evaluation questions should be set out explicitly so that other stakeholders are aware of them. Grantees then will understand the evaluation perspective of the program officer and be in a position to discuss and possibly modify this, based on their own perspective.

Stakeholders Outside the Foundation. For any foundation-funded project, there are at least four groups of stakeholders outside the foundation to consider: (1) the grantee organization, (2) the project staff, (3) the direct participants in the project, and (4) others interested in the project (for example, members of the larger community in which the project exists, policymakers, researchers, and journalists). Next, we discuss the types of evaluation questions these stakeholders may have and the likely primacy of their questions.

The grantee organization and its staff members are primary stakeholders because they are fiscally responsible for the project. Depending on their role in the actual project, however, the grantee organization's staff may have either limited or extensive evaluation questions. Some grantee organizations, for example, serve only as fiscal agents who subcontract to others to undertake project activities. In this case, the grantee organization may be interested only in the extent to which the subcontractor expends funds in the proposed manner, with limited or no interest in questions about processes or outcomes. In other cases, even when its role is limited to fiscal agent, the grantee organization may be interested in monitoring the project's activities and documenting outcomes and effects. The grantee organization might, for example, have evaluation as one of its goals and consider it part of its regular activities, across all its projects and funders; it might therefore have an evaluation framework that should be incorporated into evaluation planning. In planning evaluation for a particular project, consequently, it is important that the grantee organization's interest in the evaluation be clarified so that its views can be incorporated, if necessary.

The grantee organization often has a role in a funded project that goes well beyond being the fiscal agent; it actually carries out the project. In this case, members of the grantee organization—those involved in implementing the project—become part of the second group of outside stakeholders to consider in evaluation planning. The project staff members, whether in the grantee organization or in another organization, are the people who implement the project on a daily basis and, as such, are another primary stakeholder group to consider for evaluation. Project staff may have interests in knowing more about those whom the program is serving, about the extent of program activities they receive or participate in, about the participants' assessment of the activities and their effects, about changes in participants' status on important dimensions (for example, education level or employment status), and about the most and least effective parts of a program—just to list some of the evaluation concerns that project staff typically have. As with other primary stakeholder groups, project staff's evaluation questions should be considered at the outset of evaluation planning. In addition, as the list of questions (likely a long one) is developed, it is important for these stakeholders to understand that the final set of evaluation questions will be determined after the input of all primary stakeholders has been solicited and frequently will not include all possible evaluation questions. This issue is discussed in more detail later in the chapter.

The third group of outside stakeholders is the participants in the funded project. Like the project staff, program participants are automatically considered primary stakeholders. The extent to which program participants' views should be considered in evaluation planning varies, depending on the program, the funder, and the grantee agency. Some (including the authors of this chapter) argue that participants' views must be considered in evaluation planning to help ensure valid, useful, and ethical evaluation findings. Others would not go this far and might consider project staff's evaluation views to be sufficient, particularly when the project staff has a long-term relationship with the participants, has worked with them extensively, and can reflect and represent their views. From a foundation funder's perspective, the status of participants' roles, not only in evaluation but in program development, should be considered and explicitly set out. Some foundations (for example, the California Endowment and the Woods Fund of Chicago) put participants and their views at the center of grant planning and evaluation. In this case, participants' evaluation questions are not only primary but they may be the most important to consider, surpassing those of the other primary stake-holders, including the foundation. Many other foundations consider participants' views more indirectly, via grantee organizations with relationships to participants. In this latter case, the grantee organization's evaluation questions are assumed to incorporate and reflect participants' viewpoints.

The final group of outside stakeholders includes others who are outside the project or grantee organization but who are interested in it (for example, policy-makers, researchers, journalists, or members of the larger community in which the project exists). These individuals can be a diverse and undefined set, so it can be challenging to obtain evaluation questions in a systematic way from this group at the outset of evaluation planning. For most foundations, these are con-sidered to be secondary stakeholders; their evaluation questions, if they can be ob-tained, are considered and possibly incorporated into the evaluation plan, but they are not considered essential. There are exceptions, however. For example, foun-dations that have broad policy change as one of their goals may consider policy-makers as a primary audience for their work; in this case, the evaluation questions of policymakers should be considered at the outset of evaluation planning. An-other example would be foundations that view community-level changes as one of their important goals. For these foundations, the larger community in which a project is situated would be a primary audience and stakeholder; its views would be among the most important to consider in evaluation planning. (See Chapter Fourteen for an analysis of audiences for evaluation communications.)

Prioritizing Stakeholders and Their Questions. Once stakeholder groups have set out possible evaluation questions, the next step requires a prioritization among the questions before a final set of evaluation questions is developed. The priorities should be set among the primary stakeholders themselves, not by the inside or outside evaluation planners. This process is usually not a quick or easy one, but its successful conclusion can have advantages throughout the evalua-tion and foster the use of evaluation results. A foundation about to undertake an evaluation of a project with a diverse set of stakeholders should plan for this consensus development process, knowing that it will take extra time and re-sources but that it will pay off, not only in a stronger, more useful evaluation but frequently in a stronger, more coherent program. The process of raising eval-uation questions causes everyone associated with a project to think more deeply about what the project is intended to achieve and how it will be accomplished. The benefits of evaluation planning with diverse stakeholders can have results long before the final evaluation report, in terms of improving program theory and implementation.

Conclusion

We have discussed four important dimensions that are part of the foundation context surrounding evaluation. Two are structural factors: the resource level within the foundation and the focus of evaluation efforts. Two others are cultural: the organizational climate regarding the purpose of evaluation and the diversity of stakeholders involved in the foundation's work. For the foundation-based reader considering introducing evaluation into his or her foundation, it is important first to consider these structural and cultural aspects of the foundation and then to develop evaluation capacity in coordination with them.

Implementing evaluation within any organization is a complex and challenging undertaking. Foundations have different histories, local cultures, grantees and partners, programmatic priorities, and ways of approaching social challenges. These realities affect all that happens inside foundations and how they react when changes of any type are introduced, including implementing evaluation activities. Organizational research and theory (Scott, 2002; Galaskiewicz, 1985; Meyer and Rowan, 1977) have demonstrated the important influences of these contextual factors. Foundations, like all social organizations, are affected by system-level characteristics, and when they institute a change in the system, those characteristics will affect the way the change proceeds.

One important insight from a systems or organizational view is that, if there is a change in one part of a system, it can affect other parts, even distant ones, as the system adapts to the change and its parts come to a new equilibrium. Instituting any change in a system like a foundation, therefore, is not as simple as attaching a new component "on the side," as it were. Particularly when the change is as potentially significant as the introduction of evaluation procedures, other aspects of the system will adjust to the change, sometime facilitating it and sometimes impeding it. Consequently, when planning for the introduction of evaluation, for repositioning of the evaluation function, or for the institution of major changes in evaluation guidelines or procedures, the reader is encouraged to consider the relevance and current status of each of the four factors discussed earlier within his or her own foundation.

It is also important to note that each foundation context is dynamic, with changes occurring rapidly at some times and slowly at others. A one-time assessment of the importance of the four factors is necessary but not sufficient for the successful implementation of an activity like evaluation, which is an ongoing process rather than a one-time event. The four factors, therefore, need to be assessed and reassessed periodically if evaluation is to take root, grow, and be sustained. If this is done, evaluation activities are more likely to develop productively and to be useful to the foundation's operations and to its future projects, initiatives, and strategies.

References

Atienza, J. (2002). *Foundation staffing: Update on staffing trends of private and community foundations.* New York: Foundation Center.

Bickel, W. E., Nelson, C. A., & Millett, R. (2002). Challenges to the role of evaluation in supporting organizational learning in foundations. *Foundation News and Commentary, 43,* 2.

David, T. (1999). *Reflections on strategic grantmaking.* Woodland Hills, CA: California Wellness Foundation. Available at http://www.tcwf.org/reflections/2000/nov/.

Foundation Center. (2002). *Foundation giving trends.* New York: Author.

Foundation Center. (2003). *Foundation yearbook: Facts and figures on community and private foundations.* New York: Author.

Galaskiewicz, J. (1985). Interorganizational relations. *Annual Review of Sociology, 11,* 281–304.

Kuo, V., & Henry, G. (2002). *Mapping evaluation investments 2000 and 2001.* Paper presented at the annual meeting of the American Evaluation Association, Washington, DC.

Lipman, H., & Wilhelm, I. (2003, May 29). Pressing foundations to give more. *The Chronicle of Philanthropy. 7,* 10–11.

Meyer, J. W., & Rowan, B. (1977). Institutionalized organizations: Formal structure as myth and ceremony. *American Journal of Sociology, 83,* 340–363.

Patrizi, P., & McMullan, B. (1998). *Evaluation in foundations: The unrealized potential.* Unpublished manuscript. Battle Creek, MI: W. K. Kellogg Foundation.

Pew Charitable Trusts. (2001). *Returning results: Planning and evaluation at The Pew Charitable Trusts.* Philadelphia: Author.

Preskill, H., & Torres, R. T. (1999). *Evaluative inquiry for learning in organizations.* Thousand Oaks, CA: Sage.

Sanders, J. R. (1997). Cluster evaluation. In E. Chelimsky & W. R. Shadish (Eds.), *Evaluation for the 21st century* (pp. 396–404). Thousand Oaks, CA: Sage.

Scott, W. R. (2002). *Organizations: Rational, natural and open systems* (5th ed.). Englewood Cliffs, NJ: Prentice Hall.

Senge, P. M. (1990). *The fifth discipline: The art and practice of the learning organization.* London: Random House.

Snow, P. E., & Baxter, L. W. (2002, June). Framing the big picture: Cluster reviews. *Returning Results.* Available at http://www.pewtrust.org/return_results.cfm?content_item_id=1108&page=rr1.

W. K. Kellogg Foundation. (1998). *W. K. Kellogg Foundation evaluation handbook.* Battle Creek, MI: Author.

CHAPTER NINE

FIELD-BASED EVALUATION AS A PATH TO FOUNDATION EFFECTIVENESS

Patricia Patrizi and Edward Pauly

Whether a philanthropy has big money or small, each grant signifies a particular concern about improving society and can trigger action. At times, foundations have enormously ambitious goals, as exemplified by one foundation's Nobel Prize–winning work in yellow fever and another's investments in the eradication of trachoma. Other foundations display deep concern for the strength of the public and nonprofit institutions in their communities. Whether the aims are global or local, the critical question is, What are the most effective ways to accomplish these aims? Unfortunately, many ambitious philanthropies are stumbling within a cloud of uncertainty, seeking to provide benefits for society but with little knowledge systematically drawn from their work to guide their selection of strategies and their grantmaking.

In this chapter, we advocate for a strategy we are calling field-based evaluation. We define a *field* as the broad organizational sector within which a foundation selects particular organizations for its grantmaking. For example, in the health-care field, a foundation may make grants to a small fraction of the leading organizations. A community foundation, whose field is the nonprofit sector in a city or region, may make grants to many of the nonprofits in its area.

Our strategy calls for field input throughout the evaluation process. Initial questions of interest are identified, based on the input, as are procedures for putting evaluation results to use to optimize philanthropy's effectiveness in promoting social change. We believe that foundation effectiveness depends on foundations' ability to hear and understand the dialogue and debate among field leaders about (1) the challenges and opportunities they face, (2) the knowledge gaps that, if filled, would enable them to make important breakthroughs in their work, and (3) the results and lessons that emerge from their work.

Field-based evaluation is in sharp contrast to more insular approaches that rely primarily on institutional memory, the occasional expert consultant, and foundation officers' grantmaking judgments to frame problems, identify strategies to address them, and understand the results of their work. Although these are important sources of knowledge, they are often subjective and narrowly focused. As a result, foundations may miss opportunities to be of consequence to society.

In our discussion of the field-based approach to evaluation, we cover the following topics:

- Philanthropists' frustrations with evaluation
- The value of multiple perspectives in guiding philanthropic endeavors
- Our perspective on what constitutes effective philanthropy
- Limitations of an exclusive focus on project-based (as opposed to field-based) evaluation
- The importance of remaining patient with the gradual, step-by-step process of change
- The notion of informed inquiry and action
- Benchmarks for the cost of evaluation
- Implications of the field-based approach for foundation leadership and evaluators

We conclude with a section that summarizes our key positions on field-based evaluation and provides recommendations for using field-based evaluation to identify and address important social problems.

Frustration with Evaluation in Philanthropic Settings

It is no secret that evaluation has fallen short of philanthropy's expectations. A survey of foundation evaluation directors (Patrizi and McMullan, 1998) identifies the following issues related to evaluation and philanthropy:

- Many program evaluation reports are not useful, are completed too late to be relevant, or are too costly in comparison to the modest insights they provide.
- Program evaluation designs often neglect important questions (such as imple-

mentation lessons), fail to identify lessons or insights of interest, or fail to adapt when the program is modified midstream.

- Program evaluations sometimes fail to take account of key features of the program approach or the context in which the program is conducted, greatly limiting their value.
- Failures to obtain necessary data (such as outcome data) sometimes greatly reduce evaluations' usefulness and validity.
- Foundations often initiate program evaluations well after the grantees' work has begun, thereby missing the opportunity to gather crucial baseline data.
- Program evaluations are often implemented in ways that lead to dissatisfaction and conflict with grantee organizations, which may view the program and the relevant outcomes differently from the way evaluators do.
- Foundation staffs often avoid or fear program evaluations because they perceive them as criticizing the work of grantee organizations or as criticizing a foundation staff's decision that the program should be funded.
- When a program evaluation focuses on short-term outcomes, grantees and program staff object that a grant's larger purposes have been neglected (and simultaneously argue that the larger purposes cannot be accurately assessed at an affordable cost).

A shift to a field-based approach does not, by itself, completely eliminate these sources of frustration but does constitute a potentially powerful step in the right direction.

The Value of Multiple Perspectives

By definition, field-based evaluation expands the number of perspectives shaping an evaluative process. As Bertrand Russell famously explained, the members of a class cannot describe the class because they lack perspective on it. Perspective adds voices that have been excluded, analysis and knowledge that have been neglected, and new ways of framing problems so they can be solved. In other words, perspective adds new and complementary voices to the established voices of foundation staff members, the old hands, and the usual suspects.

Foundations have the distinctive perspective that comes from not being a government agency, a legislature, a nonprofit service provider, or a for-profit company, while working with all those organizations. Foundations can use their independent, "outsider" perspective to listen to the needs of field leaders and policymakers, find the groups that can meet those needs, and support the development and implementation of innovative ways to meet identified needs. Then they can use evaluations to gather the lessons about what works, why, how, under what conditions, and at what cost.

Because of their independent perspective, foundations are able to solicit, hear, and recognize issues and opportunities that are important to their community, their region, the fields they serve, and the nonprofit organizations they support. They can also hear and recognize the needs of policymakers and other leaders at the local, state, and national level for innovative and effective solutions to important problems, and for the information and evidence they need to incrementally implement those solutions.

Opening up its planning, decision-making, and learning processes to new sources of information and perspective will make a foundation more effective and truly accountable. This will require foundations to take their partnerships with the field more seriously and anchor their programs in objective indicators of performance, forged in collaboration with leaders of the fields they seek to influence.

To incorporate the field perspective, foundations need to dialogue with field leaders about the most important questions central to their work and the challenges facing the fields in which they are active. Foundation strategies should draw heavily on the views of field leaders who are not likely to receive a grant from the foundation and are thus independent of pressures to raise funds. Questions to explore jointly include the following:

- What are the desired outcomes for the philanthropic sector, the fields of work, and the grantees? Do the field's desired outcomes require innovation?
- What do they need to learn in order to improve their organization's effectiveness?
- How could the field be more effective in meeting society's needs?
- What is the evidence about which approaches are most effective?
- Where are the most promising opportunities for intervention?
- Do government leaders, constituents, community members, and field leaders endorse the desired outcomes?

Getting answers to these questions will enable the foundation to harness its work to an evolving body of knowledge and practice needed to engage leaders in using new knowledge and practices.

This crucial component of foundation effectiveness, which we sum up as *grounding the foundation's work in the needs of the field, as seen by field leaders who will not receive foundation funding*, provides an independent "external validity test" for a foundation's strategies and funding that stands in stark contrast to the internal, private, and closely held processes used by many foundations to determine their grantmaking and related activities. We believe that the process of grounding the foundation's work in the field should include a thorough review of the positions of the leaders and innovators in the field, the inclusion of debate by outsiders, and the vetting of foundation strategy papers by field leaders. This process of scanning and commentary provides an early market test for how the work will resound with the field and the larger public. The process also greatly expands the potential impact of a foundation's work beyond the knowledge or interests of any single foundation officer or any single grantee organization; foundation-supported discoveries, innovations, and practical lessons will be useful to the field as a whole, including non-grantees, rather than just to the grantee organization. It draws on the interaction of organizations, constituents, government agencies, and the diverse private sector to create a richer understanding of the evolving problems and ideas in a given field. The value of this process emerges directly from the dialogue and debate among field leaders. The more this is done, the more philanthropy can develop and partner with constituencies who are not beholden to them.

The foundation-field dialogue we have in mind is not a one-time event but instead commits a funder to ongoing engagement with the field. As programs are conceived, designed, and implemented, foundations would work closely with field leaders to vet and check ideas, frame and reframe questions, and gather useful lessons to ensure that the work is going in the right direction to reshape programs. The goal is to ground foundation social change efforts in a continuing dialogue with field leaders and affected parties. Societal needs, not foundation-dominated, hierarchical processes, would shape the imperative to create and use knowledge in the processes of societal change.

What Is Foundation Effectiveness?

In our opinion, the most effective foundations are those that listen best, are active in identifying the problems and opportunities for which effective approaches are most needed, and synthesize and make public the evidence that shows why those approaches are effective. Consequently, this means that the most effective foundations are likely to be those that use evaluation best.

Effective philanthropies are likely to engage in self-reflection regarding questions such as these: How well do our investments advance an agenda based on needs of the field? Is our work influential? Is it beneficial to society or self-serving? Is it based on a single foundation officer's experience and networks or governed by knowledge from the field? Is it built on assessments made independent of the search for grants or reflective of an unequal economic power relationship?

In addition to internal questioning, we believe that foundations can strengthen their effectiveness, as well as their public accountability, when the following characteristics hold true:

- Trustees place the examination of their efforts toward effectiveness at the center of institutional incentives.
- The often messy situations of grantees are accepted as a reality of social change.
- Evaluations provide credible and reliable evidence about the foundation's work; resources are applied where evidence can contribute real value; evidence comes from varied sources, including commonsense judgment.
- The experience of the foundation's work and the lessons from that work are accurately communicated to grantee organizations, non-grantees who are leaders of the field, relevant policymakers, and the public. Evaluations consider and are commissioned with these audiences in mind.
- Lessons from the foundation's work are used as the basis for the development of new strategies and new grantmaking. The history of experience is accessible and in a usable form.
- Existing knowledge is used in the process of making grants. The experiences of others—in and outside the foundation world—are accessed.

Effective foundations build their work, both grantmaking and evaluation, on an external referent, focusing their attention beyond their internal needs and those of their grantee partners. They design their work to fill the action and knowledge gaps that prevent field leaders from solving society's problems. When foundations work to fill both action and knowledge gaps, they provide the missing pieces of the puzzle, as well as the tools that enable progress toward solving social problems.

As foundations increase their focus on evidence, and as they share this evidence publicly, it follows that accountability and effectiveness will be directly enhanced in tangible and powerful ways. At least two large foundations—The Wallace Foundation and The Robert Wood Johnson Foundation—have for several years released all or most of their evaluation reports to the public (and have posted the reports on their Web sites) without damage to the reputations of their grantees and with substantial benefits for the many organizations that have used the evaluation findings to strengthen their work.

Limitations of an Exclusive Focus on Grantee Proposals

We believe that a traditional, or project-focused, approach to evaluation misses the mark because it narrowly and exclusively focuses on an individual project, without taking into explicit account the larger context in which the project operates. A project-focused evaluation strategy focuses on a foundation-supported activity or program and measures the degree to which goals specified in a project's proposal were achieved.

But are these goals reflective of true needs in the field? All too often, we see that proposals to foundations are the fruit of conversations and negotiations between a revenue-seeking nonprofit organization focused on meeting its own organizational needs and pursuing its own organizational goals, and a foundation that seeks to support effective nonprofit organizations. Grant negotiations are only indirectly and partially related to the question of how a significant social problem can be solved, which is what field leaders and policymakers really want to know.

Results of a project-focused evaluation are necessarily limited in scope. Evaluators gather data that reflect the activities conducted in pursuit of the specified goals, along with data that capture the degree to which the goals were reached. The evaluation concludes by analyzing and assessing the degree to which specified goals were achieved, that is, whether the grantee did what it had planned to do and whether its activities resulted in the effects that were laid out in the grant proposal.

Although there is a modest degree of diversity in the evaluation approaches popular among foundations, we have observed that project-focused evaluation's emphasis on whether the outcomes specified in the grant seeker's proposal were achieved or not remains a dominant, even a controlling, image of why and how foundations need to use evaluations as part of their work.

Foundations often concentrate on making the next grant and meeting payout requirements, whereas grantees often focus on securing funds. This emphasis on distributing funds fosters proposal writing that contains high hopes and optimistic projections to facilitate and justify the making of grants. Modesty about likely outcomes and realism about step-by-step, incremental progress are rarely found in grant proposals. It follows that when grant proposals become the basis for evaluations, the near-inevitable result is disappointment and a dearth of useful lessons.

Alternately, we have seen that when foundations have created evaluations tailored to support learning by field leaders, they *have* achieved some signal successes. For example:

- The Robert Wood Johnson Foundation has used evaluation evidence to stimulate changes in policies and practices throughout the public health and allied fields, including in spreading effective school health clinics and reducing binge drinking by college students.
- The Heinz Endowments have based their broad strategies for improving the quality of preschool programs on evaluation evidence.
- The John S. and James L. Knight Foundation uses evaluation evidence to compare the outcomes of a broad range of programs that improve the readiness for school of young children in low-income communities; the information forms the basis for the funding choices of its twenty-six local grantmaking committees.

- The Wallace Foundation has used evaluation evidence to inform congressional legislative decisions on teacher training and after-school programs, and to inform the broad range of activities by organizations seeking to build participation in the arts.

Field-based evaluation and the knowledge it produces enable foundations to share important lessons with leaders and the public, and can strengthen foundations' program design work, strategic planning, and midcourse reviews of existing grants. Evaluation insights can contribute directly to the foundation's critical thinking about how its work can be more effective.

The Step-By-Step Process of Change

Important social change doesn't occur overnight or at the conclusion of a single grant or a single evaluation. Yet philanthropists can be impatient and frustrated by this reality. By definition, a field-based approach to philanthropy and its evaluation looks at the big picture. It looks beyond a count of the number of children served through a particular program to whether or not the program successfully addressed an important field need. Complexities of this nature are understood, and progress is achieved in a step-by-step manner.

Consider this: the issues tackled by effective foundations typically involve both a *knowledge gap* (a failure to solve a problem due to a lack of understanding) and an *action gap* (a failure to connect resources, methods, constituencies, and opportunities for movement). Typically, these issues are experienced first as gaps in action, but a lack of knowledge often lies beneath. (If there is sufficient knowledge to solve a significant problem, yet the action gap remains, there must be barriers to action that will likely require more political change than foundations can muster.) Well-crafted, field-based evaluations can enable foundations to be more effective because they provide new knowledge that fills gaps and promotes action. This affects the foundation's approach, its grant designs, its constituency building, and its engagement with leaders and the public.

Thus the reality of work in foundations' fields is one of, at best, gradual and step-by-step progress in improving professional practices, framing problems, building consensus and support, using mistakes as the basis for learning and transformation, working together in strategic alliances and other forms of association, and publicly identifying approaches that have the greatest potential to move the needle on effects.

To understand how this incremental learning process works, consider how managed health care was first imagined, then implemented and assessed, as a response to the health insurance problem as it existed twenty years ago. Now society's problem is how to fix managed care. And so the cycle of incremental action and knowledge goes on. (Some steps are bigger than other steps, of course, and not all steps are taken in the same direction.) Today, evaluation and learning are needed to improve on managed care.

Field-Based Evaluation to Inform Inquiry and Guide Action

Field-based evaluation, if it is to inform inquiry and successfully guide action, is not for the faint of heart. Evaluators and their grantmaking colleagues need to listen to the field and be unabashed about accommodating those who speak truth to power. They need to assess and make clear where knowledge plays a central role in a foundation's decisions, as distinct from the issue areas where the foundation's longstanding commitments and values determine its decisions. They need to gather the experiences and the evidence that emerge from foundation-supported activities. In essence, they need to facilitate the very difficult discussion regarding the power that funders hold, and the tradeoffs to philanthropy for being what has been called the "fat boy in the canoe." Evaluators may be able to improve the decision-making process, but they can sink it as well.

Good foundation evaluation staff will bring in information from many and varied sources, including from practitioners and researchers. Evaluation staff can raise alternative views, make disputes productive, and illuminate the outcomes and lessons from the foundation's work. The goal is to keep the conversation going. This is a prescription for marrying informed inquiry with action.

Perhaps most important, the evaluation staff can assist in framing the *right questions*—the questions that, if answered, are most likely to advance practice. This is quite a challenge, because in foundations no one ever objects or tells you that you have a bad idea. (An old foundation insiders' joke asserts that no foundation staffer was ever fired for making bad grants, but many have been fired for being late with their paperwork or unresponsive to the trustees' requests.) The external focus and perspective are essential, because no good ideas ever emerge from complacency.

So what are the questions that evaluators can address? Here are a few:

- What knowledge gaps block action in a field? How can those gaps be filled by combining innovative work by organizations that are positioned to advance the field's practices, with targeted learning about the implementation and outcomes of the work?
- What are the emerging practices in a field? Can they be studied as a type of natural pilot experiment? What lessons about the emerging practices and issues are most needed by the field's leaders?

- Can debate be advanced through explicit experimentation, where alternative positions are deliberately staked out and studied?
- Who are the productive actors, what are their roles and contributions, and what are their limitations in a given field? Who shapes the major decisions? Who controls the purse strings? Who controls communication with media?
- Which of the field's key ideas have had exposure in the media? How have the issues been treated? Can independent, objective information and analysis add light and reduce heat in the media's treatment of these issues?
- What can be learned from patterns of similar programs from other fields? For example, since *civic participation* has been used productively in many issue areas, are there some common experiences to study, learn from, and apply to the foundation's developing work?
- Can the conversations among those in the field occur contemporaneously with programming such that programs can be altered as path-breaking evaluation information comes in from the field?

These are some of the relevant questions that advance the work in a field and thus advance the work of effective philanthropy. The goal is to keep foundations relevant and grounded, and their work accountable in its commitment to advancing discourse.

Implications for Foundation Leadership

Foundation trustees, managers, and program officers can be influential with regard to the role and use of evaluation. In many cases, however, shifts in their perspectives and expectations regarding evaluation and philanthropy are needed.

Trustees and Management

For a foundation to work in this way, the trustees and top management must embrace field-based evaluation and accountability for results and send clear, unconflicted signals to staff and grantees about this interest. Far removed from the tyranny of rigid "outcomes-based-evaluation" jargon that has become commonplace in philanthropy, the complex pathways to results should inspire serious conversations about the difficulty, challenges, and realism of the social change process at hand. Field leaders and other constituents should have access to foundation leaders and foundation evaluations because they are usually in the best position to identify the important gaps in action and knowledge.

The more persistent challenge for foundation trustees and top leadership is to counteract the all-too-human overoptimism that is attached to many foundation grants. Lovallo and Kahneman (2003) have described the tendency in the business world for new projects (products, plants, mergers) to be launched with too little skepticism about their chances for success. The chances for success are quite uncertain for many foundation grants, and foundation management can use plans for evaluation and learning to balance and inform discussions that may tend to highlight only the positive aspects of grant proposals.

We must also shift the culture away from the kind of highly packaged rationales and PowerPoint presentations that sometimes dominate discussions with trustees about grantmaking and strategy development. We believe that the work of field-based evaluation can add useful perspective by introducing the independent, externally validated perspectives on the needs of the field and the evidence of results. Moving toward the kind of qualitatively nuanced interaction required by results-oriented work involves a profound shift in foundation culture. It is difficult, long-term work; it requires brave foundation executives to work with their boards to create better tolerance for uncertainty and risk.

Trustees and top leadership also need to recognize that some of the most important things staff do have nothing to do with making a grant. Rather, they involve having the perspective to oversee many actors, bringing to the table people who otherwise might never speak to each other, and seeding a robust market of ideas. Staff also observe unfolding grant-funding efforts and capture lessons for leaders and the public. Holding the purse strings can help, but some of the most powerful work requires little money and a great deal of interpersonal capacity.

Program Staff

There is no shortage of talent and knowledge in most of the foundation staff we know. However, program staff are distracted by confusing incentives, opportunities, and pressures to move money out the door. Many have discussed the front-loading of foundations' intellectual capital, which causes the development of new grant ideas to displace learning from the results of unfolding grants. The ongoing management of a grantmaking strategy requires a great deal of convening, listening to the field, and capturing evidence of accomplishments, barriers, and results. It requires honest responses to what is heard. Program staff need to create the kind of climate in which grantees can assess foundation ideas and report on challenges and unexpected, problematic outcomes frankly and directly. This kind of exchange may require an interlocutor—a potential role for evaluators or evaluation staff in foundations.

Time and again, we are brought back to the idea that many of the best program staff do their best work by immersing themselves in the fields they work with and in the performance history of these fields. The goal becomes not to have the world adopt the foundation's program but to get the best field-based ideas into the quotidian practice of fieldwork.

Implications for Field Leaders

Field leaders need to challenge the operating assumptions of foundations and keep the discourse firmly focused on results. Foundation staff have accoutrements of power that can get in the way of objective thinking and discussion. Instead of acting as grant-seeking supplicants, field leaders must candidly discuss and debate the action and knowledge gaps that inhibit their effectiveness. Field leaders who do not depend on foundations' largess—leaders of government-funded agencies, intermediaries supported by fee-for-service work, university-based analysts, and journalists—have a particularly important role to play in identifying the challenges that foundations should address.

Implications for Evaluators

Perhaps there is a degree of codependency in the sometimes troubled relationships between evaluators and the foundations that hire them. Some evaluators may overpromise and underdeliver, with the convenient excuse that their foundation clients do not really want to assess the results of their grantmaking. Similarly, some foundations may avoid accountability for results by commissioning weak evaluations that gather data but provide few insights and no useful lessons; these evaluations may confirm the suspicion that evaluations are inconclusive and not worth the money they divert from the coffers of deserving nonprofit organizations. Both sides of the transaction protect themselves by keeping the completed evaluations private and thereby beyond the reach of critics, citing the need to protect grantees from damaging negative publicity.

Disappointment in the usefulness of foundation evaluation has left some foundation evaluation staffers in a confused, uncertain, and discontented state. Turnover is high, and foundation leaders do not know what to do with their evaluation staff. Some have experimented with jury-rigged and conflicting roles for these staff members (Patrizi, 2002), leading to intractable tensions around the purpose of evaluation. Sometimes evaluation specialists are asked to be part-time auditors or fill-in grant managers. When other foundation staff members object to these unexpected evaluation roles, great energy is expended on diplomacy, fence mending, and conciliation, with few accomplishments to show for the effort.

With the field-based approach, foundation evaluation staff will have clearer roles; they can take on the role of interlocutor with outside groups and, inside the foundation, the role of teammate who is skilled in the methods needed to build useful evidence and craft solutions. Staffers can also provide forums where evaluators, field leaders, managers, and program staff can address difficult issues in the field.

Whether as foundation staff or external consultant, all evaluators need to work to set the questions right and not allow for complacent, rote data collection and analysis. They need to energize their thinking and writing to be compelling enough for a wide audience; they should take on the challenge to be verbally persuasive on paper, writing more succinctly and clearly. They should see their roles primarily as those of teacher and facilitator within the frame of empirical evaluation.

The evaluations that have contributed the most to foundations' effectiveness have not sought to assess whether the optimistic claims of grant proposals have been fulfilled in practice. The evaluations that have improved practice have been those that assessed how significant changes were implemented, described barriers they encountered, and detailed the circumstances under which those barriers were overcome. The evaluations that have changed policy have yielded new insights about the results of innovative actions or the results of well-known actions in new contexts. The new knowledge that has enabled leaders to fill action gaps has been knowledge about costs, performance, the effectiveness of innovations, the engagement of people in self-improvement activities, and the logic of programmatic effectiveness.

Evaluators must work hard to link new knowledge from evaluations with action. Because most grantmaking foundations seek to fill action gaps, their work provides an ideal opportunity to illuminate action with understanding. By listening to the needs of the leaders struggling to close the many action gaps that surround us—for example, in health care, education, youth services, and the arts—evaluators can hear field leaders voice the questions the foundation's evaluation studies should address. Instead of asking, "Did the project go according to the plan?" evaluators need to direct their research to determine what insights the project can provide and how improved results can be obtained.

Getting Value for Money

Foundation leaders often worry that evaluation expenditures take money away from grantmaking that will directly benefit people in need, and they are often correct (although not all grants actually benefit people in need, partly because the lack of evaluation knowledge means that a grant's outcome can be uncertain). We believe that evaluations should be held to a clear standard: *they should produce lessons of practical value that is greater than the practical value of the grantmaking they displace.* This is a high standard. It can be met when evaluations provide knowledge that improves the work of service providers (both grantees and non-grantees), identifies efficiencies, and contributes knowledge to policymakers that improves services.

Foundations' evaluation staff can work to keep evaluation costs down and can explain why some evaluation approaches cost more than others. The key factors that drive evaluation costs are often controllable:

- *Multiple sites.* The more sites, the greater the costs of data collection, travel, and quality control. Having more than one site can often add value to an evaluation, but there may be declining returns to scale, so a representative sample of sites can be as useful as a study of all sites.
- *Multiple questions and multiple data sources.* The more questions and the more data, the greater the cost. Identifying the questions that the foundation can most usefully answer and leaving other questions for later can greatly reduce costs.
- *Longitudinal data collection.* The longer an evaluation must track sites and people, the greater the cost (following an individual participant can cost as much as $500 per year). Longitudinal studies can have great value, but not every study needs to gather data over long periods of time.
- *Skilled analysis.* A challenging study often needs a particularly skilled and experienced research team, and research quality is costly. Carefully matching the study to the appropriate researchers leads to the most cost-effective use of scarce funds.

It is important for evaluators to remember that as long as foundation-commissioned evaluations are perceived as being useless, *any* cost is too great and will result in resentment and resistance to further evaluations. The most effective justification for funding more evaluations is a strong track record.

Understandably, foundation leaders and trustees, as well as staff members, want to know how much an evaluation should cost. Of course, the answer is, "It depends on what you want to buy." But lurking behind this question is the much larger one raised throughout this chapter: *What do the foundation and the field want to learn?* If the foundation cannot give a clear answer to this question, evaluators may propose a general-purpose, diffusely focused project evaluation that touches lightly on many questions and costs hundreds of thousands of dollars. If the foundation has a clear understanding of what the field wants to learn, for what audiences, at what level of priority, then cost issues can be assessed with a much better sense of value and utility.

In our experience, it is possible to spend $25,000 on evaluation and get a lot (for example, by using a "visiting committee" of experts who review operational data, assess accomplishments and disappointments, and identify the lessons from a project central to the supporting foundation's mission). It is also possible to spend $1 million on an evaluation and get very little (for example, by gathering multi-site, longitudinal data for a report that answers questions left vague by the foundation and whose audience is not well specified). Similarly, this experience can and has been reversed as well. The point, however, is that there is a wide variety of ways that foundations can gather useful information and analyze it, at price tags from $25,000 to over $1 million, depending on what the foundation and the field want to learn.

Conclusion

If foundations are to be more effective, we believe it is imperative for their evaluations to pay much more attention than they do now to the perspectives and needs of field leaders, particularly non-grantee leaders, as well as those whose lives are affected by the field. Far too often, evaluations focus on narrowly defined projects, with little understanding of the larger context in which they operate.

Further, if the field is to improve its effectiveness, evaluations should contribute practice-based knowledge. Foundations need evaluations that capture the lessons of experience, whether those lessons are encouraging or discouraging, because they can strengthen field leaders' understanding of the goals, tactics, and practices on the leading edge of the field's work. Evaluation should be designed to answer questions of importance to practitioners, field leaders, and policymakers.

The process of learning about societal problems, crafting potential solutions to those problems, and learning from the work that is built from these efforts begins when foundation staff and smart field leaders meet to discuss an unmet service need, an action gap, or a need for a new organization or for new structures and capacities within existing organizations. These needs reflect problems that may exist because the knowledge to solve them is lacking or because political barriers block the adoption of a well-understood solution.

Action gaps are often tied to knowledge gaps. Solutions are never perfect and certain; they are educated but inevitably imperfect guesses. Yet foundation grants all too often fail to use existing knowledge and fail to produce new knowledge from their own labors, drastically limiting the grants' effectiveness.

If evaluations are to support foundation effectiveness, they will necessarily look very different from one foundation to the next, from one social problem to the next, and from one context to the next. Community foundations, regional and national foundations, smaller staffed foundations, and foundations with a highly specific focus will conduct different kinds of evaluations because they operate in different contexts. Their evaluations will differ because they are based on listening to the needs, goals, and approaches that matter in a particular context.

Philanthropic visionaries sometimes encounter disparate perspectives among field leaders. They must strive to comprehend these disagreements, particularly involving the non-grantee leaders who are economically independent of foundations' grantmaking. Airing the issues, listening to alternative approaches and priorities, assessing the key issues that field leaders see as most important for their future effectiveness, and explaining the foundation's decisions are essential for accountability. When this happens, the foundation's subsequent actions will shed light on alternative pathways to important and valued outcomes.

References

Lovallo, D., & Kahneman, D. (2003, July). Delusions of success: How optimism undermines executives' decisions. *Harvard Business Review, 81*(7), 56–63.

Patrizi, P. (2002, April 4). *Briefing notes to the Evaluation II Roundtable.* Paper presented at the Grantmakers Evaluation Network meeting, Council on Foundations, Washington, DC.

Patrizi, P., & McMullan, B. (1998). *Evaluation in foundations: The unrealized potential.* Unpublished manuscript. Battle Creek, MI: W. K. Kellogg Foundation.

CHAPTER TEN

STRATEGIES FOR SMALLER FOUNDATIONS

Marli S. Melton, Jana Kay Slater,
and Wendy L. Constantine

It is the greatest of all mistakes to do nothing because you can only do a little. Do what you can.[1]

SYDNEY SMITH (1771–1845)

Many topics discussed in this book are most applicable to large or medium-size foundations. These foundations tend to fund larger-scale initiatives, are more likely to invest in evaluation to improve programming and demonstrate program effectiveness, and often have evaluators on staff or access to external consulting evaluators. But what about the many smaller foundations—family, community, small-company, and independent foundations—that typically provide smaller amounts of funding to their grantees? Many of these foundations have few or no staff and often have limited, if any, access to evaluation support. Yet they are a major source of funds for innovative services in their home communities and a key sponsor of needed services and other investments not covered by larger funders. They may not be the big guys on the block, but the vast majority of foundations are small, and their grants amount to more than

---

[1] Our opening quote, from an English clergyman, gives sage advice to smaller foundations as they consider introducing evaluation into their ongoing activities.

$8 billion annually. Staff in these foundations care as much about achieving public benefits as do those in larger foundations, and they too can benefit by thinking systematically and evaluatively about the work that they and their grantees do. We must note here that, regardless of size, foundations want to know how they are doing as grantmakers, and to feel confident that their strategies are consistent with their mission and that their grantees are achieving their goals. As compassionate skeptics, foundation staff may ask themselves, Are we spending our money wisely? Are the grants we fund producing meaningful public benefits in the field we care about? Thinking evaluatively and systematically collecting information can help answer these questions.

This chapter discusses commonsense strategies for systematically collecting and using information to help smaller foundations assess the effectiveness of their grantmaking and to help their grantees better achieve their goals. It is aimed primarily toward readers who are relatively new to evaluation and interested in getting started with some evaluation activities, even though available resources might be limited. The strategies described are low-cost, can provide valuable information for the foundation and its grantees, and can be carried out by foundation staff, grantees, or volunteers.

We define *evaluation* as *using systematically collected information to help foundation and grantee efforts achieve meaningful public benefits*. We first describe strategies to shore up internal foundation practices and effectiveness and then turn to strategies that are useful at the grantee level. We conclude with some suggestions for using evaluative thinking when conducting site visits and for using the information obtained from these varied sources. We suggest no formal evaluation models, just practical strategies for identifying the important questions to answer, systematically collecting information to answer those questions, and using this information to improve the likelihood that goals for social betterment are met. Ample resources exist for those interested in learning about traditional models of program evaluation. (See, for example, *The 2002 User-Friendly Handbook for Project Evaluation*, available at www.nsf.gov/pubs/2002/nsf02057.)

Adopting an Evaluative Way of Thinking Within Your Foundation

Adopting an evaluative way of thinking and acting can contribute to a positive learning environment within the foundation and among its grantees. Board members, volunteers, and staff (if there are any) of smaller foundations bring tremendous passion and commitment to their activities. They care about their work and the causes they serve. Evaluation can increase the effectiveness of their efforts and those of their grantees, as well as provide information on whether their shared hopes for positive change are being realized. Three approaches to adopting evaluative thinking within a foundation are presented next.

Review and Update the Foundation's Mission and Grantmaking Strategies

Grantmaking should be solidly connected to the foundation's mission and goals. Sometimes smaller foundations adopt a set of grantmaking strategies without a systematic consideration of whether they are most appropriate for the goals the foundation wants to achieve. It is helpful to elucidate *what* the foundation wants to accomplish and *how* it wants to make a difference. It is also important to state how it expects that it will be able to create the changes it seeks.

A first step is to review the mission and vision statements and identify priority focus areas and the people or groups to be served. All stakeholders—the board, staff, donors, members of key committees, and other important partners—should be involved in the process of developing initial understandings and agreements about foundation priorities.

Questions about allocation can stimulate thinking about the foundation mission and its alignment with grantmaking practices. For example, What proportion of grant dollars do we want to allocate as follows:

- Among the different foundation priority areas (for example, arts, education, environmental protection, health care)?
- For operating support, project support, equipment and capital campaigns, and organizational development?
- Responsively versus proactively (that is, in response to unsolicited proposals or to specific requests for proposals or other foundation-generated requests)?
- For small, moderate, and large grants (defined as appropriate for your foundation)?
- For grants of short and longer durations (for example, one year or multiple years)?
- To projects that are part of a collaborative funding effort (for example, multiple funders supporting the same project or initiative)?

The unique foci of each foundation will spark additional questions to discuss. For example, one foundation may wish to target programs serving specific groups such as youth, people of particular ethnicities, or low-income families. Another may select high-priority regions for funding, such as inner-city, rural, or county-wide areas. Still another may place a high priority on funding new applicants rather than previously funded applicants or on grassroots, as opposed to well-established organizations. Structured conversations about these issues and questions can guide the creation or revision of foundation mission and vision statements and subsequent grantmaking strategies.

Conduct a Grants Analysis

Once mission and vision statements have been reviewed, and modified if needed, a grants analysis can provide valuable information about the degree to which foundation priorities and interests are being served. Conducting a grants analysis is a straightforward process: identify questions about top priorities (ask, for example: What percentage of our funds are being used to support the arts?) and extract from your files the information needed to answer these questions. Start with a paper-and-pencil grants analysis "summary form" (a series of questions based on foundation priorities) and complete one form for each currently funded grantee. You may also wish to review your files on grants funded in the past. As you design your own summary form, the following types of information about each grant may be relevant:

- Organization or program name
- Contact person
- Duration of grant (date began, date ended, total months of grant)
- Grant amount
- Grant classification (for example, responsive or proactive)
- Project type (project support, general operating support, capital campaign, equipment, and so on)
- Project goals
- Program or interest (for example, environmental education or youth development, which can be compared with the foundation's defined priorities for funding)
- Cofunders, if any, and amounts they have provided
- Collaborative funding (and amounts provided to other grantees collaborating on this grant)
- Population served (described, for example, with regard to characteristics such as ethnicity, age, gender, income groups, or community size)
- Geographic region served
- Self-reported success indicators (for example, impressionistic ratings of success such as "Achieved Goals," "Some Progress," "Not Successful," or "Unknown," based on communication with the grantee and other information on file). Much of this information may be subjective, but it will indicate how grantees are viewing their program outcomes and achievements.

Modify the summary form, if necessary, as more is learned about the range and breadth of grantees. After you are satisfied that your summary form captures important priorities and practices, it will be time to create a database for managing and analyzing the information. Fortunately, spreadsheet and database management software have become more user-friendly over time, and numerous packages can be used to create worksheets, enter and analyze data, and generate charts and graphs.

Special software for managing foundation grants is also increasingly available, flexible, and affordable. MicroEdge and the Bromelkamp Company were early industry leaders in grants-management software; these forerunners have now been joined by a number of other software developers, including Arlington Group, Cybergrants, eGrant, Foundation Source, and NPO Solutions. Although grants-management software is most often used by larger foundations, small foundations may benefit from the increased efficiency these programs offer.

Once a database is established, reports or charts can be generated that reveal patterns of grants awarded. Figures 10.1 and 10.2 provide examples.

Simple charts can help illuminate important funding patterns and short-term trends such as the congruence between the foundation's goals and its current grant-making policies and practice. For example, Figure 10.1 displays a sharp decrease in funding for health, with a concomitant increase in funding for elder care from 2003 to 2004. Was this shift intentional? Is the increased attention to elder care consistent with the foundation's mission? Should a higher proportion of funds be directed to the arts? If you learn that 65 percent of your funds went for health but your foundation mission calls for supporting health and the arts equally, you'll be able to adjust your future funding patterns accordingly.

As another example, the graph in Figure 10.2 shows a hypothetical pattern in which only a small proportion of foundation funds were allocated to education in recent years. Furthermore, the figure reveals a dramatic decrease in the proportion of funds allocated to education over a five-year period. The board may be able to put this information to good use as they consider future funding decisions.

Funding patterns will change over time, and this is especially true when a foundation has accepted new restricted donations or set aside funds for special initiatives. This often occurs at community foundations when they manage special-purpose endowments or restricted special-purpose or project funds. The type of grants analysis described in this chapter will reveal funding trends and illustrate whether or not the trends match the vision and intent of the foundation's board. We recommend that separate analyses be conducted for restricted and unrestricted funds.

FIGURE 10.1. EXAMPLE GRANTS ANALYSIS: PERCENTAGE OF FUNDS ALLOCATED ACROSS FOUNDATION PRIORITY AREAS, 2003 AND 2004.

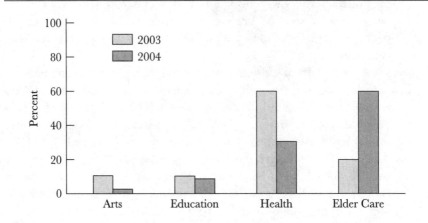

FIGURE 10.2. EXAMPLE GRANTS ANALYSIS: DECREASE IN PERCENTAGE OF FUNDS ALLOCATED TO EDUCATION, 1999 THROUGH 2003.

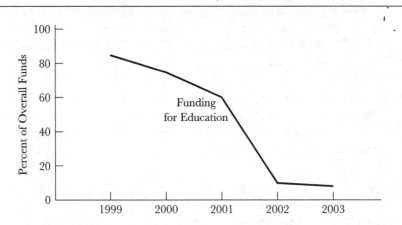

A Case Example

A midsize foundation on the West Coast is a significant funder in its region but is usually just one of many funders for the grantees it supports. As a matter of general practice, the foundation frequently awards grants at a lower level than requested. Members of the board have often debated whether this strategy of funding a higher number of grantees at levels that are lower than requested is more or less effective than awarding fewer grants at a higher level. Was the foundation's grantmaking strategy of "lending a shoulder to the wheel" to help sustain programs effective? The foundation conducted a grants analysis and evaluated the effectiveness of its own partial funding strategies to determine whether foundation expenditures were being spent as intended and producing public benefits.

The foundation already routinely collected, as part of its grant-reporting process, a brief assessment by grantees of how well key goals of the grant were met. The review of grants funded over a two-year period suggested that organizations receiving less than 80 percent of the amount requested had a difficult time completing their projects, even when goals were adjusted downward. This suggests that it might be advantageous to award fewer grants, with each one funded at a higher percentage of the amount requested.

Finally, looking at the information provided by a basic grants analysis can raise additional, higher-level questions. For some foundations, it is also desirable to look at financial characteristics of grantees. Some important financial variables are (1) grant award as a percentage of the total budget for the funded program, (2) budget size for the funded organization, and (3) whether or not the organization is operating in the black.

When the foundation wants to determine whether it is providing the bulk of the support for a particular program, calculating the grant award as a percentage of the grantee's total budget for the funded program will provide that information. You can then generate a report showing that information for many of the foundation's funded organizations, and see whether the foundation typically provides, say, 5, 20, or 50 percent, or more, of the overall support for the programs it funds.

When the foundation wants to determine whether it funds mostly large, established organizations or smaller ones, creating an additional field for the organization's total annual budget is useful. Do most funded organizations have annual budgets under $250,000? $250,000 to $500,000? $500,000 to $1 million, or more?

Some foundation personnel may wonder what portion of their grantees are financially stable and have reserves to carry them through a bad year (for example,

whether or not the organization has enough cash, over and above its current liabilities, to operate for three months or more). A grantee's financial statement will
detail revenues and expenses and show whether the organization was able to break
even or generate a modest surplus, or whether it ran a deficit and had to borrow
or draw on past reserves to pay its bills. A data field added to the database can be
used for entering a simple categorical definition of financial status for each grantee
(for example, adequate reserves, breaking even, or running a deficit).

Shoestring Strategies and Practical Tips

• Prior to convening stakeholders, important issues can be identified by asking board members, volunteers, and key constituents to provide questions they
have about the grantmaking process and results.

• A consultant on database management can provide useful training. The cost
is likely to be the same, regardless of the number of individuals attending. Dollars
spent for this purpose up-front may save a lot of wasted effort, disappointment,
and frustration later.

• Restrict your first grants analysis to no more than three to four priority areas
that are of highest interest to the board. Simply collecting, summarizing, and thinking about information currently hidden away in project file folders (for example,
in grant proposals and applications or notes from telephone calls) may improve
your grantmaking.

Think Evaluatively About Financial Issues

Foundations typically collect substantial financial information about the organizations they fund. This allows them to assess readiness for funding and, when a
grant is made, to monitor the uses of funds awarded.

The basic financial information that foundations typically collect about
grantees during the grant application process is used to determine whether applicants have the capacity to manage funds well and complete their proposed projects. For each funded grantee, then, a foundation should have on file financial
reports that detail assets, liabilities, revenues, expenses, and cash flows. To provide
an even more complete picture, many foundations also collect information about
the total current organizational budget, staffing levels, major sources of funding,
vulnerability to changes in government funding priorities, extent of private contributions, and extent of in-kind support such as volunteers.

Financial information you request from grantees both during and immediately
following the grant period is usually more limited. As a foundation, to support your
own organizational financial accountability, you need information from your grantees

to demonstrate that their funds were spent as intended. A comparison of the applicant's proposed project budget (and actual funds awarded) with its report of expenditures is often sufficient for accountability purposes. In fact, for many of your grantees, a financial report documenting that funds were used as intended may be your only evaluation requirement. For example, when funds are used primarily to purchase equipment or materials or to provide general operational support, documentation that the funds were expended appropriately is usually sufficient.

Most grantees know they will be required, at a minimum, to provide a report on their use of funds. Nonetheless, provide specific information in the grant award letter about your expectations and format for the financial component of their interim and final reports. When grantees know up-front what and when they are expected to report, they will be better able to gather information systematically throughout the grant period.

Helping Grantees Think Evaluatively

After basic questions have been answered through your grants analysis and collection of financial reports, you can turn your attention to the ultimate question: Are our dollars achieving the intended public benefit? To address this question, you will need to know whether grantees are meeting *their* stated goals. What outcomes are they achieving for the individuals or causes they serve? To answer these questions, grantees must be involved in the evaluation process.

If your foundation has not previously required evaluation activities of its grantees, introduce the concept gently. Grantees' first reaction may be to assume that you do not trust them or are suspicious of their actions. Some may worry that you will discover a reason for discontinuing their funding. The mutual respect you have shared in the past may, in their minds, be cast into doubt. It can be helpful to point out benefits that the grantees themselves may derive from the evaluation activities. Real-life stories about grantees who have used evaluative information to support their own work can be persuasive. Collect and share anecdotes about grantees who have used evaluative information to

- Focus staff efforts around particular goals and outcomes
- Document that they have done what they said they would do
- Recognize the achievements of employees, volunteers, and other key stakeholders
- Document that programs are achieving the goals and objectives outlined in their funding application

- Communicate what they do and how they make a difference
- Continue or expand successful programs and strategies
- Change or eliminate programs and strategies that are not working
- Effectively leverage additional or future funding
- Encourage others to reflect on their findings and explore wider change

Despite these beneficial uses, some grantees may resist evaluative activities because they are stretched thin trying to complete their basic objectives. They may resent the additional burden of collecting and reporting information. If you, as the grantmaker, are doing evaluation on a limited budget, chances are that many funded grantees confront budgets that are even more constrained. Even when grantees understand and embrace the importance of evaluation, they may have a hard time finding resources to implement it. Front-line staff who might be trying to tutor youth after school, provide services to disabled adults, treat individuals with substance addiction, negotiate for habitat preservation, conduct swim therapy, find adoptive homes for shelter animals, and so on, may view evaluation as a set of requirements imposed by outsiders to make their lives more difficult. Make sure that you are committed to keeping the evaluation process as simple as possible and learning with them. If possible, provide additional, earmarked financial support to offset the added responsibility and time required to collect and report data.

Think Evaluatively About Program Implementation and Effectiveness

When should you ask a grantee to provide evaluative information beyond basic financial reporting? Ask yourself: What additional information do we need from this grantee to determine whether our grantmaking strategies are successfully supporting the foundation's mission? For some grantees the answer will be clear. They are those whose programs have already been evaluated by others, who have collected evidence of their success, or whose results are widely recognized and respected. In these cases, simply request a financial report on grant expenditures and, if you are interested, a copy of the evaluation report that describes program effects. Little additional information will be needed unless their programs change significantly.

From some grantees, you'll want information beyond the basic financial report. If the grantee provides services or treatment to clients, how many clients were served? Were clients satisfied with the services they received? Grantees must be funded at a high enough level, however, to justify diverting funds away from service delivery to evaluation. One common rule of thumb is to allocate 10 percent of a total program budget to evaluation. But is it reasonable to expect a grantee who receives a grant of $20,000 for operating support to divert $2,000 for evaluation? In many cases, one could argue that it is not. At this level of funding, the foundation may decide that the only items needed are basic financial information plus observations made by the program officer. An exception might occur when a few thousand dollars can purchase technical assistance, hardware, or software to improve the grantee's existing information systems in ways that strengthen both program management and evaluative reporting to funders.

If your funds are the primary support for a program or intervention, it is reasonable to request evidence that the program was implemented as planned and that its effects were examined. Be sure to inform each grantee about your evaluation expectations during the application review process and again when funds are awarded. As you explain your foundation's interest in evaluation and the reasons you want to engage in a learning process with your grantees, ask what data they already collect. Most organizations collect program delivery statistics such as attendance, participant characteristics, frequency and type of activities or services delivered, assessments of participant status, and follow-up records. If the grantee is new to evaluation, short of staff, and limited in its resources, or if the grant itself is modest, these data, along with financial data on expenditures, may be all that is needed. (The section on standardized reporting forms discusses how to collect this information from your grantee in a format that will be useful to the foundation.) More in-depth evaluation may be warranted if the foundation has made a large grant, a multiyear grant, or multiple grants for related purposes.

Program Implementation. Some organizations may focus so intently on immediate, urgent concerns that they do not have an overall logic model for their project. In other words, they cannot explain clearly the pathways through which their activities are expected to lead to short-term achievements and, in turn, to long-term impacts. Therefore, it can be helpful to think through, with the grantee, the logic model that applies to their program. This is one time when it makes sense to look ahead first to the ultimate goal and then to work backward from there.

Start the conversation by asking, "What are your long-term goals? What activities and steps will lead to short-term, intermediate, and long-term goal achievement?" For example, in a community with a high rate of teenage pregnancy, one long-term goal of a sex education program may be to reduce the teen pregnancy rate; short-term goals may be to increase teens' knowledge about contraception and to improve their skills for negotiating contraceptive use with partners. In order to achieve any of those goals, however, the program activities and services must first be developed and delivered. How will the grantee document these activities and services? What are the intended benchmarks for success at each stage? Conversations such as these may eventually lead to a model illustrating the logic of the program. An example of a logic model for the sex education program is presented in Figure 10.3.

The example provides an illustration of the logical sequence involved in thinking through all steps associated with program implementation and leading to the short- and long-term outcomes of that program. To learn more about logic models, we suggest visiting a Web site developed by the University of Wisconsin Cooperative Extension Service (http://www1.uwex.edu/ces/lmcourse/). This Web site walks you through an interactive logic model.

Once the logic model for a grantee's program is identified, a checklist can be used to document that the program activities were carried out as planned. This list, annotated with narrative comments about challenges and successes associated with each activity, can be used to document implementation. It can also serve as a useful guide for discussions between the foundation and the grantee about issues related to program implementation.

Program Effectiveness. Measuring outcomes to determine program effectiveness can be challenging and expensive; the topic is addressed in several other chapters

FIGURE 10.3. EXAMPLE LOGIC MODEL.

The situation: A community in which there are high rates of teen pregnancy

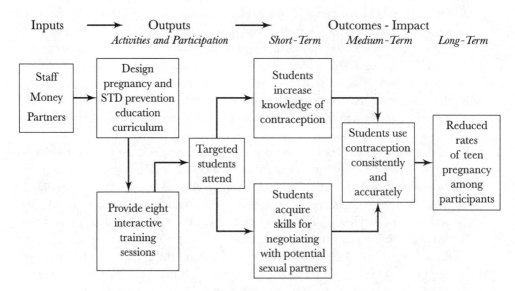

of this book (see Chapters Eleven, Twelve, and Thirteen). Generally, the most widely accepted way to learn whether a program is effective in achieving its intended outcomes is through a comparative study, such as comparing results from a treatment group (made up of people who received the program or services) with results from a comparison group (made up of people who did not). Numerous variations on this basic concept have been elaborated, and such evaluation designs can be difficult to implement in program settings.

Another challenge to measuring effectiveness is that many potential short-term and long-term outcomes are complicated and expensive to measure accurately. For example, consider the logistics involved in defining and measuring outcome data for these two programs: (1) The evaluation of a pregnancy prevention program may look first for increased knowledge about contraceptive use for all participating teens and, for sexually active teens, increased contraceptive use (short-term outcomes), followed by a reduction in unplanned pregnancies (long-term outcome); (2) the evaluation of a chronic-disease treatment program may look first at improved compliance with treatment (short-term outcome), followed by increased survival time (long-term outcome). How could these outcomes be measured? What forms of information can be used? Many options are potentially available, but the planning process requires experience and expertise.

Even when the resources are available to measure outcomes, careful consideration must be given to deciding which are most important to measure. Some outcomes are unreasonable to expect following a ten-week or even one-year program. Change is incremental and typically takes place in small, not always linear, steps. Skilled and seasoned evaluators approach the task of measuring outcomes with a great deal of care.

We have found that some activities that are viewed as valuable in themselves may be unreasonably expected to produce additional outcomes for program participants, especially children. For example, learning to play a musical instrument is a valuable end in itself. Though it may also improve mathematical ability in some students, it is probably not reasonable to burden a musical program with the responsibility for producing that outcome. Similarly, playing soccer is valuable for sportsmanship, physical conditioning, and enjoyment, but it may be overly optimistic to expect it to promote academic achievement or reductions in problem behaviors. Too often we expect that just one activity, in itself, will prevent young people from joining gangs or using drugs. Though this may sometimes happen, in our experience it is usually not realistic or useful to evaluate these programs as if gang or drug prevention were their primary purposes.

Because of these complex issues and considerations, evaluation of program effectiveness is usually reserved for higher-cost, large-scale projects and is beyond the scope of this chapter. If you are interested in conducting a rigorous evaluation that examines program effectiveness, the assistance of a professional evaluator will be very helpful.

Supplement Numerical Data with the Power of Story

Stories or narrative descriptions about program implementation and effects on participants can enrich what you learn from the grantee's program statistics and financial data. By *stories* we mean factual observations and personal perceptions, not fiction. When writing or telling stories, people begin to think evaluatively about the program they have administered or delivered, or services they have received. What worked well? What didn't? The process of writing and sharing stories can be provocative and stimulate discussion that ultimately strengthens program implementation and effectiveness.

To increase your confidence in the veracity of the narratives and to learn about the broad range of a program's effectiveness, ask grantees to gather stories about program effects from multiple sources—program administrators, service providers, and participants. Grantees can collect well-developed and thoughtful stories by brainstorming useful prompts for the storytellers. An example might be, "Describe in detail the most important thing you learned last month about providing outreach to HIV-positive persons. How has what you learned changed the way you provide outreach to this population?" Note that gathering narratives via e-mail can be an informative, low-cost source of data. Data collection can be carried out very efficiently using e-mail and group address lists. Although some personal communication is important for encouraging high-quality data, most regular communications such as requests for stories, writing prompts, follow-up reminders, and notes of appreciation can be completed with a single click. Best of all, there are no expenses for data entry.

As part of an evaluation of a school-based poetry education program, e-mail was used to gather stories from poets (who served as guest teachers) and classroom teachers to learn about the effects of the program on special-needs students. A comparison of the two points of view (classroom teachers and poets) revealed shared perceptions of benefit, as well as unanticipated effects.

Develop Standardized Evaluation Reporting Forms to Encourage Systematic Thinking

The essence of thinking evaluatively is being systematic and consistent. When grantees think systematically about the programs they are implementing, that is, when they develop a logic model and collect information about program implementation and outcomes, they are better able to provide information about their own successes and the degree to which shared goals have been met. Grantees should be informed well in advance about the questions that you, as a funder, want answered and the required frequency of reporting (for example, quarterly, annually, or at the end of a funding cycle), so that they can collect the needed information accordingly.

Designing an evaluation report form is an iterative process. In the end, you'll want a form that encourages grantees to collect, compile, organize, and report information consistently and provides the information that you will *both* find useful. When first developing the form, ask grantees what types of data they already collect and find most useful themselves. Once you have a working draft, invite feedback from long-term grantees. See if some would be willing to test out the draft form based on a recent grant. Their "test run" of the form will reveal whether people interpret the questions as you intended and whether their answers contain the type of information you seek.

Expect wide variability in the quality of reports that you will receive. Funders often need clarification and added context in order to make sense of a report. For example, what do "high," "medium," and "low" really mean? How should numbers be interpreted? For example, is selling seventy-five tickets to a dance performance a sellout crowd, or were only 25 percent of the seats filled? Request needed information in writing, indicating that it is required before the evaluation report will be considered complete.

Some grantees have substantial capacity to conduct useful evaluations and provide detailed reports. Others may have a more difficult time complying with reporting requirements due to lack of experienced staff or volunteers to write the report. These grantees may require additional support and guidance from the foundation.

Shoestring Strategies and Practical Tips

• Spend some time reviewing the Web sites of foundations similar in nature to yours. What questions do they ask of their applicants? What are their reporting requirements for grantees? Many Web sites contain grant application and reporting forms that can be downloaded. With permission, you may be able to modify the forms for use by your own foundation.

• It may be cost-efficient to bring in a database consultant to develop standard reporting forms and advise on database management.

• Tell grantees up-front that evaluation is required. Revise your foundation's grant application guidelines to include evaluation. Ask every organization to include an evaluation plan as part of its proposal. Specify which types of grants will require reporting basic implementation and financial information for purposes of accountability and which must collect more in-depth information and why. Include a standardized form and accompanying directions when a grant contract is mailed, so all grantees know in advance what data they are expected to collect and report.

• Consider a short-term evaluation consultant to help you and your grantees get a handle on the concept of the logic model that illustrates how their program's activities are related to intended short- and long-term outcomes.

• Often grantees collect quite a bit of information but do not compile it or write a report summarizing their statistics and looking for trends. For example, many grantees collect attendance forms but do not analyze the data to learn about the characteristics of attendees or how often they participate. Assisting grantees as they learn about the process of collecting and compiling data may strengthen your relationships with the grantees, the quality of program they implement, and the quality of data you receive.

• To conserve time, limit reporting requirements to just the few questions that your foundation would like answered. Develop supporting materials and data-collection forms to help your grantees collect and report that information to you. For example, if you have funded a program that provides teen health services, work with the grantee to devise a form to record clinic attendance and services. If serving Hispanic or Latino populations is a priority for your foundation, be sure the attendance form asks about participant ethnicity. Are participant age, sex, and county of residence important to the board? If so, include these elements as well.

• Restrict your evaluation requirements to current grants. Asking organizations that have been funded in previous years to go back and evaluate past grants is unrealistic. Data are unlikely to have been collected and recorded systematically, and recreating old records is time consuming, if not impossible, because of mobility among clients.

• Collecting information electronically can save time and money for both you and your grantees. For example, grantees could ask program participants with access to e-mail to answer open-ended questions about the strengths and weaknesses of a particular program or intervention. As another example, an environmental group could include a survey in its semiannual electronic newsletter to collect information about its members' knowledge, opinions, and practices on key issues. Though not statistically reliable, anecdotal data collected via e-mail can be a source of ideas for more systematic exploration.

• If you require an evaluation plan as part of your grant proposal, you may discover that some grantees are already engaged in an evaluation effort for a different funder or as part of a local, regional, or national collaborative project. These grantees may already be working with professional evaluators. Their existing evaluation efforts may well be fully adequate for your needs.

• If you and your grantees are new to evaluation, it may be helpful to bring in an evaluation consultant to introduce the concept of evaluative thinking and its potential for improving success in reaching your shared goals. Check with colleagues in other foundations about consultants they have used. In addition, national and local foundation affinity groups or regional evaluation associations may sponsor trainings on evaluation that will be helpful for you and your grantees.

Thinking Evaluatively During Site Visits

In addition to the information grantees provide in applications and reports, you can learn a good deal about your grantees' programs and successes by conducting site visits. A site visit provides the opportunity to strengthen relationships with grantees and to show that the funder values the program and its work with clients. Site visits may occur at any time—before, during, or after the grant is awarded. Obviously, the type of information collected during a site visit will vary, depending on the timing and purpose of the visit.

A site visit during the proposal review process sets the stage for thinking evaluatively about the project. Visit the program delivery site, not the administrative offices, so you can see how the staff actually conduct the activities they propose. Usually, the program officer conducts the site visit, but it can occasionally be useful for board members who have read key parts of the proposal to visit as well. Board participation frequently broadens the range of observations and relevant questions that are asked.

In addition to discussing proposal details, site visits allow for discussion of the larger context. Listen to descriptions of what the grantee does and what different staff members care most about. Listen as they identify and discuss the assets they bring to the issues they want to address, as well as their most urgent needs for the coming year. Ask questions about their long-term vision and goals, as well as the reasons they have chosen to offer their particular mix of programs, activities, and services. It is also helpful to learn about current priorities for developing the capacity of their organization as a whole, as well as their priorities for developing particular programs.

A standard site visit protocol form can be a useful guide for your visit. For example, elements included on the form used by the Community Foundation for Monterey County for initial site visits (prior to funding) include the following:

Background

• Agency name
• Agency contact person

- Project or proposal number
- Brief description of the project
- Amount requested
- Duration of funding requested (in months or years)

Questions for Project Personnel

- What are the goals of this project?
- How do these goals align with the overall organizational mission?
- Who is administering the project?
- What are her or his qualifications and experience?
- What are the key sources of financial support for this project?
- What are the long-term funding plans?
- How will success be measured?

Space for Staff Notes

- Overall strengths of the program
- Areas needing further improvement or clarification
- Other ways the foundation could assist the agency
- Other comments
- Recommendations

After funding has been awarded, you can use site visits as an opportunity to observe program implementation as well as evaluation activities. If a site visit is impossible because of distance, virtual site visits via telephone conference calls and e-mails, supplemented with photos, can be very helpful. A site visit provides the program officer with an opportunity to encourage grantees to modify their work plan or logic model based on what has been learned during early implementation stages. Written program goals and strategies often must be revised as front-line staff members learn what works. Encourage them to write down what they are learning and note the data that led to their decisions. For example, in a human service program, resources for group counseling may have been reallocated for more individualized health care instead. Drug testing, at first resisted, may later be adopted for practical reasons. These revisions mean that different services are provided and that participants may need to be assessed differently. In such instances, it may be important to revise the evaluation design. Do the new strategies call for revised data forms, spreadsheets, and reports? If so, it is better to change these early, so you can measure progress accurately.

A site visit at the end of the grant can be a useful way to allow grantees to celebrate their successes and show off their achievements, or to shed light on barriers.

Once again, it is often helpful to involve board members. Attending a graduation ceremony, panel discussion, or simply taking time to meet and thank program staff and participants personally can build morale on both sides of the funding equation. It can also lead to stronger planning for future grants or to a better conclusion to the funding relationship if the grant is unlikely to be renewed. The following section contains additional ideas about activities to consider at the end of the funding period.

Using What You Have Learned

He not only overflowed with learning, he stood in the slop.

SYDNEY SMITH

Eventually, written reports will arrive from the grantees you have funded. Some of the information in the reports will be truly useful. Other information, however, will be "slop" (in the spirit of our epigram), possibly because your guidance to grantees about collecting and reporting data was unclear, grantees did not follow your specified reporting guidelines and provided unnecessary information, or grantees were sloppy or inconsistent in their data collection.

Even though you may have pilot-tested your forms, key information may be missing from reports. If you asked a grantee to report on attendance, the report may state that twenty seniors a day came to the senior center. Now that you have what you asked for, you may still be puzzled. Are twenty seniors a day more or fewer than the average daily attendance of six months ago? Could more people have been served? What were the ages of those who attended? You'll need to revise the reporting form next time around to address these questions. Without a context for the attendance figures, they are difficult to interpret. Alternatively, perhaps the grantee only reported on senior attendance for three out of the twelve funded months of the program. Where are the missing attendance reports? If attendance is not consistently gathered and reported, the resulting data will be difficult to use.

Fortunately, a substantial number of the evaluation reports are likely to be complete. This will be more likely to happen if you have provided specific guidelines and examples of well-documented grantee reports that you have received previously. These can serve as models for what you hope to achieve for the other grantees in the next round.

When success is documented in a report, it can be helpful for you to conduct a follow-up site visit or telephone interview. Ask grantee staff what factors they believe contributed to their positive outcomes. Though many people may mention the higher level of funding from the foundation, try to draw out more. For example, factors may include:

- Stable, experienced staff
- Effective leadership
- Good partnerships with others
- Better space or new equipment
- Active board giving and fundraising
- Well-trained, consistent volunteers

When successful practices are documented, encourage the grantee to share them. If the grant results are especially promising, what other groups could benefit from learning more about the program or project?

The completion of a significant, successful grant is a good time to encourage others to join in sustaining the success achieved. Can your foundation prepare a joint press release with the grantee as part of the dissemination plan? Is it appropriate to arrange a presentation to your full board, or a meeting with other funders and public officials? Can seminars or panel discussions at conferences be scheduled with other grantees and practitioners? You may want to provide some additional postgrant funding to help grantees further document and disseminate the information.

Sometimes success or failure occurs because of factors beyond local control, especially national trends or events. During the 1990s, many communities enjoyed a positive economic climate with high levels of employment. At the same time, violent crime fell, graduation rates increased, and teen pregnancy declined. Foundation support for nonprofit activities grew at unprecedented rates, and most nonprofits were able to reach more people and provide more comprehensive programs. Some of these trends reversed as the economic picture declined. Thus, if the same program that previously produced strong results now appears less effective, be mindful of the strong roles that job growth, optimism, and a sense of security may have played. Most funders, especially small ones, cannot claim that they *caused* success, but they may present a case that they contributed to it. As a relatively small funder, even if your grant added key resources that other funders could not supply, it is hard to determine what additional levels of success can be attributable to your specific grant. Nevertheless, you can still share the story of promising results, watch for similar funding opportunities in the future, and encourage other funders with similar interests to support this project and others like it.

If a foundation is taking reasonable risks in its grantmaking, even as a limited funding partner, some grants will not achieve their goals. Grantees, of course, don't fail on purpose; in most cases, they feel much worse about falling short of their goals than you do. Because you are their partner in learning, as well as funding, try to understand the barriers they encountered. Ask yourself:

- Did other anticipated funding and resources fail to materialize?
- Were there changes in key staff? Were they able to hire and retain the people they needed at the level of funding they had?
- Were there changes at key organizations that work as program partners?
- Could they gain access to the desired population (schools, child-care centers)?
- Did competing organizations draw clients or resources away?
- What is the state of scientific knowledge in this field? Is it advanced enough to identify successful strategies?
- Do recent advances in scientific knowledge point to the need for a change in strategy or for additional staff training?
- How can stories about almost-but-not-quite-successful clients inform program improvement?
- Were other positive results achieved with the grant dollars that this report does not capture?

It also can be helpful to ask the following:

- Did we at the foundation know enough about the issue to make this grant?
- Were our goals and expectations realistic?
- Was our funding sufficient?
- Did we understand the other resources, collaborations, staff training needs, equipment, or technical expertise needed for success?

You may be asked to fund this same organization or program again in the future. Evaluation will not provide a definitive answer, but the process can yield valuable information to help guide your decision.

Conclusion

A modest yet systematic approach to thinking evaluatively about granting practices will enable a foundation to better answer these questions: Did we fund the right people? Did they have reasonable success in meeting their goals? Did we and our grantees make positive strides toward our shared goals of meaningful public benefit? If success rates were low, you want to understand why. The key is to have enough systematically collected information on hand to support reasonable decisions about your grantmaking activities.

Like other financial investment strategies, it is often wise to give your grantmaking investment strategies time to work before changing them. As you and your board members learn together, you will gain a better understanding of your role in supporting greater success for your grantees. You may decide to focus on longer-term relationships to sustain work that you most value. You may adjust the mix of large, small, new, established, mainstream, and grassroots groups in reaching people who are most likely to be underserved. You may decide it is safe to venture into areas and issues that you had not previously considered.

One of the great advantages of evaluation is that you can begin learning more about the things you most care about. You will gain new understanding about immediate needs in your priority funding areas and see the bigger picture about longer-term possibilities such as organizational development and capacity building, collaboration and partnerships, and how you might advocate for changes in systems or laws that affect what you want to achieve.

At first, you and the board may feel uncomfortable with all the possibilities you are discovering. You may find yourselves wondering, "Wasn't it easier when we just made grants to established organizations and didn't look so deeply at what they were trying to achieve? Wasn't it more comfortable when we relied on assertions that a program made a difference without feeling the need for data to document those assertions?" This tension is real. It *is* frequently difficult to find the right balance between trust—in good people with good intentions—and a systematic search for documented, positive results. Despite best intentions, from time to time, one will still award a grant based primarily on gut instincts and trust (and secondarily on whatever limited information about program effectiveness is available).

Yet being alert for new developments, looking for patterns, and drawing conclusions based on reliable evidence can be the source of progress. Over the long term, if you stick with even a simple, shoestring evaluation process, you should see the benefits for your foundation and your grantees in terms of more satisfying and supportive relationships, more realistic expectations about results, a higher proportion of successful outcomes, and more powerful programs.

CHAPTER ELEVEN

STRATEGIES FOR COMPREHENSIVE INITIATIVES

Debra J. Rog and James R. Knickman

It has been said that most foundations have one or more core traditions at the base of their philanthropic mission—to fund for purposes of relief, improvement, and social reform (Nee and Mojica, 1999). Within these broad traditions are a variety of specific reasons for funding specific initiatives. These can include:

- Seeding efforts and hoping that they will spawn sustainable initiatives
- Building capacity, whether through individual skill building and education, organization support, or community support
- Generating information and research needed to solve social problems
- Funding initiatives that the federal government either cannot or will not fund
- Testing or experimenting with new approaches to existing problems (for example, de-categorizing children's health services) (Newacheck, Halfon, Brindis, and Hughes, 1998)
- Filling funding gaps for grantees who have support from other funders
- Bringing attention to important causes or the work of innovative leaders (which may be referred to as "symbolic grantmaking")
- Building a field

Consequently, what foundations fund is often complex and multidimensional and has many components. The initiative may be focused on longer-term outcomes that cannot be achieved in the short run or on outcomes that are at best "fuzzy" goals that are difficult to measure; the funded project may be implemented in multiple sites with varying degrees of uniformity. This is especially the case when collaborative grantmaking occurs between two or more organizations, such as funding partnerships like the National Funding Collaborative on Violence Prevention or the National Community AIDS Partnership (Rog and McCombs, 1996; Nee and Mojica, 1999).

Comprehensive community initiatives (CCIs), in particular, are one example of complex, dynamic, initiatives that have become popular in the larger foundations (Connell, Kubisch, Schorr, and Weiss, 1997; Fulbright-Anderson, Kubisch, and Connell, 1998). CCIs are typically intended to strengthen individuals and families, as well as the overall communities and the various systems and sectors within them. They are described as being complex and intangible, with ever-changing relationships (Annie E. Casey Foundation, 2000). Two examples are The Annie E. Casey Foundation's Jobs Plus Initiative and The Robert Wood Johnson Foundation's Fighting Back Initiative (Saxe and others, 1997); the objective of each was to reduce substance abuse in targeted communities by creating systems of prevention, treatment, and aftercare.

Although the majority of philanthropic initiatives are not the subject of an outcome evaluation (Walker and Grossman, 1999), the pressure to have accountability, as well as the push to develop an evidence base to support practice, has increasingly meant that evaluation is part of many funded initiatives.

Evaluators are typically faced with one or more challenges. This chapter describes the most common ones and then offers five strategies that foundations and evaluators can use to address the challenges. The aims of this chapter are to (1) highlight the aspects of the foundation-funded initiatives that present difficulties for evaluation practice and (2) identify situations in which evaluation may not be the best strategy to use. The recommendations that are offered to deal with these problems and situations should help both foundation officers and evaluators maximize the contribution that evaluation can make to philanthropy.

Foundation Features That Pose Challenges

Clearly, foundations fund a range of initiatives, and any broad characterization runs the risk of oversimplification. When examining community initiatives, however, there do appear to be a number of evaluation challenges that are common to many of these efforts. Seven of these challenges are noted here.

Contextual Influences and Changes Over Time

When foundations apply money to problems that are entrenched in a particular social or community context, the efforts they fund can be influenced by context, often in unforeseen ways. These contextual challenges, in turn, present difficulties for evaluation and necessitate strategies for either controlling the influence of these contextual factors or, at a minimum, examining their role in influencing the initiative and the outcomes.

Similarly, there are often multiple initiatives in place in a community, which may influence that community and the individuals who live there. For example, in the evaluation of the Casey Jobs-Plus Initiative, the evaluators realized that individuals who were working with the Jobs-Plus case manager were also working with case managers from other programs (see Annie E. Casey Foundation, 2000). This multiplicity of initiatives and efforts makes it difficult to cleanly tie outcomes to one specific initiative. In addition, it is difficult, at times, to know all the efforts that may be in operation and the extent to which individuals are participating in them.

Community Initiatives Evolving

Evaluation, both structurally and methodologically, is not well suited to studying the outcomes of changing interventions, especially if expected outcomes themselves evolve over time. The dynamics within the intervention also require some flexibility for adjustment in the evaluation, which is sometimes difficult to accomplish, especially in quantitative studies. Having sufficient forethought before undertaking the evaluation, with respect to its structure, funding, and methods, is key to ensuring that some flexibility can be built in. This may mean collecting a broad range of measures and anticipating that some may not be used if outcomes change. It may also mean adding measurement along the way if new goals are adopted that were not anticipated during the design. However, it is important to avoid "fishing" for outcomes that might have changed. Concluding that a program affects an outcome requires that there be some logical connection between the logic of a program and an outcome. Moreover, it is important to identify this logic before looking at the data.

In the evaluation of the community collaboratives funded under the Institute for Community Peace (formerly the National Funding Collaborative for Violence Prevention), for instance, what could be reasonably expected from the collaboratives over time was better understood after the collaboratives were in the field for a while and the realities of the broader contexts and other demands were realized. In addition, the funders realized that the process of how the collaboratives were developing was not only critical to benchmark but to examine in connection with the progress of the local site's programmatic work (for example, if role clarity was not there, the chances of other "programmatic" outcomes occurring was reduced). Finally, by working in the area awhile, the funders had a better understanding of what their theory of change was, which, in turn, helped them identify more appropriate benchmarks for programmatic success and more appropriate evaluation and research questions. For example, the theory of change then began to articulate appropriate multilevel change indicators. However, the evaluation systems were already in place and could not capture all aspects of the theory that was now articulated.

At times, it may be prudent for the evaluator to spend the first phase of an initiative focused on process and implementation and let the initiative "shake down" before finalizing the outcome measurement. This can be best accomplished if there is a specific pilot phase for the initiative before it is considered in place. The danger, of course, is that in cases where there is not the benefit of a pilot phase, it may be difficult to obtain good baseline measures that can provide a good indication of any change that does occur.

There is often a developmental aspect to community initiatives, especially comprehensive initiatives, that may require the evaluator to take on the role of technical assistant and actually help in developing the intervention (Nee and Mojica, 1999). An ethical challenge may emerge in how the evaluator juggles his or her role and provides for an objective assessment of outcomes, if called for.

Demonstrations Designed from the Bottom Up

Foundations often design broad frameworks for initiatives, outlining theories of change or action but leaving much of the program design to the individual grant recipients. This nonprescriptive stance is typically very purposeful (for example, Rog and McCombs, 1996), allowing sites to design programs and initiatives that fit their own local circumstances. This program approach gives sites the opportunity to maximize their strengths and fill their own gaps but presents the evaluators with initiatives that may vary a great deal and may be only loosely tied to the theory of action set out by the foundation.

In the case of Fighting Back, for example, the foundation believed there were common elements that the fourteen funded communities needed to have in order to develop effective solutions to alcohol and drug problems, but the foundation also believed that the communities needed to have considerable latitude in their program implementation to respond effectively to the particular population, community needs, and other local factors (Saxe and others, 1997). This approach led to substantial variation in the activities that sites engaged in, to the extent that many of the program operators felt that site data should not even be aggregated in statistical analyses.

Multiplicity in Programs, Populations, Context

As noted earlier, multisite initiatives, which are often what foundations support, present evaluators not only with the potential challenge of having multiple, varied programs developed from the ground up, but multiplicity as well in the populations served and in the nature of communities involved. In one instance, a program may be implemented in a neighborhood, while in another site multiple communities across a state may be involved. As a result, there may be as much variation within a site as across the sites. Therefore, designing evaluations that can accommodate all these differences, especially evaluations that are attempting to measure change over time, can be a formidable challenge. In The Robert Wood Johnson Foundation's Community Partners for Older Adults, grantees focus on building delivery systems that are more flexible and comprehensive for addressing the care needs of frail elders. Some grantees are county governments, some are regional collaboratives, and some are Area Agencies on Aging that do not necessarily follow governmental boundary lines. From an evaluation perspective, this variation in the type of grantee makes the program more a series of case studies than a multisite demonstration. However, a limited number of common outcomes have been identified.

Goals That Are Difficult to Quantify and Measure

Constructs of complex programs funded by foundations are often not well specified and lack standard definitions (Annie E. Casey Foundation, 2000). Concepts such as *social capital, violence prevention, community efficacy,* and *citizen empowerment* are all fuzzy terms that are hard to operationalize and that can have multiple meanings. Therefore, the task of identifying and developing measures that fully capture the concept in a valid manner that is agreed upon by all key stakeholders is not easy.

Systems change, for example, is a nebulous concept that means many things to many people (Rog and Gutman, 1997). It can mean any change that occurs, such as a change in how agencies work with each other, or it can mean a specific set of collaborations that need to take place, such as that resources and data are to be shared. In addition, it is not clear what the essential ingredients are in achieving systems change (Saxe and others, 1997) or even specific approaches to take to begin to change systems (Rog and Gutman, 1997). If agreement on a definition or even more clarity on the concept cannot be reached, the evaluation may require a multipronged and often more exploratory approach in which multiple methods and measures are used to look at a multitude of possible indicators and outcomes.

Phenomena That Do Not Lend Themselves to Random Assignment

Walker and Grossman (1999) point out that outcomes and impacts are not the same. A study can measure outcomes (such as reported changes in high-risk behaviors by students in schools with health clinics), but without a strong basis of comparison, it will have difficulty linking the outcomes to the initiatives, that is, determining whether having exposure to clinics in their schools had an impact on youths' high-risk behaviors. In the case of the RWJF School-Based Health Centers Demonstration—a nineteen-site demonstration of high school and middle school health clinics (Knickman and Jellinek, 1997)—neither randomization nor the inclusion of a matched comparison sample of schools was deemed possible. Instead, a national sample of urban youth was used as a reference sample. However, baseline rates between the groups were not comparable; rates of high-risk behaviors increased as the students got older and then leveled off, making it difficult to interpret the patterns.

Initiatives focused on changing communities and neighborhoods do not lend themselves easily to comparative evaluation approaches, let alone random assignment. It is difficult to find places that are similar enough in context and history to provide a sufficient counterfactual for the initiative that is being studied. Moreover, communities can be similar at one point and then change in nonparallel ways over the course of the initiative (Walker and Grossman, 1999). And when communities are essentially the unit of analysis in an evaluation, sample sizes are generally small, making valid comparisons especially difficult.

There may be other programmatic issues that hinder randomization. For example, in the case of the School-Based Adolescent Health Centers Demonstration, schools had already been selected for the initiative without agreeing to the rigors and constraints of randomization. In addition, the foundation did not want to make the clinics available to some students and not others. However, examples of finding useful comparison groups, even when program design does not make comparison a priority, are emerging in evaluation literature. For example, when designing evaluations of CCIs it is often difficult to find appropriate comparison groups. This is because communities are chosen, not randomly but based on their readiness for change or other strengths and characteristics. In the case of the Urban Health Initiative (UHI), cluster analysis was used to identify comparison groups that matched some of the baseline features of the cities participating in UHI. Based on underlying social and economic conditions, cluster analysis allowed for the identification of a group of American cities similar to the

UHI cluster and thus useful as a comparison group (Weitzman, Silver, and Dill-man, 2002).

Finally, most comparisons are not "untreated" in the sense that there is a complete absence of what is being examined in the intervention. For example, in the federal Access to Community Care and Effective Services and Supports (ACCESS) program, intervention sites were provided funds to coordinate their services for individuals with severe mental illness (Johnsen and others, 1999). Despite not having the specific funding, the comparison communities still had some level of coordination and may have even increased it by being part of a study. The challenge is that the activities between the intervention and comparison may not be distinct enough to allow for a sensitive assessment of the intervention's impact.

The Effects of Timeframe

Initiatives are often funded for three to five years, although there are noteworthy exceptions (for example, RWJF's Urban Health Initiatives, which was funded for ten years). This standard timeframe is generally insufficient to develop models, develop trust with communities, individuals, and other entities that are needed to implement the models, and still have time to see the changes that are expected (Silver, Weitzman, and Brecher, 2002). And if programs experience missteps in the early years (for example, change in leadership, failed initial implementation, or misunderstanding of the foundation's model), the evaluation of a three- to five-year program could confuse a failed implementation with a failed concept (Rossi, Lipsey, and Freeman, 2004).

Solutions for Addressing the Challenges

Some of the challenges that exist in foundation initiatives can be avoided, others can be minimized, and still others just need to be endured. We offer a few recommendations for both foundation officers and evaluators for dealing with these situations in a manner that will maximize the contribution evaluation can make to philanthropy.

Don't Evaluate the Nonevaluable

Although evaluation is not in the portfolio of all foundations, when it is included it is often used widely. Unfortunately, not all initiatives are ready or even appropriate for evaluation. *Evaluability assessment,* championed by Joe Wholey and colleagues in the late 1970s (Wholey, 1979), was developed specifically to examine the readiness of a program for outcome evaluation. Often, a program may be too nascent and undeveloped, its goals may not be measurable, and there may not be universal agreement on what is expected from the initiative, especially if the reasons for funding were multiple.

There has been a call for a strategic rethinking of when to conduct outcome evaluations. There is increasing pressure in foundations, as well as the federal government, to see what works, but that may not always be feasible or reasonable. Too often, expectations are set that are unreasonably high for the initiative and for the evaluation. At times, the initiative is a concept with no operational model. For example, in The Robert Wood Johnson Foundation Homeless Families Program (Rog and Gutman, 1997), a major goal of the program was "systems change for homeless families." Yet there was no articulated theory of how to accomplish that change or what its achievement would resemble. There was also no perspective of what the ideal system for families would look like; there was no assessment of the needs, gaps, and strengths in the system and what would need changing; and there was no explicit strategy for bringing about change.

As Wisely (2002, p. 16) notes, "A dose of realism will benefit both philanthropy and evaluation." It is important to acknowledge the weaknesses in programs, abandon the lofty goals, and set realistic expectations—then ask if those expectations are worth the effort (Walker and Grossman, 1999). Using the Summer Training and Education Program (STEP) as an example, the authors describe how the STEP youth experienced strong, immediate changes in their educational outcomes, compared to a control group, but the effects did not hold over time. The question is whether those short-term effects are worth it or what could be built on them to make them worth it.

In addition, as in the case of the School-Based Health Clinics (Knickman and Jellinek, 1997), if a legitimate basis of comparison cannot be included in the evaluation, continuing to conduct an outcome evaluation may not be worthwhile if it cannot provide results in a definitive manner. Moreover, the authors note that rigorous evaluations are typically only practically possible when that level of evidence is needed to inform the decision-making process.

Clarify the True Reason for the Initiative

Not all initiatives are designed to further knowledge. In some instances, as noted earlier, the money is symbolic—recognizing past good work or providing funds directed to an important cause. For example, the RWJF Community Leadership Program is designed to bring attention to the important role local leaders can play in fostering positive social change. This goal is logical but rather intangible

(Mantell, 2003). In these instances, evaluation in any form is likely to be inappropriate and fraught with difficulties.

In the case of the School-Based Health Clinics (Knickman and Jellinek, 1997), the foundation was primarily interested in getting the clinics up and running in the schools. There was a fear that having an evaluation that included questions on high-risk behaviors and that attempted to include comparison schools could lead to negative parental concerns and cause districts to resign from the project. Thus the authors note that if the foundation's main goal for an initiative is program viability, then evaluations that pose their own requirements in order to achieve rigor may not be suitable. In many cases, foundations provide core support to nonprofit organizations judged to be important contributors to social well-being. Or advocacy projects may be funded to push for social improvements. Again, these types of investments are not "testing hypotheses" about what works. Traditional evaluation often misses the point in such situations.

Incorporate More Planned Variation in Multisite Initiatives

Foundations are often in the position of balancing interests, including those of their board, their internal staff, outside parties, and the programs they fund. Initiatives are often designed around these interests, rather than based on lessons from the literature and past efforts. Once an initiative is designed and a broad theory of change is articulated, it is a rare foundation that stipulates exactly what a grantee should do. Rather than prescribe, foundations often guide applicants with broad parameters. A common philosophy is to allow grantees to develop program approaches that accommodate local needs, assets, and other features. The result in a multisite initiative is often a variety of loosely connected sites that are thrown together under one evaluation. Planned variation studies, used over twenty years ago in the field of education, may provide a reasonable compromise for foundations and a way to strengthen what an evaluation can offer (Rivlin and Timpane, 1975). These studies outline possible approaches that can be followed by applicants and fund a set number of sites within each type of approach, to provide the ability to cluster approaches as well as to produce more systematic distinctions.

Fund Measurement and Development Efforts

A key struggle in evaluating many of the broad-based initiatives of foundations is identifying or creating measures that are valid, reliable, and agreed upon by the many stakeholders. Much of this development work has to be accomplished within the timeframe and support of a specific evaluation. In these instances, rarely is there time to do the careful work that is needed to test multiple approaches or to conduct reliability and validity tests. Moreover, because these project-specific efforts are not always tested, this kind of measurement-development exercise is conducted over and over again on the same or highly similar constructs in different contexts.

Foundations would do well to fund efforts designed to work on elaborating specific constructs (such as systems change or empowerment) and developing measurement systems that can work with (or at least be adapted for) a variety of content and context areas. These efforts could include both qualitative and quantitative measurement approaches and would focus on establishing reliability, validity, and sensitivity to change.

In addition to focusing on the outcome constructs, efforts could also be funded that focus on articulating and measuring the mechanisms for creating the outcomes. These would likely be much more difficult projects and would need to build on past demonstration efforts. For example, in the case of systems change, the goal would be to empirically validate the theories of change that are in place by compiling study results from a variety of investigations and to begin to identify or propose features of the efforts that are key to changing systems.

All of these theory-building and measurement efforts would be best supported through partnerships among foundations. Coordinated measurement and development efforts would more likely result in measures and articulated concepts that are generalizable and acceptable across a range of projects sponsored by different funders. Moreover, the benefit of such efforts could extend to smaller foundations that otherwise lack the ability to fund these kinds of projects, yet could use the products to make their own demonstrations more efficient.

Fund and Encourage Mixed-Method Approaches

Finally, there is a need in development efforts, as well as in demonstration evaluations, to have more mixed-method projects. Because the phenomena that foundations are interested in are typically complicated, ever changing, and nested within complex contexts, it is both difficult and undesirable to have a purely quantitative approach to measuring the process and outcomes of an effort. More flexible qualitative methods are needed in order to be sensitive to the often subtle changes that are occurring, as well as unanticipated events and other potential developments. Mixing qualitative and quantitative approaches provides sensitivity, as well as solid benchmarks that can be traced over the course of a project, and permits communication of results that are both quantifiable and interpretable.

Consider Alternatives to Formal Evaluation

Even when formal evaluation is not appropriate for assessing outcomes of a foundation's investment, a range of alternative analytical tasks can assist learning. Tracking outcomes related to a funded program may help funders and grantees keep their eye on what they hope to achieve, even if causal relationships between a program and the outcome cannot be determined. If, over time, an outcome of interest is not improving, the funder might realize the need to expand the effort or perhaps think of other outcomes or social problems to focus on. Self-evaluation techniques, including the use of logic models, may help grantees recognize whether they are accomplishing organizational objectives over time that are judged important to make progress toward an ultimate social outcome. And the "stories" of how grantees go about their business—often the focus of qualitative learning tools—can be helpful for those who wish to replicate what an organization is attempting with philanthropic support. In general, it is helpful for the evaluator to start with two questions: (1) What can we learn from an investment a philanthropy is making? and (2) What evaluative or analytic techniques can assist important learning?

Conclusion

Two goals of this volume are (1) to educate evaluators about the nature of philanthropic work and how it can shape their own work and (2) to inform foundation officials of evaluation's potential and its limits. In this chapter, we have focused on the specific nature of many of the philanthropic initiatives themselves—their many purposes, their comprehensive scope, their dynamic nature—and the implications of these features for evaluation practice. In some instances, an evaluation can offer a great deal to the understanding of an initiative if flexibility and creativity are incorporated into the study. In other instances, evaluation cannot meet a foundation's expectations due to the purposes or developmental status of an initiative. Having evaluation become a more standard part of philanthropic work to guide and improve the usefulness of foundation efforts is indeed an important goal. However, in promoting evaluation, there needs to be strategic thinking about the types of initiatives that would profit most from rigorous study, as well as the other ways in which foundations can support the goal of learning about their efforts (for example, fostering measurement development).

The practical implications of this chapter's discussion focus on the importance of being realistic on the one hand about how complicated a demonstration can be if rigorous evaluation is the goal or, on the other hand, how rigorous an evaluation one should design if a funded initiative is complex and not well defined in terms of expected outcomes. If a funder wants to develop strong evidence about the effectiveness of a new idea for improving some social outcome, then care and discipline are needed to design a multisite initiative that is evaluable. However, when a funder wants to be flexible about the local designs of initiatives and expected outcomes, as well as about letting an initiative evolve over time, then evaluators must not overpromise the abilities of evaluation to come to definitive conclusions. In these situations, the more practical approach to evaluation often starts with the question, What can be learned from an initiative? rather than, How can I evaluate success and failure?

References

Annie E. Casey Foundation (2000). *Transforming neighborhoods into family-supporting environments: Evaluation issues and challenges.* Research and Evaluation Conference, March 1999.

Connell, J. P., Kubisch, A. C., Schorr, L. B., & Weiss, C. H. (Eds.). (1997). *New approaches to evaluating community initiatives: Concepts, methods, and contexts.* Washington, DC: The Aspen Institute.

Fulbright-Anderson, K., Kubisch, A. C., & Connell, J. P. (Eds.). (1998). *New approaches to evaluating community initiatives: Theory, measurement, and analysis* (Vol. 2). Washington, DC: The Aspen Institute.

Johnsen, M., Samberg, L., Calsyn, R., Blasinsky, M., Landow, W., & Goldman, H. (1999). Case management models for persons who are homeless and mentally ill: The ACCESS demonstration project. *Community and Mental Health Journal, 35*(4), 325–347.

Knickman, J., & Jellinek, P. (1997). Epilogue: Four lessons from evaluating controversial programs. *Children and Youth Services Review, 19,* 607–614.

Mantell, P. (2003). The Robert Wood Johnson Community Health Leadership Program. In S. L. Isaacs & J. R. Knickman (Eds.), *To improve health and healthcare* (Vol. 4, pp. 203–224). San Francisco: Jossey-Bass.

Nee, D., & Mojica, M. (1999). Ethical challenges in evaluation with communities: A manager's perspective. In J. L. Fitzpatrick & M. Morris (Eds.), *Current and Emerging Ethical Challenges in Evaluation,* New Directions for Evaluation, no. 82. San Francisco: Jossey-Bass.

Newacheck, P. W., Halfon, N., Brindis, C. D., & Hughes, D. C. (1998). Evaluating community efforts to decategorize and integrate financing of children's health services. *Milbank Quarterly, 76*(2), 157–173.

Rivlin, A., & Timpane, M. (1975). *Planned variation in education: Should we give up or try harder?* Brookings Studies in Social Experimentation. Washington, DC: Brookings Institution.

Rog, D. J., & Gutman, M. A. (1997). The Homeless Families Program: A summary of key findings. In S. L. Isaacs & J. R. Knickman (Eds.), *To improve health and health care 1997.* San Francisco: Jossey-Bass.

Rog, D. J., & McCombs, K. (1996). *The national funding collaborative on violence prevention: Beginnings.* Report prepared for the National Funding Collaborative on Violence Prevention, Washington, DC.

Rossi, P. H., Lipsey, M. W., & Freeman, H. E. (2004). *Evaluation: A systematic approach* (7th ed.). Thousand Oaks, CA: Sage.

Saxe, L., Reber, E., Hallfors, D., Kadushin, C., Jones, D., Rindskopf, D., & Beveridge, A. (1997). Think globally, act locally: Assessing the impact of community-based substance abuse prevention. *Evaluation and Program Planning, 20,* 357–366.

Silver, D., Weitzman, B. C., & Brecher, C. (2002). Setting an agenda for local action: The limits of expert opinion and community voice. *Policy Studies Journal, 30*(3), 362–379.

Walker, G., & Grossman, J. B. (1999). *Philanthropy and outcomes: Dilemmas in the quest for accountability.* Philadelphia: Public/Private Ventures Brief.

Weitzman, B. C., Silver, D., & Dillman, K. N. (2002). Integrating a comparison group design into a theory of change evaluation: The case of the Urban Health Initiative. *The American Journal of Evaluation, 23*(4), 371–385.

Wholey, J. S. (1979). *Evaluation: Promise and performance.* Washington, DC: Urban Institute.

Wisely, D. S. (2002). Parting thoughts on foundation evaluation. *The American Journal of Evaluation, 23,* 159–164.

Wright, J. D. (1991). *Methodological issues in evaluating the national health care for the homeless program.* New Directions for Program Evaluation, no. 52. San Francisco: Jossey-Bass.

CHAPTER TWELVE

APPRAISING EVIDENCE ON PROGRAM EFFECTIVENESS

Norman A. Constantine and Marc T. Braverman

Rarely do we find simple or conclusive answers to our questions about the effectiveness of a program intended to address a complex social problem. Yet well-designed and skillfully implemented evaluations can and often do provide compelling evidence in this regard. To make best use of this evidence requires a healthy dose of constructive skepticism, as well as an understanding of common sources of ambiguous results and misleading conclusions that frequently pervade program evaluations.

Our intent in this chapter is to provide some basic guidance on the critical appraisal of program effectiveness evidence. We begin with a discussion of the nature of ambiguous results and misleading conclusions, followed by an illustration based on an influential national study on adolescent virginity pledge programs. Next, we discuss essential tools for strengthening effectiveness evaluations—experimental and quasi-experimental designs, and program theory. Well-known evaluations from the areas of youth violence prevention and teen pregnancy prevention are used to illustrate challenges often encountered in the use of statistical significance tests to draw conclusions about program effective-

We gratefully acknowledge the constructive skepticism and helpful suggestions provided by Melvin Mark, Wendy Constantine, Mark Lipsey, and Joel Moskowitz, and the indispensable library support provided by Mieko Davis.

ness. We then make a case for transparency and accessibility in providing full evaluation results for critique. Discussions follow of interpreting null or negative results and of the cumulative nature of knowledge about program effectiveness. The chapter closes with a reiteration of the importance of critically examining evidence about program effectiveness.

Although we invoke a few technical concepts in the course of our discussion, the ideas and examples presented rely primarily on the processes of carefully reasoned argument. We hope that this chapter will be useful to readers of diverse training and roles, and that it will support the critical appraisal of effectiveness evidence among evaluation professionals and consumers alike.

Evaluation can be defined broadly as *the systematic collection and use of information to answer questions about programs.* Depending on each unique program and stakeholder situation, different types of questions are commonly addressed within this overarching evaluation framework, including questions about the need for a program and about program development, implementation, improvement, effectiveness, and potential reach, among others. Several alternative perspectives have been articulated on what evaluation is and what it should be (Shadish, Cook, and Leviton, 1995; Mark and Smith, 2001; Cronbach, 1982). These perspectives vary on a number of dimensions, including the emphasis placed on direct questions about program effectiveness, that is, trying to determine whether a collection of program activities caused desired outcomes in a specific sample of participants in a particular setting and context, and to what extent results can be generalized to similar but nonidentical program activities, recipients, settings, and outcomes. Although certainly not the only types of questions that evaluation can deal with, these are the fundamental questions of program effectiveness evaluation.

Ambiguous Results and Misleading Conclusions

At heart, questions about program effectiveness are about causation: Did a program *cause* the intended results? And answering questions about causation is seldom a straightforward task. This complexity can open the door to results that are ambiguous and conclusions that are spurious or misleading. We distinguish here between *ambiguous results* as those that are open to multiple conflicting conclusions and *misleading conclusions* as those that are inappropriately supported by either dubious results or the questionable use of results. Ambiguous results are common in program effectiveness evaluation, as in all areas of scientific inquiry—social and natural sciences alike. Depending on the nature of the questions asked, the resources available, the skill of the evaluation team, and many other factors, effectiveness evidence and conclusions will be of greater or lesser certainty, but rarely does any one study conclusively answer an effectiveness question. It is the nature of science that confidence in a hypothesized relation (such as between a program and a potential effect) must develop over time and through replications, and always remains subject to possible modification or refutation. Science advances iteratively, often through skepticism, criticism, and debate. The same is true for evaluation. Under the right circumstances, good outcome evaluations do provide useful evidence to inform program investment decisions, especially when results are interpreted within the context of a strong theoretical grounding together with previous evaluations of similar programs. Depending on the particular situation, the necessary level of confidence required for our results and conclusions will vary. Over time and through additional studies of similar programs, these conclusions might be either weakened or strengthened; at times, a program investment decision might require reconsideration.

Divergent values and ideological views within our society about social problems and their solutions can foster the distortion of effectiveness evidence, especially when the evidence is ambiguous. For example, after decades of evaluation on programs to prevent adolescent pregnancy and sexually transmitted infections, deep ideological divisions among proponents of abstinence-only versus comprehensive sexuality education programs appear to have hardened. Both sides appeal to program evaluation "evidence," often ambiguous at best, to make their case (see several illustrations that follow). Another motivation for the misuse of evidence is the real or imagined pressure on grantees and external evaluators to show positive results and definitive conclusions that will please the funders (Braverman and Campbell, 1989; Moskowitz, 1993). Biases that might result can range from the largely unconscious to the blatantly obvious. And we are all potentially susceptible—evaluators, program staff, foundation program officers, and other evaluation consumers.

To further complicate these challenges, modern statistical and methodological tools are becoming increasingly difficult for nonspecialists to understand. Most evaluators can't keep up with the full range of methods available, while statisticians often specialize in esoteric areas or techniques. When complex statistical methods are employed, evaluation consumers might be inclined to "trust the expert" as a coping strategy and assume on faith that the evaluation results and conclusions are valid. In truth, complex statistics can sometimes strengthen a good evaluation design, but the principle doesn't hold for a weak one. As Light, Singer, and Willett (1990, p. v) note, "You can't fix by analysis what you've bungled by design." Fortunately, evaluation designs can be easier for a nonexpert to understand and critically appraise than are complex statistical methods; in many cases, this will be the most important area to assess when considering the validity of any conclusions about effectiveness.

Causation, Correlation, and Alternative Explanations

The essential nature of causation and the types of evidence necessary to demonstrate a causal relation, such as the effect of a program on an outcome, have been long debated (for example, Bunge, 1979; Mackie, 1980; McKim and Turner, 1997). In spite of these ongoing debates, it is safe to say that a pragmatic view of causation is most appropriate to intervention effectiveness studies. Most program outcomes of interest are the result of numerous and interacting causes—some that are potentially changeable (such as home environment) and some that are much less so (such as genetic influences). What we expect of the best interventions is to partially influence some outcomes, under specific conditions and circumstances, by modifying one or more causal factors. But how do we know when this has happened?

According to the nineteenth-century philosopher John Stuart Mill, at least three criteria must be invoked in justifying casual claims: (1) *association* (or correlation—the cause is related to the effect), (2) *temporality* (the cause comes before the effect), and (3) *elimination of plausible alternative explanations* (other plausible explanations for an effect are considered and ruled out). The key is that *all three* are necessary, yet sometimes the second and often the third of these criteria are neglected in the design and interpretation of evaluation studies. And even when the third criterion is explicitly addressed by the evaluation, it is often arguable whether or not a sufficient number of the most likely plausible explanations have been considered.

It is widely recognized that correlation does not necessarily imply causation, yet erroneous causal attributions are commonly made based on association or correlation alone. Consider the potential conclusion that adolescents' levels of psychological attachment to their families are a cause of observed differences in problem behavior levels, based on a correlation between these two variables. Although this conclusion might in fact be valid, the correlation alone does not provide sufficient supportive evidence for its validity; any number of alternative explanations could fit the observed relationship. For example, lower levels of problem behavior might strengthen family attachment rather than the other way around. Or a third factor, such as patterns of parental conflict, might independently influence both attachment and problem behavior.

When both of Mill's first two conditions (association and temporality) hold, it can be even more tempting to erroneously infer causation without considering other plausible explanations. As an example, consider the National Longitudinal Study of Adolescent Health, commonly known as the Add Health study (Resnick and others, 1997).[1] This large correlational study has yielded uncountable *associations* among adolescent behaviors, background conditions, health outcomes, and other factors. And because it was longitudinal, involving linked measurements over time from the same participants, some of these associations have been examined for the *temporality* expected for a cause-and-effect relation. Yet little effort has been invested in addressing the third critical criterion for causality: identifying and ruling out plausible alternative explanations.

A compelling illustration is provided by a widely publicized Add Health study conclusion that virginity pledge programs "cause virginity," that is, delay initiation of sexual intercourse (Bearman and Bruchner, 2001). Complex statistical methods, such as survival analysis and logistic regression, were used to reach this conclusion. Several qualifications regarding the program setting were appropriately discussed, most notably that to have an effect, the pledge must occur in a community of other pledgers that is neither too small nor too large relative to the total student population in the school. The authors, however, neglected sufficient consideration of plausible alternative explanations. Foremost among these would be the possibility that a pre-existing disinclination to initiate sex might have been a primary causal factor behind both signing the pledge and delaying intercourse. If true, this alternative explanation implies that signing the virginity pledge serves as a marker to identify those youth who delay intercourse for any number of other reasons and that, in the absence of pledging, the pattern of sexual initiation would be largely unchanged. This alternative arises from the likelihood of a strong self-selection effect, meaning that participants determine for themselves whether they will be part of the intervention group (in this case, those who pledged) or the control group (those who did not). It is likely that pre-existing differences between those who chose to pledge and those who didn't—most notably differences in the intent to delay intercourse—are not only related to the intervention group assignment but are arguably among its most important determinants.

A statistical adjustment procedure intended to remove the effect of self-selection was described in an appendix to the article, but this procedure was both logically and statistically inadequate (see Pedhazur and Schmelkin, 1991, pp. 295–296, for a discussion on the futility of this type of adjustment). Instead, the researchers' conclusions regarding a pledge effect suggest a criterion for causality of *post hoc ergo propter hoc* ("after this, therefore because of this"), a fundamental fallacy of logic, known since classical times, that involves inferring a causal relation on the basis of correlation and temporality alone.

This study, nevertheless, has generated extensive media coverage and policy discussion (see, for example, Boyle, 2000; Nesmith, 2001; Schemo, 2001; Willis, 2001) and has had a substantial influence on federal policy about sexuality education. Prior to this study, the U.S. Department of Health and Human Services had required as performance measures for the evaluation of federally-funded abstinence education programs the "proportion of program participants who have engaged in sexual intercourse" and the birth rate of female program participants (Federal Register, 2000). Two years later, on the heels of extensive media attention to Bearman and Bruchner's (2001) study, these sexual behavior and birth rate measures were replaced with "the proportion of youth who commit to abstain from sexual activity until marriage" (U.S. Department of Health and Human Services, 2002). Thus, virginity pledging has become the primary behavioral outcome to be measured.

If one reads the various critiques and summaries of the pledge study and its conclusions, it is remarkable to find no mention of the obvious plausible alternative explanation of a pre-existing disinclination among pledgers. Instead, the critiques tend to focus on the limited conditions under which the intervention is believed to be effective and the negative side effects observed (for example, that pledgers who break the pledge were less likely to use contraception than nonpledgers). Yet in considering the original question—Do virginity pledges cause the initiation of sexual intercourse to be delayed?—the answer remains that they might or might not. This particular study adds little or nothing to our knowledge of this wished-for effect.

Experimental and Quasi-Experimental Designs

The pledge study example sets the stage for a brief review of experimental and quasi-experimental study designs. A more comprehensive overview of this topic is provided by Reichardt and Mark (1998), and a definitive coverage can be found in Shadish, Cook, and Campbell (2002). The critical missing design element in the pledge study was a *controlled manipulation,* that is, random or other controlled assignment of the pledge program to some schools or classrooms and not others. Random assignment would be characteristic of a true experimental design, whereas nonrandom assignment strategies could be part of a quasi-experimental design. By contrast, the virginity pledge study design was purely correlational, in that no manipulation of intervention delivery across schools, classrooms, or other units took place. With a good experimental or quasi-experimental design, the plausible alternative explanation for the virginity effect could have been ruled out or rendered unlikely, and then the potential effectiveness of pledging could have been examined more appropriately. The admonition "no causation without manipulation" (commonly attributed to Paul Holland) might be somewhat exaggerated for effect, yet it is a useful heuristic for raising a red flag whenever one encounters claims of program effects based on self-selected participation in an intervention program. Correlational designs do have a variety of appropriate and important uses, such as developing hypotheses to be tested in subsequent studies. However, their utility in eliminating plausible alternative explanations is limited.[2]

Both experimental and quasi-experimental designs are intended to help address common threats to *internal validity,* that is, causal attribution of effects to the program. Eight of these threats are discussed by Shadish, Cook, and Campbell (2002), including the selection-related threat illustrated by the virginity pledge study. Briefly, these are

- Selection (pre-existing differences between intervention and control groups that could explain the effect)
- Ambiguous temporal ordering (which variable occurred first?)
- History (extraneous events occurring during the intervention that could explain the effect)
- Maturation (naturally occurring changes in participants over time that could explain the effect)
- Regression (natural movement on subsequent measurements toward the overall group average—applicable for groups selected on the basis of extreme scores)
- Attrition (differential loss of participants in the groups studied)
- Testing (practice or other effects based on exposure to the assessment instrument)
- Instrumentation (changes in the function or meaning of the measures used over time or between groups)

Some or all of these threats to validity can be addressed by various randomized-experimental and quasi-experimental designs. However, the two types of designs differ in important ways and are appropriate in different circumstances.

Randomized experiments (sometimes referred to as true experiments, randomized controlled trials, or randomized field trials) involve the random assignment of units (for example, persons, schools, clinics, or communities) to intervention versus comparison conditions. This is done to control or minimize some of the major potential threats to validity and can be especially powerful in reducing or eliminating selection effects.

Quasi-experiments do not involve random assignment to intervention and comparison conditions but employ some combination of other design features to help rule out alternative explanations of observed effects. These include nonrandom assignment strategies such as matching or stratifying, scheduling of multiple pre- and post-intervention measurements, multiple treatment and comparison groups, and intervention timing. A variety of quasi-experimental designs involving one or more of these strategies have evolved over time (Campbell and Stanley, 1966; Cook and Campbell, 1979) and are discussed in depth by Shadish, Cook, and Campbell (2002).

It is sometimes stated that randomized experiments are the "gold standard" for evaluating program effectiveness. In some ways, this might be true, but with important contextual qualifications (perhaps "bronze standard" would be a more appropriate designation). In the real world of intervention program environments, quasi-experimental designs are often the more cost-effective choice—sometimes the only logistically possible approach—and frequently can provide a basis for equally or more valid causal conclusions than a randomized experiment would provide. For example, an experiment in which some participants refuse to accept their randomized assignment, as often occurs, can yield a weaker design than a good quasi-experiment. And a randomized experiment is often contraindicated until a program has sufficiently matured. As Shadish and colleagues (2002, p. 277) caution: "Premature experimentation can be a great waste of resources—indeed it can undermine potentially promising interventions for which there has not been time to develop recruitment procedures, identify and fix implementation problems, and serve the clientele long enough to make a difference."

Conversely, in some situations a smaller-scale randomized experiment might appropriately be conducted under ideal circumstances at one site prior to implementing a larger-scale, quasi-experimental multisite design under more realistic circumstances (see Glasgow, Lichtenstein, and Marcus, 2003). The key is that both randomized and quasi-experimental designs offer the potential to reduce the likelihood of some or many alternative explanations for a suspected effect, but to be realized, this potential requires skillful application under the right circumstances and conditions. It is the evaluator's responsibility to argue and sufficiently document the case that an appropriate design has been skillfully applied. And it is the evaluation consumer's responsibility to critically appraise this argument, together with the associated results and conclusions. In spite of the potential power and elegance of both randomized and quasi-experiments, neither offers immunity to ambiguous results and misleading conclusions. To assume that results and conclusions are valid simply because they arise from a particular type of evaluation design perpetuates a common but inadequate substitute for critical appraisal.

Examples of Randomized and Quasi-Experimental Designs

The Hutchinson Smoking Prevention Project (Peterson and others, 2000) illustrates an exemplary (and expensive) long-term randomized trial of a school-based tobacco-use-prevention intervention. In this rigorous evaluation, forty Washington school districts were randomly assigned to the intervention or the control condition. More than eight thousand third-grade students were enrolled and followed until two years beyond high school. High program implementation fidelity was achieved, and 94 percent of the enrolled students were retained through the last follow-up assessment. No significant differences were found in smoking rates between intervention and control students, and the authors conclude with confidence that "there is no evidence from this trial that a school-based social-influences approach is effective in the long-term deterrence of smoking among youth" (p. 1979).

Although the Hutchison study provides a compelling illustration of the randomized trial as "gold standard," the gold here might refer not only to the quality of the study but to its cost as well. It would be a mistake, unfortunately, to believe that this level of rigor is typical among randomized evaluations in school and community intervention studies.

As a more fiscally modest example, consider the Around the Clock Mobile Crisis Intervention evaluation (Reding and Raphelson, 1995). This was a much less expensive but wonderfully elegant local evaluation of a community intervention program. It was based on a creative combination of quasi-experimental design elements. Here, the design elements of multiple measurements over time (interrupted time series), intervention timing (introduction and withdrawal of the intervention), and an intact comparison group were efficiently combined to provide compelling evidence of intervention effectiveness (discussed in more detail in Shadish, Cook, and Campbell, 2002, pp. 188–189). Arguably, the conclusions of this quasi-experimental evaluation are just as convincing as are those of the randomized Hutchison study, for a small fraction of the cost. Of course, the costs of these two studies were not set arbitrarily but depended on the evaluation questions, the nature of the interventions, and their contexts.

Program Theories and Social Science Theories

Strictly speaking, an outcome evaluation need only consider the effects of an intervention on one or more outcomes, without addressing how or why these consequences occurred. Yet outcome evaluations that are built on a clearly specified program theory can have many advantages (Lipsey, 1993; Cook and Shadish, 1994). Perhaps most important, a good program theory "enables evaluators to eliminate rival hypotheses and make causal attributions more easily" (House, 2001, p. 311). Furthermore, as Hughes (2000, p. 324) explains,

> A willingness to entertain rival interpretations, an ability to place knowledge within broader contexts, and an openness to new ways of conceptualizing problems are essential to scientific inquiry. Theory serves these functions as well as directs inquiry, unifies and systematizes knowledge, and makes sense of what (might) otherwise be inscrutable empirical facts.

In general, a program theory is the specification of what must be done to achieve the desired program goals, what side effects might also be produced, and the mechanisms through which these goals and effects are generated (Chen, 1990). More specifically, a complete program theory specifies several critical elements: (1) the problem condition to be addressed, (2) the intended intervention populations and relevant background circumstances, (3) the critical program components and their interrelationships, (4) the key aspects of the process by which the program achieves its effects, (5) the intended and potential unintended effects of the intervention, and (6) the interrelationships among these effects (Lipsey, 1993). To help illustrate a program theory, the hypothesized interrelationships among the various theory elements are sometimes portrayed in a diagrammatic format, commonly referred to as a causal diagram.

A program theory is sometimes based on an existing social science theory of change. Glanz, Rimer, and Lewis (2002) provide a comprehensive review of social science theories applicable to health behavior and health education interventions. As an illustration, the theory of reasoned action (Fishbein and Middlestandt, 1989) specifies a network of influences among beliefs, attitudes, perceived social norms, behavioral intentions, and behaviors, and has been used to design and evaluate intervention programs in HIV-AIDS prevention and other areas. Constantine and Curry (1998) documented the process of a school-based violence prevention evaluation in which a program theory was elicited through a series of participatory activities with program staff and other stakeholders, and overlaid on a higher-level theoretical framework derived from the theory of reasoned action.

More commonly, however, the program theory is built around the program designer's assumptions and expectations, with little or no connection to an existing social science theory. Instead, it reflects a thoughtful analysis of how and in what contexts the program is expected to work and what intermediate events need to happen if it is to be successful. This type of locally developed program theory is often referred to as a *logic model* or *theory of change*.

Uses and Abuses of Statistical Significance Testing

In a recent critique, Gorman (2002) describes a randomized trial of the Second Step violence prevention curriculum published in the *Journal of the American Medical Association* (Grossman and others, 1997). Based on this evaluation, the program was certified as an exemplary program by a U.S. Department of Education expert panel (Safe, Disciplined, and Drug-Free Schools Expert Panel, 2001). The department's guidelines for a program to be classified as "exemplary" include the criterion of "at least one evaluation that has demonstrated an effect on substance abuse, violent behavior, or other conduct problems one year or longer beyond baseline" (Safe, Disciplined, and Drug-Free Schools Expert Panel, 1999, p. 5). As a result of this certification, a program is recommended for use in federally funded Safe, Disciplined, and Drug Free Schools programs and exempted from requirements of further outcome evaluations at the local level. The problem that Gorman points out, however, is that the results of the published study are much more consistent with chance findings than with evidence of program effectiveness. The intervention and control groups were compared for statistically significant differences on a total of twenty outcomes (for example, teacher-reported aggressive behavior, parent-reported social skills, and so on) at one-year post-baseline. With the statistical significance level (alpha) set at .05, only one of the twenty comparisons showed the groups to be significantly different from each other—exactly the result that would be expected by chance alone if, in fact, there were no effects of the program.

As another example, consider *Reducing the Risk*—a prevention curriculum designed to reduce the incidence of teen pregnancy and sexually transmitted infections (Barth, 1996), developed in part through foundation funding. This curriculum also was recognized by a federal review panel, in this case through the Centers for Disease Control and Prevention as a "Program That Works." This recognition required that a program had been "proven effective in reducing HIV risk behaviors" (Centers for Disease Control and Prevention, 2001). The "Programs That Work" designation was assigned to *Reducing the Risk*, based on an outcome evaluation (Kirby, Barth, Leland, and Fetro, 1991) that included thirty-two initial significance tests of risk-behavior outcome comparisons (involving nine behavioral outcome measures and various combinations of time of measurement and subgroups based on prior sexual experience levels). Of these, three were significant at the .05 alpha level, involving only the students who were sexually inexperienced at the time of program entry. Thirty-six additional outcome comparisons were conducted to test effects within gender, ethnicity, and risk-level subgroups for the three significant outcomes; of these additional tests two were significant at the .05 alpha level.

Up to this point, sixty-eight significance tests of potential differences between the intervention and control groups were conducted, yielding five statistically significant results. Once again, this is very close to what would be expected by chance in the face of no program effects and given the specified statistical significance criterion of .05. Moreover, a reader who carefully studies the article will be able to identify numerous additional comparisons that were tested but were not systematically reported, further compromising any conclusions of program effectiveness based on this study.

All of this is not to say that these two evaluations show their respective programs to be ineffective. *Absence of evidence is not evidence of absence* (this theme is explored further in the section on interpreting null or negative effects). In fact, the *Reducing the Risk* evaluation yielded an overall pattern of differences between the intervention and control groups suggestive of potential behavioral effects within some subgroups that would be worthy of further study. Yet for neither evaluation do the results justify conclusions of "proven effectiveness" according to the standards of evidence associated with the statistical significance testing approach employed, nor by the criteria of the federal review groups that certified the two programs.

The practice of testing large numbers of potential outcomes for statistical significance, while ignoring the increasing likelihood of finding spurious effects as more tests are added, is often referred to as a *scattershot approach* or a *fishing expedition*. When only the significant results are reported and nonsignificant tests are held back, the term *cherry picking* is sometimes applied (see, as an example, the replication evaluation of *Reducing the Risk* [Hubbard, Giese, and Raney, 1998]). And published fishing expeditions are often cherry picked at a later stage in summary reports or other distillations provided by external review panels, program advocates, or program critics.

These problems are not unique to the *Second Step* or *Reducing the Risk* evaluations. For example, Dar, Serlin, and Omer (1994) report that only 21 percent of 111 reviewed studies of psychotherapy effectiveness compensated even minimally for performing multiple significance tests. We used these particular evaluations as illustrations because of the direct influence they have had on public policy and the fact that they are erroneously considered by many to be methodologically rigorous outcome evaluations with unambiguous conclusions of program effectiveness.

Appropriate Strategies for Multiple Significance Tests

There are three well-developed strategies for addressing the multiple significance test problem: (1) conduct fewer and more focused significance tests, (2) employ a more stringent statistical significance criterion (that is, the alpha level) for those that remain, and (3) supplement statistical significance testing with alternative indicators of effects.

Conduct Fewer and More Focused Significance Tests

The best way to avoid engaging in a fishing expedition is to use the program's theory to inform the specification of a small number of tests of theory-derived hypotheses regarding expected differences on particular outcome measures. The theory also should guide the designation, in advance of conducting the analyses, of a few selected tests as primary, allowing the others to be designated in advance as secondary or exploratory. The primary tests are those involving the outcomes the program is betting on—the ones that will be most important in reaching conclusions about a program's effectiveness. The program theory also can be used to specify particular subgroups of the sample in which to conduct additional tests of significance, rather than testing all possible combinations of subgroups. Subgroup tests should be used cautiously and, in general, only conducted in two situations: (1) following a significant full-group test or (2) if suggested by the program theory or past results and planned in advance of seeing the data, in place of full-group tests.

Employ a More Stringent Statistical Significance Criterion

To control for the likelihood of erroneously obtaining statistically significant results by chance, it is sometimes recommended to make the significance criterion more conservative by dividing the desired alpha level by the number of significance tests to be performed. Thus if one were conducting twenty tests and desired an alpha level of .05, each test would then be conducted at a more conservative level of .0025 (.05/20). This strategy, known as the Bonferonni correction, works well in studies with large samples where statistical power is strong. In smaller studies, however, it can overcorrect and excessively reduce the test's power of finding a potential effect to be significant (Shaffer, 1995).

The overcorrection problem can be addressed by applying corrections separately to smaller subsets of significance tests that are logically defined. This might involve content-specific *families* of tests. For example, if a study employs thirty measures equally divided among knowledge, attitude, and behavior outcomes, these three content categories could define three families of ten outcome tests each. Corrections then could be based on the ten tests per family rather than the total thirty tests, thereby reducing the risk of overcorrection. Another way to define families of tests would be through *nesting* of subgroups following a significant full sample test. For example, if for a particular outcome a full sample difference is found to be statistically significant, then within subgroup tests for this same outcome could be corrected only for the number of subgroups, again reducing the risk of overcorrection. The logic and methods involved in these and other approaches to correcting for multiple significance tests is discussed by Shaffer (1995). In general, these approaches tend to be good compromises between uncorrected multiple significance tests and the overcorrection that often results from a blanket Bonferonni correction across all tests.

Supplement Statistical Significance Testing with Alternative Indicators of Effects

Another important strategy involves going beyond the usual reliance on statistical significance tests and the arbitrary .05 alpha level to focus on other indicators of program effects. A movement has been growing among methodologists to do so (for example, Cohen, 1994; Wilkinson and the American Psychological Association Task Force on Statistical Inference, 1999), although its effect on practice is developing slowly. At a minimum, an *effect size* should be calculated to indicate the actual size of an effect in a metric that can be compared across studies. A commonly used effect size is the difference between the intervention and control group means, divided by the combined group standard deviation (Cohen, 1969). Discussions of this and other measures of effect size can be found in Lipsey and Wilson (2001) and Rosenthal and DiMatteo (2001). A confidence interval should be provided around each effect size, indicating its likely lower and upper bounds, given a specified degree of confidence, typically 95 percent (which is equivalent to a .05 alpha level). Another advantage of providing effect sizes is that this facilitates later studies, or meta-analyses, that attempt to quantify average findings across multiple studies of the same or similar interventions. It is hard to imagine an outcome evaluation for which reporting effect sizes and confidence intervals would not be appropriate.

It is also important to consider the practical meaning of a particular effect in terms of its clinical, programmatic, or policy significance. For example, one supplemental measure that might be employed to help assess clinical significance is the proportion of individuals in the intervention group versus the control group who reach a specified level of normal or healthy functioning (Jacobson and others, 1999). This provides a fundamentally different type of knowledge than does the statement that a significant difference between the two groups was found on a measure of healthy functioning.

In most outcome evaluations involving multiple statistical significance tests, evaluation consumers should expect to see some combination of the strategies discussed above. Often all three can be applied together. This is illustrated in the Infant Health and Development Program (1990) study, a foundation-funded national randomized evaluation of a child development intervention. Eight primary outcome variables were selected early in the evaluation (and prior to any data analyses) from a pool of several hundred measured outcomes, and primary versus secondary tests were clearly distinguished in the published report. A correction was applied to the desired significance level of .05 for these eight primary tests, yielding a more stringent corrected criterion of .006. Finally, effect sizes were calculated for all outcomes, and these were given equivalent emphasis to the statistical significance tests in the report.

Transparency and Accessibility

A preliminary draft of the virginity pledge study discussed earlier was released by the authors in July, 2000—six months prior to its official publication date (January 2001) in the *American Journal of Sociology*. However, this printed journal was not mailed to libraries or subscribers until June of 2001, creating, in effect, a one-year interval in which the report was extensively discussed in the national media and among policy advocates on both sides of the issue, yet without access to the final published version of the article. Many discussants were limited to commenting on the press release or the few selected details reported in the media reports.

As another example, consider a legislatively mandated evaluation of a statewide teen pregnancy prevention program in California (Cagampang and others, 2002). An executive summary of this foundation-funded evaluation was widely disseminated by the state of California six months prior to the public release of the full report. This evaluation contained several policy-relevant but questionable claims of positive program effects, yet by the time the full report was released the opportunity for meaningful discussion and debate had largely passed (see Constantine, 2003, for a methodological critique of this evaluation and its conclusions). These two cases are not isolated examples. Indeed, it can be argued that this type of situation, involving release of evaluation conclusions to the media or directly to policymakers prior to availability of the documentation necessary to critically appraise the conclusions, is becoming increasingly prevalent and might already represent the norm. Why might this be so?

During the last decade, health and social program evaluation has grown to unprecedented levels. Academic journals have proliferated, while other means of disseminating findings, including electronic methods, have grown exponentially. At the same time, the popular media appear to have insatiable appetites for reporting abbreviated findings from "the latest studies." When it comes to information, however, more often means less (Brown and Duguid, 2000). In many ways, we are drowning in information and increasingly challenged to use this information effectively. At a minimum, this requires separating the proverbial wheat from the chaff, that is, critically appraising the validity of evaluation conclusions and the evidence they rest upon. Yet when the popular media serve as the gatekeepers, critical appraisal of validity is often replaced by intuitive appraisal of newsworthiness or, increasingly, of potential entertainment value. And the piecemeal release of summaries or selected results can deprive legitimate stakeholders of the information needed to critically appraise results and conclusions.

There are no easy answers to this challenge. Publication of an evaluation in a peer-reviewed scientific journal provides a stamp of approval, yet peer review can be a notoriously slow process, with low inter-reviewer agreement commonly found among peer reviewers (Cicchetti, 1991; Cole, 1992; MacCoun, 1998; Peters and Ceci, 1982). And, in any case, peer-reviewed journal publication is beyond the means of many smaller evaluations. Some foundations use their own external or internal review panels. Depending on the ability and objectivity of the reviewers, this can be a very constructive approach. Often, however, we must appraise conclusions without the benefit of prior professional and rigorous review.

Program evaluation results released to (and reported by) the news media or policymakers without the benefit of a published and readily available peer-reviewed article, or at minimum, a publicly available comprehensive report, should raise a red flag. At the same time, it is important to recognize that peer or other professional reviews are not a sufficient condition to establish the validity of reported conclusions. Executive summaries might be all that a busy professional is willing and able to read, but summary authors are remiss if they do not provide a Web link or other convenient access to a full report that includes a thorough description of the context, methods, assumptions, limitations, and complete results of the evaluation. Ultimately, the evaluation consumer must take responsibility for critically appraising evaluation results, or else finding a trusted and qualified colleague to provide this service. In either case, timely access to a comprehensive report is essential.

Interpreting Null or Negative Results

So far, we have discussed some of the issues involved in interpreting program evaluations that appear to provide evidence in support of program effectiveness. There are also challenges associated with making sense of evaluations that find no evidence of the intended effects (null results) or effects that are opposite of those intended (negative results). It can seem natural to conclude from such a study that the program is not effective, and critics of a controversial program might be especially inclined to embrace this conclusion. However, such a stance is often premature. In the face of no-effect findings, a careful examination of the study is warranted to understand which alternative explanations are most likely (Lipsey, 1993).

Several possible reasons for failure to find positive results lie with the evaluation study itself. First, a weak evaluation design can obscure the effectiveness of a program. A common design weakness is the use of unreliable measures or measures lacking sufficient validity or sensitivity for their evaluation use. As Lipsey (1988) concluded in a review of a random sample of 122 published evaluation studies, "In most studies the quality of the outcome measure cannot be assumed, nor is it typically demonstrated in the study itself" (p. 15). Another common design weakness is insufficient statistical power. Power relates to the likelihood of an actual program effect being accurately captured in a test of statistical significance (as opposed to a "false negative" finding). Power problems often result from too few participants, as well as from use of measures with low reliability or validity. A study with inadequate power is likely to fail to demonstrate the statistical significance of actual effects or to yield effect size estimates that are imprecise. It has long been recognized that insufficient power is a serious and widespread problem in the evaluation literature, even among published studies (Lipsey and others, 1985).

A second set of problems relates to the implementation of the evaluation: the evaluation might have been well designed but poorly conducted. An example would be inadequate training of the study's data collectors, especially if the data collection process requires substantial skill, such as for conducting individual or group interviews. Another example applies to evaluations that have long time-frames, involving multiple waves of data collection over time. These evaluations are vulnerable to attrition (participants dropping out of the evaluation) from the later data points, and to the extent that such attrition occurs, it potentially weakens the ability of the study to identify program effects (alternatively, the study might yield spurious positive results). In evaluations with multiple data-collection points, efforts must be made to motivate continued participation and to track participants who move, as well as to analyze and disclose the potential effects of the attrition on evaluation results (see Constantine and others, 1993).

Several other possible explanations for no-effect results are related to the program itself. First, a potentially effective program might have been poorly implemented—a possibility that occurs often in the field. Program staff might not have been adequately trained, participants might not receive the full intervention, or there might be large variations in implementation across different program sites. Such problems produce an inadequate test of the basic program theory.

Intervention programs rarely remain in a constant state over time. In their development and implementation, they typically progress through a maturation process (Berk and Rossi, 1999). Immediately after the planning phase, in the initial period of implementation there is often a considerable amount of unstructured experimentation going on. During this time, the program can be evolving rapidly. A program that grows in this way will not serve its clientele most effectively until it has reached a certain stage of maturity, at which point its operations become more stable. It would be of questionable value to subject this type of program to a full-scale effectiveness evaluation during its first year, although this sometimes happens. In interpreting the meaning and usefulness of an outcome evaluation, two questions related to a program's developmental trajectory should be asked:

- Was this evaluation conducted at an appropriate time in the development of the program?
- What is the relevance of this evidence for understanding the program in its current form?

These questions do not speak to the quality of the evaluation itself but rather to the relationship of the evaluation to the program and to its developmental course.

Finally, the null effect finding might instead result from a failure of the program theory—the concept underlying the program might be inadequate, even if program implementation and evaluation implementation are strong. Failure of program theory can result from an insufficient understanding of the critical intervening processes, leading to an emphasis on the wrong kinds of program activities. This can also result from inadequate specification of the program's most appropriate target population.

Following findings of no effects, a comprehensive review of the results from the perspective of the program theory can inform the program designers in making necessary adjustments to the program, its delivery, or its evaluation so that an improved version can be tested. Alternatively, they might decide that the challenges are too fundamental to justify the investment of further resources in another round of program refinement and evaluation. Whatever course of action is followed, the decisions leading up to it should involve a full consideration of all relevant factors.

Understanding Results in a Broad Context

In most areas of scientific inquiry, the replication of results across multiple studies is an important component of the knowledge-generation process. Similarly, evaluation studies should be interpreted in light of the larger context of what else is known about the intervention and the program theory behind it. An individual study represents one particular set of decisions about how to measure the critical variables and how to time the observations, as well as one implementation, for better or worse, of the observation procedures. Furthermore, if the study involves only one program delivery site, it also represents only a single instance of program implementation. These factors—measurement, timing, program implementation, and others—often can be varied without undermining the basic theory of the program. Thus a single evaluation study, compelling though it might be, should be considered only one piece of a gradual process of knowledge accretion. Conclusions from an evaluation cannot be considered robust until there is evidence that the findings would be similar under varying contexts and conditions of program implementation, or documentation of the specific conditions, settings, and populations associated with effectiveness.

Sometimes there may be a large discrepancy between the findings of a given evaluation and the findings that were expected, based on past studies. A study may show dramatic results when previous studies have shown little effect, or it may show no results when other evaluations were positive. These discrepant patterns can be potentially interesting and revealing. They call for a more careful examination of the findings and the program theory, often suggesting the need for further investigations.

With these considerations in mind, one important question that arises when interpreting findings is where to go next. A good study typically raises new questions as surely as it answers existing ones. Sometimes it will be useful to pursue new or refined evaluation questions, systematically varying aspects of the program or the evaluation design. In other cases, a study may be so consistent with previous investigations that it is deemed fully justified to make important program-related decisions on the basis of what has been learned up to the present point. In all these cases, examination of the evaluation findings within a broad context, that is, beyond the single study, provides a stronger level of confidence for whatever decisions or courses of action are eventually pursued.

Conclusion

In this chapter, we have covered a range of issues with regard to appraising evidence about program effectiveness and using this evidence with validity and integrity. Our discussion has been necessarily incomplete. There are many other issues that an evaluator must master and an evaluation consumer needs to understand in order to do full justice to the business of making sense of effectiveness evidence and conclusions. We have presented some of the most important and frequently encountered issues—those that often lead to ambiguous results or misleading conclusions. Our aim is to raise awareness of some of these challenges, to motivate foundation evaluators and evaluation consumers to ask the right questions about effectiveness evidence and conclusions, and to provide a basic understanding to help support constructive skepticism and critical appraisal.

Program effectiveness evaluation is built largely on social science methodology. As with most science-based endeavors, it provides imperfect answers to our questions about reality. Yet these answers can improve over time with continued study and debate. For program effectiveness evaluation to realize its full potential, it is incumbent upon evaluators and evaluation consumers to demonstrate competence in logical and critical approaches to appraising evidence. And this includes, at its core, asking the right questions and considering the answers with appropriate skepticism. As Patton (2002, p. 11) advises,

> Evaluators and the people we work with have to critically and thoughtfully examine the evidence that is purported to be "scientific" and draw their own conclusions. . . . Consumers of evaluations need to attend to "truth in packaging." Look beyond the label or assertion that some proposal is "science-based" to examine where the evidence comes from and what it really shows.

Only when we heed this advice are we able to reap the powerful potential benefits that program effectiveness evaluation has to offer.

Notes

1. In the spirit of constructive criticism and rational debate, written responses will be sought from the authors of all studies critiqued in this chapter and posted at www.crahd.phi.org/evidence.
2. The skeptical reader might ask whether path analysis or structural equation modeling approaches to the analysis of correlational data can be used to demonstrate causal relationships. These analyses can be applied to any type of design—correlational, experimental, or quasi-experimental; they typically suffer from measurement error and model misspecification error problems and, in any case, "the model does not 'confirm' causal relationships. Rather, it assumes causal links and then tests how strong they would be if the model were a correct representation of reality" (Shadish, Cook, and Campbell, 2002, p. 398).

References

Barth, R. P. (1996). *Reducing the risk: Building skills to prevent pregnancy, STD, and HIV.* Santa Cruz, CA: ETR Associates.

Bearman, P. S., & Bruchner, H. (2001). Promising the future: Virginity pledges and first intercourse. *American Journal of Sociology, 106,* 859–912.

Berk, R. A., & Rossi, P. H. (1999). *Thinking about program evaluation* (2nd ed.). Thousand Oaks, CA: Sage.

Boyle, P. (2000, November). The score on teen virginity pledges. *Youth Today, 1,* 16–17.

Braverman, M. T., & Campbell, D. T. (1989). Facilitating the development of health promotion programs: Recommendations for researchers and funders. In M. T. Braverman (Ed.), *Evaluating health promotion programs.* New Directions for Evaluation, no. 43. San Francisco: Jossey-Bass.

Brown, J. S., & Duguid, P. (2000). *The social life of information.* Boston: Harvard Business School Press.

Bunge, M. (1979). *Causality and modern science* (3rd ed.). New York: Dover Publications.

Cagampang, H. H., Brindis, C., Peterson, S., Berglas, N., & Barenbaum, M. (2002). Making the Connection: How School-Community Partnerships Address Teenage Pregnancy Prevention (Statewide Evaluation Report for the California Department of Education's Teenage Pregnancy Prevention Grant Program). San Francisco: UCSF Center for Reproductive Health Policy Studies.

Campbell, D. T., & Stanley, J. C. (1966). *Experimental and quasi-experimental designs for research.* Chicago: Rand-McNally.

Centers for Disease Control and Prevention. (2001). *Programs That Work.* Atlanta: Author.

Chen, H. (1990). *Theory-driven evaluations.* Thousand Oaks, CA: Sage.

Cicchetti, D. V. (1991). The reliability of peer review for manuscript and grant submissions: A cross-disciplinary investigation. *Behavioral and Brain Sciences, 14,* 119–186.

Cohen, J. (1969). *Statistical power analysis for the behavioral sciences.* Hillsdale, NJ: Erlbaum.

Cohen, J. (1990). Things I have learned (so far). *American Psychologist, 45,* 1304–1312.

Cohen, J. (1994). The earth is round ($p < .05$). *American Psychologist, 49,* 997–1003.

Cole, S. (1992). *Making science: Between nature and society.* Cambridge, MA: Harvard University Press.

Constantine, N. A. (2003). *Review of the TPPGP statewide evaluation report prepared for the California Department of Education.* Berkeley, CA: Public Health Institute. Available at http://crahd.phi.org/TPPGPreview.pdf.

Constantine, N. A., & Curry, K. (1998, November). *Collaborative development of a theory-based assessment instrument for a school-linked violence prevention evaluation.* Paper presented at the 1998 American Evaluation Association Annual Conference, Chicago. Available at http://crahd.phi.org/papers/collab_development.pdf.

Constantine, W. L., Haynes, C., Spiker, D., & Constantine, N. A. (1993). Recruitment and retention in a multisite clinical trial for low birth weight infants. *Journal of Developmental and Behavioral Pediatrics, 14,* 1–7.

Cook, T. D., & Campbell, D. T. (1979). *Quasi-experimentation: Design and analysis issues for field settings.* Chicago: Rand-McNally.

Cook, T. D., & Shadish, W. R. (1994). Social experiments: Some developments over the past fifteen years. *Annual Review of Psychology, 45,* 545–580.

Cronbach, L. J. (1982). *Designing evaluations of educational and social programs.* San Francisco: Jossey-Bass.

Dar, R., Serlin, R. C., & Omer, H. (1994). Misuse of statistical tests in three decades of psychotherapy research. *Journal of Consulting and Clinical Psychology, 62,* 75–82.

Federal Register. (2000, November 17). 65 Federal Register 69562–65.

Fishbein, M., & Middlestandt, S. E. (1989). Using the theory of reasoned action as a framework for understanding and changing AIDS related behaviors. In V. M. Mays, G. W. Albee, & S. F. Schneider (Eds.), *Primary prevention of AIDS: Psychological approaches* (pp. 93–110). London: Sage.

Glanz, K., Rimer, B. K., & Lewis, F. M. (2002). *Health behavior and health education: Theory, research, and practice* (3rd ed.). San Francisco: Jossey-Bass.

Glasgow, R. E., Lichtenstein, E., & Marcus, A. C. (2003). Why don't we see more translation of health promotion research to practice? Rethinking the efficacy-to-effectiveness transition. *American Journal of Public Health, 93,* 1261–1267.

Gorman, D. M. (2002). Defining and operationalizing "research-based" prevention: A critique (with case studies) of the U.S. Department of Education Safe, Disciplined, and Drug-Free schools exemplary programs. *Evaluation and Program Planning, 25,* 295–302.

Grossman, D. C., Neckerman, H. J., Koespell, T. D., Liu, P. Y., Asher, K. N., Beland, K., Frey, K., & Rivara, F. P. (1997). Effectiveness of a violence prevention curriculum among children in elementary school: A randomized trial. *Journal of the American Medical Association, 277,* 1605–1611.

House, E. (2001). Unfinished business: Causes and values. *American Journal of Evaluation, 22,* 309–315.

Hubbard, B. M., Giese, M. L., & Raney, J. (1998). A replication study of Reducing the Risk: A theory-based sexuality curriculum for adolescents. *Journal of School Health, 68,* 243–247.

Hughes, J. N. (2000). The essential role of theory in the science of treating children: Beyond empirically supported treatments. *Journal of School Psychology, 38,* 301–330.

Infant Health and Development Program. (1990). Enhancing the outcomes of low birth weight, premature infants: A multisite, randomized trial. *Journal of the American Medical Association, 263*(22), 3035–3042.

Jacobson, N. S., Roberts, L. J., Berns, S. B., & McGlinchey, J. B. (1999). Methods for determining the clinical significance of treatment effects: Description, application, and alternatives. *Journal of Consulting and Clinical Psychology, 67,* 300–307.

Kirby, D., Barth, R. P., Leland, N., & Fetro, J. V. (1991). Reducing the risk: Impact of a new curriculum on sexual risk-taking. *Family Planning Perspectives, 23,* 253–263.

Light, R. J., Singer, J. D., & Willett, J. B. (1990). *By design: Planning research on higher education.* Cambridge, MA: Harvard University Press.

Lipsey, M. W. (1988). Practice and malpractice in evaluation research. *Evaluation Practice, 9,* 5–24.

Lipsey, M. W. (1993). Theory as method: Small theories of treatments. In L. B. Sechrest & A. G. Scott (Eds.), *Understanding causes and generalizing about them.* New Directions for Program Evaluation, no. 57. San Francisco: Jossey-Bass.

Lipsey, M. W., Crosse, S., Dunkle, J., Pollard, J., & Stobart, G. (1985). Evaluation: The state of the art and the sorry state of the science. In D. S. Cordray (Ed.), *Utilizing prior research in evaluation planning.* New Directions for Program Evaluation, no. 27. San Francisco: Jossey-Bass.

Lipsey, M. W., & Wilson, D. B. (2001). *Practical meta-analysis.* Thousand Oaks, CA: Sage.

MacCoun, R. J. (1998). Biases in the interpretation and use of research results. *Annual Review of Psychology, 49,* 259–287.

Mackie, J. L. (1980). *The cement of the universe.* New York: Oxford University Press.

Mark, M. M., & Smith, M. F. (2001). Special issue on the future of evaluation. *American Journal of Evaluation, 22*(3).

McKim, V. R., & Turner, S. P. (1997). *Causality in crisis: Statistical methods and the search for causal knowledge in the social sciences.* Notre Dame, IN: University of Notre Dame Press.

Moskowitz, J. M. (1993). Why reports of outcome evaluations are often biased or uninterpretable. *Evaluation and Program Planning, 16,* 1–9.

Nesmith, J. (2001, January 4). Teens who pledge not to have sex stay virgins longer, study finds. *San Francisco Chronicle,* p. A5.

Patton, M. Q. (2002, Spring). A conversation with Michael Patton. Interview by J. Coffman. *The Evaluation Exchange Newsletter, 8,* 10–11.

Pedhazur, E. J., & Schmelkin, L. P. (1991). *Measurement, design, and analysis: An integrated approach.* Hillsdale, NJ: Erlbaum.

Peters, D. P., & Ceci, S. J. (1982). Peer-reviewed practices of psychological journals: The fate of accepted published articles submitted again. *Behavioral and Brain Sciences, 5*, 187–195.

Peterson, A. V., Jr., Kealey K. A., Mann, S. L., Marek, P. M., & Sarason, I. G. (2000). Hutchinson Smoking Prevention Project: Long-term randomized trial in school-based tobacco use prevention—results on smoking. *Journal of the National Cancer Institute, 92,* 1979–1991.

Reding, G. R., & Raphelson, M. (1995). Around-the-clock mobile psychiatric crisis intervention: Another effective alternative to psychiatric hospitalization. *Community Mental Health Journal, 31,* 179–187.

Reichardt, C. S., & Mark, M. M. (1998). Quasi-experimentation. In L. Bickman & D. J. Rog (Eds.), *Handbook of applied social research methods.* Thousand Oaks, CA: Sage (pp. 193–228).

Resnick, M., Bearman, P., Blum, R., Bauman, K., Harris, K., Jones, J., Tabor, J., Beuhring, T., Sieving, R., Shew, M., Ireland, M., Bearinger, L., & Udry, R. (1997). Protecting adolescents from harm: Findings from the National Longitudinal Study on Adolescent Health. *Journal of the American Medical Association, 278,* 823–832.

Rosenthal, R., & DiMatteo, M. R. (2001). Meta-analysis: Recent developments in quantitative methods for literature reviews. *Annual Review of Psychology, 52,* 59–82.

Safe, Disciplined, and Drug-Free Schools Expert Panel. (1999). Guidelines for submitting safe, disciplined and drug-free schools programs for designation as promising or exemplary. Washington, DC: U.S. Department of Education.

Safe, Disciplined, and Drug-Free Schools Expert Panel. (2001). *Exemplary and promising safe, disciplined and drug-free schools programs.* Washington, DC: U.S. Department of Education. Available at www.ed.gov/admins/lead/safety/exemplary01/exemplary01/pdf.

Schemo, D. J. (2001, January 4). Virginity pledges by teenagers can be highly effective, federal study finds. *New York Times.* Available at www.nytimes.com/2001/01/04/science/o4VIRG.html. Accessed January, 18, 2001.

Shadish, W. R., Jr., Cook, T. D., & Campbell, D. T. (2002). *Experimental and quasi-experimental designs for generalized causal inference.* Boston: Houghton-Mifflin.

Shadish, W. R., Jr., Cook, T. D., & Leviton, L. C. (1995). *Foundations of program evaluation: Theories of practice.* Thousand Oaks, CA: Sage.

Shaffer, J. P. (1995). Multiple hypothesis testing. *Annual Review of Psychology, 46,* 561–584.

U.S. Department of Health and Human Services. (2002, December). *SPRANS Community-Based Abstinence Education Program, Pre-Application Workshop.* Available at www.mchb.hrsa.gov/programs/adolescents/abedguidetext.htm. Accessed August 14, 2003.

Wilkinson, L., and the American Psychological Association Task Force on Statistical Inference. (1999). Statistical methods in psychology journals: Guidelines and explanations. *American Psychologist, 54,* 594–604.

Willis, M. (2001). Virginity pledges work: Pledging I won't until swearing I will is helping teens say I don't. Available at www.abcnews.com. Accessed February 17, 2001.

CHAPTER THIRTEEN

EVALUATIVE THINKING FOR GRANTEES

E. Jane Davidson, Michael M. Howe,
and Michael Scriven

Evaluation is sometimes viewed as an insidious black hole that draws funds away from a program that would otherwise be spent on helping people. What could possibly justify devoting 5 to 10 percent of a program's budget to documenting results? Often, the main reason grantees give for doing evaluation is that funders require it. But viewing evaluation as a necessary evil imposed from the outside virtually guarantees that grantees and the communities they serve will miss out on the considerable benefits that evaluation can deliver.

In this chapter, we explore, from the grantee's perspective, the ways in which evaluation can be transformed from a perceived burden into a powerful tool whose benefits can far outweigh the costs. We outline four important payoffs that grantees can reap from building evaluative thinking and practice into their own projects: (1) increasing the chances that project proposals are funded, (2) increasing the chances of project success, once funded, (3) contributing to our understanding of "what works" in social change, and (4) demonstrating the value of the organization's activities to its supporters (staff, funders, governors, and communities) and critics.

Before describing how evaluation can be used to achieve the benefits listed, we begin by defining what we mean by *evaluative thinking* and how we see it as an essential ingredient for building and maintaining something called *creative tension*. The chapter closes with a phased approach for foundation-supported organizations to gradually build evaluation into their operations in a way that builds on existing strengths, minimizes evaluation anxiety, and maximizes grantees' ability to contribute to the betterment of the communities they serve.

The Link Between Creative Tension and Evaluative Thinking

The topic of this chapter is not "doing evaluations." Neither is it simply checking to see whether we've done what we said we would do ("we" being grantees and those of us thinking about evaluation from the grantee's perspective). Rather, the topic is using evaluative thinking to help create and maintain something that Senge (1990) calls creative tension, that is, the affective reaction created by the gap between our desired level of performance (the effects we are striving to achieve in the community) and our current level of performance (how much of an impact we have had so far; see Figure 13.1).

Although creative tension can be a great energizing force, Senge (1990) points out that, by its very nature, creative tension makes people uncomfortable. In order to alleviate this discomfort, people often seek to decrease the tension in one of two unproductive ways. Sometimes, we lower our goals to make the desired level of performance less distant and more achievable. This is counterproductive because modest, easily achievable goals can be considerably less motivating than challenging ones that are more difficult to achieve. Or we might close the perceived gap by overestimating our current level of performance, that is, assuming (but not checking) that we are closer to our goals than we truly are. Although both strategies will work to decrease our discomfort by decreasing the *perceived* performance gap, neither is particularly effective for helping us bridge the *actual* performance gap. According to Senge, what we need to do instead is maintain creative tension by keeping both high, inspiring goals *and* a firm grasp of where we are relative to those goals, then working to decrease the gap by improving performance.

So what is evaluative thinking, and how can it help generate and maintain creative tension? Evaluative thinking is a combination of commitment and expertise, involving an understanding of the performance gap and knowing how

FIGURE 13.1. CREATIVE TENSION.

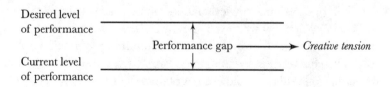

to gauge it. Put another way, evaluative thinking has two fundamental components: *passion for improvement* and *evaluative know-how*.

The *passion for improvement* part is the motivational dimension of evaluative thinking. Senge (1990) speaks of this as "a relentless willingness to root out the ways we limit or deceive ourselves from seeing what is" (p. 159). Put simply, it means being committed to knowing the truth about where the lower line is in Figure 13.1. As it applies to the performance gap, this concept is roughly equivalent to the *evaluative attitude*—a term coined by Scriven (1991) and later identified as one of the key elements of the cultures of learning organizations: "the relentless pursuit of the truth about quality or performance" (Sathe and Davidson, 2000, p. 293).

Simply being committed to knowing the truth, however, is only one part of the equation. In order to translate passion for improvement into action, we also need the *evaluative know-how* element of evaluative thinking. This refers to the ability to identify and clarify the most important potential effects of the project or program, to think through the ways in which these effects are most likely to be achieved, and to design systems that will tell us, as we need to know, the extent to which these and other effects are emerging. Those who have already had some involvement in assessing the effectiveness of projects will know that this is no trivial matter. One of the goals of this chapter is to suggest some useful strategies and resources for dealing with this challenging task.

By building both the passion for improvement and the know-how elements of evaluative thinking into projects and programs right from the start, grantees will be able to generate and maintain the all-important creative tension that drives success. In the next section, we look at how and where these elements of evaluative thinking can be most effectively incorporated to help grantee organizations get the most out of them.

Payoffs for Grantees

There are several potential payoffs of incorporating evaluative thinking and practice into project design and management. In the following sections, we explore how each of these works and share some strategies that have been used successfully to achieve these benefits.

Creating More Compelling Project Proposals

When funders look across the range of proposals they receive, one of the main things they look for is how likely each project is to achieve important outcomes that will positively affect communities in need.

How can grantees make use of evaluative thinking to build a compelling case for a project and thereby increase its chances of obtaining funding? Here are four strategies to consider:

1. Show that you have done your homework by reviewing the literature to find out what has been shown to work—and not work—in the past.
2. Get solid evidence about the nature, extent, and underlying causes of the needs you aim to address and the strengths in the community you will build on to address them.
3. Show plausibly how (that is, by what mechanisms) your proposed project is expected to meet those needs.
4. Spell out in concrete, measurable terms how and when you will know if you are successful.

Show That You Have Done Your Homework. Quite often, there is a mismatch between prevailing public opinion (or supposed common sense) and the current research. This means that program designs that appear to make good intuitive sense may actually be going over old ground that has already been found to be barren.

Here's an example to help illustrate the point. Despite their enormous popularity, many programs that seek to reduce or prevent drug abuse by teaching youth resistance skills (such as the Drug and Alcohol Resistance Education program, or D.A.R.E.) have repeatedly failed to demonstrate effectiveness (Brown, 2001; Donaldson, Graham, and Hansen, 1994; Ennett, Tobler, Ringwalt, and Flewelling, 1994; Lynam and others, 1999; Rosenbaum and Hanson, 1998). Experienced foundation personnel who have worked extensively in a particular area are often well aware of approaches or programs that have demonstrated effectiveness in certain settings and populations and those that have not. Proposals are viewed in a more favorable light if they clearly reflect and build on current knowledge about what works and what doesn't.

How does one find out what has already been documented about what works? Several avenues are available: (1) looking at the published literature (academic journals, professional magazines, and books), (2) tapping into formal and informal networks to ask about unpublished information (for example, professional associations and listservs), and (3) searching the Internet. This kind of background research can be done reasonably quickly by someone who knows his or her way around the main sources and has the evaluation expertise to quickly and critically evaluate source documents for their evidence value. Although some grantee organizations are lucky enough to have such expertise in-house, others might consider bringing in someone to help do this important groundwork (for example, a local consultant, university faculty member, or graduate student), especially if the proposed project is an innovative one that is taking the organization into a relatively new area. (See also Chapter Twelve for guidelines on critically appraising effectiveness claims about intervention programs).

Gather Solid Evidence About Needs and Strengths in the Community. More often than not, the existence of a pressing need in the community forms the basis for the development of proposals submitted to foundations for funding. To those writing a grant proposal, the need may seem obvious and the project clearly worthy of funding. Quite often, statistics can be uncovered in a needs assessment to support this claim. In its simplest form, a needs assessment is the systematic documentation of the dimensions on which a community (or a certain group of individuals) is functioning at a level that is considered less than satisfactory in a particular context. However, there are several ways one can design a needs assessment that pushes beyond simply gathering and presenting statistics about a community's current plight (an approach sometimes referred to as the "deficit model" of needs assessment).

In addition to documenting areas of unmet need, it is also important to balance this with a careful examination of a community's strengths. The strengths are what will be available to build on in order to achieve meaningful social change. By complementing information about needs with information about strengths, an applicant changes the picture from one of despair to one of hope, and it shows a good understanding of a key leverage point (or advantage) that will help a proposed project succeed.

Here is an example to illustrate the importance of strengths assessment. While planning a community nutrition intervention called *'Ai Pono* (translated roughly as "eat right") on one of the islands in Hawaii, program staff from Kamehameha Schools' (KS) Health, Wellness, and Family Education Department (part of KS's Extension Education Division) noted some of the unique characteristics of Hawaiian culture that might help them design a successful nutrition education project. These were the respect for *kūpuna* (or elders) and for tradition, the preference for face-to-face communication, the tradition of serving food at gatherings, and the existence of extensive *'ohana* (extended family) networks. The program staff were able to design a community nutrition education project that built directly on these strengths, thereby creating a more compelling proposal. For example, they involved *kūpuna* in the process of teaching children how to cook healthy food using traditional methods, ending each intervention with a family meal presentation to which the children invited all the members of their *'ohana* to sample their creations. A strengths assessment not only shows why a project is likely to be successful but demonstrates respect for the community and an understanding of its culture and resources.

The other useful strategy for designing a needs assessment that will help build a more compelling proposal is to dig beneath the surface needs to show that you understand something about the underlying causes. In the example given, the creators of *'Ai Pono* noted that some of the main reasons native Hawaiian families were not eating enough healthy food were (1) a perception that it was not tasty (and a lack of knowledge about how to make it tasty), (2) poor availability on the island of affordable ingredients for healthy food, and (3) a lack of knowledge about good nutrition and its potential benefits. Armed with this insight, they were able to design program components that specifically addressed those underlying causes (for example, talking to the families about nutrition when they came to the family meal presentation and teaching the children gardening skills and providing them with seeds and gardening implements to grow some of the vegetables that were not readily and affordably available on the island).

These strategies to enhance the depth and breadth of needs assessment to include information about strengths and underlying causes make a lot of sense from the foundation's perspective. One of the criteria foundations use when they allocate funds is to try and direct their support toward areas where there is a clearly demonstrated and important need that will be met by the proposed intervention. Proposals that demonstrate a clear and well-researched understanding of the nature, extent, and causes of the needs they plan to address will inevitably be looked upon more favorably. The same holds true for proposals that clearly identify the strengths on which they will build to achieve success.

Show Plausibly How the Program Will Meet the Identified Needs. Once you have identified the community's strengths and needs (and their underlying causes), it is a relatively modest next step to use this information to articulate a "program theory," that is, a description of the mechanism by which the program is expected to achieve its effects. A program theory can be expressed in a narrative or picture, or it can be depicted in a simple logic model (a visual representation of how, that is, through what mechanisms, you expect the program will achieve its effects). An example logic model for the *'Ai Pono* community nutrition program is shown in Figure 13.2.

The exercise of mapping out a program theory does not need to be an elaborate or deeply theoretical exercise; even the development of a fairly simple logic model can be helpful for clarifying what you are trying to achieve. The more clearly you can articulate the underlying program theory, the easier it will be to cross-check it against current research to see if it survives scrutiny. This phase is important for identifying any questionable "logical leaps" in the program theory that need further explanation, development, or background research. The process can often lead to extremely useful refinements that dramatically increase the program's chances

FIGURE 13.2. LOGIC MODEL FOR THE *'AI PONO* COMMUNITY NUTRITION PROGRAM IN HAWAII.

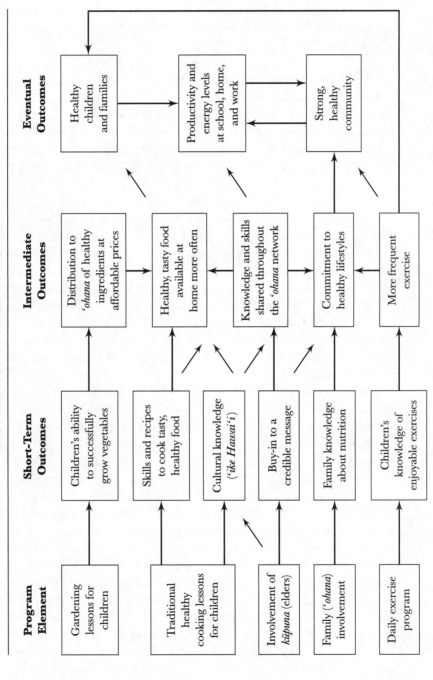

of success and that avoid the waste of plunging resources into something weaker. Further, having a plausible program theory clearly mapped out shows funders that you have thought through very carefully why and how your program should have a stronger positive impact than the alternatives.

Spell Out How and When You Will Know if Your Program Is Successful. Foundations are not in the business of dishing out money simply for generating activities; they are in the business of placing their money where there is maximum likelihood of seeing results. Therefore, a proposal that has built in a way of seeing and documenting those results (an evaluation plan) will be far more compelling than one that promises only to document activities and assumes that results will be forthcoming.

The "outcomes" section of your evaluation plan (which details the effects you hope to have on the participants and their families) may be drawn directly from your needs and strengths assessment and your program theory. These sources should be supplemented with some strategies for probing of potential unintended effects (both positive and negative). Also important in the evaluation design is some examination of the "process" side of the program—the quality of the program content and its delivery and documentation of the main process outputs (for example, the number and range of services delivered, families, and communities reached). Table 13.1 outlines a simple "process and outcomes" evaluation plan for the *'Ai Pono* community nutrition program that could be included in a proposal.

Note that the outcome elements have all been drawn directly from the logic model in Figure 13.2, whereas the process elements are listed under the three basic categories: *content, delivery,* and *outputs.* Quality of program content typically covers the extent to which the content matches participants' needs and is technically sound. Quality of program delivery usually spans such issues as level appropriateness, match of delivery method with learning styles, interest value, and effective use of resources. Outputs are the documentation of the quantity and nature of what was delivered, as well as information about recipients and others who were affected indirectly. In many cases, it may be useful to add to the evaluation plan a critical analysis of the costs of the program relative to the other main alternative interventions. This addresses the big-picture question of whether the current program is an improvement on those reviewed during program design.

The evaluation plan in Table 13.1 also includes a list of the main sources from which evaluation data might be drawn. It is important to make sure that every piece of data collected as part of the evaluation clearly serves the needs of program staff, including those responsible for collecting the data, either because it is directly relevant and useful for their own work or because it will inform decisions they know to be important. This is one of the least understood and most ignored aspects of evaluation design and implementation and is especially important to address when program staff cannot be involved in the evaluation design. If overworked staff are asked to add yet another layer of data collection onto their plates without any benefit to them, it usually means that the request will be ignored or undermined.

Some grantee organizations are lucky enough to have one or two staff members with expertise to put together a good evaluation plan as part of a proposal. When such in-house expertise is lacking, some training and technical assistance with developing this part of the proposal can be valuable. Various options are available for grantee organizations, depending on budget and current levels of expertise. These include sending one or more key staff on short courses to build evaluation skills (such as local colleges, nonprofit resource centers, support centers and foundation centers, and the Evaluator's Institute), getting hold of a good nuts-and-bolts guidebook for conducting evaluations (for example, Davidson, forthcoming; Wadsworth, 1997), and making use of good Web-based resources (see the end of this chapter for a list of useful Web sites).

For organizations that cannot afford to devote staff time to major new skill building, one option is to bring in some outside expertise. Even if you can't find an evaluator who is experienced with the exact type of program you are proposing, in most cases the combination of outside evaluation expertise and the content expertise your own staff brings to the table can work well. And with sufficient attention to skill development, at least some of this evaluative thinking can be retained in-house for future use.

Increasing the Chances of Program Success

Once your project has been funded, the next major priority is maximizing its chances of success. Some of the key areas where evaluative thinking can add value here are

- Clarifying (and focusing people's energies on) the true purpose of the program
- Helping a new program "find its feet"
- Helping mature programs keep up with ever-changing needs in the community

Clarifying the True Purpose of the Program. Studies of the world's most successful organizations show that a clear and shared sense of purpose is one of the most important factors in inspiring and motivating staff (for example, de Geus, 1997; Senge, 1990; Wind and Main, 1998). A leader's role, especially in organizations that cannot motivate people through offering high salaries, is to connect

TABLE 13.1. SAMPLE EVALUATION PLAN FOR THE *'AI PONO* COMMUNITY NUTRITION INTERVENTION.

Program Aspect	Evaluation Criteria	Key Sources of Data
Quality of Program Content	• Gardening class accurately covers all needed skills for growing selected crops. • Cooking class recipes meet nutritional requirements. • Exercise sessions are appropriate for participants' fitness level and age.	• Review of gardening class content or observation by an expert (experienced gardener) • Review of recipes by registered dietician • Review of exercise sessions by physical education teacher or other exercise specialist
Quality of Program Delivery	• Gardening and cooking classes and exercise sessions are interesting, delivered at a level appropriate for children, and consistent with Hawaiian ways of knowing and learning. • *Kūpuna* (elders) are involved in the teaching process and follow-up.	• Feedback from *kūpuna* about cultural appropriateness and about their role in the process • Feedback from children (and families) about understandability and enjoyment • Feedback from families about the family meal presentation event
Program Outputs	• Children served (numbers and details; how selected) • Families served • Geographical reach of the program	• Class enrollment records (numbers, demographics) relative to whole target group • Documentation of attendance at final (family meal presentation) event • Communities served (locations)
Short-Term Outcomes	• Children's ability to successfully grow vegetables • Children's skills and knowledge (recipes) of how to cook tasty, healthy food • Cultural knowledge (*'ike Hawai'i*) gained from learning traditional cooking methods	• Children's performance in hands-on gardening activities • Nutritional quality and tastiness of food cooked for family meal presentation • *Kūpuna* assessments of how well children acquired cultural appreciation during the experience

TABLE 13.1. SAMPLE EVALUATION PLAN
FOR THE *'AI PONO* COMMUNITY NUTRITION INTERVENTION. *(continued)*

Program Aspect	Evaluation Criteria	Key Sources of Data
	• Family knowledge about nutrition • Perceived credibility of the message about nutrition • Children's learning of enjoyable exercise routines	• Family self-assessments of (1) nutritional knowledge and (2) their understanding of the importance of nutrition before (retrospective pretest) and after coming to the final gathering • Children's ability to perform learned exercise routines themselves and reported enjoyment of them
Intermediate Outcomes	• Distribution to *'ohana* (extended families) of healthy ingredients at affordable prices • Healthy, tasty food served at home more often • Children exercising more regularly • Knowledge and skills being shared throughout the *'ohana* network • Commitment to healthy lifestyles	• Children's "food and exercise diaries" (as a school homework assignment) • Teacher and school staff reports of school lunch content (if lunch not provided at school) • Interviews with family members • Tracking the spread of skills and knowledge throughout *'ohana*
Eventual Outcomes	• Healthy children and families • Productivity and energy levels at school, home, and work • Strong, healthy communities	• Results of regular health checks of children and families • Teacher assessments of children's productivity and energy levels at school • Interviews with family members • Rates of nutrition-related illnesses in the community (especially among families involved in the intervention)

daily activities to the reason people get out of bed and come to work in the first place: making a difference.

"The practice of shared vision involves the skills of unearthing shared *pictures of the future* that foster genuine commitment and enrollment rather than compliance" (Senge, 1990, p. 9). Staff should be helped to think about the purpose of their work, who and what they are trying to affect, and how they plan to do it. The exercises mentioned earlier in mapping out program theory can be extremely valuable here.

Evaluative thinking (both the passion for improvement and the ability to clearly identify what the program aims to achieve and how it might be able to do so) is essential for building motivation and meaning and for channeling energy in the right directions. If this is done well, the resulting increase in program staff passion can dramatically increase the likelihood of early success, which in turn creates a second opportunity for building staff commitment and passion.

Helping a New Program "Find Its Feet." Rarely does a truly innovative idea work perfectly the first time it is implemented, no matter how good the intentions or how experienced the staff. In fact, there are some who say that if everything works perfectly the first time, you must not be pushing the innovation envelope hard enough! When new programs flounder soon after implementation, this usually means that either some unforeseen circumstances are preventing success or that it is just taking a while to get all the energy and resources aligned and synchronized. This is especially true for a complex program in which some parts work well and others need fine-tuning or major revision.

There is sometimes strong resistance to the idea of early outcome evaluation—the rationale being that it is "too early" to expect results and that an early review that finds little impact could damage the program. This is one of the arguments behind the notion of "evaluability assessment"—a procedure for determining whether a program is "ready" for evaluation (Smith, 1989; Wholey, 1979). But one lesson many people have learned through painful experience is that if a program is off track, the longer it takes to figure this out the worse the situation becomes and the harder it is to make improvements. The worst-case scenario is that we do not find out about the problem until the program is given a formal review and an unfavorable decision is made about continued funding. Early corrections and improvements are not only easier and cheaper to make but the milder nature of the negative feedback received early on makes it less likely to be resisted and more likely to be acted on quickly and effectively.

Another factor to consider is that the longer early implementation problems persist at the beginning of a program, the greater the time lag between implementation and the emergence of results. This can have two potentially serious consequences for a program. First, given the time it takes to achieve any sizable effects, even for a smoothly implemented program, any additional time lag may make it more difficult to justify continued or expanded support in the next round of funding. Not only will the program look less effective than it would later, it will also appear to be more expensive to implement because of the time it takes to get up to full functionality. Second, long delays between expending effort on a program and seeing any fruits of that labor can be extremely demotivating for staff. And if staff are not as energized and encouraged as they might be, the program has less than a fighting chance of reaching its full potential.

No matter what the new program, it is important to have a way of finding out sooner rather than later if anything is amiss. One of the most important tools for being able to do this is to have a good-quality early feedback mechanism in place to allow you to see which elements of the program are already falling into place and where things still need streamlining. For the *'Ai Pono* community nutrition intervention described earlier, this would mean gathering evidence from Day 1 about the quality of program content, delivery, and outputs, as well as the anticipated immediate learning outcomes (see Table 13.1). With good planning, this early data collection can be built right into program activities for the first few sessions. Program staff can review their findings immediately after each session, perhaps inviting an advisory group of elders and parents and a registered dietician to participate in the review. In this way, evaluative information can be immediately put to work for the program by providing helpful direction for improvements. Over time, the data collected will provide a cumulative body of evidence about program effectiveness and a steady track record of continuous improvement.

Here is another example to illustrate the benefits of building a data-collection system directly into program operations rather than treating it as a separate undertaking. Over the past ten years, integrated, comprehensive, and collaborative projects have become popular. The Contra Costa County Health and Social Services Departments, along with specific school districts, realized that in order to adequately evaluate their own collaborative project, there needed to be a tracking system in place that would provide evidence that the collaborating agencies were indeed changing their systems by integrating the services of the other agencies, as well as services provided to their clients. Rather than build an external tracking process (which would have generated considerable extra work), the project's entire data system was rebuilt and focused on program goals. The design of the systems was based on helping line staff obtain information that would help them serve their customers.

Three things became evident with this change. First, program staff were much more motivated to enter this information; second, line staff only had to enter the information once, and third, the information consisted of data that were needed for the evaluation. As a result, effective tracking of services allowed program staff to better serve their clients, and the evaluation data were collected in the background.

To supplement the feedback gained from ongoing tracking of program performance (often referred to as program monitoring), the judicious use of formative evaluation reviews (evaluation aimed at providing feedback for improving existing programs), both in-house and independent, can help accelerate improvements by providing more and better ideas earlier in the program implementation process. One can minimize the costs of both by building a good data-collection system right into the program operations so that any review team needs only to supplement that information rather than start from scratch.

Helping Mature Programs Keep Up with Ever-Changing Needs in the Community.
Those of us committed to building community capacity and alleviating social problems know that these are, in many ways, moving targets. Even when the basic community need remains constant, its underlying causes (and therefore the appropriate solutions) may change due to generational differences, demographic fluctuations, socioeconomic changes, and other factors. This means that even the most carefully conceived and implemented program with a strong track record to date needs to keep its finger firmly on the pulse of changes so that it can anticipate them and respond effectively.

How does one keep one's finger on the pulse of changes in communities that might affect the program? One useful strategy is to supplement regular outcome assessment with a fresh reassessment of community needs. For example, as part of a long-term evaluation of the *'Ai Pono* community nutrition program, one might include some in-depth, open-ended inquiry into both success cases and disappointments in an effort to learn about what drives eating behaviors and key health outcomes in the target population. It is important to bear in mind that the same causes may not apply to all members of the community. By keeping up with changes in what drives key behaviors and outcomes for different kinds of people (for example, males and females, different age groups, and families with different ethnic backgrounds and education levels), it is possible to adjust the program design in a timely manner and tailor it to diverse communities served.

Even in cases where community needs have not changed substantially, "tried and true" mature programs often contain multiple hidden opportunities for innovation. Perhaps a new approach to program delivery has been developed elsewhere since the program was implemented, or maybe there are opportunities for making things run just a little more smoothly. There are three main alternatives here: (1) an in-house improvement initiative, (2) an external review, or (3) a comparison-learning exercise.

An interesting and potentially useful model for generating ideas for improvement in-house is called Work-Out (General Electric, 2004, p. 1):

> The aptly named Work-Out process involves identifying an area in need of improvement and bringing people together from all sides of the process . . . to identify a better method. . . . Team recommendations are presented to the responsible managers, who must accept or reject proposals on the spot. Ideas that require further study are reviewed for a period of time agreed on by the team (usually less than a month) before a final decision is made.

Although pioneered in the private sector, this model has great potential in the nonprofit sector due to its emphasis on the values of employee participation in decision making and responsive leadership. The basic idea behind the process is the same in any context: finding ways to get rid of unnecessary obstacles so that people can channel their energies toward what they are passionate about—making a difference in people's lives.

In-house efforts at process improvement can produce substantial benefits; however, there usually comes a time when internal reviews start to yield diminishing returns, as findings become more and more predictable. At times like this, it is often well worth the effort of bringing in a fresh set of eyes for an external review. Even if you hadn't originally planned for this and funds are tight, there are some creative "shoestring" alternatives available. For example, try contacting other grantee organizations, preferably those striving to address similar problems in a different community. See if you can set up an exchange arrangement whereby their most evaluation-proficient staff member participates in the evaluation of your program, and you lend your best person to their program to return the favor.

In a comparison-learning exercise (called benchmarking in the private sector), you find a partner organization or program and invite them to participate in a learning exercise that involves a systematic comparison of the processes and practices used by each organization, with a view to learning new ideas that might improve each other's programs. It's common to find that another organization has already found an elegant solution to something you have been struggling with, and a comparison-learning exercise can help capitalize on other organizations' collective wisdom and avoid reinventing the wheel.

Building Our Knowledge Base About Social Change

Foundations and nonprofits have spent many decades striving to find creative and effective ways of strengthening families and communities and improving social conditions. Various methods have been tried and failed; others have shown considerable promise. By documenting what we are doing, why, and what we achieved, we are able to share what is learned both within and among organizations. Evaluation can support this overarching goal by

- Turning innovative projects into rich opportunities for the creation of in-house knowledge that will inform future program design within the organization
- Adding to the general body of knowledge about "what works" so that other organizations and the academic community may benefit from the lessons learned

Turning Innovative Projects into Opportunities for In-House Knowledge Creation. Every new project or program represents an opportunity to find out what works, under what conditions, and for whom. If we are systematic about gathering useful information that will inform design, we have the opportunity to use this learning to design even better programs next time. In other words, good evaluation can help build the kind of organizational knowledge that will support the grantee organization's mission.

One of the most important benefits internally for documenting what is learned from each project is that it ensures the survival of organizational memory. Often, when a key staff member resigns or retires, his or her accumulated memory of what has worked and not worked in the past can be lost forever. And even if that person is still available, human memory tends to fade over time and cannot always be tapped into. In organizations with high staff turnover, keeping track of activities, results, and lessons learned can be crucial for avoiding the wasted effort of new staff going back over old ground.

Adding to the General Body of Knowledge About "What Works." As we mentioned earlier, it is important to study the literature to see what has been tried before launching into full proposal development. But it is equally important to contribute to that knowledge base so that others (our successors within the current organization and others in the field striving to address the same issues) may benefit. One of the founding fathers of evaluation, Donald Campbell, spoke several decades ago about the need for an "experimenting society," where we try out new and innovative ways of addressing important social problems (Campbell, 1969).

A good evaluation plan built into program design conveys to foundations the potential of the project to contribute to society as a whole by providing this valuable form of knowledge. And a well-written and presented evaluation report provides both the project and funding organizations the ability to disseminate the information so that others can learn from the knowledge they gained. Even disappointing results can be helpful in this regard; recall the value of such information with respect to the D.A.R.E. program. This benefit will often require some explicit attention to dissemination of results, for example, via Internet-posted reports or announcements of their availability or by partnering with university faculty to get findings that have been published in more formal channels.

Demonstrating the Value of the Organization's Activities

A prevailing view in the nonprofit world is that even though formative evaluation might conceivably be useful for grantee organizations, summative evaluation (reporting on the overall quality or value of a program) is done solely for the benefit of funders. This is not so. The use of evaluation to demonstrate overall value can be helpful to grantees by

- Documenting a track record of success that can be shared with key stakeholders (and often critics)
- Building justified confidence (confidence that is backed by evidence) about independent evaluation reviews
- Informing decisions about which future projects grantees should expend time and energy developing or implementing

Building a Track Record of Success. Foundations fund projects that they hope will produce positive effects on society, and they often require evidence that they have received some return on their investment. This is frequently seen as the primary reason for documenting results. But gathering information about program impact doesn't just address the accountability requirement imposed by foundations; it also helps organizations build a track record of success that they can share with stakeholders, with staff, with their communities, and with funders when they request further support for the same program or funding to try something new.

Building Confidence About Formal Evaluation Reviews. One of the reasons that evaluation is sometimes seen as a demotivating force is the anxiety associated with the possibility of receiving a negative review. However, as we discussed earlier, building early feedback systems into a program or project can increase the chances of success by allowing for the early detection and correction of problems. If early feedback is available and acted on, this dramatically reduces the chances that any later formal review will be negative.

The combination of a strong body of early evidence of success, coupled with the knowledge that many areas for improvement have already been identified and addressed, can also go a long way toward allaying some of those fears. The more thorough your early evaluation efforts, the greater your (and your staff's) confidence will be when it comes time to assess the program at maturity to see whether it was worth the investment overall. Of course, evaluation *can* turn up negative evidence, but this should typically happen in the formative phase, when most problems can be fixed.

Informing Decisions About Future Projects. The other factor, from the grantee's perspective, is that each organization has a limited amount of time and energy to devote to bettering the communities it serves. Naturally, it makes sense to ensure that the programs one chooses to engage in constitute the best possible use of that time and energy. Although some of this knowledge can be harvested from the growing literature on the effectiveness of social change, there really is no substitute for seeing and knowing for yourself which of your activities was a worthwhile investment of your precious time and particular talents. Not only does this feed into organizational learning by helping you learn what works but it also helps with strategic planning when you want to channel your efforts to the areas that yield the greatest payoff.

Steps Toward Phasing in Evaluative Thinking

Given the myriad of ways in which evaluative thinking and practice might be built into foundation-funded projects, where should an organization start? The following suggestions are designed for grantee organizations that currently have little in-house evaluation expertise but would like to start using evaluative thinking to strengthen their proposals and existing programs while building creative tension and capacity for further success.

Whenever venturing into new territory, two important considerations are (1) being able to try something on a small scale first and (2) maximizing staff buy-in. For this reason, it is a good idea to start with a proposed project in an area of strength for your organization but on a topic that is not overly straightforward to conceptualize. If possible, it should also be a project that you are fairly confident will be fundable if the program and evaluation design are well presented.

The following steps outline a phased approach that starts with an injection of evaluative thinking at the point where it is most likely to yield clearly visible benefits within a relatively short period of time. Each subsequent step builds on the first, gradually building in-house evaluation capability while increasing both staff motivation and involvement and the chances of achieving demonstrable project success. The process is designed to capitalize on the notion of creative tension, that is, maintaining high, inspiring goals for social betterment while increasing the quality of the information about where the program currently is with respect to those goals. This should eventually result in being able to move closer to the organization's overarching vision than has yet been possible.

Step 1: Increase the use of evaluation expertise in the proposal development phase. If evaluation expertise is not already available in-house, it can be brought in by sending staff to training workshops, bringing in an expert coach to guide people through the process, or simply hiring an expert to do certain pieces of the proposal development work as needed. In particular, evaluation expertise will strengthen your critical review of the research, needs and strengths assessment, goal setting, development of a program theory, and evaluation design.

If exactly the right person is difficult to find, remember that if you have access to content expertise on your staff already (for example, knowledge of community development, teen drug prevention, or unemployment), you may not need the evaluation expert to also be a specialist in your particular kind of intervention. Combine the expertise from your two complementary sources.

In addition to content and evaluation expertise, make sure you have people on the team with the cultural competencies needed for understanding and addressing the concerns of the project's target populations. This might take the form of community representation on the design team, a consultation process to allow input, or bringing on someone with expertise in similar types of communities.

Step 2: Set up an evaluation data-collection and management system. A great deal of the information required for a good evaluation can be collected relatively inexpensively as the project progresses so that (1) it is available to you when you need it, and (2) it can be pulled together for progress reports and for the main summative evaluation of the project, thereby minimizing evaluation costs by eliminating the need to start from scratch. Working out what information to collect and in what form requires good evaluative expertise, as does the task of training those who will be involved in data collection. But once set up, the system removes a lot of the time burden associated with regular reporting of results.

Step 3: Get training or on-the-job coaching on evaluation for grantee staff. The most difficult task in getting the most out of a data management system is being able to turn a mass of information from multiple sources into a concise summary that can be made available quickly to decision makers, as they need it. Interpretation of evaluative data (both qualitative and quantitative) is as much an art as a science, and such know-how (if it is needed in-house) is best imparted using a combination of off-the-job training and on-the-job coaching, supported by user-friendly reference materials.

Step 4: Commission an expert to provide advice and support during an in-house evaluation. Once your in-house evaluation team has had a chance to try out the skills they have learned from training and on-the-job coaching, have them conduct their first evaluation on their own but with the benefit of access to an evaluation expert who can provide advice and support but is not involved in hands-on evaluation activities. This person would comment on the initial evaluation design, provide advice and feedback as the evaluation progresses, and make suggestions on drafts of the final evaluation report.

Step 5: Commission a review of a completed evaluation. Once the in-house evaluation team has conducted a few evaluations with expert advice and support and feels confident about the quality of their work, allow them to complete an entire project independently, then bring in someone to review the evaluation. This person would examine the final evaluation report, supplement it with some additional probing to check validity, and then provide overall feedback about the quality of the evaluation and suggestions for improving procedures.

Step 6: Commission a fully independent evaluation. If the program is looking strong after early evaluation and the implementation of midstream corrections, and if in-house evaluations are found by external reviewers to be solid, then the program may well be ready for a fully independent review. By this time, staff confidence in the quality of the program should be high, and attention should be focused less on whether the overall review will be positive or negative (the usual source of evaluation anxiety) and more on what new insights a fresh perspective will bring.

The six-step strategy described may be used by grantees to gradually phase in the use of evaluation in a way that maximizes the capacity-building benefits for grantee organizations. The general approach is to start by getting front-end help to improve program design and build in good formative feedback systems, and then build organizational confidence and performance gradually until the organization is ready to launch a "best practice" mix of internal and external evaluation.

Conclusion

As we have seen in this chapter, evaluative thinking is a powerful tool that can be used by grantee organizations to build and maintain the creative tension that provides focus and motivation and to design highly effective programs with greater chances of getting funded, thereby making a significant impact in our communities. In addition to this "internal" perspective of strengthening organizational capacity, there is an important benefit with respect to the organization's external image.

A grantee organization that is committed to building evaluative thinking into its operations conveys an important message to foundations, to staff, and to the community—that it stands for quality. Organizations that have a demonstrated commitment to and a track record of delivering the very best that their resources allow tend to attract top-performing staff—people who are motivated by the knowledge that their best efforts will be detected and appreciated. As we mentioned earlier, the true strength of a grantee organization lies in the passion, dedication, and talent of its people. Evaluative thinking can be an important way to attract, nurture, and retain that crucial source of strength.

On-Line Resources

Aspen Institute. *Measures for community research.*
http://www.aspenmeasures.org/

Callow-Heusser, C. *Digital resources for evaluators.*
http://www.resources4evaluators.info/

Canadian Centre for Philanthropy. *John Hodgson Library.*
http://www.nonprofitscan.ca/ccp_library.asp

National Science Foundation. *Online evaluation resource library.*
http://oerl.sri.com/

National Science Foundation. *User-friendly handbook for project evaluation.*
http://www.ehr.nsf.gov/EHR/RED/EVAL/handbook/handbook.htm

Shackman, G. *Resources for methods in evaluation and social research.*
http://gsociology.icaap.org/methods/

South Australian Community Health Research Unit. *Planning and evaluation wizard.*
http://www.sachru.sa.gov.au/pew/index.htm

The Evaluation Center, Western Michigan University. *Evaluation checklists project.*
http://evaluation.wmich.edu/checklists/

United Way of America. *Outcomes measurement resource network.*
http://national.unitedway.org/outcomes/

U.S. Department of Energy. *Knowledge transfer center.*
http://www.t2ed.com/

Voluntary Sector Evaluation Project (Canada).
http://datasource.vserp.ca/vserp/resources.lasso

Wilde, J., & Sockey, S. (1995). *Evaluation handbook.*
http://www.ncela.gwu.edu/miscpubs/eacwest/evalhbk.htm

References

Brown, J. H. (2001). Youth, drugs, and resilience education. *Journal of Drug Education, 31*(1), 83–122.

Campbell, D. T. (1969). Reforms as experiments. *American Psychologist, 24,* 409–429.

Davidson, E. J. (forthcoming). *The multipurpose evaluation guidebook: The nuts and bolts of putting together a solid evaluation.* Thousand Oaks, CA: Sage.

de Geus, A. P. (1997). *The living company.* Boston, MA: Harvard Business School Press.

Donaldson, S. I., Graham, J. W., & Hansen, W. B. (1994). Testing the generalizability of intervening mechanism theories: Understanding the effects of adolescent drug use prevention interventions. *Journal of Behavioral Medicine, 17,* 195–216.

Ennett, S. T., Tobler, N. S., Ringwalt, C. L., Flewelling, R. L. (1994). How effective is drug abuse resistance education? A meta-analysis of Project DARE outcome evaluations. *American Journal of Public Health, 84*(9), 1394–1401.

General Electric. (2004). *Cultural change process.* Available at www.ge.com/en/company/news/culture.htm.

Lynam, D. R., Milich, R., Zimmerman, R. S., Novak, S. P., Logan, T. K., Leukefeld, C., & Clayton, R. (1999). Project DARE: No effects at 10-year follow-up. *Journal of Consulting and Clinical Psychology, 67*(4), 590–593.

Rosenbaum, D. P., & Hanson, G. S. (1998). Assessing the effects of school-based drug education: A six-year multilevel analysis of Project D.A.R.E. *Journal of Research in Crime and Delinquency, 35*(4), 381–412.

Sathe, V., & Davidson, E. J. (2000). Toward a new conceptualization of culture change. In N. M. Ashkanasy, C.P.M. Wilderom, & M. F. Peterson (Eds.), *Handbook of organizational culture and climate* (pp. 279–296). Thousand Oaks, CA: Sage.

Scriven, M. (1991). *Evaluation thesaurus* (4th ed.). Thousand Oaks, CA: Sage.

Senge, P. M. (1990). *The fifth discipline: The art and practice of the learning organization.* New York: Currency/Doubleday.

Smith, M. F. (1989). *Evaluability assessment: A practical approach.* Boston: Kluwer Academic Publishers.

Wadsworth, Y. (1997). *Everyday evaluation on the run* (2nd ed.). St. Leonards, NSW, Australia: Allen & Unwin.

Wholey, J. S. (1979). *Evaluation: Promise and performance.* Washington, DC: The Urban Institute.

Wind, J. Y., & Main, J. (1998). *Driving change: How the best companies are preparing for the 21st century.* New York: Free Press.

CHAPTER FOURTEEN

COMMUNICATING RESULTS TO DIFFERENT AUDIENCES

Lester W. Baxter and Marc T. Braverman

With its focus on serving the information needs of intended users (Joint Committee on Standards for Educational Evaluation, 1994), evaluation is a fundamentally practical form of inquiry. This emphasis on practicality places a high premium on effective communication among all the people involved in an evaluation, including those conducting the study and those who will use the information it generates. Indeed, as evaluation approaches have proliferated (Stufflebeam, 2001), so has the potential for misunderstandings about the expectations and assumptions underlying a particular evaluation project, making the need for accurate, balanced, and clear communication stronger than ever.

This chapter is about the communication of evaluation results—an area that experience shows can frequently be neglected or devalued. Communication of results is sometimes viewed as a procedurally routine phase of the evaluation process that involves drafting and distributing a report, possibly accompanied by a meeting or oral presentation. Furthermore, many evaluation reports follow the template of a research paper, in which background, hypotheses, techniques,

We are grateful to Michael Cortés and Carolina Reyes for their contributions to the conceptualization of this chapter in the early phases of its development. We also thank Martha Campbell, Rebecca Cornejo, Victor Kuo, Garth Neuffer, Edward Pauly, and Tracey Rutnik for their insightful comments on a previous draft. The views of Lester Baxter expressed in this chapter do not necessarily reflect those of The Pew Charitable Trusts.

findings, and recommendations are methodically detailed. What sometimes seems to underlie this standardized approach to communication is the belief that an evaluation study's technical aspects (such as its adequacy of design, soundness of data-collection methods, and relevance of data analysis) require thorough consideration, whereas its human aspects (such as how the project gets communicated, what it finally means, and whether it answers people's questions) are easily managed. Of course, this view is mistaken. Good communication is neither easy nor routine, and careful attention to it can enhance the conduct of evaluations themselves and increase their usefulness to a wide variety of audiences (Patton, 1997; Torres, Preskill, and Piontek, 1996).

Our central theme is the need for sound communication planning, which involves identifying specific audiences, determining how to approach them, deciding the purpose of the communications, fashioning the messages, and considering other characteristics of the setting. Our aims are to stimulate communication planning and to help evaluators and foundation personnel take account of the interplay of factors that affect communication, with the ultimate goal of making the evaluation process more useful. The task of planning and conducting the communication of results may fall on the shoulders of foundation-based communications staff or evaluation managers, external evaluators, or grantees. We direct our discussion primarily toward these individuals, but we hope it will also be useful for readers involved with foundation-based evaluations in other capacities.

The chapter has four major sections: (1) a description of the elements of an evaluation study's communication environment, (2) a discussion of different potential audiences, (3) an overview of communication tools and approaches, and (4) implications of these considerations for communicating evaluation results.

Understanding the Communication Environment

A communication environment is established early in an evaluation study, characterized by how information is exchanged and how decisions are made. This environment might also include shared or divergent understandings about the purpose of the study, the primary and secondary audiences, the evaluation questions, the evaluation methods, and the relevant timelines. Appropriate planning can help to develop the communication environment for an anticipated evaluation in a constructive way.

In the next sections, we present six questions that are fundamental to both evaluation and communication planning. Working through these questions can help evaluators understand what types of information (delivered at what times and in what formats) will be most useful to various audiences. Pursuing these questions can also help them gauge the dynamics of the organizational setting (for example, the degree to which the environment may be collegial or adversarial). Finally, it will facilitate budget planning, because different communication strategies can vary substantially in their resource requirements. If the planners of the evaluation study are not clear about the answers to these questions, the communication of findings will be seriously hampered, and the evaluation may fail to achieve its intended purposes.

What Information Is Being Sought?

In most cases, the evaluation will be designed to address a number of discrete evaluation questions, which are the central guiding statements that will structure the information-gathering activities that follow. The answers to these questions will form a basis for the later communication of results. In addition, new questions that should be pursued sometimes emerge once an evaluation is under way. The advisability of midcourse adjustments to an evaluation, to take account of these new directions, is best assessed by keeping the needs of the study's primary intended users clearly in sight.

Who Are the Audiences for the Information?

Identifying an evaluation's primary audience is a critical objective of communication planning. As will be discussed in detail, a fundamental distinction is whether the primary audience is internal or external to the organization sponsoring the evaluation. The audiences may be supportive, skeptical, antagonistic, or indifferent. They may be sophisticated or novice consumers of evaluation. The better the audience is understood, the greater the likelihood will be of communicating with them productively.

Why Do They Want to Know?

This question addresses the intended use of the evaluation results by particular audiences. Patton (1997) describes three general categories of evaluation use: (1) *making judgments,* including questions of accountability and program effectiveness, (2) *facilitating program and organizational improvement,* which may involve helping foundations or grantees become more effective or adapt to changing circumstances, and (3) *generating knowledge* that can advance a field or be used broadly by government agencies and other foundations to improve practice and social policy.

Audience interest in evaluation findings will depend, in part, on how they might be affected by an evaluation and whether they can act on the study's findings and recommendations. For example, foundation officers receiving information about the progress of grantee programs will approach the evaluation setting differently than would grantee organizations. In addition, some groups may view the evaluation with reasonably high levels of objectivity, whereas others may be heavily invested in demonstrating program success.

In other instances, an audience may be unaware of the evaluation study or not interested in its results, yet the presenter wishes to make a case for the importance of the program or the evaluation. This can occur with secondary audiences external to the project, such as other funders or the press. In such cases, the strong motivation lies with the presenter, whether evaluator, grantee, or foundation, and the pertinent question might become, Why do *we* want them to know?

How Much Information Do They Want?

Information needs differ by audience: program staff and grantees might want all the details about the results; trustees and executives might want a brief presentation of highlights and bottom-line implications; academic audiences might want to know specifics about the scientific and technical aspects of the study. Audience members' responsibilities within their home organization or their field play a major role in shaping their information needs; the nature of these responsibilities can help guide decisions about content and presentation. Of course, individual preferences also warrant consideration, particularly if the primary audience is small, such as a board or a president. Some audience members or groups may be particularly attuned to communication via graphical, written, or oral formats.

Who Is Doing the Communicating?

If a foundation is large enough to have a communications or public affairs staff, that group may have the primary responsibility for communicating evaluation results. Typically, the evaluator will also be involved, especially for certain audiences. The foundation staff person managing the evaluation contract can be effective in framing evaluation findings and recommendations for internal audiences. Program staff can be important internal communicators, providing executives or trustees with their views on the evaluation and their proposals on how to respond to its findings. Program staff are also obvious candidates for sharing evaluative information with grantees.

In all cases, the credibility of the source must be firmly established if the audience is expected to act on the findings. If the grantee organization is communicating evaluation results about its own program, some audience members may be skeptical of its willingness to reveal negative information. Similarly, external audiences may be suspicious of a foundation that shares only the "good" news from its evaluations. In such cases, the organization must be particularly careful to convey evidence of objectivity, balance, and open disclosure.

The planning for communication also needs to consider issues of intellectual property rights. For example, who owns and controls the data and findings that will emerge from an evaluation? When an evaluation is externally contracted, this question can create problems if it has not been addressed. In some cases, the foundation may want to exert ownership and control; in others, these prerogatives might be granted to the evaluator. The best time to decide intellectual property questions is in the early stages of planning, prior to final selection of the evaluator. The terms and conditions governing the dissemination or other use of data and findings should be clearly articulated in the evaluation contract.

When Should Evaluation Results Be Communicated?

Effective communication of results is rarely a one-time event that takes place after the various analyses, interpretations, and recommendations have been formulated and packaged. On the contrary, communication can be planned to occur in phases, with target times being identified for sharing specific types of information with certain audiences. For example, the parties closest to a program evaluation study, such as program officers and grantees, might be kept apprised of findings as they become available; communication with other audiences might occur less frequently or only after the study's completion. Similarly, the information being learned about program implementation might be communicated earlier than information about program outcomes.

In cases where an evaluator discovers that a program is not being adequately implemented, and that the evaluation will therefore not be a test of the intervention as it was planned, it can be useful to share this information with the program staff. The rationale for sharing grows much stronger if the implementation issues are correctable and meaningful data could still be gathered from a properly implemented program. However, care must be taken to ensure that the plan for communicating this feedback is compatible with the evaluation's purpose and design. For example, if the study involves an evaluation of a packaged program and places high priority on the generalizability of the findings, it may be necessary to withhold evaluative information until the completion of the program delivery. This will help to maintain the generalizability of the results to other program settings that do not have the benefit of self-correcting feedback (see Shadish, Cook, and Campbell, 2002, for a detailed discussion of generalizability issues).

More generally, evaluation communication can be an ongoing exchange of information among the evaluator and various program stakeholders at well-planned points in time. As noted earlier, creative new questions or perspectives are sometimes identified only after a study has begun. This type of creative thinking may emerge, in part, because of the richness of ongoing communication and the cumulative growth of shared learning. Strong communication can also foster a sense of buy-in for the evaluation study among diverse audiences and build their anticipation to learn its final results.

Evaluation Audiences and Their Information Needs

A given evaluation study may have several potential audiences, but usually only one or two of these will be considered primary. Understanding one's audience is a key to successful communication in any endeavor, and audiences for foundation-sponsored evaluation information can be varied indeed. Evaluations should be designed, conducted, and conveyed with the needs of the primary audience in the forefront. Secondary audiences may have different needs, which may also be considered, particularly if anticipated in advance and if resources permit. But evaluation use will inevitably be limited unless the core messages are delivered in a way that can be heard by the intended primary audience.

Determining whether the primary audience is *internal* or *external* to the foundation is fundamental because these two types of audiences may have information needs and purposes that are better served by different communication approaches. When the primary audience is internal, the evaluation information usually is needed either to inform organizational decision making (for example, "Should we continue to invest in this approach or project?") or to improve programs and projects (for example, "How can this program's strengths be better deployed?" "What are the weaknesses of this program, and how can they be addressed?"). Certain external audiences may share these priorities, particularly audiences that are close to the foundation (for example, grantees or funding partners) or embarking on similar projects. For other external audiences, however, particularly those more distant from the foundation, the benefit from the evaluation is likely to entail overall knowledge generation and understanding of the issue, rather than being tied to specific decisions. The internal evaluation manager will usually have limited access to external audiences but ongoing access to most internal audiences, providing the option of using a wide range of communication tools to reach them.

We also distinguish among three broad types of information needs: (1) strategic, (2) tactical, and (3) operational. Figure 14.1 illustrates the relationships between an evaluation's potential audiences and their information needs. *Strategic* information needs are dictated by the mission, values, and goals of the organization. Evaluation findings that bear on a foundation's approach to philanthropy, its goals, or its allocation of resources, for example, may inform the organization's strategic decisions. Communications to meet strategic information needs should be concise, with what Tufte (1991) would characterize as "rich information density." The content should focus on the grantmaking context, core evaluation findings, large lessons relevant to future or ongoing work, and emergent issues.

Tactical information needs are shaped by the objectives, grantmaking approaches, and specific grants within well-defined program areas. Evaluation findings that inform either the implementation of a grant (or a collection of grants)

FIGURE 14.1. POTENTIAL AUDIENCES
AND THEIR CHARACTERISTIC INFORMATION NEEDS.

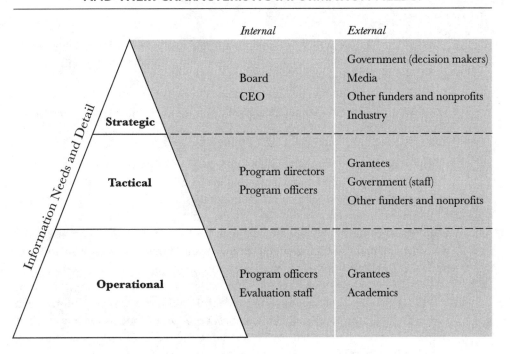

	Internal	External
Strategic	Board CEO	Government (decision makers) Media Other funders and nonprofits Industry
Tactical	Program directors Program officers	Grantees Government (staff) Other funders and nonprofits
Operational	Program officers Evaluation staff	Grantees Academics

Information Needs and Detail

or the approach to a specific issue (for example, underage drinking, wilderness protection) serve the foundation's tactical decision needs. Actors at the tactical level, such as program directors and officers, are much closer to the topics of the evaluation itself. Communication to meet tactical information needs may include regular updates during the course of the evaluation, as well as the full evaluation report and information about what strategic content will be conveyed to the organization's highest-level decision makers.

Finally, *operational* information needs derive from the activities and products expected from a grant or collection of grants. This detailed picture is often developed through a foundation's grant-monitoring or administration processes rather than through an evaluation. Nevertheless, evaluators usually become deeply familiar with the immediate work of grantees and can provide program officers and grantees with an independent perspective on the timeliness, quality, and usefulness of specific activities and products. In addition, evaluators may be exposed to personnel or organizational issues that bear on a project's progress. The specific nature of the operational information will help determine whether it should be discussed in the written evaluation report, an appendix, a separate memo, or a briefing.

Internal Audiences

Within the foundation, several audiences may have an interest in evaluation results. We cover four here: board members, executive management, program staff, and internal evaluation staff.

The Board of Trustees. Foundation trustees' stake in evaluation information lies in its potential to help them make better decisions about the foundation's mission and major directions, program areas, and funding levels. The level of their decisions tends to involve the broadest issues facing the organization, and thus their decision-making role is primarily strategic and direction setting in nature. Furthermore, their responsibility to the foundation as board members is generally not a full-time commitment. Boards typically meet for only a handful of days per year, and their meetings must cover a broad agenda of topics, including organizational governance, financial management, personnel, and public relations, in addition to decisions about program areas. Therefore, these decisions (for example, involving resource allocation or grant approval) must be managed very efficiently.

What are the implications of these considerations for trustees' information needs? In their responsibilities, they can profit most from concise information that supports their organizational role. Information shared from an evaluation study should generally include key findings, the recommendations that were offered, the larger lessons that can be gleaned for the field under examination (for example, public health, education, child development, the environment), and relevant emergent issues—those not anticipated when the evaluation was launched but that emerged during the study and are relevant to the program area or the institution at large. Trustees do not have time for detailed evaluation reports that document methods, instruments, and analyses. In most cases, asking trustees to review such reports is a poor use of their time, because drawing conclusions about evaluation rigor or similar concerns tends not to match either their expertise or their responsibilities on behalf of the foundation. (Nevertheless, of course, the full report should be readily available on their request.)

Foundation Executive Management. The foundation executive is the senior ranking staff person in the organization, with responsibility for the overall day-to-day management of the foundation. This person's title might be CEO, president, or executive director. This individual, often a member of the foundation's board, is a bridge between the board and the program officers, ensuring that the board's vision is infused in the foundation's approach to philanthropy. The senior executive's work spans organizational direction setting and operational oversight but usually not direct project oversight. The executive's decision-making responsibilities can therefore be characterized as both strategic and tactical, in the sense that he or she must participate in the board's decision making and promote the smooth functioning of the organization. Evaluation information for this audience should be oriented and organized in a way that will promote efficient action and decision making. As is true for the trustees, to do their work effectively, foundation executives need synopses of evaluation studies rather than detailed comprehensive reports. These synopses can be accompanied or augmented by memos or briefings that elaborate on selected findings or recommendations, or that raise management issues for the foundation or program. In some cases, however, the top executive may indeed need full evaluation reports on topics of particular import, for example, cluster reviews that assess a foundation's philanthropic strategy for a particular area.

Program Staff. Program directors and officers oversee funded projects and serve as the main points of contact with grantee organizations. In some foundations, the program staff make project funding decisions themselves, whereas in others they prepare funding recommendations for their board. In all cases, however, it is their responsibility to be well versed on the proposed or ongoing projects, and their judgments and opinions carry a great deal of weight. Their decision-making role is primarily tactical in nature, as their work is close to the primary ongoing function of the foundation. The grantmaking staff with direct oversight responsibilities for the projects being evaluated will also have operational information needs.

Program staff are the foundation personnel whose interests are most closely aligned with the details of the evaluation study. They frequently have a hand in the focus and design of the evaluation, either directly through collaboration with grantees or in the requirements they set for evaluation activity within projects. Program staff may also have the most interaction with the evaluators, particularly if regular briefings are part of the evaluation's communication plan. If an evaluation focuses on the performance or outcomes of a grantee project or organization, the task often falls to the relevant program officer to represent that study or the knowledge gained from it to other internal audiences of the foundation. It is generally the responsibility of the program staff to synthesize evaluation information into a format that allows the board to take appropriate action quickly and effectively. Program staff may also be in the best position to share evaluation findings that could inform grantmaking elsewhere in the foundation, because peer-to-peer learning can be an effective way to build organizational knowledge.

Our recommendation that foundation trustees and executive managers be provided with concise syntheses of evaluation studies implies that those individuals will not have the full set of background materials needed to determine whether a study has been conducted with a high degree of technical merit. The foundation needs other staff to be able to make this type of judgment, and the program staff (sometimes aided by consultants) typically fill this role in the absence of internal evaluation staff. Accordingly, program staff need to be well-versed in the details of the foundation's evaluation studies.

Internal Evaluation Staff. Several large foundations are fortunate to have evaluation expertise on-staff. These individuals can take on many of the responsibilities described earlier: helping to shape the organization's approach to evaluation, designing evaluations, judging the technical merit of evaluations, and playing an important role in communicating evaluation results. They often make recommendations to the trustees and executive management about the projects that should be selected for careful study and, most broadly, about the foundation's strategies for collection and use of information to strengthen institutional decision making. The decision-making role of the evaluation staff is tactical in nature to the degree that it supports the management of the organization and its grantmaking, though the evaluation staff may also prepare and deliver the strategic information from the evaluation to the foundation's board. Further, their role is operational in nature to the degree that it supports the operation and effectiveness of the foundation's grantmaking programs and helps the program staff acquire the information they need to track the progress of their grant portfolios.

External Audiences

Outside the foundation, the number of audiences potentially interested in evaluation results is striking. In this section, we discuss several of these, including grantees, government, news media, academia, other funders and nonprofits, and private industry.

Grantees. Both grantees and their funders have a strong stake in the success of their programs. Thus grantees are a foundation's most direct and often most important external audience. As with program directors and officers, grantees' information needs are usually tactical. Communication regarding program implementation and results is most beneficial when it is candid, collegial, ongoing, and bidirectional. This advice has been borne out by evaluators' experiences. Torres, Preskill, and Piontek (1997) canvassed members of the American Evaluation Association about communicating evaluation findings with intended users and reported that communication that is ongoing and collaborative was most successful, including informal conversations and other means of keeping in close contact throughout an evaluation. Foundations can do much to promote that kind of communication by encouraging strong working relationships among program officers and grantees.

Communication between foundations and grantees about evaluation results can take many forms: grantees can report results to their program officers; foundations can report to their grantees about all of the projects in an initiative; grantees and foundations can work together to report results to other audiences; or a foundation might communicate evaluation results to a grantee about the grantee's own programs. In these latter cases, if an evaluation report is involved the grantee should, whenever possible, have the opportunity to review and comment on a draft version. Grantees should also have the opportunity to be briefed about the evaluation's findings by the foundation's program or evaluation staff (or both) and to be informed about how the foundation will use the evaluation.

Government. Government officials and staff may be interested in evaluation results because of their policymaking, programmatic, and budgetary responsibilities. *Government* actually represents a broad cross-section of potential audiences, including government agencies and legislative bodies at the local, state, or federal level (as well as the organizations that exist to inform or otherwise aid legislatures, such as the Congressional Research Service or the National Conference of State Legislatures). Agency staff and legislative staff tend to be most interested in the findings and recommendations that arise from an evaluation, that is, the "big picture" issues. They need to have confidence in the technical adequacy of an evaluation, and those staff responsible for assessing a study's technical merits may share some of the tactical information needs of the foundation's internal audiences. Even if they are not fully equipped to make that determination themselves, government staff will want to understand the important strengths and weaknesses of a study before bringing it to the attention of decision makers such as agency executives or elected or appointed officials. Similar to a foundation's trustees, the information needs of government decision makers and their advisers tend to be strategic in nature because they are focused on policy development and implementation and broadly oversee the more detailed operations of government. Communications with these audiences need to be brief and focus squarely on the results and implications of the evaluation study, that is, what the evaluation adds to what is already known about a field, policy, or program.

News Media. Print and broadcast media can be secondary (or, on rare occasion, primary) audiences for information about foundation-funded projects. The news media represent an important communication vehicle to inform public opinion in efforts to promote policy change. In addition, communications with media can inform policymakers, who often look to media representations of important issues as markers of current public opinion or its future direction. The information needs of most media will be at the strategic level, concerned with new ideas or evidence about existing and emerging problems. For specialized media such as professional or trade press, additional information may also be relevant.

Of course, working with news media involves experience and expertise. Few evaluation reports will be featured by the media in the absence of a deliberate effort on the part of the evaluators, the foundation, or grantees. If an evaluation has been well-conducted, and its results are judged to have strong applicability to current public issues, foundations and grantees are certainly well advised to attempt to give it appropriate exposure. Outreach to the media can include issuing press releases, contacting individual reporters, identifying and preparing organizational spokespeople to discuss the evaluation and its implications, and even hiring a public relations firm. These activities can be adapted to local, statewide, or national-level communication channels.

Academic Audiences. Scholars at universities, research institutes, think tanks, and other academic locales can play a role in two important aspects of an evaluation study's dissemination and use. First, they often participate in the debate on social or policy issues. Public discourse about controversial topics such as the effects of day care on young children, effects of various HIV-prevention strategies, or local experiments in school vouchers can be marked by sharp dispute about the scientific adequacy of evaluation studies presented in support of one position or another. Through their critiques, researchers sometimes play a gatekeeper role in shaping the acceptance of a research study by policymakers or the public. Second, academics can become involved in the formulation of new research directions that follow from an evaluation study. Through the development of follow-up projects, academics often take part in shaping the long-term investigation of social issues and policy questions.

Communication to academic audiences requires careful attention to the technical details of the study. Two major avenues of potential communication are research reports, which can be issued as separate documents from the comprehensive evaluation report, and publication in peer-reviewed academic journals. Journal publication signals some degree of academic acceptability for the study (depending on the journal involved) but can carry the strong disadvantage of a long time period—sometimes over a year—between a manuscript's submission and its availability. Furthermore, many journals require that reports be embargoed until the time of publication, which delays other avenues of dissemination and conflicts with the need to share results with other audiences in a timely manner.

Other Funders and Nonprofit Organizations. Other foundations and funders that make grants in a project's general topic area may have common interests in program effects, and sharing results with them is an important way to make progress in the field as a whole. Similarly, sharing results with a range of nonprofits beyond the grantee organization can also develop knowledge about effective practice. These communication decisions require judgment about the kinds of information that will be useful. For example, an evaluation focused on the operational detail of a recently implemented project will generally not be suitable for wide distribution, except under unusual circumstances such as when the project is so novel, the evaluation so informative, or outside interest so high that dissemination is warranted.

Private Industry. A foundation's grantmaking objectives can aim to influence private sector behavior through promoting policies, changing norms for industry practices, or providing resources for new industry initiatives. Thus the private sector may be an audience for an evaluation. It will, in fact, be a primary audience when the foundation intends to alter industry behavior or when a private corporation works with a foundation or nonprofit grantee in a programmatic partnership. In the former instance, the media can be a useful avenue for communicating to different audiences about private sector practices or policies.

Communication Tools and Approaches

Several writers have described the variety of tools available for communicating evaluation results (Hendricks, 1994; Smith, 1982; Torres, Preskill, and Piontek, 1996), and we provide a brief review here. Some of the most important options are presented in Table 14.1, which describes their particular strengths and limitations and some considerations about suitable audiences. Some formats are superior for conveying technical detail; others are well suited for convenience and broad distribution; still others are preferred for facilitating decision making and stimulating an audience's motivation to follow through on a recommended action. Good communication planning matches specific approaches with audience needs. Different tools and approaches may also be needed to convey different aspects of the evaluation study.

Final Reports

The most common form of evaluation reporting is the final project report. Final reports have a reputation, probably deserved, for having limited relevance and often remaining unread. Nevertheless, this format can be a comprehensive record of the evaluation study, and it certainly does not need to be doomed to irrelevance.

Hendricks (1994) provides a series of valuable stylistic recommendations for producing final reports that are oriented toward action and meeting an audience's information needs. Among his recommendations are that the report

- Be written in an active, readable style
- Have decreased emphasis on background and methodology and increased emphasis on findings and their meanings
- Use strong visuals
- Be clear in the study's interpretations, conclusions, and recommendations

Evaluators should also be creative and flexible in designing a report's format. Rather than echoing the format of an academic research paper, the evaluation report should be planned with the information needs of the primary audience squarely in mind. One effective way to organize tactical and operational information for the internal audience is to clearly address the questions that triggered the evaluation. These answers, accompanied by the most important evidence supporting them, can form the body of the evaluation report. Details about methods, data, the history of the efforts under study, contextual matters, and the full range of evidence collected can be displayed in appendixes. We have read wonderfully clear evaluation reports that consisted of a series of well-thought-out and logically arranged bullet points that conveyed important observations, findings, and recommendations, with the various details that evaluators and academics love fully reported in technical appendixes. The challenge for this type of reporting is to be able to justify such discussion by clearly linking it to underlying evidence.

Summary Reports

Strategic information can be conveyed effectively through a written summary—a concise, engaging, and informative report geared to the audience's needs. For internal audiences (the board and CEO), the summary could consist of background (for example, the grantmaking objectives, major lines of work, resources committed, important contextual matters, evaluation objectives, brief biography of the lead evaluator, and a snapshot on methods), core findings (positive, negative, and equivocal), recommendations (guided by the author's institutional knowledge), and conclusions (the "takeaway" messages). Preparing a lucid summary that informs the audience while maintaining the integrity of the final evaluation report is challenging, but in our experience it is the rare evaluation that cannot be summarized in about three thousand words. Summaries for an external audience may need to be written with even greater economy, perhaps including only the barest of background details and revising the recommendations as appropriate (for example, recommendations prepared for an internal audience may differ from those directed outside the foundation).

Sonnichsen (2000) has written insightfully on the value and preparation of internal evaluation summaries. These are among his recommendations that resonate most strongly with our own experiences (adapted from Sonnichsen, 2000, pp. 248–250):

- The purpose of the *executive summary* is to convey concisely and meaningfully the highlights of the evaluation and the benefits to be derived from the recommended actions.
- Outline the focus of the report for the audience with emphasis on prominent organization components, individuals, or programs. Organize the report around material topics.
- Format the summary for power and impact. Put the "good stuff" up front. Be clear about the evaluation objectives and questions.
- Use data in the summary when appropriate. Use representative, descriptive quotes that convey the essence of the data collected.
- Do not mix together findings and recommendations.
- Include minority views and rival data. Being clear does not mean ignoring complexity or nuance.

TABLE 14.1. COMMUNICATION TOOLS
AND THEIR CHARACTERISTICS.

Tool	Strengths	Limitations	Audiences
Final reports	• Allow for sustained analysis and interpretation • Allow for detail and comprehensiveness in their description of the program, evaluation focus, and evaluation methods • Serve as archival records of the study	• Even if well written, are not appropriate for certain audiences • Are often shaped by the author's needs rather than those of the primary audience • May require technical expertise to fully absorb	• Are suitable for audiences that need to understand the study in detail (for example, program staff, evaluation staff, grantees, academics)
Summary reports	• Highlight the evaluation's critical items of information • Identify core findings and recommendations • Stimulate thought and action • Can be read in brief periods of time	• Pose a challenge to maintaining the integrity of the larger final report (for example, the need to guard against distortions, omissions, editorializing) • Require additional effort to prepare	• Are useful in conveying strategic content to internal and external audiences
Other written formats • Synopses • Memos • Press releases • Academic papers	• Can be read in brief periods of time • Can be customized for specific audiences • Can be released in digestible packages of material, as relevant information is generated (rather than all at the end of an evaluation)	• Can make it difficult to provide a comprehensive picture of the program and evaluation if used in isolation	• Depending on the nature of the product, can be useful for a wide range of audiences
Presentations and briefings	• Allow for human interaction, with the reporting process following the spontaneous lead of audience members • Allow for misunderstandings to surface and be addressed in the moment	• Success of the method depends on skills of the presenter • Is inflexible with regard to time constraints of individual audience members	• Work well with audiences that require relatively brief summarization of results and are oriented toward decisive action (trustees, management staff)

TABLE 14.1. COMMUNICATION TOOLS
AND THEIR CHARACTERISTICS. *(continued)*

Tool	Strengths	Limitations	Audiences
	• Encourage elaboration of follow-up ideas • Encourage audience members to discuss issues with each other • Can be customized to specific issues and audiences		• Appropriate for strategic content or narrower slices of tactical and operational information • Effective for candid exchange on sensitive issues
Periodic informal meetings	• Build rapport between evaluator and intended users • Can be useful format for presenting negative findings	• Can threaten an evaluator's objectivity due to the extended discourse involved, with negative consequences for the report's recommendations	• Very useful for communications involving ongoing relationships, especially internal foundation audiences and grantees
Internet-based resources • Web sites • E-communication (mail, alerts, news wires) • Keyword buys	• Are generally low-cost • Permit rapid dissemination • Can reach wide or narrow audiences • Allow site visitors or communication targets to customize content • Allow for ongoing updates of communications to keep information current as project circumstances change	• Effort is needed to direct traffic to site. • Web postings make it difficult, if not impossible, to identify the audience that has actually been reached. • Audiences' different hardware formats can make it difficult to know if there is congruence between the visuals as designed and as received.	• Web site postings are an excellent format to reach the general public and other audiences. However, to accommodate audience biases due to differing patterns of technology use, this method should generally be used in combination with others. • E-mail lists can be used with a broad range of audiences. • All tools are well suited for communicating with other foundations, government, media, academics, businesses, and (usually) grantees.

Other Written Formats and Graphical Displays

In addition to a single report, or sometimes in place of it entirely, Hendricks (1994) suggests the option of issuing a series of shorter reports that can each be targeted for a specific audience or cover a particular subtopic. A collection of such reports, taken together, can quite successfully represent the full scope of an evaluation project.

Of course, reports should be delivered in a timely manner. Utmost care should be taken to ensure that the timeframe for delivery is appropriate for supporting necessary decisions and other actions. This fundamental requirement is often not fulfilled in practice. Another frequent recommendation is that reports be shared with important users while still in draft form. This practice has multiple advantages. First, errors of fact or perspective can be corrected by the project staff members, who will often be the individuals with greatest familiarity about the details of the project. Second, the inclusion of the primary evaluation users in the report development process can increase their eventual buy-in and acceptance of the report. If the evaluation findings are negative or otherwise unwelcome to the users, sharing draft versions of the report may be an awkward process, but even in these cases early communication is helpful. The program staff will thereby have time to reconcile their views with the evaluation's findings and be in a better position to contribute insights about the circumstances underlying the results.

There are many other productive ways of communicating through written reports. Newsletters, bulletins, fact sheets, and other approaches can be used. The evaluator can distribute a series of memos that keep audiences updated with the progress of an analysis. Memos can convey sensitive or confidential operational information to the foundation CEO or program director that may not be appropriate to include in a summary report (for example, personnel issues or other topics that bear on the management of a grant). In addition, reports should make use of graphics to the extent possible, including charts, tables, diagrams, and outlines. These options provide the opportunity to communicate information clearly, succinctly, and powerfully (Henry, 1995; Torres, Preskill, and Piontek, 1996).

Presentations and Briefings

As is the case with written communications, there are numerous formats for delivering information face-to-face. Presentations should be geared to be clear and understandable, and encourage audience involvement. As always, information presented should be developed with the particular audience in mind, with attention given to appropriate terminology and the level of technical detail. Care must be taken to have the core messages drive the design of the presentation rather than rely on standard formats (see Tufte, 1991, 2003, for further elaboration on this point). Presentations must also allow ample time for interaction between presenter and audience, as well as between audience members themselves.

Briefings are short oral presentations that are typically geared toward the communication of specific aspects of a study, with strong emphasis on interpretation and potential applications. Oral briefings are a useful option to convey sensitive information. The Pew Charitable Trusts often conclude important evaluations with a half-day series of meetings between the evaluators, the CEO, the program director, other program staff, and the Trusts' evaluation staff. As part of these meetings, the CEO meets privately with the evaluators to give them the opportunity to discuss any issues that arose during the course of the evaluation. The CEO also participates with program staff in a briefing led by the evaluators on the evaluation's findings and recommendations.

Periodic Informal Meetings

Some evaluators schedule regular meetings with program managers or funders to update them on progress and the emerging results. This approach allows information to be shared shortly after it becomes available. Continuing engagement carries several advantages, including the opportunity for evaluation users to receive information in an informal context that encourages comment and suggestions. Regular engagement also helps lay the groundwork for the integration of evaluation results into the program under study and throughout the organization.

Communicating via the Internet

Internet communication can take the form of Web sites, listservs, discussion forums, and e-mails, to name just a few. These options provide enormous opportunities for tailoring communication, and new approaches are evolving rapidly. Electronic communication is often inexpensive and convenient. Content can be easily revised, quickly distributed, and broadcast to a wide range of audiences or narrowcast to a targeted few.

A foundation's public Web site can become its major electronic communication tool. Visitors searching for content may come to the site unbidden, or they may be steered to the site through links posted on related sites, e-mails announcing new content, or even keyword purchases at major search engines. The site can be designed to give visitors the option to indicate interest in specific issues (for example, health care or early childhood education). When new content is posted on the subscribers' topics of interest, they can receive e-mail announcements that provide links to the new content. The electronic version of a wire service can be developed to deliver even more customized content (analysis, interpretation, or opinion) to a narrowly focused target audience (for example, government or non-profit decision makers, journalists, academics). In general, the narrower the audience the more targeted the content and the dissemination tool must be.

As for potential evaluative content, a foundation can use the Internet to present its approach to evaluation, list past or current evaluation projects, summarize results from grants and specific evaluations, synthesize findings across evaluations, and discuss how it is integrating evaluative findings and recommendations into its work. For example, the reporting practice at The Pew Charitable Trusts has developed by experimentation over time. Roughly four times a year, the Trusts post material to their Web site about some aspect of planning or evaluation. To date, this content is split almost evenly between summary information on specific evaluations and descriptions of how evaluation is more broadly integrated into the Trusts' program planning and design.

Of course, the promise of electronic media also brings communication challenges. Posting full evaluation reports on a public Web site may be problematic, for example, unless it was clear from the evaluation's inception that the public was a primary intended audience. In our next section, we discuss the issue of public dissemination of evaluation reports, which carries strong implications for how the Internet might be used.

Implications for Communicating Evaluation Results

As we have described, planning for effective communication can be a complex process. In this final section, we consider several implications of our discussion for broader issues involving foundations' communication of evaluation information.

Varieties of Communicator-Audience Contact

In several respects, internal audiences will be easier for communication planners to accommodate than external audiences. Most notably, the channels between the evaluation team and the internal audiences—boards, executives, program staffers—are more likely to be open and ongoing. This characteristic accommodates the use of multiple communication approaches quite well: there can be comprehensive reports, e-mail correspondence, regular briefings, and other kinds of contact. The continuing use over time of multiple approaches allows a rich dialogue to develop. For example, a program officer can contact the evaluator for clarification of a critical point several days after a presentation and receive it via telephone, e-mail, or face-to-face contact. A board member can raise an analytical question that initiates a re-analysis of some of the data. This pattern of communication helps make it likely (though it does not guarantee) that inadvertent misinterpretations will be corrected, unanticipated questions will be pursued, and the new evaluation information will be integrated into decision making. As Rallis and Rossman (2001) describe, open exchanges between evaluators and intended evaluation users allow for areas of unexpressed knowledge to be negotiated and developed into shared understandings or, in cases marked by lack of consensus, dissenting positions that at least are clearly understood.

A corresponding depth of interaction is harder, though not impossible, to achieve when communicating with external audiences. With government agencies, news media, and other external audiences, there are fewer opportunities for dialogue, and feedback to the foundation or the evaluator is sparser. (Grantee organizations can be an exception, depending on the strength of the foundation-grantee relationship.) Many of the end-users of the communication may in fact be anonymous to the evaluator, as in the cases of readers of journal articles or visitors to a Web site. If an audience member raises a question or perspective that leads to further interpretive clarifications or new data analyses, the new information, though it can become part of the ensuing discourse about the evaluation study, might not reach the individual who originated the question. These limitations on the communication process place a great burden on the evaluator to be unambiguous, direct, and precise when communicating with external audiences. Therefore, in comparison to internal audiences, the nature of the message might need to change along with the choice of communication channel.

An illustration of this perspective is provided by Snow (2001), who explores the problems inherent in "communicating with the distant reader" (p. 33). To meet the challenge of representing and communicating the "quality" of a program or product, he notes, the evaluator can make use of both subjective and objective approaches. Subjectivity in communication involves the incorporation of the evaluator's personal reactions into the communication, which can frequently be a powerful strategy for influencing judgments or decisions. By contrast, objectivity relies on replicable descriptions and assessments. Because the value, relevance, and acceptability of subjective statements depend, in part, on the audience's familiarity with the communicator, Snow notes that objectivity and replicability must take on greater importance as familiarity within the evaluator-audience relationship decreases.

Contributing to Public Debate

The opportunity to contribute to public policy discussions through broad and thoughtful communication of findings is recognized as one important potential benefit of foundations' evaluation practice (Council on Foundations, 1993; Patton, 1997). As yet, however, there has been limited attention to it in the foundation community (McNelis and Bickel, 1996; Patrizi and McMullan, 1998). Foundations that wish to be more active in this area should take account of several considerations in their planning processes.

Variations in the Interpretations of Findings. The characteristics of limited audience access and one-way communication can lead to the evaluator's or the foundation's loss of involvement—even loss of knowledge—regarding how the audiences interpret the evaluation message. If indeed a foundation's evaluation study is relevant to a topic of high public interest, foundation personnel may find themselves unable to contribute appropriate or needed input to the variety of meanings and implications that interested parties will assign to the study, including occasional misinterpretations. Of course, this unpredictability is a natural element of public debate and suggests that the foundation may have to stay involved as the debate unfolds to guard against the inappropriate representation of evaluation findings. Communication professionals can help the foundation ensure that an evaluation's major themes are accurately portrayed.

Public Dissemination of Evaluation Findings. Foundations have taken different approaches to questions about how broadly to share evaluative information on their programs. This issue has assumed new prominence with the rise of the Internet and the powerful new capacities it presents for direct communication with the public. Complete evaluation reports might not be suitable for Web posting or other dissemination in unabridged form because of their high level of detail and potentially sensitive information about identified individuals. However, such reports can be recast for dissemination purposes, and this effort can be a good investment of resources if reaching an external audience is a primary purpose of the study.

Foundations that strongly value the open disclosure of evaluation findings may make the public release of evaluation reports a matter of standard policy, as has occurred, for example, at The Wallace Foundation. In addition, several prominent organizations that conduct evaluation research, such as the Manpower Demonstration Research Corporation, Public/Private Ventures, and the Rand Corporation make public access to results a condition of undertaking an evaluation engagement. These organizations and many other experienced evaluators are well versed in making evaluations public in ways that are sensitive to the concerns of funders and grantees alike.

Communicating Negative Findings. Evaluation studies that fail to demonstrate a program or initiative's anticipated benefits can present a special dilemma. Foundations may be reluctant to disseminate what they view as negative findings out of a concern for the potential repercussions to their reputations and those of their grantees. However, from the perspective of advancing general knowledge in a field, it is useful to know about approaches that fail to meet expectations, as well as those that do. The reluctance to share findings can result in the perpetuation of ineffective program approaches.

One distinction that may be helpful for encouraging disclosure in some cases is to consider whether an evaluation's negative findings represent a failure of *strategy* (the guiding concepts or theory on which a program is based) or of *implementation* (the degree to which the program is delivered as planned). The results from well-implemented program strategies will usually be useful, whether the program is judged to have been successful or not. Indeed, information about strategies that failed, despite faithful implementation, can be especially valuable for moving a field forward in new directions. Thus evaluation findings that reflect such new information are good candidates for sharing.

By contrast, if a program is found to have been inadequately implemented, especially if the reasons are peculiar to the specific program setting, the lessons to be learned will probably be of more purely local interest. In such cases, dissemination of the evaluation will add little to general knowledge, may cause harm to the grantee organization, and thus will probably not be warranted. (See Chapter Twelve for further discussion of the interpretation of null and negative findings.)

Conclusion

Those of us with responsibility for communicating evaluation results sometimes forget that a study will not disseminate itself, no matter how expertly it has been designed and conducted. Our overall theme in this chapter has been the need to plan for communicating results, so that the evaluation has the best possible chance of reaching its primary audiences in forms that will encourage its appropriate application. Given the amount of new information that evaluation studies produce, as well as the amount of effort and expense that they typically entail, it is remarkable how frequently this phase of the process is overlooked. The use of foundation evaluations will increase dramatically if foundations and their grantees give careful attention to the questions of what, why, when, how, and to whom they wish to communicate the new knowledge made possible by their evaluation work.

References

Council on Foundations. (1993). *Evaluation for foundations: Concepts, cases, guidelines, and resources.* San Francisco: Jossey-Bass.

Hendricks, M. (1994). Making a splash: Reporting evaluation results effectively. In J. S. Wholey, H. P. Hatry, & K. E. Newcomer (Eds.), *Handbook of practical program evaluation.* San Francisco: Jossey-Bass (pp. 549–575).

Henry, G. T. (1995). *Graphing data: Techniques for display and analysis.* Thousand Oaks, CA: Sage.

Joint Committee on Standards for Educational Evaluation. (1994). *The program evaluation standards: How to assess evaluations of educational programs* (2nd ed.). Thousand Oaks, CA: Sage.

McNelis, R. H., & Bickel, W. E. (1996). Building formal knowledge bases: Understanding evaluation use in the foundation community. *Evaluation Practice, 17*(1), 19–41.

Patrizi, P., & McMullan, B. (1998, December). *Evaluation in foundations: The unrealized potential.* Report prepared for the W. K. Kellogg Foundation Evaluation Unit.

Patton, M. Q. (1997). *Utilization-focused evaluation: The new century text* (3rd ed.). Thousand Oaks, CA: Sage.

Rallis, S. F., & Rossman, G. B. (2001). Communicating quality and qualities: The role of the evaluator as critical friend. In A. Benson, D. M. Hinn, & C. Lloyd (Eds.), *Visions of quality: How evaluators define, understand and represent program quality* (pp. 107–120). Amsterdam: JAI Press.

Shadish, W. R., Cook, T. D., & Campbell, D. T. (2002). *Experimental and quasi-experimental designs for generalized causal inference.* Boston: Houghton-Mifflin.

Smith, N. L. (Ed.). (1982). *Communication strategies in evaluation.* Beverly Hills, CA: Sage.

Snow, D. (2001). Communicating quality. In A. Benson, D. M. Hinn, & C. Lloyd (Eds.), *Visions of quality: How evaluators define, understand and represent program quality* (pp. 29–42). Amsterdam: JAI Press.

Sonnichsen, R. C. (2000). *High impact internal evaluation.* Thousand Oaks, CA: Sage.

Stufflebeam, D. L. (2001). *Evaluation models.* New Directions for Evaluation, no. 89. San Francisco: Jossey-Bass.

Torres, R. T., Preskill, H. S., & Piontek, M. E. (1996). *Evaluation strategies for communicating and reporting: Enhancing learning in organizations.* Thousand Oaks, CA: Sage.

Torres, R. T., Preskill, H. S., & Piontek, M. E. (1997). Communicating and reporting: Practices and concerns of internal and external evaluators. *Evaluation Practice, 18*(2), 105–125.

Tufte, E. R. (1991). *Envisioning information.* Cheshire, CT: Graphics Press.

Tufte, E. R. (2003). *The cognitive style of PowerPoint.* Cheshire, CT: Graphics Press.

Index